BEYOND BELIEF

BEYOND BELIEF

The American Press and the Coming of the Holocaust 1933–1945

Deborah E. Lipstadt

THE FREE PRESS
A Division of Macmillan, Inc.
NEW YORK

Maxwell Macmillan Canada
TORONTO

Maxwell Macmillan International
NEW YORK   OXFORD   SINGAPORE   SYDNEY

The Free Press
A Division of Macmillan, Inc.
866 Third Avenue, New York, N. Y. 10022

Maxwell Macmillan Canada, Inc.
1200 Eglinton Avenue East
Suite 200
Don Mills, Ontario M3C 3N1

Macmillan, Inc. is part of the Maxwell Communication Group of Companies.

First Free Press Paperback Edition 1993

Printed in the United States of America

printing number

1 2 3 4 5 6 7 8 9 10

Library of Congress Cataloging–in–Publication Data

Lipstadt, Deborah E.
    Beyond belief.
    1. Jews—Germany—History—1933–1945—Public opin-
ion. 2. Germany—Foreign opinion, American. 3. Holocaust,
Jewish (1939–1945)—Public opinion. 4. American news-
papers. 5. Public opinion—United States. I. Title.
DS135.G33L57   1986   943'.004924   85–16243
ISBN 0–02–919161–0

To my Father, of blessed memory,
and my Mother

CONTENTS

CONTENTS

ACKNOWLEDGMENTS

This book has its roots in a challenge hurled at me by a student a number of years ago. I had just told my class that during the Nazi years, detailed information regarding the destruction of European Jewry was available to the Allies. "It was no secret," I proclaimed. From amidst the mass of students came an almost angry voice: "But what did the public—not just the people in high places—know? How much of this information reached them? Could my parents, who read the paper every day, have known?" I began to argue that given all the public declarations, international conferences, and government-authorized information which was released they could have known a great deal. Furthermore, I contended, we had reporters in Germany until America entered the war. They transmitted information on Nazism, and that certainly contained information regarding the persecution of the Jews. "No," my student responded, "I can't believe people could have read about all this in their daily papers." Rather than let the class degenerate into a debating match, I determined that I would prove to my skeptical student—and he probably was not the only one—that I was right. Now, a number of years, numerous students, and many long hours of research later, I wish I could find that angry voice and say, "I was right but so were you." Therefore, first and foremost, I thank that student who prompted me to examine this issue. His name now eludes me, but his voice still rings in my ears.

I sincerely appreciate the assistance rendered me by the archival and library staffs at the National Archives and Records Center, American Jewish Archives, American Jewish Historical Society, YIVO Institute for Jewish Research, Franklin D. Roosevelt Library at Hyde Park, Manuscript Division of the Library of Congress, Mass Communications History Center of the State Historical Society of Wisconsin, University of Washington Library, UCLA Research Library, and Yad Vashem. The National Foundation for Jewish Culture, the University of Washington Scholarly Development Fund, and the Academic Senate of UCLA all provided essential financial support.

In the course of my work a number of students and research assistants have been of critical aid to me. They assisted in the tedious task of reading microfilm and aging copies of newspapers and magazines and participated in other ways in this work. My thanks to Jon Schwarz, John Fox, Judith Israel, Arlene Becker Azose, Dorothy Becker, Cindy Fein Straus, Michael Daniels, Melanie Karp, Margaret Hanley, and Esther Leah Weil, all of whom played an important role. A number of other people helped in various ways. The editorial suggestions, technical support, and sage advice of Ann Appelbaum, Bill Aron, Cynthia Chapman, Grace Cohen Grossman, Anne Roberts, Janet Hadda, Bonnie Fetterman, Ahavia Scheindlin, Barb Shurin, and Gerald Warburg were crucial elements in different aspects of the work. Arnold J. Band not only offered critically important editorial suggestions but also pointed out that I had neglected to do the obvious. I am thankful to Fredelle Spiegel for her comments on an early version of the manuscript and for saying the right thing at precisely the right moment.

My editor Laura Wolff, of The Free Press, has been both exacting and supportive. I value her advice and assistance greatly. Eileen DeWald, also of The Free Press, was responsible for the successful production of this book. Her competence, diligence, and good humor were significant factors in ensuring its timely appearance. Hunt Cole performed a herculean task in the editing of the manuscript. My debt to Sandra E. Smith is enormous. Without her assistance the preparation of this manuscript would have been far more onerous and tedious. She played a vital role in this project.

I have been blessed to have a set of friends—both here in Los Angeles and in a number of other places—who provided emotional and material support, who nurtured and nourished me and helped me through many difficult moments. They tolerated my erratic schedule and my single-mindedness and were there for me when I needed them. They are like family. My family has always had a deep and abiding faith in me. They have rejoiced in my accomplishments and by so doing have given me the strength to strive to do even more. To thank either my family or my friends seems both superfluous and inadequate.

Introduction
Shaping the News

The basis of our governments being the opinion of the people, the very first object should be to keep that right; and were it left to me to decide whether we should have a government without newspapers, or newspapers without a government, I should not hesitate a moment to prefer the latter.

Thomas Jefferson

In America, the President reigns for four years, but Journalism governs forever.

Oscar Wilde

I believe that in ninety-nine cases out of a hundred, the American people will make the right decision—if and when they are in possession of the essential facts about any given issue.

Adlai Stevenson[1]

During the 1930s and 1940s America could have saved thousands and maybe even hundreds of thousands of Jews but did not do so. This is a terrible indictment which carries a heavy burden of responsibility and also raises some difficult questions: If more could have been done, why was it not done? Why were certain rescue options deliberately ignored? And most important, who

was most directly responsible for the failure to act? Other historians have grappled with this issue, but most of the previous research on America during the Holocaust has focused on Franklin
Roosevelt, the State Department, and Congress.[2] They were the
ones with the power to rescue, and consequently, what they did
and did not do is of seminal importance. But the President, his
Cabinet, the State Department, the Congress, and other government offices and officials do not operate in a vacuum. They are
political creatures and as such are sensitive to the pressure of
public opinion. This was particularly true during the Roosevelt
Administration because, as Elmer Roper recalled, the President
was "tremendously interested in public opinion" and always
"more secure when he felt the public was behind him."[3]

It is possible that Washington's behavior would have been
different if the American public had demanded that this country
not "stand idly by" while innocent human beings were destroyed,
but throughout the period, whenever it came to rescue, particularly when the victims were Jews, the public favored inaction over
action. How can we explain such behavior? Was this a function
of callousness or prejudice? Was it a matter of other priorities?
Or is it possible that the American public did not really know
the full extent of the tragedy underway in Europe? The President
knew, the State Department knew, but did the public know? Did
it have access to the details? As this study will demonstrate, an
astonishing amount of information was available long before the
end of the war. There was practically no aspect of the Nazi horrors
which was not publicly known in some detail long before the
camps were opened in 1945. Can we say therefore that there
was no real secret, that there should have been no doubts? Can
we assume that Americans firmly knew and consciously chose not
to express concern or pressure their representatives to act? No,
for it is not enough to say that what was happening was known;
we must evaluate how the information was presented to the public.

In an attempt to understand why the American public reacted
as it did, this study turns its attention to the American press,
for the press was the conduit of information to the public. How
did it transmit this news? Did it treat it as fact or rumor? Was
the news accorded the kind of attention that made Americans
view it as something important, or was it treated as a "sidebar,"
the name given by the press to stories which are ancillary or

subsidiary to the main story? Did the press take Hitler's threats against Jews seriously? Did it consider them perhaps just bombastic rhetoric, or did it grasp that antisemitism was the keystone of Nazism? Did the press understand that what was happening to the Jews was not simply a matter of war—related privations, but something of much greater consequence? Did the source of a report affect the way in which it was treated, i.e., was news released by groups associated with the victims—Jews in particular—treated differently than that released by "impartial" bodies? Did the press believe that America had a direct interest in Nazi Germany's treatment of the Jews? If the existence of the Final Solution was no longer a secret by 1942, why was there so much doubt and confusion in the ranks of the American public regarding what was being done to the Jews? Might the way the press conveyed this news have raised much of the doubt? A reader might well have wondered why, if editors thought a report of a massacre or gas chambers was trustworthy, they placed it in the inner recesses of the paper.

The press may not determine what the public thinks, but it does influence what it thinks *about.* If the media pay particular attention to an issue, its importance is enhanced in the public's eyes, and if the media ignore something, public reaction will be nil, for as Gay Talese has observed, news unreported has no impact.[4] The way the press told the story of Nazi antisemitism— the space allocated, the location of the news in the paper, and the editorial opinions—shaped the American reaction. My analysis of the press is an attempt to shed light on that reaction. The press was not a neutral or passive observer—it almost never is. When we study the press, it may appear that we are studying the narrator, but we are really studying an actor. The press became part of the historical process by virtue of the role it played as conduit of information. Just by fulfilling its task, it became a catalyst.[5]

This analysis of the press begins with the Nazi accession to power in 1933, for the annihilation of Europe's Jews essentially began then, not later. As a veteran American journalist who had been stationed in Nazi Germany for many years observed in 1942 upon his release from internment, the Nazis' annihilation of the Jews had at that time "swept onward for nine years in a series of waves, each exceeding the previous one in ferocity."[6] It is critical that we examine how the press covered and interpreted each of these "waves," for this helped shape the American reaction to this watershed event in human history.

Roosevelt, the Press, and the Sources for This Study

The press is used by policy makers to assess and create public attitudes.[7] To succeed at this, a policy maker must know how to deal with the press. At this, President Franklin D. Roosevelt was a master. The transcripts of his press conferences demonstrate that he was extremely adroit in his relations with the press corps. A reporter who covered the White House during the Roosevelt years wrote in December 1940, "Every time one goes to a White House press conference, he is made to recognize once again that Franklin D. Roosevelt is without peer in meeting newsmen." The general consensus among reporters was that Roosevelt was a "newspaperman's President." The President had a voracious appetite for news. Arthur Krock described Roosevelt, who read anywhere from eleven to sixteen newspapers daily, as the "greatest reader and critic of newspapers who had ever been in the president's office." His concern with the press and what it was saying about his policies was almost obsessional.[8] And his interest had its effect on his subordinates. For as James Reston has observed, it is a President's attitude toward the press that "sets the pattern for the rest of the administration." If the person occupying the Oval Office carefully reviews the papers, as we know this President did, his aides will do likewise lest they find themselves unprepared for some query from him.[9]

In addition to the papers he read on a daily basis, the President received numerous articles and editorials from friends and opponents throughout the United States. Perusal of the President's files at the Roosevelt Presidential Library in Hyde Park reveals multitudes of press clippings that various correspondents sent him. He often passed these on to his subordinates and other government officials. He also had available to him a systematic and comprehensive analysis of American press opinion. One of the most important White House barometers of public attitudes was a daily digest of press reactions prepared by the Division of Press Intelligence, which had been established by the President in July 1933 at the instigation of Presidential Secretary Louis Howe. Its task was to read and clip articles from 500 of the largest

American newspapers and prepare a daily *Press Information Bulletin* which classified news reports and editorials according to their opinions on foreign and domestic matters. In the 1930s there were approximately 2,000 daily newspapers published in the United States. Thus the collection of clippings in the Division of Press Intelligence archives constitutes a sample from 25 percent of those newspapers. The *Bulletins,* designed for use by all government offices and departments, often contained a "box score" recording the number of editorials which supported or opposed certain policy decisions. These mimeographed multipaged releases "digested and summarized" the nation's editorial opinion. Each item in the *Bulletin* was assigned a number so that government officials could consult the articles directly. The Division of Press Intelligence continued this daily press service until the middle of 1942, when many of its functions were taken over by other government agencies, including the Office of War Information. The President, his press secretary Stephen Early, and key figures in the Administration "relied heavily" on this clipping and digest service.[10]

Much of the material in this book is based on news stories and editorials collected for the *Bulletin.* By tapping this rich lode, it was possible to survey a broad spectrum of press opinion and reports, the same spectrum examined by the White House, State Department, and other government offices. For those events that occurred before or after the Division of Press Intelligence was in operation, major metropolitan dailies were examined. These included the *New York Times, New York Herald Tribune, New York Journal American, New York Sun, PM, New York World Telegram, Los Angeles Times, Los Angeles Examiner, Baltimore Sun, Philadelphia Inquirer, Christian Science Monitor, St. Louis Post Dispatch, Chicago Tribune, Atlanta Constitution, Miami Herald, San Francisco Chronicle, San Francisco Examiner, Washington Star,* and *Washington Post.* A number of popular and influential magazines and journals were also reviewed, including *Collier's, Harper's, Life, Literary Digest, Look, The Nation, The New Republic, Newsweek, Reader's Digest, The Saturday Evening Post, Time, The Christian Century,* and *Commonweal.* In addition, the files of the American Jewish Committee as well as those of a number of government agencies besides the Division of Press Intelligence, including the War Refugee Board and the Office of War Information, yielded important newspaper clippings. (In those cases where an article was found *in situ,* it was possible to analyze page location. Clippings from the files of the Division of Press Intelligence, the other government agencies, and the American Jewish Committee did not indicate page number.) Finally, interviews with a number of reporters who were stationed in Berlin in the 1930s and 1940s as well as those who covered some aspect of this story from other places, e.g. Moscow, helped provide additional perspective on what it was like to tell the story of this whirlwind.

In 1942 the State Department also began a systematic analysis of public opinion on foreign affairs and used the media as one of its major sources of information. The Department prepared comprehensive analyses of the public's views based on newspaper reports, editorials and columns, radio programs, and public opinion polls. In 1943 it contracted with the Office of Public Opinion Research of Princeton to prepare studies on the public's attitudes regarding foreign policy. Wherever possible this work considers these studies and other public opinion polls.[11]

The Germans and the American Press

American officials were not the only ones who used the press as a barometer and cultivator of American public sentiment. Foreign countries did the same. From 1933 on the Germans resolutely sought ways to enhance Nazi Germany's image in America. Concerned about that image, they even hired American public relations firms and assigned them the task of fostering a "good press." (When the identity of the firms was revealed in the course of Congressional hearings, their usefulness to the Germans came to an end and they were fired.) Throughout the 1930s Germany continued to attempt to influence the press because of the key role it played in the battle to win public support.[12]

Reports by German embassy officials in Washington often discussed the attitude of the American press toward Germany. The German embassy monitored the American press on a regular basis and kept Berlin informed about how the news conveyed by particular reporters was greeted. In 1939, after the beginning of the war, the German Chargé d'Affaires in the United States informed Berlin that the "most effective tool of German propaganda in the United States is, as heretofore, the American correspondents in Berlin who give detailed descriptions of their courteous treatment in Germany."[13] On other occasions the embassy suggested that certain American correspondents in Germany be rewarded and others more severely censored or expelled. Naturally, reporters studiously tried to avoid expulsion because it angered their employers and seriously disrupted their own careers. American reporters, some of whom were present in Germany until 1942, witnessed the brutalities inflicted on the Jews, the effect of the Nuremberg Laws, the expropriation of Jewish wealth, and the forcing of Jews to wear an identifying mark. Some reporters accompanied Polish Jews who were expelled from Germany in 1938. They traveled with them to the border and witnessed their treatment by German officials. In 1941 America correspondents watched as Jews were loaded onto trains for "resettlement" in the east. On other occasions they heard soldiers on leave from the Russian front describe the massacres of civilians there. But fearing the impact of such news on themselves and their informants, reporters did not always transmit what they saw and heard. Moreover, the news they did transmit was not necessarily the story Americans read at the breakfast table, for reporters do not work alone. They pass the news to editors, who decide whether to print it at all, where to place it, and whether to publish it in its entirety or in an abridged form. At times, editors excised portions of reports they considered unreliable or unbelievable.

The State Department and the German Foreign Office were both aware of the press's power to shape events, and both suggested to reporters that they adopt a particular tone when it was considered in the interests of government policy for them to do so.* During the first months of Nazi rule, American reporters in Germany were urged by United States diplomats to moderate the tenor of their dispatches, lest public opinion against Germany be so inflamed that relations between the two countries would be irrevocably harmed. On certain occasions Berlin issued orders to German papers to refrain from criticizing Roosevelt in order not to alienate either the President or American public opinion.[14]

The Press Within the Context of Its Times

The two new fields of public relations and propaganda both had a profound impact on the way the press told the story of the

---

* When a German reporter received such a suggestion, it was an order.

persecution of Europe's Jews and help to explain the skepticism which greeted the news.[15] Initially these two endeavors, sometimes referred to interchangeably as manipulations of the public, were treated with great derision. Their rapid growth in the interwar period can be traced directly to the "astounding success" of wartime propaganda. Edward L. Bernays, one of the outstanding figures in the fledgling field of public relations, observed that wartime propaganda "opened the eyes of the intelligent few . . . to the possibilities of regimenting the public mind." In less than a decade the American government's attitude toward the use of public relations evolved from hostility to recognition that propaganda could serve government objectives.[16]

Within one week of declaring war in 1917, President Wilson established the Committee on Public Information to disseminate information regarding the war and to coordinate government propaganda efforts. The Committee, which considered its job to be "mobilizing the mind of the world," released thousands of press stories and created a vast network of writers, photographers, advertising specialists, artists, and journalists whose responsibility it was to foster a prowar sentiment. George Creel, the journalist appointed by Wilson to direct the Committee, candidly described the Committee as a "plain publicity proposition, a vast enterprise in salesmanship, the world's greatest adventure in advertising."[17] Some scholars consider the Committee's activities during World War I to have been the "first modern effort at systematic, nationwide manipulation of collective passions."[18] After the war the *Encyclopedia Britannica*'s entry "Propaganda" asserted that during the war "the conquest of neutral opinion was seen to be almost as important as victory in the field."[19]

These new approaches to the dissemination of information had a profound effect on the way news was reported by the press and received by the public. Skepticism and cynicism, which had long been the hallmarks of the experienced reporter, intensified. Propaganda proved that any story could be created; consequently every story was now open to doubt. What seemed to be empirical evidence could now be carefully engineered illusion designed to manipulate and dupe even the most experienced reporter. The "inside story" could be the product of propagandists. Reporters, whose job it was to demand "Just give me the facts," now had good cause to wonder whether the "facts" they were given could be trusted. The Belgian atrocity reports of World War I made the press all the more skeptical. Reports of the Germans' use of poison gas, the brutal killings of babies, and mutilations of defenseless women in Belgium all turned out to be products of the imagination. But these stories left their legacy. During World War II, even when reporters possessed proof of mass killings they doubted they had occurred because the stories seemed too similar to the false reports of the previous war.[20] And if the reporters believed the news, those far from the scene—both editors and public—often did not. This chasm between information and belief was one of the major obstacles to the transmission of this news.

In *Discovering the News,* Michael Schudson notes that it was precisely during this period that "objectivity" became a journalist's ideal. Unknown as an ideal prior to World War I, it became one because propaganda made subjectivity impossible to avoid.[21] Distrusting much of what they could see and, of course, even more of what they could not see, reporters and the public greeted the news of the persecution of the Jews skeptically.

If doubt about the trustworthiness of this news was one prism through which the American view of Germany was refracted, the fear of being drawn into Europe's internecine affairs was another. During the 1930s a deep-rooted isolationist sentiment permeated American public opinion.[22] It served as a standard for judging any American foreign policy action. America, contemptuous of Europe's inability to put its house in order, had no inclination to be involved in the Continent's affairs.[23] Isolationism and cynicism, the fear of being "duped" by government propaganda, revulsion at Europe's inability to police itself, and despair about the future course of democracy together formed the backdrop against which the news from Germany was presented. These sentiments affected both the way the story was told and the way it was understood.

The Press and the Historical Record

The press has been described by veteran newsman Harrison Salisbury as "holding up a looking glass to history."[24] The press does far more than passively hold up that looking glass; it positions the glass, and the way it does that serves to shape the events themselves. The mirror, as the medium, becomes part of the message. Indeed, understanding the press's behavior may tell us more about what the American people knew, believed, and felt about the persecution of European Jewry, and why the Americans reacted as they did, than will the analysis of diplomatic endeavors, however critical those endeavors may have been.

As the British journalist Claud Cockburn observed,

> All stories are written backwards—they are supposed to begin with facts and develop from there, but in reality they begin with a journalist's point of view, a conception, and it is the point of view from which the facts are subsequently organized. Journalistically speaking, "in the beginning is the word."[25]

And it is on the basis of that word that much of history is written.

The press record is a large part of the raw material from which historians try to shape a coherent whole. Both the journalist's and historian's professions consider objectivity the highest ideal and believe that facts and values can and should be separated. In reality, neither the journalist nor the historian is completely objective. Their values inform their view and understanding of events, and thus influence the creation and interpretation of the historical record. And since people's values tend to reflect those of the society they are part of, our examination of how the American journalist—both the reporter and the editor—treated the news of the persecution of European Jewry will also be an examination of the values of this society which watched from afar as the Holocaust erupted in all its fury and horror.

PART I

LAYING THE
FOUNDATION

1

Dateline Berlin: Covering the Nazi Whirlwind

As soon as the Nazis came to power, they began to institute antisemitic measures. Although the first antisemitic laws were not promulgated until early April 1933, from the earliest moments of Hitler's rule in January 1933 violence against Jews in the form of *Einzelaktionen,* or "individual" acts of terror and brutality, was an inherent facet of German life. Boycotts of Jewish shops were conducted by the Nazi storm troopers. Jews were beaten and arrested; some were killed and others committed suicide. When the Nazis strengthened and consolidated their rule in the March 5, 1933, elections, outbreaks against Jews increased in intensity. American Ambassador Frederic M. Sackett, who was then preparing to retire from his post, wrote to Secretary of State Cordell Hull that democracy in Germany had been the recipient of a "blow from which it may never recover."[1]

The First Reports of Persecution

Though the press had not previously ignored Hitler's antisemitism, most of the early reports stressed Nazi action against communists and socialists. It was only after the intensification of the attacks in March that the press began to focus explicit attention on the Jews' situation. Typical of the vivid press reports sent by reporters on the scene was that by the *Chicago Tribune*'s Edmond Taylor, who provided readers with a stark description of the "unholy fear" prevailing among German Jews.

> On the nights of March 9th and 10th, bands of Nazis throughout Germany carried out wholesale raids to intimidate the opposition, particularly the Jews. . . . Men and women were insulted, slapped [and] punched in the face, hit over the heads with blackjacks, dragged out of their homes in night clothes and otherwise molested. . . . Innocent Jews . . . 'are taken off to jail and put to work in a concentration camp where you may stay a year without any charge being brought against you.' Never have I seen law-abiding citizens living in such unholy fear.[2]

Taylor's depictions of the systematic persecution faced by Jews and those deemed "opponents" of the regime eventually resulted in his expulsion from Germany. H. R. Knickerbocker, the Berlin correspondent of the *New York Evening Post,* who was also forced to leave Germany because of official opposition to his reports, provided a similar appraisal.

> Not even in Czarist Russia, with its "pale," have the Jews been subject to a more violent campaign of murderous agitation. . . .
> An indeterminate number of Jews . . . have been killed. Hundreds of Jews have been beaten or tortured.
> Thousands of Jews have fled.
> Thousands of Jews have been, or will be, deprived of their livelihood.
> All of Germany's 600,000 Jews are in terror.[3]

As the news of antisemitic activities reached this country, newspapers in cities large and small responded angrily. The *Pittsburgh Sun* decried the "acts of revolting cruelty . . . [which] have been committed." The *Poughkeepsie News* saw a "tide of Nazi fury" engulfing German Jews and inflicting great "bodily violence" on them. The *Toledo Times* believed that conditions in Germany were characterized by an "abuse of power, . . . unrestrained cruelty, . . . suppression of individual rights, . . . violent racial and religious prejudices."[4] A midwestern paper was horrified by the reports of "beatings, torture, murder." According to the *Nashville*

Banner, sentiment in the United States was "solidified in condemnation of Hitler's atrocious policy." The *New York Times* simply wondered how a nation could "suddenly go mad."[5]

But the persecution of the Jews constituted only one small segment of the story of Nazi Germany and was never the central theme of the reports about the new regime. News of political upheavals, Hitler's jockeying for control, the Reichstag fire, the March elections, and the violence perpetrated by groups such as the storm troopers against communists and socialists took precedence. Rarely was news of the persecution of the Jews handled by journalists, particularly by those who viewed the situation from the safety of the United States, as an inherent expression of Nazism. This failure to see Nazi antisemitism as a reflection of the fundamental principles of Nazism was to have important consequences for the interpretation and comprehension of the news of the persecution of European Jewry.

A Drawing Back

When the first reports from Nazi Germany reached this country, Americans were incredulous. This was not the Germany of Beethoven, Goethe, and Schiller. The entire situation, not just that of the Jews, rang of chaos and confusion, revolution and upheaval. There were what the *Chicago Tribune* and the *New York Times* described as "wild rumors" that the Nazis planned to "massacre Jews and other political opponents." The whole Jewish population in Germany was living, according to a *London Daily Herald* report which the *Chicago Tribune* reprinted, "under the shadow of a campaign of murder which may be initiated within a few hours and cannot at the most be postponed more than a few days."[6] In addition to these extreme reports, there were eyewitness descriptions by returning Americans of what the *New York Times* described as "atrocities" being inflicted on Jews. A number of Americans were among those who were terrorized and beaten. There was a striking difference between the United Press and *New York Times* versions of this story. The United Press described "three incidents alleged to have been perpetrated," while the *Times* described "three more specific cases of molestation" about which American Consul General George Messersmith had complained to the German Foreign Office.[7]

Though the news that emerged from Germany during this initial period was not nearly as horrifying as that of subsequent years, a deep-seated American skepticism was already evident. In fact, some Americans were more skeptical about this news than they would be about news of far more terrible magnitude. Ignoring the fact that much of the news was based on eyewitness accounts, editorial boards lamented that the "stories which have trickled through cannot be checked and officially verified."[8]

It was quite common to find papers and magazines which were convinced that the situation could not be *as* bad as the reporters contended. This, in fact, would become one of the recurring themes in the press coverage of the entire period: "Terrible things may be happening but not *as* terrible as the reports from Germany would have you believe." The *Los Angeles Times,* which in mid-March carried exclusive reports of German persecution, a few weeks later told its readers that the "amazing tales of oppression" being brought from Germany by Americans who were visiting or living there were "exaggerated." On March 26 the *Los Angeles Times* featured news of a Los Angeles physician who had visited Germany and claimed that the stories were incorrect.[9] The *New York Herald Tribune* did the same on March 25. In a front-page story John Elliott of the *Herald Tribune* bureau in Berlin complained that while the situation of German Jews was "an unhappy one," it was exacerbated by the "exaggerated and often unfounded reports of atrocities that have been disseminated abroad." He dismissed ten cases of American Jews who had been "mishandled" as not an "accurate picture of the position of German Jewry under Hitler." As proof he cited both the claims of German Jewish organizations that Jews were not being molested and the fact that he was personally "acquainted with members of old Jewish families in Berlin who were so undisturbed by the political change in Germany that they had never even heard of these deeds of violence against their co-religionists."[10] Another doubter, initially, proved to be Frederick Birchall, chief of the *New York Times* Berlin bureau, who in mid-March assured listeners in a nationwide radio talk broadcast on CBS that Germany was interested only in peace and had no plans to "slaughter" any of its enemies. He acknowledged that there had been persecution but believed that German violence was "spent" and predicted "prosperity and happiness" would prevail.[11] (As the situation became worse, Birchall's doubts would be totally erased.) On March 27, 1933, five days before all Jewish shops in Germany were subjected to a one-day nationwide boycott by the Nazis, the *Los Angeles Times* announced in a page 1 exclusive "German Violence Subsiding" and "Raids On Jews Declared Over." *The Christian Century*, which would emerge as one of the more strident skeptics regarding the accuracy of the reports on Jewish persecution, called for a "tighter curb . . . [on] emotions until the facts are beyond dispute."[12]

Other papers expressed their reservations less directly. One paper acknowledged with an almost reluctant air that there "seems to be evidence to support the charges [of brutality against Jews] in the main." But it then reminded readers that "many of the cruelties charged against Germany in war propaganda were later proved not to have existed."[13] The *Columbus* (Ohio)*Journal* also associated these reports of "destruction of property, beatings and blacklisting" with the "exaggerated . . . stories the allies told about German atrocities during the war." The link with World War I atrocity reports as a means of casting doubt on the current spate of stories was to become a common feature of the American public's reaction to the news of the Final Solution. By the time World War II began, Americans had determined, according to *Journalism Quarterly*, "that they would not be such simpletons that they would be fooled again" as they had been in the previous war by the tales of German atrocities.[14]

The reports on Nazi brutality which appeared in the *Christian Science Monitor* were also decidedly skeptical in tone.[15] In March the paper noted that the *Frankfurter Zeitung* had condemned as false the stories of the persecution of the Jews which had appeared in foreign newspapers. The Frankfurt paper was described as an "outstandingly outspoken" critic of the regime. The *New York Herald Tribune*'s John Elliott also cited the Frankfurt paper in his page 1 denial of reports that Jews were being molested. The implication was clear: if a newspaper which had been outspokenly critical of the government claimed that the brutality reports were untrue, then they obviously must be.[16] The *Chicago Tribune*'s Taylor offered a very different assessment of the Frankfurt paper's denunciation of the foreign coverage. Taylor pointed out that the paper was owned and edited by Jews and noted, not without a touch of sarcasm, that even though German Jewry was "living through the most systematic persecution known since the Middle Ages, and has had a fair taste of physical violence, by its own account it has seen nothing, heard nothing, remembered nothing." To Taylor it was clear that this myopia was prompted by fear and not by a desire for journalistic accuracy.[17] Similarly, the popular and widely syndicated columnist Dorothy Thompson, who visited Germany in March 1933, assured her husband, Sinclair Lewis, that the Jews' situation was "really as bad as the most sensational papers report. . . . It's an outbreak of sadistic and pathological hatred." When she returned to the United States she repeated this theme.[18]

In sum the picture that was drawn in the American press particularly during these early days was a confused one. There was the question of the truthfulness of the reports. Once it became clear that the reports were accurate—though there were those who would never accept them as completely accurate—there was the question of what this meant. Were these attacks actually being perpetrated and directed by the Nazi hierarchy, or had they been inspired by the Nazis' extreme rhetoric? Was this the result of Nazi government policy, or was it simply an outgrowth of the chaos which often followed a revolutionary change in government? Were these events "boyish tricks" perpetrated by overzealous Nazi enthusiasts, or was this a reign of terror designed and controlled by those at the highest level of authority?

Official Lines and Lies

German authorities used a variety of tactics to reinforce American confusion. They followed a policy which the *New York Evening Post*'s Knickerbocker accurately described as "first, they never happened; second, they will be investigated; third they will never happen again." In March 1933 a reporter asked Hitler's foreign press chief, Ernst Hanfstaengl, if the reports "about alleged Jew baiting" were true. Hanfstaengl's answer was entirely false but typical of the Germans' tactics in dealing with news they did not wish to be reported. "A few minutes ago, . . . the Chancellor authorized me to tell you that these reports are every one of them base lies." Hermann Goering also attacked those who had spoken these "horrible lies," and declared that there were "no plundered, no broken up shops, no warehouses destroyed, robbed or interfered with."[19] Other German officials including Foreign Minister Konstantin von Neurath and Reichsbank President Hjalmar Schacht, who visited the United States, made a point of attacking the news reporters' credibility. When German officials could not deny the reports, they disavowed responsibility for the outbreaks and blamed them on "all sorts of dark elements" intent on pursuing "their anti-governmental purposes."[20]

These protestations of innocence were continuously contradicted by both the recurring cycle of terror and the frequent predictions by Hitler and others in the Nazi hierarchy that the Jewish community in Germany would be "exterminated." Some reporters tried to alert readers to this cycle of terror and the German duplicity in trying to disclaim responsibility for it. Edwin James, writing in the *New York Times,* pointed out that though the Germans claimed that "a few individual acts of violence have been grossly exaggerated," the situation was severe enough for Hitler to have given "official orders" to stop the recurring violence. An Associated Press (AP) dispatch from Berlin in March also took note of the contradiction in Nazi claims. While Hitler instructed storm troopers to "remember their discipline [and] refrain from molesting business life," Hermann Goering, who was described in the article as Hitler's "confidential man," was telling an audience that the police would never be used "as protective troops for Jewish merchants." At the end of 1933 *The Nation* noted that this cyclical process continued unabated. Each time violence was reported, the German government "issues denials, punishes Jews for spreading atrocity stories, expels honest correspondents and continues to encourage the very violence and confiscation it is denying."[21] Ultimately the reporters stationed in Germany grew so cynical about German disclaimers that when high-ranking officials vigorously denied a report, reporters became convinced that there was some truth to it.[22]

In June 1933 the *New York Times* described the denial of the terror as "more shocking" than the terror itself.

> Even while Hitler [is denying] that such terror ever existed . . .
> and perfect calm reigns in Germany, the *Collier* reporter found
> the Jewish persecution in full swing and life in Berlin like sitting
> on the edge of a volcano.[23]

During this early stage of Nazi rule American officials joined German authorities in shedding doubts on the press reports. In late March 1933 Secretary of State Cordell Hull pressured the press to adopt a "spirit of moderation" and suggested to reporters that conditions in Germany may not have been "accurately" and "authoritatively" reported. He believed that the "gravity" of the press reports was not borne out by the facts.[24] Hull apparently was convinced that many of the reports regarding "terror and atrocities which have reached this country have been grossly exaggerated," despite the fact that American officials in Germany were sending him news to the contrary. George Gordon, American Chargé d'Affaires in Germany, reported to Hull that "numberless sources" agreed that the Jews' situation was "rapidly taking a turn for the worse."[25] The *New York Times* and *New York Herald Tribune* placed Hull's denials on the front page under headlines which proclaimed the "end" of German violence against Jews. Actually Hull did not succeed in convincing everyone that the violence was "virtually terminated." *Newsweek* observed that "no great improvement was evident" in German behavior.[26]

Hull considered his claims that the severity of the situation had been exaggerated to be in America's best interest. He told American officials stationed in Germany of his "fear that the continued dissemination of exaggerated reports may prejudice the friendly feelings between the peoples of the two countries and be of doubtful service to anyone."[27] His objective was to "try and calm down the situation created by a lot of extremists in Germany and inflamed by a lot of extremists in this country."[28] Hull did not identify the American extremists to whom he was referring, but faulted the press for disseminating "exaggerated" stories.

Rather than exaggerate, American correspondents actually made a concerted effort to modulate the tone of their reports so as not to be accused of fomenting hysteria. Their reports were balanced, reserved and tended toward moderation, not exaggeration. Still, they were often met with skepticism in this country. The task of covering Berlin and being sure that your editors and readers would believe what you were reporting was not an easy one.

The Ordeal of American Reporters in Germany

Throughout the 1930s American reporters felt sustained pressure both from readers and editorial boards, who wanted them to substantiate their information, and from the Nazis, who denied the veracity of their reports. The Nazis repeatedly accused reporters of lying and admitted doing so. In 1933, after most leading German communists and socialists had been arrested, at a luncheon given by the Foreign Press Association in Berlin for Joseph Goebbels, the Nazi propaganda chief told the reporters that he was glad the foreign press was in Germany. They were wonderful scapegoats on whom to blame problems, "now that there was no [political] opposition" in Germany. In a letter to his daughter Betty at the University of Chicago, AP reporter Louis Lochner described problems the Berlin bureau faced in covering politically significant events such as the Reichstag fire trial. (The Reichstag was burned on February 27, 1933. The man accused of setting the fire was charged as a communist, was tried in the fall of 1933, and executed in January 1934.) If the foreign correspondents depended on German press reports, they only heard what pleased the Nazis. A correspondent who tried to present what Lochner described as a "fair picture of the trial, objectively giving what is said on both sides," was immediately branded by the German press as a *Greuelhetzer* (atrocity monger).[29] And as the decade wore on, the atmosphere the American reporters worked in became worse.

In May of 1933 Messersmith reported to the Secretary of State that ever since the Nazis' rise to power, the situation of "a number of the American correspondents in Berlin has not been easy." Because of the Nazi determination not to allow "undesirable news [to reach] . . . the outside world through the foreign correspondents," the press was often censored.[30]*

Even when there was no overt censorship, the reporters stationed in Germany had to walk a "dangerous and difficult path" in order to avoid being prevented from sending their reports, thrown out of the country, or even thrown in Nazi prisons. The Nazis would "punish" reporters they deemed guilty of sending

---

* The German policy on censorship varied. Radio transmissions were severely censored; the printed press sometimes had more freedom. C. Brooks Peters, who was assigned to the Berlin bureau of the *New York Times* from 1937 through the fall of 1941, recalled that the paper escaped strict censorship because its policy was to phone all its stories to Paris, London, and, after the war began, Switzerland, and phone transmissions were not interfered with. He did not recall any occasion on which the telephone connection was interrupted or cut off. Sometimes, material that was telegraphed to New York did not arrive.[31]

"atrocity stories" by banning their papers from Germany and preventing them from using the German mails, as was done to the
Manchester Guardian in April 1933. Reporters' lives were further
complicated by an elaborate spy system that placed Nazi sources
in their offices and homes. In *Germany Will Try Again*, the *Chicago
Tribune*'s veteran Berlin correspondent Sigrid Schultz described
how her maid became a "servant in the Gestapo system," keeping
tabs on her mail, telephone conversations, and visitors. Certain
reporters, including the *Chicago Daily News*'s Edgar Mowrer, had
SS men stationed outside their home as a means of limiting their
freedom of movement.[32] The Nazis, anxious to get Mowrer out
of Germany, first tried to pressure him to resign his position as
president of the prestigious Association of Foreign Correspondents in Berlin. When his colleagues refused to accept his resignation, the Nazis left him alone for a few months. But in August
German embassy officials began to urge Secretary of State Hull
to "facilitate or encourage" Mowrer's departure from Germany.
After some consideration, the State Department decided that it
would not be "appropriate" to approach the *Chicago Daily News*
and suggest Mowrer's removal. German officials in Washington
then went straight to Frank Knox, the paper's publisher, and with
a combination of "argument and veiled threats" convinced him
to pull Mowrer out of Berlin. Earlier in 1933 the Germans had
tried to do the same thing to H. R. Knickerbocker, but his paper
had refused to recall him. In Mowrer's case it appears that Knox,
who had visited Nazi Germany earlier that year, was genuinely
concerned about his safety and feared that the Nazis would use
the forthcoming party rally which was held annually at Nuremberg
to inflict bodily harm on him.[33]

William Shirer, who reported from Berlin for Universal Service
and for International News Service (INS), the chief Hearst wire
service, before joining CBS, described his experience in Berlin
as "walking a real, if ill defined, line." The line was real for every
correspondent, and any one of them who strayed too far on what
the Nazis considered the wrong side of it faced outright expulsion
or even jail. S. Miles Bouton, the Berlin correspondent for the
Baltimore Times for over a decade, was instructed by the German
Foreign Office in March 1934 to "change his style of reporting
or leave the country." He chose to do the latter. Howard K. Smith
has recalled another tactic of the Nazis: they would "entrap" certain reporters by making sure that they broke some obscure law

or regulation. One common maneuver was to informally tell the reporters that a certain bank was offering a particularly high rate of exchange as a service to correspondents. Reporters would use the bank freely until suddenly one would be arrested and informed that he or she was breaking a little-known law regarding exchange rates. Other reporters were sent incriminating documents and then accused of spying. Sometimes the arrest was random, as in the case of Richard C. Hottelet of the United Press, who was arrested shortly after the beginning of the German invasion of Russian-occupied Poland and held for several months prior to being exchanged for some Germans being held in the United States. Hottelet believes that this arrest had little to do with what he wrote but was in retaliation for the arrest of certain German reporters in America on charges of espionage. Howard K. Smith believes Hottelet was arrested in order to intimidate the other American reporters still in Germany.[34]

Expulsion was not a badge of honor for foreign correspondents. They were quite anxious to avoid it because they were never "sure [their] newspapers would understand" or forgive them if they were forced to leave.[35] G. E. R. Gedye, whose dispatches from Vienna appeared in the *New York Times* and *London Daily Telegraph,* described the price a foreign correspondent had to pay for the freedom to cover an exciting and controversial beat: "keep out of politics. It is a necessary price, but on occasions it is a hard one to pay. . . . When I failed to pay the price . . . [I] had no excuse to offer my newspaper if I . . . got into a mess."[36] As it happened, shortly after the Nazi occupation of Austria in 1938, Gedye was ejected from the country because of his dispatches. In his autobiography AP's Louis Lochner summarized the orders he and his colleagues received from their superiors as orders "to tell no untruth, but to report only as much of the truth without distorting the picture, as would enable us to remain at our posts." Ejection was, according to Lochner, "the one thing our superiors did NOT want."[37]*

In *What About Germany?,* written immediately after his return

* When American anti-German sentiment grew more intense, some correspondents scored big successes when they returned home and were immediately invited to join the lecture circuit, interviewed on the radio, and asked to write their memoirs. According to Sigrid Schultz, this put the Nazis in a bit of a "quandary" because an expelled reporter could do them more harm outside of Germany than inside.[38]

from Germany in 1942, Lochner described how even though he would "write a story, discuss every word of it in a staff conference, revamp and modify it" in order to avoid any challenge from Nazi officials, he would still "leave the office with the uneasy feeling that we would be called to the Wilhelmstrasse the next morning and chided for our 'offense' if not threatened with ejection." Howard K. Smith recalled how, once a story was published in America, if a local consul discovered that it contained "something objectionable," he would report to officials in Berlin, who in turn would call in the reporter and mete out punishment ranging from a "polite wrist-slap to banishment from Germany." Percy Knauth and C. Brooks Peters, both of whom worked for the *New York Times* Berlin bureau, described how they would periodically be called to the Foreign Office or Propaganda Ministry to be "chewed out" for something they included in a dispatch. Sigrid Schultz was summoned to the Gestapo and berated several times for stories that the Germans said were "insulting." Another tactic used by the Nazis was to refuse to grant a reporter a reentry visa after he or she had completed a vacation or assignment outside of Germany. They did this to Otto Tolischus and tried to do it to Schultz.[39]

The Views of Others

Correspondents knew that there was little help they could expect from Washington if they got into trouble. When State Department officials, such as Undersecretary of State William Phillips, visited Berlin, they made it quite clear to the reporters that Washington would take no action if the Nazis expelled or arrested reporters. A number of reporters, including Mowrer, Knickerbocker, and Shirer, considered Consul General George Messersmith, Commercial Attaché Douglas Miller, and Consul Raymond Geist not only good sources of information about the Nazis, but among the few diplomats likely to come to a correspondent's aid in case of difficulty with the regime. Even Ambassador William Dodd, a fierce anti-Nazi, was not always willing to aid a reporter who had problems with Nazi officials.[40]

When reporters were able to bypass the censorship and explicitly describe conditions, they still had to contend with other obstacles, most notably the concerted German effort to discredit stories critical of the Reich, on the one hand, and the American skepticism that these stories just could not be true, on the other. When Edgar Ansel Mowrer, the Berlin correspondent for the *Chicago Daily News,* reported in March 1933 that Germany had become an "insane asylum," even his brother who served as the paper's correspondent in Paris thought he was "breaking under the strain." Allen Dulles of the State Department visited Berlin and told Mowrer that he "was taking the German situation too seriously." Frank Knox, the publisher of the *Chicago Daily News,* was also convinced that Mowrer was exaggerating. Knox changed his mind when he visited Germany in 1933 and saw the situation first hand.[41]

The Germans further complicated the reporters' task by repeatedly charging that they were not telling the truth. Various sources—both diplomats and visiting American journalists—defended the integrity of the journalists. American embassy officials in Berlin assured Washington that the correspondents stationed there included some of the most respected and accomplished individuals in their field. Their reports were considered by those familiar with the situation in Germany as "more truthful and less sensational" than those of many European newspapers.[42] The *Manchester Guardian* believed that American and British reporters had understated, rather than inflated, the facts about the "terror," not because they doubted its existence, but because so much of it was hidden and difficult to document. Indicative of the care exerted by the *New York Times* was the fact that for over two months in 1933 it refused to publish a story on Jews' being subjected to various indignities until it could obtain independent confirmation.[43] Edgar Mowrer, accused by Dulles and his own brother of exaggerating the severity of developments, was also one of those who actually underplayed the German terror. His wife recalled how he often chose *not* to tell the story of concentration camp victims who returned to their homes with "horrible wounds" because he feared it would further exacerbate their situation.[44]

Mowrer was not alone in adopting this policy. At the end of March 1933 Consul George Messersmith wrote to Secretary of State Cordell Hull that "American correspondents in Berlin have brought to my attention cases of maltreatment of all sorts of persons of various nationalities which they have personally investigated and found correct but which more recently they have not been able to publish" because of fear of the consequences to themselves and the victims. Messersmith expressed his "confidence" in these correspondents and their reports.[45] Hamilton Fish Armstrong, the editor of *Foreign Affairs*, who was in Germany in 1933, described American and British correspondents as having "kept their heads in trying circumstances." Armstrong was particularly impressed by the fact that reporters sent their papers "documented accounts of specific acts of violence" and statements by Nazi leaders "explaining and justifying" this behavior. Many years later he recalled how correspondents would avoid trying to interpret events for their readers because the obvious interpretations seemed so outlandish, and instead would simply quote statements by Nazi leaders. These leaders often admitted that the events had happened just as the reporters had claimed. Ambassador Dodd's daughter, Martha, acknowledged that while reporters occasionally chased down "stories that were clearly implausible," the portrait they painted of Nazi Germany represented an "accurate picture of what was happening there."[46]

Mark Etheridge, an American journalist who spent time in Germany in 1933, wrote an impassioned defense of the reporters' accuracy. He argued that because American journalists knew that "what they wrote was being watched and criticized, [they] have not only endeavored to verify the minutest particular of what they wrote, but have leaned backward in reporting the truth."[47] This defense of the press corps was reiterated by Michael Williams of the Catholic periodical *Commonweal*, who upon his return from Germany exhorted Americans not to "be deceived by false denials concerning the persecution of the Jews under the Hitlerite regime; guard against its paid and voluntary propaganda."[48]

The *New York Times* also expressed its faith in the correspondents in an editorial in May 1933. The editorial countered public doubts about the trustworthiness of the reports from Germany by citing the findings of a "group of eminent American lawyers," including "leaders of the American bar and two former Secretaries of State," who had studied the situation in Germany. They confirmed, according to the *Times*, that judges had been "violently dragged from the bench and lawyers forced out of practice for no reason except hatred of their race or religion."[49] Despite these expressions of confidence in the reports of persecution, explicit and implicit expressions of doubt continued to be voiced in the American press.

Sometimes reporters defended themselves by letting the Nazis condemn themselves. This was what *New York Times* reporter Otto Tolischus did in August 1935 when he quoted extensively from the official German news agency's press releases describing the Nazi campaign against the Jews, which included picketing in front of stores, physical attacks on individuals, insults to customers who frequented Jewish firms, and an array of other incidents. Because it was unusual for a correspondent, Tolischus in particular, to rely so heavily on quotes from an official news source, Tolischus felt obligated to explain why he did so: "Next to the Jews the foreign correspondents in Berlin are now under fire from the National Socialist authorities." Therefore, to avoid being accused by German authorities of telling falsehoods, he used the Nazis' own words to describe the condition of the Jews.

What Reporters Saw and Where They Stood

Most of the reporters who were stationed in Germany were personally conversant with the Nazi *modus operandi* and understood Germany's deep commitment to antisemitism. They also knew that "fanaticism was the essence of fascism."[50] Many of them had interviewed Hitler and had personally watched him at close range on numerous occasions. Foreign reporters often were placed adjacent to Hitler at mass meetings and public occasions. Every year at the Nuremberg rally the press cars were, by Hitler's personal orders, "sandwiched" in between his own car and the car carrying his closest advisers—Goering, Goebbels, Hess, and Himmler.[51] Most of the foreign correspondents did not doubt that those at the very apex of power were either directly or indirectly responsible for the violence and were unequivocally committed to antisemitism. However, as we have seen, their observations were often discounted by those in the United States. Throughout the period of the Third Reich this pattern repeated itself: reliable sources told at least a portion of what was happening, and those far from the scene and unfamiliar with Nazism discounted the news as exaggerated or dismissed it as not quite possible.[52]

A variation on this theme was the disagreement between Sigrid Schultz, the *Chicago Tribune*'s bureau chief in Berlin, and her employer, Colonel Robert R. McCormick. A highly venerated journalist, she was fiercely anti-Nazi and as early as 1932 warned that there would be dire consequences for Germany and for Europe if Hitler came to power. McCormick and the *Tribune* had a very different view of Germany under Hitler: it was an obstacle to the "communist menace" and therefore deserving of strong American support. McCormick attributed antisemitism to the shortcomings of Versailles and the economic hardships created by the treaty's inequities. He explained that antisemitism was a "national psychological reaction to being officially blamed for World War I." Schultz absolutely disagreed with her boss on this point. "Our alleged unkindness at Versailles had nothing to do with Germany's dedication to another war." It also had nothing to do with Nazi antisemitism. Those who made this claim were, according to Schultz, in "quest of an alibi." Neither the publisher nor the paper explicitly approved of German antisemitism, but they were willing to tolerate it because of Germany's value as a bulwark against Russia. As late as 1938 the *Tribune* was still ignoring Germany's internal persecution and calling for a "square deal for the Germans." Incidentally, although her views were diametrically opposed to McCormick's, Schultz's articles generally appeared uncensored. And even George Seldes, the former *Chicago Tribune* correspondent who made a career of exposing the duplicity of the press and who on frequent occasions launched vitriolic attacks on McCormick, admitted that most of the foreign correspondents for the *Chicago Tribune* enjoyed "full freedom," and were not given orders on what to write and how to treat the facts—or the falsehoods."[53]

Other reporters who understood the true nature of Nazism and its fanatical hatred of Jews included Ralph Barnes of the *New York Herald Tribune;* Edgar Ansel Mowrer, Berlin correspondent for the *Chicago Daily News* until his forced departure in late August 1933; H. R. Knickerbocker of the *New York Evening Post;* Louis Lochner of Associated Press, the reporter who had been in Berlin longest and who also maintained social contacts with German leaders and seemed particularly careful to avoid antagonizing the Nazi authorities; William Shirer of CBS, who according to Martha Dodd was among the most fiercely anti-Nazi of the American correspondents; Pierre van Paassen of the *New York World;* Fred Oeschner of the United Press, and *New York Times* correspondent Otto Tolischus.[54] Norman Ebbutt, the senior *London Times* correspondent in Berlin, was also among the reporters who were most appalled by Nazi behavior. His intimate knowledge of Germany and his extensive contacts with different groups in the country gave him background for reports which, according to Franklin

Gannon, who has studied the British Press and Germany, "undoubtedly riled the Nazi authorities." But Ebbutt ran into a serious obstacle when his publisher, Geoffrey Dawson, refused to publish "anything that might hurt their [German] susceptibilities." When Ebbutt discovered that his most exhaustive, comprehensive, and critical reports did not appear in the paper, he began to feed information to Shirer, who used it in his own reports.[55]

Some reporters required only a short interaction with the Nazi system and with Hitler in order to understand them, others took longer. In certain cases initial impressions changed dramatically. Such was the case with Dorothy Thompson, whose popular syndicated column appeared in a variety of different newspapers, including the *Philadelphia Public Ledger* and the *New York Evening Post*. In 1932 Thompson visited Germany and was granted a personal interview with Hitler. She was unimpressed by the man and wrote that before she first "walked into Adolf Hitler's salon in the Kaiserhof Hotel, I was convinced that I was meeting the future dictator of Germany. In something less than fifty seconds I was quite sure that I was not. It took just that time to measure the startling insignificance of this man." (For many years Thompson's journalist colleagues reminded her of this startlingly wrong evaluation.) In March 1933 she returned to Germany for a brief visit. In her reports on this visit she confirmed that the stories of persecution were not exaggerated. She returned once again in August 1934. Ten days later she was ordered out of the country. According to Ambassador Dodd the reason for her dismissal lay in her interview with Hitler in 1932 and her reports in 1933 condemning Hitler's antisemitic campaign. Thompson explained her expulsion to readers as follows:

> My first offense was to think that Hitler is just an ordinary man.
> . . . That is a crime against the reigning cult . . . which says
> Mr. Hitler is a Messiah sent by God to save the German people—
> an old Jewish idea. To question this mystic mission is so heinous
> that if you are a German, you can be sent to jail. I, fortunately,
> am an American so I merely was sent to Paris.[56]

While most of the reporters stationed in Germany had little, if any, enthusiasm for the Nazi regime, they still maintained social ties with the German hierarchy. Some, such as Louis Lochner, whose wife was German and who spoke German in his home, held many famous elaborate parties attended by high-ranking Nazi leaders. He went to great lengths to maintain cordial contacts with German authorities. Sigrid Schultz's *Bier Abends* (beer evenings) were renowned for the array of people—from the most powerful to the "just plain common folk"—who attended. Schultz, in an interview, acknowledged that entertaining politicians such as Hermann Goering, Joseph Goebbels, and other members of Hitler's immediate circle was a most useful way to "collect news from them." And the fact that she socialized with these people did not compromise her reputation as an anti-Nazi.*

There were, of course, reporters such as Karl von Wiegand of the Hearst chain, who maintained close ties with Nazi and Prussian officials and was considered by some of his colleagues to be somewhat *too* sympathetic to German interests. Even Lochner, who certainly was no friend of the Nazis, was criticized by some of his colleagues for his strong identification with Germany. Shirer believes that Lochner occasionally "compromised" his journalistic integrity in order to ensure that he would get scoops from German authorities. In his autobiography Lochner described how, when he once discussed the "Jewish question" with Hitler during a visit to his famous mountain retreat, Berchtesgaden, the Reich leader became so agitated that Lochner "saw white, foamy saliva exude from the corners of his mouth." This description does not seem to have been included in any of Lochner's dispatches from Germany.

As I have noted, other reporters, while not sympathetic, did choose at times to mute their criticism of Nazi Germany. First of all, they desired to avoid expulsion or arrest. Second, they feared that if they told too much, they might reveal their sources, who then might be arrested, sent to concentration camps, or even killed. This was particularly the case when inmates who had been released from the camps told reporters about life inside them. Their descriptions were especially valuable because reporters were

* The writer Katherine Anne Porter, who spent six months in Germany from the fall of 1931 through the winter of 1932, also attended one of Schultz's evenings, at which she met Joseph Goebbels and Hermann Goering. Many years later Porter described Schultz, whom she called in an article "Sigrid Something-orother," as a "treacherous, devious, fiendishly clever and always scheming" ally of Hitler who was trying to secure the Nazi rise to power. She also claimed to have berated Goering for Nazi policies. No evidence exists to substantiate Porter's description of Schultz or her claims to have delivered a tirade to Goering. Schultz's articles and columns as well as the testimony of her former colleagues are absolute proof of the falsehood of Porter's claims about her. Moreover, during this period Porter's letters to her fiancé included some bitter antisemitic comments. Joan Givner, Porter's biographer, describes the writer's activities during her stay in Germany as marked by "slander and malice."[57]

not allowed to visit the camps except on rare and orchestrated occasions. Ironically, these descriptions were often not included in reports. Finally, reporters recognized that the more they were known to have an anti-Nazi attitude, the more they would be excluded from access to inner government circles. Fearful of being designated "uncooperative" by the Nazis, some reporters did not report all the information they obtained. Over the years of his stay in Germany, as his reputation of being unfriendly to Nazi interests grew, William Shirer found his access to news sources increasingly limited.[58]

Support—and Disbelief

Reporters who understood the deep and fervent Nazi commitment to antisemitism and knew that, despite occasional respites, persecution would persist had some astute backers in their field. There were editorial boards, such as the *Philadelphia Record*'s, and magazines such as *The New Republic* and *The Nation* which accepted the reporters' analyses and accurately predicted that while "Jewish beatings may stop. . . . the 'law' will be used to deprive Jews of personal and political rights."[59] There were publishers such as Frank Knox of the *Chicago Daily News,* who after his visit to Germany had no doubt about the veracity of the most extreme reports. There were commentators and authors such as John Gunther, whose immensely popular *Inside Europe* noted that the "basic depth and breadth of Hitler's antisemitism" was clear to anyone who read *Mein Kampf.*[60] Visitors such as these men understood, after a face-to-face encounter with Nazi Germany, that the country had undergone a fundamental transformation. A dispatch from the *New York Times* bureau in Berlin noted that though Nazi actions might "appear incomprehensible to observers in Western democracies," it had to be remembered that "Nazism's prestige rests on complete fulfillment of its antisemitic dogma in all its ramifications"; consequently Germany would "use all means at its disposal" to advance its antisemitic goals.[61] Yet there was in general a dichotomy in the ranks of the press between reporters stationed in Germany, who because of where they were recognized the insidious nature of the National Socialist Party, and editors, publishers, and commentators witnessing Germany from afar, who tended to be more skeptical and optimistic.

This split was mirrored in the diplomatic corps, though it was far less striking there.[62] A number of the American diplomats stationed in Germany, including Ambassador Dodd, Consul General George Messersmith, Commercial Attaché Douglas Miller, and Consul Raymond Geist, understood the nature of this regime. Even before the Nuremberg Laws were issued, Dodd and some of his colleagues contended that any amelioration in the Jews' situation, including the order against *Einzelaktionen,* or individual acts of terror, was simply a "camouflage for more drastic action based upon the plan of proceeding against the Jews by orderly, lawful means."[63] Many State Department officials at home were more optimistic about the future course of German affairs in general and the fate of the German Jews in particular. This split, which became even more striking as the situation grew more severe, may have resulted in part from the unprecedented nature of Germany's behavior, which was particularly hard to fathom when one heard about it from a distance. Never before, even in states which were unquestionably antisemitic, e.g., Czarist Russia, had the demonization of the Jew been made the *raison d'être* of the regime. Antisemitism was a fundamental element of Nazism. While officially sanctioned antisemitism was not new, the fact that this was taking place in Germany, a country where Jews were fully integrated into the fabric of society, was difficult to comprehend. It was also hard to comprehend that this was occurring in a land which attached considerable importance to foreign opinion, especially in "those countries from which she hopes to gain political or financial advantage."[64]

Another explanation for this dichotomy may well have been the ever intensifying American conviction that the country must never be drawn into one of "Europe's eternal wars." A number of reporters who returned to America after a sojourn in Germany attributed the skeptical and sometimes hostile reception their stories of terror received from the American public to the fact that Americans in "overwhelming" numbers were determined to stay out of Europe's affairs and therefore resented being made uncomfortable by these stories. Even when they accepted the reports as accurate, they often argued that this was "no business of ours."[65]

Voices of Praise: Tourists, Students, Businessmen

Reporters also faced an obstacle in the stark contrast between their accounts and what Tolischus described as "the eulogistic statements about conditions in Germany made by returning American tourists."[66] Germany was neat and clean. There were no slums, and people were well dressed. In contrast to America in the early 1930s, in Germany no jobless were visible on streetcorners selling apples or pencils, and no homeless were to be seen living in shantytowns or gathered in desolate corners of large cities. Visiting Americans, impressed by Germany's spectacular achievements, repeatedly complained to reporters about their pessimistic and critical news reports. It was acutely difficult to convince visitors who did not witness overt acts of persecution and discrimination that there was more to the new Reich than its economic renewal, rebuilt physical plant, substantial sports achievements, and gracious welcome accorded those from abroad. Edgar Ansel Mowrer's wife Lilian found it exasperating to hear people who paid a short visit to Germany fervently deny the fact that anything unusual was happening. "But you *must* be exaggerating, everything is so calm here, there is no disorder, and the Germans are such pleasant people . . . how could they allow such things to happen?" After his expulsion from Germany, Edgar Mowrer toured the United States and found many people unwilling to believe his description of life in Nazi Germany. In 1933 *The Nation* complained that it was "difficult to restrain the silly people who after a week or two in Germany, during which they have seen no Jews beaten up in the streets, go back to their own countries and declare that the stories told in the papers about Germany are all untrue." These visitors often said they knew things were not that bad because "the Nazis had told [them] so." (One reporter developed a foolproof method for countering this impression. She would have any of her American or British visitors who "fell victim" to the Nazis' "charms" or propaganda accompany her to an interview with the Nazi leader Julius Streicher. Listening to him, particularly when he spoke about Jews, was enough to "cancel out all their good impressions.")[67]

When Norman Chandler, the publisher of the *Los Angeles Times*, visited Germany during the Olympic Games, he berated Ralph Barnes of the *New York Herald Tribune* and William Shirer of CBS for their critical and alarming stories on Germany. Other businessmen in his group told these two reporters that they had never seen a people so "happy, content, and united," as one put it, and that the violence which had been reported was exaggerated or had not even occurred. When the reporters asked who had told them this, they responded that it was Hermann Goering.

Upon her return to this country Martha Dodd, the Ambassador's daughter, complained about the "naivete" of Americans who dismissed the reports from Germany as "gross exaggeration."[68] Throughout the 1930s American students continued to go to study in German universities, and many of them were deeply impressed by what they found there. They too served to counter the reporters' pessimism.[69]

But it was not only tourists and students who praised conditions in Germany. Americans with business there did so as well. Sometimes this resulted from what the American Consul General in Berlin described as "real pressure" placed on American businessmen and exchange professors by German officials to "send statements which would not give a really correct picture of the situation."[70] When these Americans returned home, they often told their local paper a very different and far more positive story than the one being carried by the news services. The praise by some came of their own volition and they had no ulterior motive; others had an economic motive for praising Germany. Sigrid Schultz claimed that many American businessmen were lured into snapping up "lucrative contracts" proffered by Nazi business interests and then threatened by Nazis that irregularities in these deals would be exposed if they failed to publicly extol Germany.[71]

The American business community was impressed by the way in which Hitler was directing Germany's economic recovery.[72] *Business Week* believed that in terms of economic programs, "in many ways the Hitler administration is paralleling the Roosevelt administration." By the end of 1934 there was a general consensus in much of the American business community that the recovery in Germany was healthier than in the United States. Germany managed to reduce the number of jobless from 6 million in 1933 to 1.17 million by the summer of 1936. The armament program, road-building projects, and forced sharing of work continued to whittle away at the number of unemployed, so that by 1937 joblessness was not a problem for Germany. The American business world envied the increasingly improving economic conditions enjoyed by the Reich. (By the mid-1930s, however, many business publications, while strongly isolationist, were critical of German economic affairs because of their highly controlled nature. The business press was also disturbed because of the demise of a free press in Germany.)[73] There were numerous American firms with extensive business interests in Germany. One American company was making more than half of all the passenger cars in Germany, another was building the ambulances for the Wehrmacht, still another had 20,000 filling stations, and many others had millions of dollars invested in all sorts of plants and equipment. According to Douglas Miller, American Commercial Attaché in Berlin, all these firms were "peculiarly subject to pressure and threats from Nazi quarters."[74]

Contrasts in the Press

Thus, even as much of the press was telling one story, visitors, businessmen, and German propaganda mills were telling another. But they were not the only ones who related wondrous accounts of life in Germany. The *Christian Science Monitor* seemed particularly intent on describing life in Germany as "normal and serene." Praise of Germany's natural beauty and social order was to be frequently found in its news and editorial columns. In August 1933 a two-part, unsigned series entitled "A Traveler Visits Germany" told of a satisfied, industrious, contented nation whose populace was fully devoted to the Nazis: "The train arrived punctually. . . . traffic was well regulated. . . . An occasional mounted policeman in smart blue uniform was to be seen. . . . street cafes are busy." Even the infamous Brown Shirts emerged in a benevolent light. They behaved like they were "members of some student corps." Little seemed amiss: "I have so far found quietness, order and civility." This traveler found "not the slightest sign of anything unusual afoot." Doubts were also cast upon the tales of Jewish suffering. The "harrowing stories" of Jews "deprived of their occupations" applied, the reporter assured readers, "only to a small proportion of the members of this . . . community." Most Jews were "not in any way molested."[75]

Other papers and journals were reporting a strikingly different story. At the same time that the *Christian Science Monitor*'s traveler was painting a portrait of a Germany peaceful, joyous, on the road to recovery, and above all united behind Hitler, who was bringing to a "dark land a clear light of hope," *Newsweek* reported the arrest of 200 Jewish merchants in Nuremberg who were accused of "profiteering," beatings inflicted on American Jews who were in Berlin, and the closing of Jewish Telegraphic Agency offices in Germany.[76] Hamilton Fish Armstrong described the red proclamation affixed to the door of the Jewish research institute, the Berlin Hochschule, and the doors of similar institutions throughout the Reich proclaiming the Jew as the enemy of German thought and culture. By this time the *Los Angeles Times* had reversed its stand, and now branded Hitler's denial of antisemitic persecution as "feeble and unconvincing." The *Los Angeles Times* carried the harrowing description of how a young German woman was publicly humiliated for spending time with a Jewish man. Her head was shaved clean, and she was forced to march through a hostile crowd wearing a placard stating "I have offered myself to a Jew." The incident was witnessed by a number of American correspondents including Quentin Reynolds, who was touring the area with Ambassador Dodd's children. In a series of front-page stories the *Los Angeles Times* described the "campaign of indignities" against German girls who kept company with Jewish boys. It featured "documentary evidence" of this campaign in the form of a card given to these girls threatening them with violence if they continued this practice.[77]

Some papers and journalists who acknowledged that persecution existed still maintained a benevolent attitude toward Nazi Germany. This was particularly the case when their support of Germany had an ideological basis. Colonel Robert McCormick, the publisher of the *Chicago Tribune,* visited Germany in August 1933 and wrote a series of three articles about what he saw. He found a reign of terror which placed "suspected Communists, members of former opposition parties and all Jews . . . in constant danger." McCormick's comments are particularly important in light of the fact that the *Tribune* considered Hitler a force against communism and supported him as such.[78]* Even *The Christian*

---

* In a taped interview prepared for the Tribune Company's archives on its foreign correspondents, Sigrid Schultz offered some interesting comments on McCormick's initial willingness to criticize Nazi Germany, as he did in these articles. She accompanied him during this visit to Germany in 1933. At one point she grew concerned that McCormick was becoming enthralled by the gracious treatment accorded him. Moreover, his military background predisposed him to be sympathetic to the military demeanor of the Germans. At a Nazi rally and celebration in Berlin she sat next to the colonel and watched how mesmerized he was by the military display. "I could see his soldier's heart throbbing—the way they marched was just absolutely beautiful." Fearful of the effect of the parade, Nazi military precision, and the hospitality he was being shown would have on him, she turned to the colonel, who insisted that the *Tribune*

Century, which had been and would continue to be skeptical about the accuracy of the reports of persecution, momentarily set aside its dubiousness when Paul Hutchinson, an editor of the journal, returned from visiting Germany to report that "the actual brutalities inflicted on Jews, socialists, communists and pacifists have been even more severe than the American press has published."[80]

The Triumph of Doubt

But these negative assessments of German life did not dispel the doubts of some of those who had not personally witnessed these developments. As late as 1935, when America's participation in the Olympics was being vigorously debated, some papers opposed the boycott because, they said, the news from Germany regarding the treatment of Jews was unsubstantiated "hearsay" on the basis of which it would be wrong to withdraw. A similar argument was made in the summer of 1935 by the *Minneapolis Tribune* after AFL President William Green recommended that Americans boycott Germany. Ignoring the numerous eyewitness accounts of events in Germany, it argued that a boycott would mean "involving this country in a dispute about which it has little accurate information." Earlier that year, in January, an article in *Harper's* observed that when it came to press reports of Nazi persecution of Jews "what relation the news we get on the subject bears to the truth cannot be accurately calculated."[81]

By this point in time extensive accounts of the riots and other violent outbreaks in Germany, many of which SS officials had verified, had appeared in the press. Various legal and quasi-legal

---

was a "respectable . . . family newspaper," pointed to where the high-ranking Nazi leaders were assembled, and said, "Colonel, the little man there right beside Roehm is his former lover, and his other lover, the new one, is standing right behind there." Schultz believed that McCormick was willing to criticize the Nazis at this point because of aversion to homosexual behavior and his impression that leading Nazis engaged in it. She believed that subsequently, when Hitler murdered Roehm and those around him, for McCormick back in Chicago "it meant that that nice man [Hitler] had nothing to do with the homosexuals." This, Schultz believed, made it easier for the Nazis to ultimately win McCormick's complete sympathies: once the "perversion" was eliminated McCormick's feelings about the Nazis improved and he was able to see them as simply engaged in fighting communism.[79]

actions against Jews had been announced by German officials and reported by the German news agency. Nonetheless, there was a feeling in much of the press that America did not really have completely "accurate information" about the persecution of the Jews. There were papers, such as the *Philadelphia Record* and *New York Evening Post,* which dismissed German attempts to deny the persecution as "absurd statements."[82] More prevalent, however, was a state of skepticism and confusion about whether things were *as* bad as reported. Even while they condemned the Nazis' brutality, editorial boards expressed reservations about the accounts of brutality because they seemed beyond the pale of believability. Initial doubts regarding the veracity of the reports notwithstanding, the abundance of detail and eyewitness accounts constituted strong evidence of persecution. Most papers were never totally swayed by German denials and generally agreed that the accounts of what had been perpetrated upon a "defenseless Jewry" were too numerous and similar to believe "the *blanket* denial" offered by German officials. However, they also seemed never to fully accept the accuracy of the reports.[83] Newspaper stories and editorials increasingly echoed the *St. Louis Post Dispatch*'s assessment that while the reports of persecution, including looting and even murder, might be "somewhat exaggerated," they nonetheless demanded attention because they were so "uniform in tenor." The press did not doubt that terrible things were happening, but its belief was a grudging belief, sometimes bordering on disbelief. As one paper expressed it, "when there is so much smoke there must be some fire."[84]

This persistent incredulity would not fade with the passage of time, but would instead come to characterize the American reaction to Nazi persecution. Often this skepticism persisted in the face of detailed information to the contrary. In February 1939, three months after *Kristallnacht,* Quentin Reynolds, writing in *Collier's,* noted that since that pogrom, which had been described in great detail in practically every American paper and magazine, the "plague of hate" against Jews had grown "in intensity every day." Nonetheless "there are those," he complained, "in England and in America who shrug complacent shoulders and who say: 'Oh things can't be as bad as we hear.' " The truth was, Reynolds observed, the Jews' plight was "actually much worse than we have heard."[85]

Over the course of the years to 1945 the details would multiply, but the doubts would never be completely erased. By early in the Nazis' rule a pattern had emerged which would characterize the reaction of the press as well as the public to the entire Nazi persecution. Americans did not doubt that things were difficult for the Jews but seemed reluctant to believe that they were as bad as reporters on the scene claimed. Whether the story was of Jewish judges being dragged from their courtrooms or Jews being rounded up and shot en masse, the news was greeted with both horror and disbelief, condemnation and skepticism.

2

Making Meaning of Events

As reports of the beatings and legal disenfranchisement of the Jews continued to flow out of Germany, it became increasingly clear that physical and juridical antisemitism had found a secure niche in Nazi Germany. Now that persecution was occurring with frightening regularity, the press sought to explain why it was happening. The events being reported sounded so fantastic that condemnation alone seemed insufficient. The determination to discover "what is behind it" and "what's it all about" was also characteristic of the press response to Nazi antisemitism. Ironically, the more it sought to explicate, the more it tended to obscure reality.

Analysis of the explanations offered is illuminating because it is in them, more than in the condemnations, that the press's perception of what was happening to Jews in Nazi Germany can best be discerned. In a certain respect these explanations shaped the way in which both contemporary analysts and future scholars would understand German behavior. Had the American press and other Western observers understood the central role of antisemitism in Nazi ideology, they would have been less perplexed by the violence, which seemed to run counter to Germany's intention to win investing nations' confidence in the Reich. During this period it was common knowledge that Germany wanted "above all things to make a favorable impression on the outside world"; why then, the press wondered, did it allow antisemitic outbreaks to mar its image?[1]

Why Antisemitism? Seeking a Rational Explanation

The press's confusion was heightened in the summer of 1935 when the quiet of Berlin's fashionable Kurfürstendamm was shattered as groups of rowdy and destructive Germans—exactly who they were and who instigated their actions remained a matter of contention in the press—stormed up and down the boulevard. They brutally beat up Jews, and all those they assumed were Jews, who were frequenting the famed ice cream parlors and outdoor cafes on the tree-lined avenue or promenading in the cool summer evening breeze. The riots lasted through the evening and were repeated a number of times in the following days.

Witnessed by summer strollers, foreign correspondents stationed in Berlin, and tourists from various nations, the outbreaks were prominently featured on the front pages and in the editorial columns of the American press, even though they were not the most violent actions to occur since the onset of Nazi rule. World interest was heightened by the fact that unlike earlier violence, these riots took place not in a small town, village, or provincial city, but in the German capital, the seat of the German government. These disruptions could not, therefore, be dismissed as local aberrations or blamed on the excesses of overly zealous provincial storm troop leaders. Observers were particularly perplexed by these events because they occurred during the American debate over participation in the Olympic Games and while the British Minister of Trade was in Berlin negotiating with the Germans. Western commentators assumed that Germany would bar anything that might jeopardize the Games' success. A strong foreign reaction to these riots could increase the likelihood of a boycott.

Because they appeared to contravene German objectives, the press was all the more motivated to find a rationale for them.

The explanations offered in various editorials for these and other similar incidents fell into a few basic categories. The most commonly accepted motive was that Hitler wished to "divert attention" from domestic problems and to camouflage the steadily worsening economic situation. One editorial argued that by focusing attention on the Jews, the German government could "flimflam on matters of vital concern."[2] "Frenzy . . . [and] hysteria are vented upon minorities," one paper concluded, to "keep public attention away from the [economic] crisis."[3]

The riots, as well as the many other antisemitic provocations, were also seen as an attempt to unify the German people. The Jews "have always made excellent 'whipping boys' . . . and [have] provid[ed] an outlet for a resentment" which otherwise, for "lack of a scapegoat," might be directed at the government. The *Dallas News* believed Hitler was "bolstering his position by playing to anti-Jewish sentiment."[4] Similar explanations would be offered by the American press eight years later to explain the deportations of Jews from Germany.

German antisemitism was also commonly interpreted as a reflection of the country's dissatisfaction with the Versailles treaty. The *Houston Post* argued in April 1933 that while "a dictatorship for Germany is regrettable, it was inevitable" because of the peace pact. Though various papers and commentators subscribed to this position, it was argued most persistently by the leading isolationist paper, the *Chicago Tribune.* If the inequities from Versailles could be rectified, then, the paper contended, Hitler's diatribes and the internal violence they provoked would be eradicated. The *Cincinnati Enquirer* echoed this view. These rationalizations and explanations gave Nazi behavior an aura of inevitability. Blaming the persecution on Versailles or on the German balance of payments relieved the Nazis of responsibility, making it appear that they were simply being carried along by events beyond their control. Second, such explanations placed ultimate responsibility for the violence on those who had imposed the treaty on Germany.[5]

But external forces were not all that was blamed; the victims were blamed as well. One common interpretation offered during this period, and still heard many years later, was that the Jews had brought this on themselves. The *Christian Science Monitor* was among those who found Jews, both inside and outside of Germany, responsible—at least in part—for the Reich's brutality. It suggested that the reports of violence were "exaggerated" by those "inclined towards hysteria," including reporters and Jews in America and England. In its editorials and commentaries on the April 1, 1933, German boycott of Jewish stores and businesses, the *Christian Science Monitor* argued that Jewish, not German, excesses needed curbing. The *Monitor's* front-page columnist, Rufus Steele, placed the responsibility for the German boycott on foreign Jews' calls for a boycott of German goods: this forced the Nazis' hand and prompted retaliation in the form of the April 1 action, which was a "rebuke to false propaganda about atrocities." Once again Germans were depicted as responding to a situation that was neither their fault nor their responsibility. The same approach to the boycott was adopted by the *New York Herald Tribune* and its Berlin correspondent John Elliott. They were convinced that Jewish protests were inflaming the situation. On a number of occasions in March 1933 Elliot argued that Jews were not being persecuted because of their "race," but because they were "political" opponents of Hitler. Einstein, he contended, was "detested by the Nazis more for his pacifism than for his Jewish blood." On March 27 the paper carried two front-page stories on the Jews' situation. One reported Hull's assurances that the violence had ended, and the other discussed how American Jews were determined to protest conditions in Germany "despite assurances" from Hull and representatives of German Jewry that there was no violence. The impression left by both stories was that American Jews were exacerbating a difficult situation which, according to United States government officials, had been ameliorated. According to the *New York Herald Tribune* German Jews had "beg[ged]" American Jews to end their protests but the latter had adamantly "refuse[d]." The *New York Herald Tribune* presented the curtailing of the boycott as dependent on "Jews" ceasing to spread "atrocity tales." The *Literary Digest* was noncommittal as to who was most to blame and faulted both Germans and "Jewish sympathizers abroad" for the "double edged sword" of boycotts.

> Round and round in a dizzying circle of atrocity reports, denials of atrocities, protests, counter-protests, apprehension, boycotts and counter-boycotts, revolve Chancellor Hitler of Germany, his Nazis, German Jewry and Jewish sympathizers abroad.[6]

The most vituperative attack on Jews' protests appeared three days after the April 1 boycott in the lead editorial in the *Christian Science Monitor*. It accused American Jews of exacerbating the situation by demanding that official bodies such as the State Department and the League of Nations condemn Germany. German people, the editorial argued, had the right not only to be indignant over "atrocity" stories but to punish "rumor mongers." The *Christian Science Monitor* not only placed the word "atrocity" in quotation marks, thereby indicating its doubts about the accuracy of the reports, but reiterated almost verbatim the Nazi explanation for the boycott: "Stringent measures against those who spread lies against Germany are easily justified." In contrast to the *Monitor*'s justification of the boycott, the *New York Times* believed the boycott proved that the Nazis were "acting blindly and almost . . . with a touch of insanity."[7]

Relying on Biblical imagery, the *Christian Science Monitor* accused Jews in America and England of practicing the "ancient code of an 'eye for an eye.'" Had Jews heeded Jesus' commandment to "love one another" and Spinoza's saying that "it is rational to repay persecution with love," this "misunderstanding" might have been avoided. Who misunderstood whom was not clarified.

Among the most telling aspects of the editorial was a brief statement that illuminated the *Christian Science Monitor*'s general attitude toward Jews. It exonerated the non-Jewish world of responsibility for its antisemitism by declaring that it was Jews' "commercial clannishness which . . . gets them into trouble," and recommended that Jews both "within Germany and without might give some attention to this problem."[8] The entire editorial reflected the tradition of the modern Protestant critique of Judaism, whose source was in a school of scholarship which portrayed Judaism as a soulless religion of dry legalisms and national particularism.[9] The paper revealed a latent hostility toward Jews and Judaism by raising the specter of *lex talionis,* accusing Jews of failing to adhere to Jesus' commandment and attributing Jews' sorrows to their supposed economic propensities and to protests by American and English Jews. The editorial indicated that the *Christian Science Monitor*'s view of the Jews' contemporary suffering was refracted through the prism of Christianity's long-standing theological view of Judaism.

The *Christian Science Monitor* was not the only representative of the Protestant press to suggest that Jews were responsible for their suffering or to express a subtle animus toward Jews and Judaism. The *Reformed Church Messenger, Lutheran Companion, Moody Bible Institute Monthly,* and other publications echoed these views.[10]

The Christian Century, also suggested that the root of the problem was Jews' behavior and accused Jews in Germany and abroad of exacerbating the situation. Ironically, whereas the *Christian Science Monitor* faulted Jews for their commercial activities, *The Christian Century* faulted them for their radical activities.

> May we ask if Hitler's attitude may be somewhat governed by the fact that too many Jews, at least in Germany, are radical, too many are communists? May that have any bearing on the situation? There must be some reason other than race or creed— just what is that reason? It is always well to try to understand.

The Christian Century, the most prominent Protestant journal in the country, had already responded to these questions a few weeks earlier in an article by a German Jew living in America. He accused German Jews of bringing their present suffering on themselves by supporting "reactionary parties," setting themselves off as aliens, eating particular foods, keeping Saturday as a holiday and doing other things which aroused "suspicion and envy."[11]

A similar view—that Jews had caused their own suffering— was voiced by Walter Lippmann, at the time considered by many to be America's most influential columnist and commentator. Lippmann had severely criticized Hitler when he assumed power, but his fears were allayed by a conciliatory-sounding speech Hitler delivered in mid-May 1933. Convinced that the German leader was intent on pursuing peace, he dismissed claims that Hitler was insincere and described Hitler's speech as the voice of a civilized people coming through "fog and the din, the hysteria and the animal passions of a great revolution." He urged his readers not to judge Germany on the basis of the Nazi radicals and argued that people possessed a "dual nature": they could be good and evil. "To deny," he argued in defense of Germany, "that Germany can speak as a civilized power because uncivilized things are being said and done in Germany, is in itself a deep form of intolerance." He bolstered his argument by citing other peoples' defects.

> Who that has studied history and cares for the truth would judge the French people by what went on during their terror? Or the British people by what happened in Ireland? Or the Catholic church by the Catholic church of the Spanish Inquisition? Or Protestantism by the Ku Klux Klan *or the Jews by their parvenus?*[12]

Lippmann's desire to call attention to what he considered legitimate German grievances about the Versailles treaty did not, as his biographer Ronald Steel has noted, require him to describe Hitler's speech as "statesmanlike" and the "authentic voice of a genuinely civilized people."* Most disturbing was his gratuitous equation of the French terror, the Ku Klux Klan, and Nazi brutality with Jewish "parvenus." Coming from one of the most influential opinion makers in America, it was an offensive, if not insidious, comparison. Coming from a Jew, it indicated an ambivalence, if not outright hostility, about his Jewish identity. Most significantly, however, it suggested that Jewish behavior was ultimately the cause of antisemitism.**

After defending Hitler's supposed peace-loving qualities, Lippmann never acknowledged that in the weeks immediately following the "conciliatory" speech violence had occurred which, the *London Times* correspondent in Berlin pointed out, could not be excused as the inevitable accompaniments of "first revolutionary fervor," as violence in March and April had been excused by many foreign observers. Lippmann simply ignored these subsequent outbreaks.***

---

* The speech *was* a powerful one—in a letter to his daughter, who was a student at the University of Chicago, Louis Lochner described it as the "best thing I have heard Hitler do."

** There are numerous examples of Lippmann's discomfort with his Jewish identity. To honor Lippmann on his seventieth birthday, a group of his colleagues published a collection of essays in his honor. Carl Binger, a well-known psychiatrist and a good friend of Lippmann's, was invited to contribute an essay on Lippmann's youth. He agreed to do so but with one condition. He could not mention that Lippmann was a Jew because if he did, Lippmann would never speak to him again.[13]

*** This was not the first time Lippmann had suggested that Jews provoked antisemitism; he had done so a decade earlier. In fact, in the spring of 1922 Lippmann contributed an article to a special issue of the *American Hebrew*, in which he openly charged that this was the case. "The Jews are fairly distinct in their physical appearance and in the spelling of their names from the run of the American people. . . . They are, therefore, conspicuous. . . . sharp trading and blatant vulgarity are more conspicuous in the Jew because he himself is more conspicuous." Lippmann's recommendation was that the Jew work to ensure that he not be noticeable. "Because the Jew is more conspicuous he is under all the greater obligation not to practice the vices of our civilization." Lippmann then attacked *nouveaux riches* Jews in a tone that reflected the classic attitudes of many wealthy established German Jews who had come to America in the mid-nineteenth century toward the more recent immigrants, particularly those from Eastern Europe. The "rich and vulgar and pretentious Jews of our big American cities are perhaps the greatest misfortune that has ever befallen the Jewish people." They were, in his opinion, the "real fountain of antisemitism. When they rush about in super-automobiles, bejeweled and furred and painted

Ultimately Lippmann's views would be echoed by many Americans, as was evidenced by an April 1938 poll in which approximately 60 percent agreed that the persecution of European Jews was either entirely or partly their own fault. Nevertheless, Lippmann's column shocked many readers, including Felix Frankfurter, his mentor and supporter, who was so incensed that he did not communicate with Lippmann for over three and a half years.[15]

The tendency to find the cause of Jewish suffering in Jewish behavior was not unique to Lippmann and sectors of the Christian press. An analysis of antisemitism which appeared in *Harper's* argued that Jews in England "do better" than in most countries in terms of social standing and non-Jews' attitudes toward them because that country never was "overrun by crowds of them. . . . Any group of people that in the long run seems to be getting more than its share of what is accessible will come in due time to be disliked by observers who are less fortunate."[16]

The belief that Jews were responsible for their suffering was not necessarily indicative of a pro-Nazi or pro-German attitude. Even papers which unequivocally condemned Germany's action still attributed the persecution of the Jews to something they had done. The *Columbus Dispatch,* which warned German Ambassador Luther that Americans would not tolerate Germany's antisemitism, believed that Hitler's policies were directed against the "large Jewish element in the financial, commercial, professional and official life of present-day Germany."[17] Franklin Roosevelt also succumbed to this kind of reasoning. In January 1943 at the Casablanca conference he proposed that North African resettlement projects restrict the number of Jews allowed to practice such professions as law and medicine. The President argued that "his plan would further eliminate the specific and understandable complaints which the Germans bore towards the Jews in Germany, namely that while they represented a small part of the population,

---

and overbarbered, when they build themselves French chateaux and Italian palazzi, they stir up the latent hatred against crude wealth in the hands of shallow people; and that hatred diffuses itself."

Steel notes that the "crudeness" and the "cruelty" of Lippmann's attacks on his fellow Jews are in marked contrast to the sensitivity he displayed toward other minority groups and those suffering discrimination. It is "inconceivable," according to Steel, that Lippmann would have written anything similar about the Irish, the Italians, or the blacks, despite the fact that none of these groups was without its own *nouveaux riches.*[14]

over 50% of the lawyers, doctors, school teachers, college professors, etc. in Germany were Jews."[18]

Defining antisemitism as a *quid pro quo* for Jewish behavior
was one of the ways observers tried to make sense of events in
Germany. In reality it only belied the true nature of Nazism and
made it more difficult for observers from afar to understand it.

The Question of Government Responsibility

During these early years the press struggled to determine if the
government had instigated, condoned, or simply been unable to
contain these outbreaks. If it was not responsible, what other
group—inside the Nazi Party or outside of it—might be held ac-
countable? The more irrational the violence appeared and the
more it seemed to contravene German goals, the more the press,
particularly the newspapers analyzing the situation from the American side of the Atlantic, was inclined to try to hold some non-
governmental entity responsible.

The tendency of some of the press to blame ancillary entities
was graphically illustrated in 1933 when the earliest outbreaks
were described by various editorials as the "unauthorized sallies
of irresponsible mobs of youthful Nazis" and the work of "overen-
thusiastic and poorly disciplined followers."[19] By designating
those engaged in violence as "mobs" or "followers," the press
not only exonerated Hitler but differentiated between him and
those who indulged in such behavior. The press also exonerated
Hitler by claiming that Nazi violence was a reflection of strife
between party moderates and radicals. Generally the proponents
of this internecine-warfare theory placed Hitler in the ranks of
the moderates and surmised that the violence was committed over
his protests or unbeknownst to him. United Press believed that
it reflected the extremists' displeasure with Hitler's attempt to
pursue a moderate course and proof that that the radical elements
had "gained the upper hand for the time being." United Press
representatives in Germany subscribed to the idea of this moder-
ate-versus-radical dichotomy and dismissed the entire Nazi antisemitic campaign as "just a side show" organized and tolerated
for the benefit of extremist elements. Catholics and Jews, they
explained, were bearing the "brunt of the Nazi party struggle
between conservatives and extremists." The United Press theory,
which appeared in numerous papers, apparently shaped many

editorial responses to the riots. Readers of the *Canton* (Ohio) *Repository* were told that "Chancellor Hitler, personally, is committed to a policy of moderation" and that events such as the July 1935 riots were proof of the difficulty he was experiencing in "controlling the action of subordinates."[20] The *Boston Post* wondered if such outbreaks were a sign that Hitler was "in trouble."[21] The *Boston Evening Transcript* speculated that the rioters were able to work unhindered because "the Government . . . did not dare to interfere with the lawless among its followers." *Literary Digest* also believed that the outbreaks reflected "divergence in high Nazi circles" regarding the drive against Jews.[22]

Other papers did not totally exonerate Hitler but only held him responsible for creating the climate that produced the outbreak. His rhetoric started something which was now being carried along "by the force of its own momentum." The proof of this was that despite the fact that "officialdom . . . frowned" upon the riots, they had persisted.[23] A similar explanation was posited by the *Trenton* (New Jersey) *Times Advertiser* in an editorial entitled "Hitler's Frankenstein." The monster created by Hitler had grown "out of control." The riots were the product of "subordinates who, apparently, disobeyed orders and did exactly what they wanted to do." News of the riots, the paper informed its readers, "brought dismay to Hitler," who, another paper believed, remained "on the sidelines." The *New York Herald Tribune* echoed this view and blamed "violently worded anti-Jewish" propaganda for creating the atmosphere for these "cruel excesses." A *Dallas Times Herald* editorial also cast Hitler as the passive actor in this scenario. It praised him for having many of the good qualities a dictator must have in order to prevent the country from "suffering all the ill effects of tyranny," but could not overlook the fact that "the Nazi leader *permits* a defenseless minority to be persecuted."[24] Once again Hitler was cast not as instigator, but as bystander, the one who failed to prevent persecution.

This inability to believe that Hitler was directly responsible was a manifestation of the press's difficulty in accepting that his antisemitism was not rhetoric, but a deep-seated ideology. This difficulty persisted as late as *Kristallnacht,* when the *Atlanta Constitution* and the *Hamilton* (Ohio) *Journal News* both surmised that Hitler must have been "deceived by those around him because no man possessed of sanity would have brought upon his nation the condemnation of the world."[25]

Some papers which subscribed to the notion that the government was not directly involved changed their minds when immediately after the 1935 riots Count Wolf von Helldorf, who was known as a "violent antisemite" and a "pogrom leader," was appointed Berlin's chief of police.[26] The *Baltimore Sun,* which had previously absolved the government of at least a portion of the responsibility, now implicitly admitted that it had been wrong. His appointment, the *Sun* observed,

> removes from serious consideration the idea that the recent beating and kicking of Jews in the Kurfürsten-damm was the result of young men getting out of hand.[27]

In contrast to many other papers, the *New York Post* was not ambivalent about the source of the riots or, for that matter, the entire range of antisemitic policies. In an editorial entitled "Not Hooligans but Hitler," the *Post* designated anyone who believed that the riots were "spontaneous" and "unofficial" either a "Nazi sympathizer or a fool."[28] Other papers offered similar arguments. "Hitler's hand appears only indirectly in the latest campaign to suppress the Jews. . . . He is its source, one may be sure." "Hitler is wholly and completely responsible for it [antisemitic violence] and . . . since it persists, it must represent his personal views."[29] "There is every reason to view them [the riots] as having been of official origin. They could not have happened without the knowledge and consent of the Chancellor."[30] American Ambassador Dodd shared the conviction that the riots, as well as other antisemitic incidents, were sanctioned by the government, which dispatched *agents provocateurs* to do the work.[31]

However, unequivocal association of the governmental leaders—Hitler in particular—with the violence and brutality was the exception to the rule during the first years of Nazi rule. Generally the press remained confused, recognizing that someone with power was behind these attacks but not quite believing that it was Hitler or those around him. After the Nuremberg rally of 1934 William Shirer was convinced that the west in general and "our newspapers above all had underestimated Adolf Hitler." Yet while the press generally refrained from pointing the finger of blame directly at Hitler, it did not accept the government's protestations of innocence. When German authorities told journalists that thanks to the "cooperation of the police" the riots had been stopped, their claims were dismissed with derision. Numerous eyewitness reports were cited telling of studied police disinterest while rioters had free reign over one of Berlin's most fashionable boulevards. *Time* and *Newsweek* both informed their readers that the Berlin police took "little interest in the Jew hunt" and just "looked on calmly" as the rioters proceeded with their work.[32]

Seeking a Moderate Hitler

This confusion regarding Hitler's responsibility for the campaign of terror was reflective of a broader debate then being conducted in the United States and Europe. Many people, including those responsible for formulating policy, could not decide how committed Hitler was to realizing his threats to nullify the Versailles treaty, rearm Germany, expand its borders, and fulfill his numerous other objectives. During these years there were many optimists who counseled that once the Nazi leader solidified his rule, eased Germany's economic crisis, and redressed the balance of power, he would moderate his tone, abandon his extremist and hyperbolic rhetoric, and assume a respected role as a head of state.

The isolationist *Chicago Tribune* and some other papers, including the *New York Times*, were optimistic about Hitler's ability, in the words of the *Christian Science Monitor*, to act like the month of March—"come in like a lion" and soon become a "lamb." Once Hitler "becomes more used to his job," the *Los Angeles Times* predicted, he would surely become less "theatrical."[33] In his front-page column "March of Nations," the *Monitor*'s Rufus Steele reassured readers that "power tempers the Chancellor's ready tongue." Steele reached this conclusion in the same column in which he cited Hitler's Reichstag announcement that the German government "will attempt to exterminate communism, . . . ruthlessly punish treason . . . not tolerate adherence to a religion or race that [was not] lawful," and give the German people a "moral purging." Somehow Steele managed to extrapolate from this that Hitler was becoming more moderate.[34] In mid-March 1933 Frederick Birchall, who was then serving as *New York Times* Berlin bureau chief, was in the United States. In a nationally broadcast CBS radio speech he denied that Hitler was a dictator. He described him as a "bachelor and a vegetarian and he neither drinks nor smokes. His whole life, his whole thought are given to this National Socialist movement and he has taken upon himself the hardest job that ever a man could undertake." He also urged listeners to dismiss the thought that the Nazis would engage in "slaughter of the[ir] enemies or racial oppression in any vital degree."* On March 12 the *Times* ran an editorial complimenting Hitler for urging his followers to "refrain from acts of individual terrorism." In July *Times* columnist Anne O'Hare McCormick offered readers a benign, almost enraptured description of her interview with the Chancellor. She described his "curiously childlike and candid" blue eyes, his voice which was "as quiet as his black tie," and his frequent smile, and concluded that when he talked he was "undubitably sincere." In his conversation with her, Hitler declared that acts of discrimination were not directed primarily against Jews, but "against the Communists and all elements that demoralized and destroyed us."[35]

Shortly after the Nazis' nationwide boycott against Jews, Hitler's speeches were interpreted by many editors as showing "an unexpectedly moderate tone." His claim to be interested only in "peace" and "reconciliation" was described by one midwestern paper as "fine and conciliatory words." The *St. Louis Post Dispatch* believed that Germany would soon return to democracy. The *Detroit News* argued that the world "in fairness must wait and see what the new regime accomplishes before it hastens to condemn it."[36]

In the fall of 1933 Kurt Schmitt, Minister of the Economy, censured the boycott of Jewish business establishments. *New York Times* reporter Guido Endreis believed that Schmitt's remarks were an indication that more "responsible elements in the Hitler government are taking sane counsels on this issue." In a reversal of the norm, the *New York Times*'s editorial board took a somewhat more skeptical stance than its reporter and argued that the recurring cycle of terror in Germany raises doubts about acts of seeming moderation such as Schmitt's promises or Goebbels's statements to the foreign press that "Jews had not been treated as inferiors." The *New York Times* observed that "hitherto. . . . any sign of relaxation in one place has been counterbalanced by an outburst of unreason along another section of the anti-Jewish front." The *Times* wondered whether these developments would not be followed by a "new display of spiritual ferocity against the Jews." *Newsweek,* which also doubted the genuineness of Schmitt's statement, suggested that his comments be understood as a German

---

* Birchall later became somewhat more critical about the Nazis.

attempt to "further its reemployment program" since, as Schmitt acknowledged, the boycotted stores and businesses employed too many people to be "simply wiped out."[37] But much of the press continued to hope that moderation was in the offing and that Germany was on the verge of abandoning its violent behavior.

This expectation of impending moderation persisted even after the Berlin riots and the 1935 Nuremberg Laws. It was part of a broader set of expectations regarding Germany's policies and symptomatic of the attitude which led Neville Chamberlain to the disastrous Munich agreement. Until *Kristallnacht,* and even to a small degree thereafter, much of the press continued to be optimistic regarding Nazism's treatment of the Jews. It condemned the violence and then predicted that this particular act—whatever it might be—marked the end of the terrorist campaign against the Jews. It never did; in fact, the following act usually escalated the degree of brutality. After the July 1935 riots, when German authorities announced that those who engaged in individual actions against Jews would be subject to arrest, AP claimed that the "Nazi chieftains had called off their drive on 'state enemies.' " Newspapers which a few weeks earlier had lamented the madness prevailing in Germany now hailed Germany for "show[ing] sense." The *Washington Star* believed that "reason" had returned to the Teutonic state.[38] There was satisfaction that Germany seemed to be responding to foreign opinion.[39] The optimism may have been a reflection of the American desire to stay out of the cauldron of European problems. As long as it could be argued that Germany might eventually adopt a rational and respectable path, then it could also be argued that the world would remain at peace and America would not become entangled in foreign battles as it had less than two decades earlier.

"Signs of Weakness"

Some papers found a different reason for hope in the outbreaks. Their interpretation was indicative of the degree to which they were anxious to view the situation in a positive light. They argued that the Berlin riots as well as other antisemitic incidents reflected Hitler's weakness, not his strength, and were signs of the imminent collapse of his rule.

In some circumstances this argument would have had a certain logical foundation. Violent upheavals in the capital of a nation—particularly when the authorities attributed them to enemies of the regime—could be indicative of a threat to the government's stability. But these were not such circumstances.

The *Troy* (New York) *Record* concluded after the Berlin riots that "Nazi rule is crumbling," and a southern paper, convinced that the handwriting was on the wall, declared that "the days of the Hitlerite rule are numbered; there can be no doubt about that. Any regime which makes its appeal for popular favor on the basis of a philosophy of hate cannot survive." The *Washington Post* believed that the riots were a "precedent" to Germany's imminent collapse.[40] A New York paper believed the riots proof that things were "going badly" for the Nazi regime. According to the *Oakland Tribune* the Berlin riots revealed the existence of movements which "endanger the regime" and rendered Nazi leaders' positions precarious at best. The *Cleveland Plain Dealer* concluded that Hitler's opportunity "to create the Teutonic new age [is] fast slipping way." The *Syracuse Post Standard* found the riots a cause for celebration, for the "fact that violent measures are undertaken prove [sic] that censorship and the iron fist cannot crush for long the spirit of free men."[41] Such interpretations transformed the riots into a revolt against persecution rather than an expression of it.

Even the *New York Times,* whose front-page headline proclaimed "Antisemites Firmly in the Saddle" and whose reporters had been arguing that it was Hitler and his followers' power, not vulnerability, which led them to this new radical offensive, fell prey to the "weakness, not strength" interpretation. In an editorial it surmised that "all is not going well" within Hitler's regime and the *Reichsführer*'s "power seems to be waning."[42]

Similar interpretations had been offered in the wake of the murder of Hitler's chief lieutenant, storm troop leader Ernst Roehm, and many of Roehm's followers in 1934, which Hitler had engineered.* After that and a futile Nazi attempt to precipitate

* Roehm and the leadership of the *Sturmabteilung,* or *SA* (the storm troops), were purged in June 1934 after Roehm had demanded of Hitler that the *SA* become a part of the German army and eventually be made its central force. Roehm's interpretation of Nazi ideology was rooted in his populist, antiaristocratic ideas. By this time Hitler was working hard to attract the support of the

a civil war in Austria which would lead to imposition of Nazi rule, there was speculation in the press that Hitler's position of power had become more symbolic than real. Actually his power was realer than ever. *Chicago Daily News* correspondent Wallace R. Duel subsequently characterized repeated reports that Hitler was weakening as part of the "nightmare" with which he and other journalists had to contend. Every crisis or upheaval in Germany produced such reassuring claims from those far from the scene, and each time they proved "more false . . . than before."[43]

Of course not everyone associated with the press succumbed to this optimism. Skeptics pointed to the increasing power of Julius Streicher, publisher of the pornographic antisemitic weekly *Der Stürmer*, the persistent spread of antisemitic violence in Germany, the appointment of a known antisemite, Wolf von Helldorf, as Berlin police chief, and the rumors of forthcoming antisemitic legislation and argued that these developments did not augur well for improved treatment of Jews and were no cause for optimism.[44] The *Milwaukee Journal* interpreted German actions as a change in tactics and not policies. Germany might shun overt physical violence but would relegate Jews to a "living death" and "slow starvation" by cutting them off "entirely from [their] place in the community."[45] The *Baltimore Sun* was also unconvinced that any amelioration was in the offing. It cautioned readers against being blinded by maneuvers designed for foreign consumption and pointed out that German leaders claimed they wanted to "halt or at least 'modify' " the drive against the " 'enemies of the state' . . . but every dispatch from Germany brings fresh tales of coercion and repression [and] of new attacks upon Jews, Catholics and other groups." This view was echoed by the *New York Post,* the *Washington Post,* and the *Chattanooga Times.* The latter, which was owned by the Sulzberger family, as was the *New York Times,* had previously been rather optimistic about Germany's ability to return to a path of reason. Promises of a change in policy notwithstanding, statements by Nazi leaders indicated to the *Washing-*

---

wealthy upper class and to ensure the loyalty of the *Reichswehr* (army) leadership, which was composed of Prussian aristocrats. Despite his long-standing relationship with Hitler, Roehm was no longer useful to the party, and on June 30, 1934, he and the *SA* commanders were murdered.

ton Post that the country was "within striking distance of . . . complete terrorism."[46]

Nothing but . . .

All of the various explanations in the press about who precisely was responsible for and what were the ulterior motives behind the antisemitic violence were attempts to make sense of a situation that seemed fraught with irrational behavior. Such efforts to explain and rationalize antisemitism spring out of what has been termed the "nothing but" theory of antisemitism.[47] It is a theory that defines antisemitism as *nothing but* a means of accomplishing something else, e.g., a smokescreen designed to divert attention from other more complex problems, a means of uniting disparate groups, or a pressure valve for venting social or political discontent. Such an interpretation made it difficult, if not impossible, to understand that for the Nazis antisemitism was a, if not *the,* keystone of their ideology.

This is not to suggest that the Nazi leadership had no ulterior motives when it pursued its antisemitic campaign or that there were no variations of opinion among Nazi leaders. The struggles of 1934, including the murder of Ernst Roehm and his followers, revealed the volatility of such differences of opinion. During the early years of Nazi rule, Germany, in many respects, was still in the throes of an internal revolution as different segments of the party and government hierarchies jockeyed for power. The press was correct in arguing that antisemitism sometimes did serve as a smokescreen and that Jews were often useful as convenient scapegoats. Certain antisemitic acts *were* timed to divert attention from other problems, and some reflected divisions of opinion between competing Nazi factions. For example, there was serious debate in the Nazi ranks about the efficacy of actions such as the April 1, 1933, boycott of Jewish stores. There were officials, such as Reichsbank President Hjalmar Schacht, who were opposed to precipitous measures that might both "inflame opinion abroad" and "create economic and financial disturbances," and who were upset by the Berlin riots and the vulgar and *public* tactics of individuals such as Julius Streicher. At the other end of the spectrum there were Streicher and others who sought the "complete subordination" of the Jew, including citizenship restrictions, loss of property rights, and prohibitions upon business and social relations with non-Jews.[48] The press did not totally misread the situation; different factions were jockeying for position. However, its inclination to attribute outbreaks of antisemitism to *nothing but* the Nazi leadership's desire to placate one side or another or to divert attention from other problems obscured the degree to which antisemitism was central to Nazi ideology.[49]

Of course the press was not alone in its optimism or it adherence to "nothing but" explanations. Many Germans, Jews and non-Jews, and foreigners, including diplomats and journalists, believed that the Jews were simply serving as scapegoats. Many German Jews themselves believed that each antisemitic act marked the culmination of the Nazi campaign against them. At the time of the Nuremberg Laws some German Jews argued that because their status was now formalized by law, the situation would stabilize and improve.[50]

Yet it remains difficult to justify the press's failure to understand Nazi antisemitism. It might have required a quantum leap of the imagination to comprehend that Nazism was fundamentally different from other conventional systems of government particularly in its policies and conduct regarding the Jews. But Nazi leaders constantly reiterated their antisemitic ideology, openly promised to rid Germany of its Jews, and made no attempt to hide their visceral hatred of Jews and Judaism. In June 1932 *Literary Digest* unequivocally observed that "antisemitism is an outstanding feature of the Hitler philosophy." In 1933 Edgar Ansel Mowrer argued in his book *Germany Puts the Clock Back* that the aim of the Nazis' "barbarous campaign was the extermination, permanent subjugation or voluntary departure of the Jews from Germany."[51] But as the reaction to the 1935 Nuremberg Laws would demonstrate, few, particularly among those viewing the situation from afar, shared Mowrer's understanding.

The Nuremberg Laws

When the Nuremberg Laws, which officially disenfranchised Jews and classified them as noncitizens, were issued in September 1935, the press tried to make meaning of them in the same way that it had tried to interpret many antisemitic acts during the preceding two and a half years. It explained, rationalized, and interpreted them as the Nazi *quid pro quo* for the actions of others and rarely understood their true significance.

The laws divided the German population into two classes— Reich citizens, who had to be of "Aryan" ancestry, and state subjects, i.e., Jews, who could no longer secure employment in government positions, serve in the army, vote, marry non-Jews, engage in extramarital sexual relations with "Aryans," hire female non-Jewish domestic workers, or fly the German flag, which, as a result of the laws, was now the swastika. Shocked by the laws, many papers condemned them as the embodiment of "the bigotry of the Middle Ages." Jews were commonly described as a "people without a country."[52]

Adhering to a pattern that we have seen was established as early as 1933, the press not only condemned but tried to explain the reasons why the Nazis issued the laws. Once again, the way the press explicated the laws revealed its perception of conditions in Germany. One common interpretation was that the decrees constituted the German response to an incident that had occurred in New York City on July 26, when demonstrators boarded the German ship the SS *Bremen,* which was anchored in the harbor, and ripped down the swastika from its mast. German authorities demanded an apology from the State Department and punishment of the perpetrators. They were infuriated when Louis Brodsky, the New York magistrate who heard the case against the demonstrators, admonished them for their actions but dismissed the charges on the grounds that the sight of this "pirate" flag would naturally incense them. Press interest in events in this New York City courtroom was heightened by the fact that a few days earlier the colorful mayor of the City of New York, Fiorello LaGuardia, had refused to renew the license of a German masseur on the grounds that Americans doing business in Germany were being treated unfairly and that he was reciprocating Germany's policy toward them. Brodsky's and LaGuardia's forays into the arena of foreign relations were severely criticized by the press. Many papers, including the *New York Herald Tribune, New York Sun,* and *Washington Post,* reminded the mayor that treaty rights were outside the bounds of his authority. In addition to criticizing the mayor and the magistrate, the press hastened to interpret the laws as *nothing but* Germany's response to the magistrate's "unnecessary" remarks and a *quid pro quo* for the desecration of the Nazi flag.[53]

Many papers featured the change of flag in their headlines

and relegated the Jews' loss of citizenship to a secondary or even tertiary item of interest. *Newsweek*'s heading said this:

> HITLER DECREES SWASTIKA REICH FLAG;
> Bars Intermarriage;
> Relegates Jews to Dark Ages[54]

Los Angeles Times readers were confronted with a headline that truly obscured the issue and made it sound as if citizenship rights had been "limited" in some oblique fashion.

> DEFIANCE TO JEWS OF ENTIRE WORLD
> HURLED BY HITLER
>
> SWASTIKA MADE SOLE GERMAN FLAG BY SPECIAL
> REICHSTAG SESSION;
>
> Citizenship Limited[55]

The *Washington Herald* was mute regarding the Jews' change of legal status:

> HITLER ASSAILS LEAGUE AND JEWRY AS EUROPE SEETHES
>
> German-Jew Marriage Banned;
> Swastika Made Official Flag[56]

The *New York Times* interpreted the laws as instigated and motivated by the New York City incident:

> REICH ADOPTS SWASTIKA
> AS NATION'S OFFICIAL FLAG;
> HITLER'S REPLY TO 'INSULT'
>
> Anti-Jewish Laws Passed
>
> 'Non-Aryans' Deprived of Citizenship and Right to Intermarry.
>
> Forbidden to Show Flag
>
> They are Warned by Hitler
> Further 'Provocative' Acts Will Draw Reprisals.[57]

There were headlines that stressed the deprivation of citizenship rights and did not portray the action as a response to the Bremen incident or focus primary attention on the adoption of the swastika as a state emblem.

Baltimore Sun:

> HITLER DEPRIVES JEWS OF CITIZENSHIP RIGHTS,
> BANS INTERMARRIAGES

THREATENS OTHER STEPS TO SOLVE RACE PROBLEM

Laws Restricting Rights of Hebrews
Voted By Special Session of Reichstag—
Swastika Proclaimed Only Reich Flag[58]

Christian Science Monitor:

REICH BANS JEWS FROM CITIZENSHIP

Hitler's Reichstag Speech Prelude to Enactment of Three New Laws

Swastika Adopted[59]

Readers who read past the headlines in any of these and numerous other American papers were generally given enough information to understand the laws. However, the presentation of them as a *quid pro quo* for the *Bremen* incident and the stress on the swastika obscured the fact that the laws represented the embodiment of Nazi ideology.[60]

Some papers acknowledged that the decrees were a new step in severity but still reverted to the "nothing but" approach. They interpreted the laws as a means of deflecting the attention of the German people from their domestic problems. The *Cleveland News* declared them an "escape mechanism for tyrants who seek to divert the minds of their subjects."[61] In fact, however, the laws were quite different from earlier proscriptions. The Jews' unprotected and permanent second-class status was now "formally rooted in law," and, as Ambassador Dodd reminded Secretary of State Hull, law was regarded with great "sanctity" and observed with much "discipline" in Germany.

Other papers, intent on finding a rational explanation for the laws, argued that the decrees were nothing but an attempt by Hitler to pacify extremist Nazis. Because the laws did not completely exclude Jews from Germany's economy and did not physically subjugate them, some press analysts optimistically argued that the moderate elements in the party had prevailed.[62] J. E. Williams, editorial columnist for the *Christian Science Monitor,* typified those who recognized the laws' severity but found them cause for optimism because "radical" Nazis had been forced to surrender their freedom to conduct "individual isolated actions against Jews."[63] This interpretation made it seem as if Jews and extremists had each been forced to make some concessions.

In an editorial the *Boston Transcript* interpreted the laws as indicative of the "failure of measures already taken to keep the

German Jews in subjection."[64] What indication the paper had of the failure of Jews to be kept in "subjection" it did not reveal. It ignored the numerous documented reports of Streicher's increasing strength and autonomy, the spread of antisemitic boycotts and rioting, the expulsion of Jews from German schools, and the mass migration from towns and villages where persecution was unbearable to places such as Berlin where it was often barely tolerable.[65] This editorial conveyed the impression that the Jews were managing to cope successfully with Hitler's rule.

Some papers reverted to the "weakness, not strength" approach and argued that Hitler needed the laws to bolster his precarious position. The laws, they concluded, were symptomatic of internal difficulties.

> It is hardly possible to explain the drastic laws on any broad basis except the assumption that Hitler's domestic situation must be extraordinarily precarious and shaky.[66]

These interpretations—those that saw compromise between extremists and moderates and those that saw Nazi weakness, not strength—reflected the failure of the press to see the Nuremberg Laws as an inherent expression of antisemitic ideology. The editorial boards that offered these interpretations ignored the observations of reporters on the scene such as Otto Tolischus of the *New York Times,* who even before the laws were issued dismissed the discussion of moderates versus extremists as "largely academic" because the campaign against the Jews was in "such an advanced stage" that all that remained to be done was to "legalize what is already accomplished." American officials in Berlin also dismissed the idea that moderation could be anticipated. They looked in vain for any sign of a tempered attitude toward Jews and found no "opposition to the swing towards radicalism." Ambassador Dodd confidentially reported to the Secretary of State, a few days after the 1935 Nuremberg rally, that things seemed to be getting even worse for the Jews and that there was "a tendency in the direction of severer measures" in order to ensure "complete separation of the Jews from the German community."[67]

Press failure to grasp that antisemitism had become official state policy was exemplified by the reaction of the *Los Angeles Times,* which did not believe the laws made that much difference. The paper argued in a rather matter-of-fact tone that Jews had simply been deprived *de jure* of what all other Germans had lost *de facto.* It noted that "generally speaking, nobody has any civil rights in Germany, . . . and nobody votes in the sense in which voting is understood in democratic countries," so that the laws did not entail any real change in the Jews' situation. In a similar vein, after decrying the Jews' loss of citizenship, the *St. Louis Post Dispatch* argued that there "are no citizens of Nazi Germany . . . whose rights are unimpaired" and that Jews were really being treated no differently from most other Germans. According to the paper this was a case of a dictatorship treating one segment of its population somewhat more harshly than others. The "penalties imposed on the Jews, official scapegoats of the Nazi regime, are only a part of the burdens borne by all the people under their Fascist dictatorship."[68]* This argument—that the persecution of the Jews was not qualitatively different than that of a multitude of other groups—would be repeatedly expressed by press, public, and policy makers during the course of the next decade.

In a way, the *Los Angeles Times* and the *Post Dispatch* were correct. Democracy in Germany was no longer extant. Many Germans had lost their rights and were subject to physical attack. But while much of what had previously occurred could be dismissed as unauthorized actions or individual laws designed to make life difficult for Jews, these Nuremberg decrees were different. They took Nazi ideology and made it the law of the land.

Despite its condemnations most of the press did not grasp that this legal program for the "blood and honor" of the German Reich was categorically different from previous antisemitic acts; the ultimate effect of these 1935 laws was to be more profound and ominous than Nazi efforts to force Jews out of certain professions or to prod them to leave Germany.[70] The Nuremberg Laws were the point of departure for the terror that followed. Those who interpreted them as "nothing but" a response to a minor incident in New York, a concession to extremists, or a smokescreen for other woes made it almost impossible for the American public to understand their full import: they constituted the basic legalization of Nazi hatred of the Jew. In 1935 biological criteria became the determining factor for citizenship. In 1941 they would become the determining factor for survival.

* At least the *Post Dispatch* had abandoned its previous reluctance to criticize Hitler and Germany. In May 1935 it had hailed the German leader for his "virtues of peace."[69]

3

The Olympic Games: Germany Triumphant

In 1931 the International Olympic Committee (IOC) designated Germany as the site for the 1936 Games. The winter Games were to take place in Bavaria's Garmisch-Partenkirchen and the summer Games in Berlin. For the Germans the Games were both a propaganda and sporting event. The Nazis used them to enhance their international image and to convince visitors that the terrible things reported in the press were figments of correspondents' imaginations. Tourists and visiting reporters—there were over 1,500 of the latter at the Games—were so impressed by what they saw that many dismissed the stories of brutalities as exaggerated. The glowing press reports from the Olympic Games helped shed doubts on the earlier reports of persecution. As was so often the case during this period, truth was disdained as falsehood and fiction accepted as fact. Americans cite the 1936 Olympic Games as an event which, thanks to Jesse Owens's amazing achievements, disproved Hitler's "Aryan" theories. In truth, the victory was Hitler's. The Games were the ultimate propaganda triumph for him, a triumph facilitated by the press.

The Move to Boycott the Games

Within a few months after the Nazi assumption of power, America began to debate its participation in the Olympic Games. The press wondered whether Germany's domestic persecution was America's concern. The battle over the Games was, at least in part, a microcosm of the fight between interventionists and isolationists over how America should react, if at all, to developments in the Reich.

When the Nazis began to exclude Jews from various aspects of German life, they also barred them from the sports arena. In May 1933 the Reich sports commissar, Captain Hans Tschammer und Osten, explicitly declared that "German sports are for Aryans. German youth leadership is only for Aryans and not for Jews."[1] In June 1933, when the IOC met in Vienna, Brigadier General Charles H. Sherrill, a member of the American Olympic Committee (AOC) and the American representative to the IOC meeting, extracted a promise from the Germans that "as a principle . . . German Jews would not be excluded from German Olympic teams."[2] Sherrill claimed that it had taken an arduous and "trying" effort to get the Germans to accede to this point.[3] In the following months Germany simultaneously discriminated against Jewish athletes and repeatedly pledged that all promises made to the IOC would be fulfilled. Despite the Reich's assurances to the contrary, Jews were slowly but deliberately excluded from a wide array of sports activities and training facilities. As early as April 1933 *Newsweek* reported that "anti-Jewish feeling [had] spread through German sport." This sentiment intensified as Jews were barred from international track and field matches, Germany's best amateur tennis player was dropped from competition, and the chairman of the German Sports Federation was fired because of his Jewish ancestry.[4]

In the fall of 1934 AOC president Avery Brundage visited Germany and also obtained a German commitment that Jews would be included in Olympic tryouts. Richard Mandell, in his study of the Berlin Games, described Brundage as "one more important personage dazzled by the order, relative prosperity and joy that most travelers observed in Germany in those years." Brundage's assurances that the spirit of the Olympic Games was being assiduously observed by Germany and that German Jews wanted the competition to take place as planned convinced the AOC to accept the invitation to the Games.

Brundage and Sherrill both had strong pro-German feelings. Sherrill, who had served as Hoover's Ambassador to Turkey, was known among his colleagues in the State Department for his pro-fascist views. Upon his return from a meeting with Hitler regarding the Games, he described him as an "undeniably great leader." In 1935, in a speech before the Italian-American Chamber of Commerce, he expressed his admiration for Mussolini, a "man of courage in a world of pussyfooters." Sherrill publicly expressed the opinion that Mussolini should come to the United States and eliminate the communists as he had in Italy.[5]

Sherrill and Brundage portrayed the boycott movement as an insidious effort orchestrated by American Jews. Their claims that the "demand of prejudiced groups" threatened American participation were reiterated by various publications, including the *Literary Digest,* which attributed the boycott movement to "wealthy American Jews and Catholics." Sherrill and Brundage also used scare tactics to prevent American Jews from supporting the movement. In 1933 Sherrill warned American Jews against organizing a boycott because it would "provoke antisemitic feeling" in the United States. On a number of different occasions during the Olympic debate Brundage and Sherrill repeated this thinly veiled prediction *qua* threat. On his return from Germany Sherrill warned the press that,

> We are almost certain to have a wave of antisemitism among those who never before gave it a thought, and who may consider that about 5,000,000 Jews in this country are using the athletes representing 120,000,000 Americans to work out something to help the German Jews.[6]

When Sherrill and Brundage were criticized for such statements, they responded by arguing that *they* were acting in Jews' best interests. Their behavior was reminiscent of a familiar tactic of "saving" Jews or any other minority group "in spite of themselves." At best such behavior is paternalistic in nature; at worst it is prejudicial, and in this case it was antisemitic.

In the months that followed it became increasingly obvious that the situation was not improving. Participation in special pre-Games training programs was denied to Jewish athletes, and of the twenty-one Jews "nominated" for Olympic training camps, none were ultimately "invited." By May of 1935 Jews were excluded from the gardens of Bad Dürkheim, the swimming pools and baths of Schweinfurt, the municipal baths of Karlsruhe, Frieburg Gladbach, and Dortmund. Even the streetcars of Magdeburg were closed to Jews.[7] Nonetheless, Brundage echoed German claims and emphatically reassured critics that Germany would abide by its "unqualified assurances of non-discrimination." In August 1935 Brundage assured the press that he had heard nothing about discrimination against athletes of any race or religion since Germany had pledged to allow Jews to participate and that there were no "reports whatsoever official or otherwise that Germany has failed to give Jewish athletes a fair opportunity."[8] As long as Germany abided by its promises, Brundage argued, then the AOC could not interfere in its internal political, religious, or racial affairs. Sherrill declared that it did not concern him "one bit the way the Jews in Germany are being treated, any more than lynchings in the South of our own country."[9] The views of Sherrill and Brundage were buttressed by the claims of Frederick W. Rubien, secretary of the American Olympic Committee, that

> Germans are not discriminating against Jews in their Olympic tryouts. The Jews are eliminated because they are not good enough as athletes. Why, there are not a dozen Jews in the world of Olympic caliber.[10]

While Brundage, Rubien, and Sherrill were arguing that everything was fine, the *New York Times's* Fred Birchall was reporting a very different story. The headline constituted a sharp rebuttal to Brundage:

NAZI OLYMPIC VOW KEPT TECHNICALLY
In Theory Even Jews May Try For Team,
but All Except Hitlerites Are Handicapped.

In its reports to the State Department the American embassy also contradicted Brundage's claim that there were no reports "official or otherwise" that Germany was discriminating against Jewish athletes.[11] By this time the Germans had managed by deft manipulation and sheer terror to transform the question of Jewish participation into a theoretical and not a practical matter. Many Jews who were potential competitors had left Germany because they knew they would not be able to train in the manner demanded of an Olympic contender. Lacking financial means and communal support, two critical components of Olympic preparation, those who remained faced such substantial psychological and personal handicaps that qualifying for a berth on a team became a virtual impossibility.

Despite these developments, the press paid relatively sporadic attention to the question of American participation during the first two and half years of Nazi rule. It was only after the Berlin riots and the Nuremberg Laws that the issue of whether Americans should go to the Olympics acquired a new prominence. The debate about the Games now spilled over from the sports pages, where it was first raised, to the editorial pages, and from the meetings of the Amateur Athletic Union (AAU) to the Congressional floor.[12] The presence of an American team at the 1936 Olympic Games became a matter of national significance and remained so until the day the team set sail for Germany. In the twelve months preceding the Games reporters, columnists, sports writers, and editorial boards debated how an American presence at the Games would be interpreted and what was more likely to violate America's neutrality: boycotting or participating in the Games.

Those papers which opposed a boycott generally shared Brundage's view that what occurred in Germany, as deplorable as it might appear, was none of America's business and that it was not America's responsibility to approve or disapprove.[13] Moreover, they contended, since no country, including the United States, had a blemish-free record regarding minority groups, it was hypocritical to single Germany out for its treatment of Jews. Japan's treatment of China, the *Norfolk* (Virginia) *Pilot* believed, would rule it out of Olympic contention; Rome would be eliminated because of its Ethiopian escapade, London because of its treatment of Indian nationalists, Russia because of forced labor, Dublin for its religious riots, and the United States because of the lynching of blacks. It was not, the *Pilot* declared, "the function of the Olympic Games to distribute clean bills of political health. Too many glass houses are involved."[14]

When it learned that antisemitic signs had been posted in Garmisch-Partenkirchen, the site of the winter competition, the *Pilot* changed its stance and advocated a boycott because Germany does not "seem to be in a position to guarantee the proper physical arrangements for the Olympic festivals."[15] But the paper's fundamental position had not changed. It still believed that America should avoid anything which might force it to become entangled in Germany's affairs. The signs at the winter site indicated that Jews' safety could not be guaranteed. If something happened to an American Jew or if an American non-Jew was attacked in the course of some action against Jews, this country would be forced to respond. Therefore remaining at home was prudent and the best way to guarantee that America would not be forced to violate its neutrality.

Ultimately this noninterventionist position became one of the more frequently voiced arguments against participation. Irrespective of a paper's views about events in Germany, there was a possibility that something could occur during the Games which would severely strain American-German relations.[16] Some noninterventionists advocated a boycott because they feared that participation might necessitate involvement in German affairs, and some noninterventionists argued against a boycott because they feared a protest would, *ipso facto,* involve us in German matters. Although the practical considerations differed, the motivation was the same: ensure that America distance itself from a troublesome situation.

The Scripps-Howard chain's *New York World Telegram* expressed the views of those who advocated a boycott for noninterventionist reasons, when it acknowledged that, while it opposed "gestures" which could be interpreted as a protest because they were an "irritant" for an already difficult international situation, it believed it "imperative" that America not attend. It would be a practical mistake to do so because it would invite "bad friendship, embarrassing incidents and involvement in controversy."[17] The *Boston Globe* counseled that holding the Olympics in Nazi Germany created a "risk" which was probably not worth taking.[18] The *Trenton Gazette* contended that the atmosphere in Germany was anything *but* conducive to promoting "friendship" and "sportsmanship" among nations.[19] These papers all feared that if an American Jewish competitor narrowly bested a German, the crowd might subject the American to abuse and obloquy, which in turn might necessitate an official American response. It was prudent, therefore, to stay on the sidelines rather than risk becoming embroiled in a potentially volatile situation.

Sports, *Kultur,* and Politics

Some of the proparticipation editorials reverted to the "differentiation" approach utilized earlier, but with different villains. In a switch from exonerating the Nazi leaders and blaming their overzealous followers, editorials now exculpated Germans at large and argued that not all Germans were Nazis, but many were "law abiding, hard working people" who were not culpable for the party's wrong doings. A boycott, the *Springfield* (Illinois) *Journal* claimed, would convince the German people that they are "universally disliked" when it really was their leaders who were at fault.[20] Even if the "outrages" in Germany were fostered by the government, the paper claimed, the government was not the people and the people "deserved" the Olympics. Overlooked in these arguments was the fact that the German people would and rightfully did interpret the world's participation in the Games as a sign of its legitimization of Hitler's policies. As a result opposition and resistance to the Nazis became even harder. The differentiators also argued that sports and politics were two separate issues. The athletes were, in the words of Brundage, "pledged to good clean competition and sportsmanship. When we let politics, racial questions, religious or social disputes creep into our actions we're in for trouble."[21] This argument ignored the fact that from the outset the Nazis had not only let politics "creep" into the sports arena, but had created a symbiotic relationship between the two.

Differentiating between the German people and the Nazi Party and German government or between sports and politics demonstrated the press's failure to understand the inherent value of a pageant such as the Olympic Games to a totalitarian regime. The German people may have enjoyed the Games, but it was the state that reaped the bounty. In Germany sports, like all forms of *Kultur,* were transformed into state propaganda intended to glorify the "Aryan" race, the German nation, the Nazi Party, and, above all, the Führer as the embodiment of all that was Germany and Nazism. The Nazis repeatedly used ostensibly nonpolitical events in a blatantly political fashion, and there was no reason to assume that they would act differently when it came to the Games. Germans leaders had already acknowledged that sports were a means to an end. In May 1933 Dorothy Thompson, in an article in *The*

Saturday Evening Post, cited the view of the official Nazi newspaper, the *Voelkischer Beobachter,* on this topic. "It should always be remembered that sport merely for recreation fails to fulfill its essential purpose, which is to produce hardy man power for the state."[22] Immediately before the Games Sigrid Schultz reported in the *Chicago Tribune* that a handbook published by the office of the Reich sports commissioner stated that "nonpolitical sportsmen are unthinkable." According to the book, which was required reading for all German competitors, every organized activity in Germany had to be part of "Hitler's movement." In the Third Reich nothing was "nonpolitical."[23] Most Americans who visited Germany, including the reporters who came for the Games, failed to grasp this fact.

There were, of course, observers who understood that the Games were designed to legitimize Germany in the eyes of the rest of the world. According to the *Des Moines Register* the real reason for not participating was that to do so would convert the 1936 Olympic Games "into a falsified proof that Nazi concepts are endorsed by the sportsmen and athletes of the world."[24] Proboycott papers rejected Brundage and Sherrill's claim that a boycott would exacerbate Jewish disabilities and argued that it might force an improvement of the Jews' status.[25] It would serve, the *Atlanta Constitution* argued, as "timely notice to Germany that the world does not approve of her campaign of terrorism."[26] America's not competing might prove to be, according to the *Milwaukee Herald,* "a wholesome lesson for the Nazi scoundrels." *The Christian Century* agreed: moving the Games would "tell Germany" what the world thinks.[27]

Albion Ross of the *New York Times* noted that the Reich expected the Olympic Games "to accomplish nothing less than its rehabilitation in the eyes of a still largely hostile world." Ambassador Dodd and George Messersmith, former American Consul in Berlin who was then American Minister in Vienna, felt similarly. Germany, Messersmith predicted, would use the Games "not only as a political instrument within Germany but also as a propaganda instrument throughout the world." Because press reports about German brutality had increased in severity in the wake of the riots and the Nuremberg Laws, Ambassador Dodd believed that Germany would use the Games "to rehabilitate and enhance the reputation of the 'new Germany' " and to convince foreign tourists, particularly non-German-speaking ones, who would visit only

Berlin, "to reject as libel press reports respecting such unpleasant occurrences as Jewish persecution which they have previously read in their home papers."[28]

A number of papers argued that the most efficacious thing America could do would be to send a team to Germany which included, in the opinion of the *Minneapolis Star,* the "best Jewish and Catholic talent the country has to offer." Let them "swamp . . . the Germans, cleanly and sportingly, in every event on the program," the *St. Joseph* (Missouri) *Gazette* advised. Some editors and sports columnists were swayed by the argument that an American boycott would leave the playing field uncontested and Germany would then capture the victor's laurels. Ed Bang, sports editor of the *Cleveland News,* said that the United States should go and "force the bitter dregs of defeat down the throats of the Hitlerites." It was the German performance, not the American one, that was to win the accolades and do the swamping. The Germans won nine more gold medals than did the Americans and surprised most experts with their achievements.[29]

There were those who counseled that until there was an "affront" to American athletes, this country would not be justified in declining to attend. A boycott, they believed, should only be instituted if *American* Jewish athletes faced some disability; otherwise the treatment of the Jews remained a German domestic matter. The *Lansing Journal* argued that "either all Americans must have full privileges and recognition in Berlin, irrespective of creed, race or color, or else all Americans should refuse to participate."[30] The argument was, again, that what took place in Germany was none of America's business per se, and that only when German affairs impinged on Americans' rights was a protest in order.

Another argument popular with those in favor of an American presence at the Games had also been voiced before, and would be heard again, in connection with foreign protests about Nazi behavior: Rather than improve matters for Jews, a boycott would make them worse. Germans would blame the Jews for marring the competition and would only persecute them more severely. At best such an action would be of "little practical value." In the 1930s this argument was marshaled against an economic boycott or diplomatic protests. In 1944 it was taken to its most ludicrous extreme when State Department officials used it to explain their refusal to bomb the death camps. (John McCloy of the State Department somehow concluded that bombing Auschwitz would inflict worse punishment on the Jews interned there, Jews *who he knew* were destined for the gas chambers.)[31]

This argument, that action would make things worse, ignored Germany's desire to enhance its international stature and the fact that it had already proved responsive to foreign criticism. One of the grandparents of the president of the German Olympic Committee (GOC), Theodor Lewald, had been Jewish, and as a result the Nazis had forced Lewald to resign in 1933. Ensuing world criticism and German fears of an Olympic boycott led to his reinstatement as GOC "adviser." The new head of the German Sports Committee acknowledged that the reinstatement as well as the announcement that Jews would not be excluded from the Games was due to the "foreign political situation."[32]

The years 1935 and 1936 were a crucial period for the Nazi rulers, who, increasingly confident that they had consolidated their domestic rule, were now intent on improving Germany's economic and political status. Dodd described this as a time when the Nazis were committed to introducing the "New Germany" to the family of nations and were, therefore, still susceptible to foreign criticism and pressure.[33] While a boycott of the Games might not have changed the Nazis' ideological commitment to antisemitism, it might well have prompted them to moderate their antisemitic policies.

Although the July 1935 riots and their aftermath strengthened the opposition to the Games, the opposition tended not to last. The *Charleston Post's* doubts about participating were dispelled because Germany had provided "satisfactory assurance" regarding the treatment to be given "its own and visiting athletes."[34] Other papers regained their optimism about Germany's intentions to abide by these promises when it invited two Jews, Helen Mayer, a fencer who had won a gold medal as a member of the German Olympic team in 1928 and who in 1935 was living in Los Angeles, and Rudi Ball, one of Germany's best ice hockey players, who was then in France, to join the German teams. Although it had taken two years of prodding by Brundage and others to get Germany to issue these invitations, they convinced a number of papers that Germany had softened its attitude toward Jews in general. This new faith in a repentant Reich came in the fall of 1935 at the same time that Germany had disenfranchised the Jews and Joseph Goebbels had removed the names of 1,200 Jews from the honor roll of Germany's war dead.[35]

Ironically, some of the most fervent advocates of American participation were cognizant of German intentions. Bill Henry, sports editor of the *Los Angeles Times* and an outspoken proponent of the Games, returned from a visit to Berlin and admitted that Germany saw the Games as an opportunity to show the world the "possibilities of the new Germany."[36] The *Los Angeles Times* editorial board followed its sports editor's lead and strongly supported the Games. Ignoring the fact that Henry himself had openly acknowledged Germany's propaganda and political goals, the paper denied that the Games were a political institution. They were neither German nor Nazi, but "one of the world's greatest institutions." Hitler, the paper predicted, would have nothing to do with them. Ignoring numerous reports to the contrary, many of which it had carried in its pages, the *Los Angeles Times* argued not only that the eligibility rules were "impartial" but that "there has been nothing to indicate prospective discrimination against any athletes because of race or religion."[37] By this point not only Jews but Catholics and even certain Protestant youth were feeling the pressure of Nazi discriminatory actions. Even when the Nuremberg Laws were issued two days later, the *Los Angeles Times* did not change its stance. Other papers reacted similarly. In November, two months after the promulgation of the first phase of the Nuremberg Laws and four days before the second phase of the laws were announced, the *Mobile* (Alabama) *Register* came out in favor of the Games. Its doubts had been eased by Hitler's "personal assurance that Olympic athletes and visitors would be treated courteously no matter what their religion or race."[38]

Westbrook Pegler, columnist for the Scripps-Howard papers and the featured columnist of the United Press syndicate, strongly opposed the Games, which he termed an "official project of the Nazi government." He was particularly critical of Bill Henry of the *Los Angeles Times,* who not only laudatorily described the preparations for the Games but argued that "nothing would be gained" by a boycott and promised that there would be "fair treatment for Jews, Catholics and everybody else." Pegler dismissed Henry's claims by noting that the sports writer had served as an adviser to the German government on the planning of the sports extravaganza. He had visited Berlin as a "sort of guest" of the government and was obligated to say that the event would be a "rousing success."[39] Pegler eventually infuriated Goebbels at the winter contest when, instead of discussing the hospitality and good will of the German hosts, he told readers about the war maneuvers of some "5,000 to 10,000 hard looking disciplined troops."[40]

One of the most interesting aspects of the *Los Angeles Times's* position on the Games was that it was absolutely contrary to its position on Nazi Germany in general. At the same time that it vigorously advocated sending Americans to the Games, it accused German authorities of "directly and openly inspiring" the July riots. It contended that a government, such as Germany's, which "publicly sponsors and encourages hooliganism becomes itself a hooligan."[41] Though these international sporting events would enhance this "hooligan" government's prestige in the eyes of its own people and those of the myriad of visitors who came from abroad, the *Times* continued to support participation. This kind of dissonance was not, of course, unique to the *Los Angeles Times*. In fact much of the press reaction throughout the period was characterized by optimistic interpretations and expectations even when the evidence indicated that optimism was not in order; e.g. a conciliatory speech by Hitler negated the persecution and incarceration of thousands of innocent Germans, Jew and non-Jew. Assurances of fair play and equal treatment of Jews rendered the reality of the Nuremberg Laws moot.

William Shirer recalled that reporters in Germany "could scarcely believe it" when they read statements by Americans claiming that the Germans were not discriminating and would not discriminate against Jews.[42] Fifty years later, in an interview, he again expressed his utter amazement at how some Americans were able to ignore what Germany had become under the Nazis. The July riots, the Nuremberg Laws, the exclusion of Jewish athletes from training facilities, and the progressively harsher treatment being meted out to Jews throughout Germany did not shake the faith of the pro-Games faction that Hitler and the Nazis were abiding by their promises to behave as a civilized nation and observe the Olympic code of sportsmanship.

Fall 1935: The Final Heat

Although it took some papers until November to decide to do so, ultimately close to two-thirds of the papers that commented on the Games opposed going. The press favored a boycott of the Games far more enthusiastically than it ever favored any form of economic boycott. This was understandable, for a trade boycott had the potential to cause economic repercussions in America, while a sports boycott demonstrated contempt for the Nazi system at little direct cost to America. Furthermore, while an economic boycott constituted a political statement, an Olympics boycott could be interpreted as a commitment to neutrality.

In the period following the issuance of the Nuremberg Laws, opposition to the Games increased markedly. By mid-October the fight began to gain momentum as the number of papers advocating a boycott increased. The *New York Times* cautioned that it was not necessary to "indulge in violent denunciations of what the Nazis are doing and proposing to do." Just refusing to send players to the Games would be "the application of a moral sanction which could not be hidden from the German people and which they would not fail to understand."[43] Though in comparison with some other papers' editorials during this period the *New York Times* was reserved, the fact that the leading newspaper in the country advocated a boycott as a form of moral protest was significant.[44] As the date for the AAU's final vote on whether to certify athletes for the Games grew near, press opposition became increasingly vocal and the list of prominent Americans and American organizations demanding a boycott grew apace.[45]

The tenor of the fight also became more vehement. Sherrill again predicted an outbreak of American antisemitism upon his return from Germany, and the AOC published a pamphlet in favor of the Games which posited that the opposition was "essentially Jewish and Communistic." These claims elicited a number of editorial responses which argued that it was not Jews who were leading the fight against participation and that Jews were not Hitler's only victims. Brundage also introduced the Jewish issue, sometimes by innuendo. He called the fight one between "principles and dollars" and claimed that there was a million-dollar war chest so that the fight for a boycott could go on "whether or not there was any truth to the reports (from Germany)." On another occasion he claimed that newspapers—which by November were two to one against going—had been warned that if they did not oppose the Games, they would lose millions of dollars in advertising, and that the colleges which sent athletes would lose substantial donations. Brundage's stress on the existence of powerful monied forces anxious to halt the games was clearly intended to raise the specter of "Jewish money" in the minds of the public. The threat of loss of advertising dollars was linked to the popular notion of Jewish department store owners who controlled the press with their monies. Sherrill later reiterated his premonitions about domestic antisemitism in a letter to the editor of the *American Hebrew*. In an admonitory tone he warned American Jews that there existed a "present danger of increased antisemitism . . . among thousands of young Americans . . . once [they] get the idea that Jews are scheming to get America to boycott the Berlin Games."[46]

The opposition of prominent non-Jews and publications such as the Protestant *Christian Century* and the liberal Catholic journal *Commonweal* made it more difficult, but far from impossible, for Brundage and Sherrill to suggest that the Jews were behind it all. *Christian Century* and *Commonweal* took Sherrill to task for his warning to American Jews.

> Reading accounts of torture and oppression, of hunger and degradation, which are the daily fate of hundreds of thousands living under the Hitler lash, Jews are bidden remember that silence alone can preserve them from a like fate here.[47]

The Committee on Fair Play in Sports, a proboycott group whose chairmen and members included secretary of the Federal Council of Churches Dr. Henry Smith Leiper, prominent theologian Dr. Harry Emerson Fosdick, former owner of *The Nation* Oswald Garrison Villard, the president of Mt. Holyoke College Mary Woolley, and Governor of Massachusetts James M. Curley, chastised Sherrill because he "gratuitously" tried to turn the debate over the Games into a "purely Jewish issue."[48] Until the participants set sail for Germany, Brundage and Sherrill continued to blame Jews—both directly and by innuendo—for placing obstacles in the team's path.

Sports writers were also debating the propriety of American attendance. The *Column Review* polled sports writers and found a strong division of opinion. A survey by the United Press was almost evenly divided. Of the thirty writers polled, thirteen supported participation, eleven opposed it, and six were undecided. (The close nature of the United Press results did not prevent the pro-Games *Los Angeles Times* from headlining its story "SPORTS SCRIBES FAVOR SENDING OLYMPIC TEAM.")[49] Among the sports writers who favored participation were Fred Digby of the *New Orleans Item Tribune*, Maurice O. Shevlin of the

St. Louis Globe Democrat, and Richard Vidmer of the *New York Herald Tribune,* who made a special point of attacking Jeremiah T. Mahoney, former New York State Supreme Court justice and president of the AAU, who opposed the Games because of his conviction that Jewish athletes were not being given a fair chance. Harry Smith of the *San Francisco Chronicle* and Tom Laird of the *San Francisco News* gave guarded approval to participation if strong assurances of fair play could be obtained. Ralph McGill of the *Atlanta Constitution,* Shirley Povich of the *Washington Post,* and Bill Cunningham of the *Boston Post* all opposed participation, as did most of the New York dailies. Cunningham wondered whether the Germans planned to "declare a moratorium for six weeks and then go back to their beatings, sluggings and boycott?"[50] *Christian Century,* which had adopted an anti-Olympic editorial stance within a few weeks after the riots, considered the sports writers' opinions important enough to urge its readers to write to their local papers to protest United States participation and address their letters to the sports writers because they might pay more attention than editorial boards. The influence of *Christian Century* was reflected by the fact that the *New York Times* reprinted its statement in full and by the number of different editorials— both those for and against participation—which cited the Protestant journal's stance. Some felt compelled to take issue with it, while others cited it as support of their own position.[51]

By the beginning of November the Anti-Nazi Federation had collected 30,000 protest signatures.[52] Shortly after the announcement of the second phase of the Nuremberg decrees, 138 Protestant leaders called for an American withdrawal from the competition. They were joined by Ernst Jahncke, the American representative to the IOC. His decision to "do all I can to persuade my fellow Americans that they ought not take part in the Games if they are held in Nazi Germany" elicited a strong response from the press.[53] It seemed to prompt many papers that had been ambivalent about American policy to take an anti-Olympic stance. The *Washington Post, Philadelphia Record, Brooklyn Citizen, Troy* (New York) *Times Record,* and other papers that were opposed to the Games, considered Jahncke's decision the "most important" anti-participation action. Ever the proponent of participation, the *Los Angeles Times* deprecated Jahncke's opposition by casting it in a blatantly political light. Jews, columnist Warren B. Francis argued in a *Los Angeles Times* exclusive, were distressed by Roosevelt's failure to intervene in Germany and the Republicans were intent on "profiting" from the situation. Therefore, "Jahncke, former *Republican* Assistant Secretary of the Navy," was making "overtures" to American Jews.[54]

The popular journalist and commentator Heywood Broun registered his opposition to the Games on his radio show and asked listeners to express their opinion in a postcard poll. The response was overwhelming, surprising even Broun, who, in an article in *The Nation,* admitted that he had "never said anything on the air in any other discourse which caught and held a single ear" as this had. Despite the unscientific nature of his poll, it is significant that responses were more than 99 percent against going to the Games.[55]

The Vote

By early December, immediately prior to the AAU meeting, an impressive list of civic, political, religious, and sports figures had joined many American newspapers in opposition to the Games. Proboycott petitions with 500,000 names and resolutions by organizations with 1.5 million members were presented to the AAU in the final days prior to its convention. After more than five hours of debate and speeches the boycott resolution lost by the tiny margin of two and a half votes. (The half vote was possible because of the AAU procedure for allocating votes.)[56]

But the opponents did not give up. Mahoney announced that he would continue to fight for a boycott. The *Philadelphia Record* called for a continuation of the fight, as did a number of other papers. The *Indianapolis Star* advocated a boycott if the persecution did not cease in the period remaining prior to the Games. One of the few national newspapers to openly praise the vote was the *Christian Science Monitor,* which believed that "competition on the playing field (would) . . . lessen unnatural animosities." In contrast, the *Washington Post* regretted "loss of this great opportunity to let the Germans see what the outside world thinks of their present rulers."[57]

Despite the fact that the fight was lost, some papers believed that significant gains had resulted. The *Wheeling* (West Virginia) *Register* observed that "no issue has been so widely discussed through the news columns and so persistently eschewed editorially as the United States' participation in the Olympic Games" and consequently Americans had been enlightened regarding conditions in Germany.[58] The *Philadelphia Record* expressed a similar sentiment. As a result of the Games there was now "awakening American awareness of the menace of Fascism."[59] Alan Gould, sports editor for Associated Press, predicted that the strong sentiment both within and outside the AAU would place insurmountable obstacles in the path of an American team.[60] All these evaluations and predictions proved far too optimistic. The team sailed on schedule for Germany, where, instead of vanquishing the Reich's representatives, which some proponents of participation had claimed would constitute a fitting response to Hitler, they watched the athletes of the "new" Germany claim an unexpectedly large share of the honors.

The *Philadelphia Record* was probably right; many Americans were now more aware of German persecution. Discussion of the issue on both editorial and sports pages resulted in increased American exposure to German fascism. Never had there been such sustained nationwide debate about events in Nazi Germany. The boundaries between domestic and foreign policy issues had been blurred. But in all likelihood if Americans had a negative image of Germany as a result of the debate, it was obliterated by the glowing reports brought back by those Americans who attended the Games.

The Games and Their Legacy

In addition to winning the top medals on the field of competition, the Germans won warm praise from many of those who came to witness the events. The American press corps, many of whom were in Germany just for the Games, lauded the Reich's accomplishments on and off the field. Much of what had been reported over the preceding years was ignored or forgotten. Newspaper and magazine readers were provided with lavish and extensive coverage of the Games. The sports competition was a massive exercise in propaganda and public relations, and many American reporters were uncritical about all that they saw. As Ambassador Dodd had predicted, Americans—particularly non-German-speaking ones who only knew Germany from the Games—departed convinced that the revolutionary upheavals, random beatings, and the murders of political opponents had been greatly exaggerated or were a thing of the past. Those bedazzled included not only the athletes and tourists, but personages such as newspaper publisher Norman Chandler and numerous American businessmen. This period marked the beginning of Charles Lindbergh's love affair with the Reich. One reporter was convinced that as a result of the Games visitors would be

> inclined to dismiss all anti-German thought and action abroad as insipid and unjust. [The visitor] sees no Jewish heads being chopped off, or even roundly cudgeled. His popular conception of the aspect of post-revolution is shattered. The people smile, are polite and sing with gusto in beer gardens. Board and lodging are good, cheap, and abundant, and no one is swindled by grasping hotel and shop proprietors. Everything is terrifyingly clean and the visitor likes it all.[61]

Visitors to Berlin described it as a warm, hospitable place and Germany as a country well on its way to solving the economic and unemployment problems which still plagued America. Few of the descriptions of the Games touched on the darker side of the German record. Three consecutive issues of *Time* magazine carried extensive reports on the Games. They mentioned various nonathletic details such as the fact that the Games were covered by 1,500 reporters, which was more than generally covered the activities of the League of Nations, but never cited the Jews' absence from German teams or from the spectator stands. While unsure whether they promoted international understanding, *Time* did believe that the Games, at the very least, "afford harmless amusement to participants and spectators [and] a valuable chance for ballyhoo to the nation which holds them."[62]

The general tone of the press coverage was described by *Literary Digest* as "mild and tolerant." Actually it was quite tolerant and not all that mild. Sports writers, reporters, and visitors waxed rhapsodic about the Germans' attention to detail and their concern for the athletes' and spectators' comfort.[63] Reporters such as William Shirer and Sigrid Schultz reported that Germany used the Games to "make propaganda as never before," but praise was far more common. The Germans' efforts were described as "amazing" and the provisions they made for the athletes, visitors, and the press were called "luxuriant."[64] The Games and the atmosphere in which they were held were, United Press (UP) reporter Edward Beattie wrote, "certain to surpass all others" and be "rated tops for all times." The press paid particular attention to the hospitality accorded the American team. The AP described the welcome given the Americans as the "most rousing" and declared it to have set the record for greetings to foreign teams.[65]

Not surprisingly, the *Los Angeles Times,* a strong supporter of the Games from the outset, described Berlin as a "gala city" and paid special tribute to German efforts. Even its fashion editor exuded enthusiasm: "Zeus, in his golden days, never witnessed a show as grand as this." Part of the press became more and more convinced that the competition would redound to the world's benefit. During the Games an editorial in the *Los Angeles Times* expressed the conviction that the "spirit of the Olympiads" would "save the world from another purge of blood." Immediately prior to the Games an AP dispatch predicted that the Games would help "assure peace" in Europe.[66]

Foreign visitors who came to witness the sporting events saw far more than sports. Although the militaristic aspects of German life were not unduly emphasized during the winter or summer Games, they were evident nonetheless. During the week prior to the winter Games one of America's most prominent sports writers, Paul Gallico, reported in the *Washington Post* that "the anxious Germans are rehearsing for the next war right next door to where the athletes are . . . practicing to win the great peace games of 1936." The *Los Angeles Times* sports writer Braven Dyer dismissed Gallico's report—one of the few to stress this theme—as a "scare story." In Berlin Nazi military might was demonstrated to many visitors as thousands of helmeted soldiers paraded in front of spectators. Nonetheless, a UP reporter at the Games claimed that there was "nothing military about the atmosphere of these Olympic summer games," a conviction that from all accounts was shared by most visitors to the competition.[67] This view proved to Germany's ultimate benefit, for now it had lots of vocal American support in its efforts to discount the "exaggerated" reports of its military might which were relayed to the American public by reporters stationed in Germany who, Reich leaders claimed, were anti-Nazis. How could a nation, readers may well have wondered, which went to such lengths to see to visitors' needs be accused of preparing to precipitate war? Subsequent depictions of violence and persecution that were dispatched to America seemed to bear no relation to the Germany of the Olympic Games.

In the general enthusiasm about the Games even Germany's pre-Olympic elimination of all non-Nazi sporting groups and of all "non-Aryans" from competition was reinterpreted by *Literary Digest* as nothing more than an energetic attempt by Germany to "reorganize German sports and gymnastics." According to this widely read magazine, it was *nothing but* an administrative move to eliminate disparate athletic groups and "bring them into one organization."[68]

Even the *New York Times,* which had opposed participation, was affected by the pageantry and atmosphere of the competition. Immediately prior to the Games it had warned readers about Germany's intention to use the competition to resurrect its image.

> For the duration of the Olympic Games the German people . . . go upon a special regimen. A good German citizen during these two or three Olympic weeks will . . . give up reading Herr Streicher's newspaper stories about how Jews kill little children for Passover, refuse to buy anti-Catholic cartoons, remove from hotel lobbies and village roads all signs and posters likely to give offense.

Once the Olympic flame was extinguished and the visitors were gone, then, the paper predicted, the good German citizen could "get right back to normal."[69] During the event itself, though *New York Times* reporters recognized that the competitions were designed to effect Germany's "rehabilitation in the eyes of a still largely hostile world," the tone of both its editorials and its news dispatches changed. Fred Birchall, Arthur Daley, and Albion Ross sent extensive reports to the paper describing in great detail German hospitality, enthusiasm, and, above all, efforts to transform the contest from a "sporting event into a world pageant and international spectacle." Even when some reporters, such as Ross, acknowledged that Germany might be "abusing" the Games, they still could not contain their own enthusiasm. On the eve of the winter Games Fred Birchall declared not only that the Germans were doing "a pretty close to perfect job" as hosts, but that "not the slightest evidence of religious, political or racial prejudice is outwardly visible here." *Time* magazine was quick to cite Birchall's observations and to note that Birchall worked for the paper which gave "the loudest bursts of publicity" to the boycott movement. Obviously his praise of Germany carried even greater weight than it would have if it had come from a paper with a record of support for the Games. By the end of the summer Games *New York Times* reporters had become even more generous in their praise as they predicted that the event would further "the undoubted improvement of world relations and general amiability."[70] The *New York Times* had succumbed to the very propaganda it had warned readers about. An editorial expressed the hope that the Games "may come to be one of the greatest of all agencies in the promotion of fairness in all human relations." At the end of the Games Birchall praised Germany's "good will" and "flawless hospitality" and called attention to the fact that people were leaving with a "bright hope."[71]

Even Paul Gallico, who had been so pessimistic, was impressed. On the eve of the opening of the Berlin competition he observed that "Berlin is magnificently dressed for the great show. Every house on every street is beflagged and the decorated streets are jammed with people. The Germans are being wonderfully polite and cordial and helpful to the Americans. The English language is the passport to all the courtesy and consideration possible."[72] Alan Gould, AP's sports editor, was so taken with the German hospitality that he questioned the American team's refusal to give the Nazi salute at the opening ceremony, as many other foreign teams had done. According to Gould, the Americans would have received an even warmer welcome had they adhered to the rule "when in Rome do as the Romans do."[73]

The critics were not entirely silenced. The *Washington Post* described the winter Games as the "biggest publicity stunt in recent history." On the eve of the summer Games the *San Francisco Chronicle* published a cartoon, which the *Washington Post* reprinted, showing Hitler hanging a sign which read "We Stand for Racial Equality! No Discrimination!" The caption underneath read "Just During the Olympics."[74] During the summer competition Westbrook Pegler continued to fulminate about the mix of sports and politics. According to him, the Games were "degenerating into a Sporting League of Nations," and the same calculations which stopped America from joining the League should have prevented America from participating in the Games.[75]

Pegler and Shirley Povich of the *Washington Post* were particularly critical of the Germans' treatment of American black athletes. On the day that Jesse Owens won his third gold medal, the German paper *Der Angriff*, which was published by Goebbels's Propaganda Ministry, wrote that America had been compelled to "enlist her black auxiliary forces" in order to withstand German competition. Povich believed such "race insult" marred the Games and wondered "what price Olympic glory?"[76]

Owens's accomplishments received front-page attention in

many papers, including the *New York Times* and *Washington Post.*
Time dubbed him "no. 1 hero of the world's no. 1 sports event,"
and Gallico described him as the "coolest and best-prepared party
on the American team." Even before the Games were over, Owens's mythic identity as the man who confounded Hitler's "Aryan"
principles had firmly taken root.[77] It was as if his victories alone
validated America's decision to participate. The truth was that
Ambassador Dodd's predictions, made over eight months before
the Games, that they would "rehabilitate and enhance" Germany's
reputation and that foreigners, including the American visitors,
would dismiss as "libel" the reports of persecution, were correct.
The laudatory stories and press reports proved more significant
than Owens's victories. The returning Americans even managed
to impress Roosevelt with their laudatory reports. Revealing an
incongruous degree of innocence, the President told Stephen
Wise that the tourists who had been to Germany "tell me that
they saw that the synagogues were crowded and apparently there
is nothing very wrong." Wise explained to him that the Nazis
had told people not to "let foreigners see anything wrong in
the relations of the people to the Jews." Wise doubted whether
he had convinced Roosevelt that all was not in order and appealed
to Felix Frankfurter to write a special report for the President
because the "tourists had made an impression on him."[78]

William Shirer bemoaned his inability to persuade American
visitors who were charmed by the splendor of the Games and
the Nazi system that "behind the glittering appearances [was] a
regimented antisemitic militaristic nation."[79] Recently in an interview Howard K. Smith, who broadcast for CBS from Berlin, described the Olympics as a "triumph for Hitler," possibly his greatest prewar propaganda triumph.[80] Rare was the mention of Jews
or of their absence from the Games in any of the reports which
American newspaper readers received. The press was impressed.
Visitors were beguiled. The world was becalmed. And Hitler's
conviction that the other nations of the world, America in particular, would adhere to their noninterventionist behavior was
strengthened.

Hitler had reinstated conscription in March 1935 and begun
a program of rearmament shortly thereafter. He disenfranchised
an entire portion of his population in the fall of 1935 and reoccu-
pied the Rhineland in March 1936, thereby committing a *casus
foederis* under the treaties Germany had signed.[81] Despite all this

the world came to compete and Hitler drew the correct conclusion.

The greatest irony may well have been that the Americans who went to the Games—tourists, reporters, sports writers, and dignitaries—had fallen prey to German propaganda. They returned convinced that Germany was at peace and on the road to economic and industrial triumphs. The truth about German persecution, which they were not shown, they dismissed as propaganda and beyond belief. The dissonance which permeated America's perception of Nazi Germany took firmer hold during this sports spectacular. A few years later other stories about German behavior—tales of mass executions, death camps, and gas chambers—would be so unbelievable that *they* would be dismissed as propaganda.

4

1938: From *Anschluss* to *Kristallnacht*

Between 1936 and 1938, as the situation of Jews in Germany grew progressively worse, increasing numbers of Jews left Germany. Those who sought to enter the United States found a multitude of obstacles in their path. The worldwide flood of refugees would be made much greater and more intense by the events of 1938, beginning with the German invasion of Austria in March and culminating in *Kristallnacht,* the night of broken glass, in November. During this eight-month period the American press responded to Germany's behavior with increasing horror. But its outrage did not alter its attitude regarding immigration and refugee rescue. Negative sentiments toward Germany intensified, but no softening of the American attitude toward refugees occurred. In fact, it stiffened. Faced with a potential flood of German Jews trying to escape the Reich, various papers noted that in light of the increased pressure on Jews to emigrate, now was the time for America to *raise,* not lower, its protective barriers; now was the time for increased vigilance. The press did not permit its disdain for Germany to compromise its conviction that there should be no changing of our immigration laws.

The *Anschluss* and Its Reverberations

On March 13, 1938, the German army crossed the Austrian border in order to "unify" these two countries. Unlike German Jews, who had five years to adjust to their indignities, Austria's 185,000 Jews were subjected to Nazi antisemitism overnight. Instantly they became a pariah people and swelled the rolls of those seeking refuge. As *New York Times* correspondent G. E. Gedye observed in a front-page article after he was expelled from Vienna by the Nazis for his reports:

> The plight of the Jews in Austria is much worse than that of the Jews in Germany at the worst period there. In Austria, overnight, Vienna's 200,000 Jews were made free game for mobs, despoiled of their property, deprived of police protection, ejected from employment and barred from sources of relief.[1]

The *Anschluss,* as this action was known, was but the initial step in a series of events which made Central European Jewry's situation even more desperate than it had previously been. Beginning in 1938, Germany accelerated the imposition of restrictions on Jews and expropriation of Jewish businesses and assets. The deterioration of the condition of Reich Jewry and the surge in the number of refugees seeking a haven forced the United States to confront more seriously that which it had previously tried to treat as a German "domestic issue." The tragic irony was that the indifferent response of the United States and most other nations of the world intensified the difficulties the Jews ultimately faced. The nations' actions, or lack thereof, served as a "green light" to Germany and a sign that though the world might condemn its behavior, it would do nothing to stop it or to materially aid the victims.

The *Anschluss* propelled the fate of Jews under Nazi rule onto the front pages and into the editorial columns of the American press. During the days and even weeks following the invasion, German actions were front-page news in the vast majority of American papers. According to the *Press Information Bulletin,* which analyzed the news coverage of over 400 different papers, more than 1,400 editorials on the subject appeared in the two weeks following. Close to half of them specifically mentioned or were entirely devoted to the plight of the Jews.[2] German Ambassador Dieckhoff, well aware of the press's influence on public opinion, tried to convince reporters and publishers in Washington and New York of the "absurdity of this whole commotion." However, as he correctly observed in his report to Berlin, his protestations "rarely penetrated the columns of the newspapers." Though he attributed his failure to the fact that the press was under either "Jewish or hostile control," the truth was that the sudden horror of the Nazification of a country and the persecution of a segment of its population shocked the press in a way that prior events in Germany had not.[3]

In the first few days following the *Anschluss* the abusive treatment meted out to Dr. Sigmund Freud was the topic of many editorials and the lead item in reports on Nazi activities. The *Detroit Free Press* observed that the news that the Nazi authorities in Vienna had taken Sigmund Freud's passport and impounded his money in order to prevent him and his wife from leaving Austria "would be unbelievable if the Nazi record in Germany were not already stained by a long record of persecution of members of the Jewish race."[4] Other papers found it hard to fathom that Freud's home could have been raided at night by "thugs cloaked in the law's vestments," and that Freud himself could have been "persecuted and suppressed without reason."[5] For the press as well as for other Americans including President Roosevelt, Freud's "subjugation" was "one of the most appalling incidents of Hitler ordered atrocities."[6] Many editorials believed it epitomized Nazi behavior and reflected the incomprehensible aspect of Nazi persecution.[7] The oppression of one individual, particularly one who was so prominent, elderly, and "harmless," evoked a more horrified reaction than did more intense brutalities inflicted on a larger number of faceless and nameless persons.[8]

It was against this background of intensified American outrage that President Roosevelt told the press that the German and Austrian immigration quotas would now be fully allocated, and Secretary of State Hull called for the convening of an international gathering to facilitate the emigration of political refugees from Austria and Germany.[9] In previous years the entire allotment of quota slots for Germany had not been distributed—due not to any lack of applicants, but to the many roadblocks placed in their path by State Department immigration officers.[10]

While Hull's proposal was quite vague regarding the conference's objectives, it was quite specific about what would *not* be done. America would neither increase the size of the quota for Germany and Austria nor liberalize existing immigration legislation. In addition, no cost would be incurred by the United States taxpayer for any programs the conference might adopt. The proposal's absence of detail about the way the conference would aid the refugees was not accidental. The State Department and White House did not have any specific ideas in mind beyond filling the existing German and Austrian quotas, but, aware of the growing public and press interest in the issue, Hull and his close aides and associates decided it "would be far preferable to get out in front and attempt to guide the pressure, primarily with a view toward forestalling attempts to have the immigration laws liberalized."[11] This was the first and only time the State Department took the initiative regarding the refugee situation.

Despite the fact that most Americans were strongly opposed to the immigration of refugees, the press greeted Hull's announcement with a chorus of hosannas. Newspapers from all regions of the country hailed it as "splendid and timely action" consonant with the finest American tradition of "act[ing] as a haven" and as "praiseworthy a proposal as President Roosevelt has made in a long time."[12] *Time* described its reception by the press and various public figures as "magnificent."[13] In the past whenever suggestions for liberalizing immigration laws had been posed, the press had discussed the burden immigrants placed on America. This time the reaction was different. Newspapers cited Freud and Einstein as typifying the Jewish refugee and counseled the nation to consider itself more "the benefactor than the benefited" by these people who could strengthen America.[14] One southern paper even took the dramatic step of indicating a willingness to have some of the Jewish refugees come to live in its region.[15]

Of the more than 400 editorials which discussed Hull's plan, over 75 percent favored it. At first glance this positive response is quite striking and might be interpreted as indicating a change in the traditional press opposition to any increase in the immigration quota; this, however, was not the case. Analysis of the press response to the *Anschluss* and the other critical events of 1938 reveals that while the press was horrified, its outrage had definite limits. As appalled as the American press was over German behavior, anger did not change its basic opposition to allowing refugees to enter this land. Hull had placed so many strictures on his proposal, including his promise that "any financing of the emergency

emigration referred to would be undertaken by private organizations" and that quotas would not be expanded, that the press
felt safe in approving it.[16] It had been stipulated that two main
concerns of the press—increased immigration and cost—would
not eventuate. Unfortunately, these stipulations virtually nullified
the chance that the proposed conference might substantially alleviate the problem.[17]

Actually, that did not matter to the press because its reasons
for supporting the plan had little or nothing to do with refugees.
The American press perceived Hull's proposal as a means of regis-
tering American opposition to the invasion of Austria. It was a
"stinging rebuke" to Hitler which would demonstrate American
contempt for "statesmen who . . . act like gangsters" and would
serve as America's means of reproaching Germany.[18] The press
approved of the plan because it would do these things without
materially involving the United States in the European quagmire
and did not appear to compromise America's neutrality. Even
the *Chicago Tribune* felt reassured enough to support it. Ironically
the opposite perception prevailed in Europe, where the conference proposal was greeted joyously because it appeared that
America was, at last, involving itself in the international situation.[19]

The press's euphoria obscured the major problems associated
with the plan. If no extension of quotas was contemplated, there
would be no real chance of alleviating the distress of persecuted
Jews. Though most papers ignored the issue, a few pointed out
that a conference which entailed no commitment to additional
asylum and an expanded quota would falsely raise the expectations
of a vast number of people. At best, one editorial observed, Hull's
proposal "restated a basic American principle" but envisioned
no change in the refugees' situation.[20] Typical of those papers
that viewed the idea and the fanfare that greeted it with cynicism
was the *Salem* (Oregon) *Journal,* which categorized the conference
as something which appeared at first glance to be a "fine humanitarian gesture" but upon closer inspection proved to be "wistful
thinking or a gallery political play." *Time* magazine was unsure
whether it amounted to "much more than a grandiose gesture."[21]

Even the President privately indicated that these were accurate
assessments. When Felix Frankfurter praised him for setting up
the proposed conference, Roosevelt told him that the majority
of the victims "won't find a haven of refuge, either here or elsewhere," but the conference would "help sustain their souls in
their material enslavement."[22] Actually the press recognized that

the President had an additional more political and less humanitarian objective. A number of papers and periodicals, including both *Time* and *Newsweek,* correctly discerned that the conference was an attempt "to think up a practical way to express the U.S. Government's disapproval" of German behavior, and to move American public opinion away from isolationism toward "active opposition to 'international gangsters.' " *Newsweek* accurately noted that the administration was "manifestly more interested in belaboring Hitler than in offering asylum to masses of German refugees."[23] Though the conference may have served the administration's purposes, ultimately it served Hitler's even more by demonstrating that the world's commitment to rescuing Jews was negligible at best. Afterward the Nazis were able to ask, with some justification, why the nations of the world berated them for wanting to rid the Reich of its Jews when they were no more anxious than Germany to have them in their midst.

Anti-Immigrant or Antisemite? Blurring the Line

There were a substantial number of papers which, despite the promises of private financing, international cooperation, and strict maintenance of quota limits, opposed the conference. In a strongly worded editorial, "Keep Up the Bars," the *Jackson* (Michigan) *Citizen Patriot* argued that there should not be expansion of quotas nor "should the customary bars against undesirable aliens be lowered."[24] A New York State paper took a strongly isolationist stand and described the plan as symptomatic of America's tendency to stick "her little pug into matters which did not in the least concern her and from which only trouble ensued."[25] Most of the plan's opponents cited the standard economic reason for opposing immigration: the United States could ill afford to admit limitless numbers of people, for "until work is found for our unemployed we must not complicate that difficulty by bringing in others."[26] The other standard argument, raised each time discussion of *any* alteration in the immigration laws was proposed, was that this would open the proverbial Pandora's box of liberalized quotas. The *Milwaukee Journal* cautioned that the "real danger in the present situation is that, overcome by our solicitude, we may forget to apply the protecting tests and to keep the numbers within quota limits."[27]

In reality many of these arguments had an antisemitic foundation. The premise was that Jews—their actions, interests, economic endeavors, in short, their very presence—cause antisemitism and that Hitler, therefore, had legitimate reason for his antipathy toward them. Editorials that condemned Nazi outbreaks often went on to justify the hostility from which they sprang. Two days after it first expressed its opposition to Hull's proposal, the *Milwaukee Journal* contended that Pandora's box had already been opened as a result of the visit of a delegation of Jews to the State Department to request that the quotas be liberalized until the international program for rescue that seemed to be in the offing was formulated and placed into operation. The paper attacked "American citizens of Jewish parentage" who were asking for special privileges for European Jewry and accused them of doing "neither their country, nor themselves, nor their kin a service." Their greatest sin was that they threatened the future of something the paper described as *"homogeneous* America."[28] Although the meaning of "homogeneous" was not spelled out, its implication was clear: Jews were different, and an influx of them threatened the nation's "racial" and "social" composition. The *Portland* (Oregon) *News* also mixed economic and antisemitic arguments. America, beset by problems of unemployment and barely able to take care of its own, could not afford to be "a dumping ground," particularly for refugees who might not "make real Americans" and who might not subscribe to "American principles of democratic government." Rather than admit more people, it was time to force "these trouble making aliens to go back from whence they came."[29] The *Detroit News,* without ever mentioning Jews but clearly referring to them, also objected to the potential flood of Jewish immigrants.

> Further refugees would largely settle, as the others have, in cities and particularly New York, where their presence has not been to the best interests of those of their own people, already settled, whose compassion and active sympathy they have enlisted.[30]

During the 1930s the press generally couched its opposition to immigration in terms of unemployment, a depressed economy, and burdens on already overburdened taxpayers, all of which were supposedly exacerbated by immigration. On occasion the xenophobic sentiments and social and racial antipathies which undergirded the standard economic arguments were revealed. This was not the first or last time that such feelings were displayed. As has been shown, during the first years of Nazi rule Jews were often blamed for bringing their suffering upon themselves. A similar argument was repeated in November 1938 after *Kristallnacht*, when *The Christian Century* argued against increased immigration. The journal admitted that it was more concerned about the social than the economic implications of a change in immigration policy. The United States, it argued, already had to contend with the problem of integrating nationalities and races who "are wholly irrelevant to our common national life." Permitting entry of additional Jews would be a "tragic disservice to the Jews in America" because it would "exacerbate" what *Christian Century* described as America's "Jewish problem."[31]

Other less prestigious press voices also blamed the Jews. The *Holyoke Times Telegraph* accused Jews of provoking their persecutors by "adhering too closely to city life." The *Allentown* (Pennsylvania) *Chronicle and News* attributed Jews' suffering to their "inability" to assimilate with "any other race" and to an innate "aggressiveness" which had always caused the Jews' "downfall."[32]

Despite these pockets of dissent and hostility toward Jews, however, most of the papers which commented on the idea of a conference were swept up in the enthusiasm of a "rebuke to Hitler" at little cost to America. And those who feared that it would produce a wave of newcomers had little cause for real concern, for this was the politics of gestures, as the conference itself would soon demonstrate.

Evian: A None Too Trustful Poker Game

For eight days in July the delegates of thirty-two nations, the representatives of thirty-nine private organizations, two hundred newspaper reporters, and a myriad of unofficial observers and supplicants gathered at the luxurious Hotel Royal at the French resort of Evian-les-Bains on Lake Geneva near the Swiss border. Evian's mineral baths had long been a favorite of Europeans in search of cures for various ailments. On this occasion Evian's healing powers would fail to cure any of the ills plaguing those who were the subject of the conference—the refugees.

By this time much of the enthusiasm for the conference had evaporated and a keener recognition of the problems faced was to be found in news stories and editorials. Since the *Anschluss*

Germany had increased the economic pressure on Jews, forcing them into what *Newsweek* described on the eve of the conference as "an isolation unequaled since the Middle Ages." It was now clear that few nations wanted immigrants at all and fewer still were willing to provide places for those who were both penniless and Jews.[33] Clarence Streit, writing in the *New York Times*, described the atmosphere which prevailed at this tranquil resort as "so much like a poker game . . . a none too trustful poker game particularly as between the three great democracies, the United States, the United Kingdom and France"—a poker game in which each of the players refused to even contemplate raising the stakes. This gathering, supposedly dedicated to helping refugees, was permeated by an "air of inhospitality" to them.[34]

During the conference various editorials energetically explained why the United States, despite its deepest sympathies, could offer little additional aid. Some papers vigorously protested, possibly a bit too much, that this was due to economic and not racial or religious considerations.[35] They contrasted the contemporary situation with earlier times when "farmers needed more consumers for their products; railroads wanted new settlers along their rights of way, . . . [and] mills had room for common labor at low wages." The press argued that while this was America's mythic identity, reality was quite different. According to the *San Francisco Chronicle,* even skilled refugees were not wanted in this country, where there was not only a surfeit of common laborers but "already as many doctors as can make a living, perhaps more."[36]

Some papers ignored the issue of whether refugees should be allowed to enter the United States and simply echoed the demand of the "Big Three" powers—the United States, Great Britain, and France—that Germany permit the refugees to take a substantial portion of their income and belongings with them to facilitate their resettlement. Editorials repeatedly argued that Germany could hardly "expect other countries to admit the Jews" who had been cast "abroad penniless."[37] A New Orleans paper bluntly informed Berlin that if it was more "interested in getting rid of these people than in confiscating their property," then the rule that Jews could only take 5 percent of their income should be eased.[38] These demands seemed strangely unrealistic. Germany had previously done nothing to ease Jewish emigration, and there was no reason to expect it to begin to cooperate with other nations now. A few press observers recognized the ludicrousness of expecting German cooperation and dismissed it as a "naive suggestion."[39] One commentator cynically mused that life would certainly be easier if the Nazis would "give each refugee a cow and a horse, seed and farm implements, as well as some cash!"[40] The *Baltimore Sun* wryly and accurately pointed out that the fact that Jews' reception in other lands was made "doubly difficult" by their penniless state would be no "shock" to Nazis because expelling them in this condition was "part of their plan."[41]

There was nothing to indicate that Germany would change its tactics without a strong incentive such as a decision at Evian to impose economic pressure on Germany. The few editorial suggestions for explicit action—e.g., countries which owed Germany money should withhold payments as a form of protest and leverage until Germany "acquiesces"—were the exception.[42]

As the conference progressed, press appraisal of it grew progressively harsher. The great expectations of March dissolved in the realities of July. The *Detroit Free Press* decried the behavior of the various delegations, dismissed the reasons they gave why they could do nothing as "immaterial," and branded the gathering a "sad commentary" on the willingness of the world's democracies to resolve one of the "most serious problems" the world faced.[43] Another paper aptly categorized the meeting as a polite game of "passing the buck."[44] According to yet another paper the delegates had all but nullified their "profound sympathy for the tortured victims of Europe's totalitarian tyranny" with their various excuses why they were unable to provide asylum.[45]

The *New York Herald Tribune* declared the gathering "not exactly a pretty spectacle" as it got "nowhere with great dignity but at a high rate of speed." Demonstrating both pessimism and insight, the *Tribune* observed that Evian was enough to justify the "scorn" which the fascist governments of the world "delight in pouring out" on the other nations. *Time* described Evian as a place which had heard "many warm words of idealism and few practical suggestions."[46] The "air of inhospitality" and undercurrent of antisemitism prevalent at Evian were most dramatically exemplified by Australia's representative, who declared that "we have no real racial problem [and] we are not desirous of importing one."[47] Once again Jews were explicitly and implicitly held responsible for their suffering. *The New Republic,* one of the most ardent critics of the failure to rescue, observed that the delegates' annoyance at the Nazis seemed to proceed fully as much from the fact that they had presented the rest of the world with an awkward problem of absorption as from the cruelty practised toward the exiles, past and future.[48]

An even sharper condemnation was contained in a query by the *Richmond* (Virginia) *News Leader:*

> When the conference adjourns and a permanent commission is established in London to aid in mass migration, what will the United States do? Will this country set an example and modify immigration laws carefully and wisely to permit the entry of a considerable number of these intelligent refugees? Or will we simply play politics, hide behind nationalism, and insist that South America is the proper home for these people? As between the two questions, the answer is nearly obvious. The United States will be content with friendly gestures and kind words. That is why some of us not only are cold to the report of the conference but also are a bit ashamed of our country.[49]

The *Richmond News Leader*'s response was unique in explicitly taking the United States to task for refusing to act. Generally press condemnations of the world's intransigence excluded the United States. Victor Wilson of the *Philadelphia Record* assailed the "indifference if not downright hostility" of the conference in a lengthy article under a telling headline:

> Humanitarianism Suffers a New Blow as Evian Parley Fails to Provide
> System for Aiding Europe's Unhappy Exiles—France and Britain
> Maneuver to Shunt Burden on U.S.

As the headline indicates, Wilson's ire was directed at other nations, France and Britain in particular.[50] Similarly *Newsweek* noted that when other nation's governments heard *American* calls for prompt action, they responded by "promptly . . . slamming their doors against Jewish refugees."[51] The *Washington Star* also castigated Evian's participants, with the exception of the United States, for their "yes-but" behavior. The delegations "vied with one another in deploring the plight . . . faced by [the] oppressed"; the problem was that when it came to the "brass tacks . . . for facilitating emigration . . . Evian emulated a famous region paved with good intentions."[52]

Then, during the meeting's final days, when the participants managed to agree on the establishment of a permanent intergovernmental commission charged with the task of finding a solution to the refugee problem, some of the press's sharp critique was tempered.[53]

The vast majority of the critics in the American press refused to consider that America's refusal to change its quota laws might have been responsible in some measure for the limited results of Evian. When the United States promised that the status quo would be maintained, Evian's eventual outcome could well have been predicted. In truth, had America expanded its quota allotments or assumed responsibility for a greater number of refugees, the press would have condemned its actions just as relentlessly as it now condemned the inaction of the rest of the world. The press had supported the idea of a conference because it guaranteed no increase in immigration. In fact its stance was entirely consistent with—if not slightly more liberal than—public sentiments. A *Fortune* survey taken earlier in the year revealed that less than 5 percent of Americans favored expanding the quotas while 67 percent favored trying to keep refugees out. Only 18 percent of the public—but most of the press—favored the status quo.[54]

In the opinion of the press America had done enough, and some even wondered if it had not done too much. Though this was a European matter, America had convened the conference, had promised full quota allocations, and and had already taken in more refugees than many other countries. An American, Myron C. Taylor, had served as the conference's president. America had come to France and England's aid just two decades earlier and now was being asked to do so again. A number of papers cautioned that it was not America's responsibility to "remake Europe."[55] The burden was on others to respond.

For the American press, the failure of Evian was the failure of the rest of the world to shoulder its share of the burden. Press reaction to the *Anschluss,* Evian, and, as shall be demonstrated in the pages that follow, *Kristallnacht* exemplified the way in which American contempt for German behavior coexisted with an unwavering commitment to isolationism and anti-immigrationism. Though the press was increasingly hostile to Nazi Germany, this did not preclude its strengthened commitment to the maintenance of American neutrality. Its sympathy for the victims and its contempt for the perpetrators did not negate its conviction that the gates of this land must remain firmly shut.

The Sound of Breaking Glass

When on the night of November 9, 1938, the glass was shattered in Jewish homes, stores, and places of worship throughout the Reich, along with it were shattered American hopes about the possibility of achieving stability for Jews under Nazi rule. The Munich pact, concluded but six weeks earlier, now seemed to be a mockery of the notion "peace in our time." Any expectation that Hitler and his government intended to abandon their policy of terror and physical persecution now seemed naive.

As a result of *Kristallnacht* the official and popular attitude toward Germany hardened. Roosevelt, genuinely repulsed by Nazi behavior, used *Kristallnacht* as a means of justifying his requests for increased defense allocations. The boycott of German goods regained its momentum, while those who had advocated a liberal attitude toward Germany or who had previously remained silent about events in that country condemned "this march backward into medieval terror."[56]

For the first time since the Nazi accession to power a nation-wide antisemitic action had taken place in full public view. In the past, even when the government's "hand" showed as the force behind similar violence, the violence had never occurred on such a national scale. Whereas the Germans had often dismissed foreign news reports as unreliable rumors based on "lies," this time there was no denying. As Lionel Kochan has observed, "every newspaper correspondent in Germany and Austria could see and hear what was taking place, and through him his readers." In reporting on *Kristallnacht,* the press transmitted to the American public first-hand, unimpeachable evidence of what it meant to be a Jew in Nazi Germany.

The shock waves which reverberated through all segments of the public were so severe that Ambassador Dieckhoff described the reaction as a "hurricane . . . raging here" and urged Foreign Ministry officials to understand the change of attitude in America. He warned that many Americans who had previously "maintained a comparative reserve and had even, to some extent, expressed sympathy toward Germany, are now publicly adopting so violent and bitter an attitude."[57] NBC and CBS radio broadcast condemnations by former Governor of New York Al Smith, New York District Attorney Tom Dewey, former President Herbert Hoover, former Presidential candidate Alf Landon, Secretary of the Interior Harold Ickes, and an array of other prominent religious, political, and educational leaders. Hoover's participation was particularly significant, because earlier in the year he had castigated the press for conducting what he felt was an anti-German campaign. Throughout the United States local, county, and state government officials expressed their horror. One southern governor wrote to Roosevelt that "it is time for America to stand four-square for humanity."[58]

Nowhere was the criticism stronger and more sustained than in the press. In the weeks following *Kristallnacht,* close to 1,000 different editorials were published on the topic. Virtually every paper listed in the *Press Information Bulletin,* the White House's barometer of press opinion, carried a series of news stories and editorials on the issue. For over three weeks following the outbreak, eyewitness reports from Germany could be found on the front pages of numerous papers. Practically no American newspaper, irrespective of size, circulation, location, or political inclination failed to condemn Germany.[59] Now even those that, prior to *Kristallnacht,* had been reluctant to admit that "violent persecution is a permanent fixture in Nazism" criticized Germany. During the early years of Nazi rule the most influential German-language newspaper in America, the *New Yorker Staatzeitung und Herald,* had defended Hitler's antisemitic measures. Its publisher and owner, Bernard Ridder, who also owned other American papers, returned from Germany in 1933 with the claim that when Hitler came into power he "found 62% of all governmental offices filled with Jews." (The *Nation* hastened to deprecate Ridder's charge by pointing out that since Germany employed 970,000 salaried officials, this would mean that 601,400 of them were Jews, or "more than 40,000 [Jews] more than there were Jewish men, women, and children in the Reich.")[60] Subsequently the *Staatzeitung* was virtually silent about the persecution in Germany. Now even it joined in the chorus of condemnations. Its condemnation was news in itself and was cited by numerous papers as evidence of the fact that even German Americans who had long maintained an uncompromising loyalty to their homeland would not tolerate such outrageous acts.

But the press did not only condemn; once again it sought rational explanations for this apparently senseless course of events.[61] Some papers reverted to the "weakness, not strength" theory that was common during the early years of Nazi rule.[62] Various papers, including the *New York Daily News,* posited that *Kristallnacht* was an expression of anger and resentment on the part of those Germans who lacked funds and were under severe financial strain. The *New York Daily News* went so far as to conclude that Hitler "can no longer control his people, that he is losing his grip"; he had "turned so much German wealth into armaments that he can no longer provide for the rockbottom necessities of all his people."[63] This attempt to define *Kristallnacht* as an expression of popular anger turned the pogrom into a riot conducted by what the *Daily News* described as "hungry mobs" intent on plundering Jews. The paper's isolationist sentiments may have led it to this interpretation; if Nazi Germany was on the brink of collapse, there was no need for the United States to involve itself in this affair.

In sharp contrast, a significant portion of the press believed that it was strength, not weakness, which led to *Kristallnacht.* The Nazis had dealt with the world without penalty and felt that as concerned the Jews they could continue to do so. World leaders who had granted Hitler's every territorial wish certainly did not appear likely to penalize Germany for an attack on Jews. The *Wilmington* (Delaware) *News* dismissed those who would "read into [Kristallnacht] signs of Nazi weakness. The evidence points the other way." *Newsweek,* concurring, noted that *Kristallnacht* came at a "moment of great international triumph and not as the refuge of a weak regime trying to foment hatred as a stimulant."[64] The most recent and possibly greatest German international success had come at Munich just six weeks earlier, and it was this, much of the press contended, that had given the Nazis the hubris to act in this manner.

According to much of the press, the timid and misguided policies of Neville Chamberlain had resulted in *Kristallnacht.* Because of the English "surrender" at Munich, various papers warned, Jews in Germany and German-dominated countries may have to be "rescued" or left "to suffer" Czechoslovakia's fate.[65] The *Virginian Pilot*'s observation that "peace in our times . . . seems certain only to insure an ever increasing measure of beastliness in our time" typified the reaction of numerous papers.[66] There was a tendency, particularly on the part of isolationist papers, to use *Kristallnacht* as a means of clearly demarcating between American and British interests.[67] Generally the isolationists condemned

Britain and advised the Administration to avoid all dealings with it, including dealings on matters relating to refugee resettlement.[68]

The *Gary* (Indiana) *Post Tribune,* in addition to declaring that *Kristallnacht* proved that appeasement was wrong, reminded readers, in what amounted to an almost gratuitous slap at Britain, that during World War I Americans had been "deceived by our Allies into believing a lot of atrocity tales." The underlying message of the editorial was clear. Britain had deceived us once before and would do so again in order to entangle us in European affairs.[69]

The press's conviction that Munich had led to *Kristallnacht* resulted in part from its willingness now to view Nazi antisemitic actions as part of a broader context. This contrasted sharply with the way in which the press generally had treated Hitler's antisemitism as separate and distinct from his overall policies. This time the press linked Germany's domestic antisemitism to the conduct of its foreign policy. It did not argue that the two were different spheres with no connection, but recognized that the way the world treated Germany in the international arena could have a direct influence on how Germany behaved in the domestic arena. (Some papers had understood this at the time of the Olympics; many others had not.)

But while the press was able to link Germany's domestic and international policies, it still had difficulty grasping that one of the primary motives for *Kristallnacht* had been to destroy organized Jewish life and to make the Reich *Judenrein.* Instead the press, irrespective of its political outlook, interpreted *Kristallnacht* as a reflection of German financial exigencies; namely, this was said to be a way of extorting money from Jews.[70] This view gained credence after the Nazi government announced that a fine was to be levied on the Jews. The *Cleveland Plain Dealer* believed the "confiscation of Jewish wealth and property [to be] a revelation of the government's need of new funds" and the primary objective of *Kristallnacht.* Numerous papers dismissed the idea that the Nazis were motivated by racial hatred or the desire to transform Germany into an "Aryan" land. Greed had prompted them to act as they did: these were "pogroms for profit" designed to strip all "Jews in Germany of their wealth and savings."[71] The *St. Louis Post Dispatch* described *Kristallnacht* as the "looting of a people," while the *Baltimore Evening Sun* termed it a "money collecting enterprise."[72] The *New York Times* also adopted this view. In an editorial entitled "Profit from Persecution" it condemned Germany's plan to "make a profit for itself out of legalized loot."[73]

The chance to acquire "easy loot" may well have motivated or encouraged some of the participants. *Kristallnacht* doubtlessly helped many German citizens and authorities to line their pockets. However, the potential cost to the economy as a result of loss of trade and destroyed property offset many of these "gains." Had those who organized the pogroms been only or even mainly interested in fattening German coffers, they would have chosen a less costly way of doing so. The motivating factor was not financial gain, but deep and abiding antisemitism. Even at this stage, after five and a half years of Nazi rule, much of the press and even more of the public did not understand that antisemitism was a, if not *the,* keystone of Nazism and not a by-product of Nazi greed or a means of deflecting the German people's attention from other troubles.

There were some commentators who did understand, as an analysis of *Mein Kampf* which appeared in *The Saturday Evening Post* a few months after *Kristallnacht* demonstrated. The author of the article argued that if Americans wanted to understand Hitler and the regime he led, they could not "blink the fact that hatred of the Jews is the mortar which binds together into one house all the bricks of Hitler's other hatreds."[74] Those reporters, editors, and readers who adhered to economic interpretations would fail to understand this.

Incidentally, the version of *Mein Kampf* which was sold in America did not contain many of the more virulent references to Jews. Senator Alan Cranston, who in the 1930s served in Italy and Germany as a reporter for International News Service, returned to America shortly after *Kristallnacht.* When he discovered that the sanitized American edition of *Mein Kampf* was "purged of its most vitriolic ravings," he translated and published an unexpurgated version which was sold at cost. Before the American publisher sued him for violation of copyright—something the publisher, by Cranston's own admission, had every right to do—his edition sold over 500,000 copies.[75]

There were papers, including *Staatzeitung,* which after *Kristallnacht* reverted to differentiating between the people and the party and branded the pogroms the work of "fanatics in the ranks of the party in power who are trying to drag a great people into the mire of their sadistic lowness." The advocates of this approach refused to believe that a nation of apparently civilized people could condone a modern-day pogrom.

> It is impossible to avoid the conclusion that the German people, as humane in general as any nation, are under the control of a government with the morals of a lynching party at its worst.[76]

Many of the papers which followed this line and exculpated the German people cited former President Hoover's CBS broadcast, which castigated Nazi officials but absolved the German public. That one should separate the German people into two groups, those who committed such acts and those who did not, was an attitude that had been manifested consistently since 1933. Rather than dissipate with the passage of time, it seemed to grow stronger. The more outrageous German behavior became, the more likely some Americans were to argue that Hitler was an "aberration in German history." Many Americans, particularly scholars and diplomats who had studied in Germany during their university careers, tended to divide German society into "bad Germans," the dregs of society recruited from the gutter, and "good Germans," those of the upper-class university-educated elite, who would neither commit nor sanction brutal acts. They remained committed to this view despite repeated eyewitness accounts, particularly from American reporters, that the German people were united behind the Führer. Some of them would not abandon this idea of two Germanys until the Nuremberg trials, when it was conclusively demonstrated that the upper-class elite was as much part of the "bad Germany" as any other group was. This natural American sympathy for the good Germany, the Germany of art, culture, and storybook charm, persisted through the war. Jan Ciechanowski, Polish Ambassador to the United States during the war, was perplexed by this "basic kindheartedness" Americans felt toward Germany even *after* its "ruthless" war methods were public knowledge.[77]

The tendency to absolve the people and condemn the leaders was not universal. A few papers argued that the German people had to bear the full responsibility for the persecution rampant in their country. They had at least silently acquiesced if not energetically participated in all manner of acts of persecution and had to bear the consequences. The *Chicago Daily News* declared the Germans an "uncivilized nation"; the *New York Herald Tribune* described Germany as a "nation possessed."[78]

This time the vast majority of the press recognized that Germans from the highest level of government were involved. Claims that *Kristallnacht* occurred contrary to the government's wishes and without its approval were dismissed as implausible. However, as noted earlier, there were still some papers, including publications such as the *Atlanta Constitution,* which could not fathom that Hitler would sanction such an event and believed that he must have been deceived by those around him.[79] Even the *Manchester Guardian,* long in the forefront of British opposition to Nazi anti-semitism, refused to believe that the government was involved.[80]

Irrespective of whether a paper pointed the finger of blame directly at Hitler or believed that he had "inspired" but not staged the pogrom, there was almost absolute agreement that the uprising was not, as the official explanation claimed, a "spontaneous" expression of wrath by the German people.[81] *Time* referred to the "so-called mobs," while *Newsweek* was quizzical about the ability of supposedly spontaneous gatherings to wreak such "methodical destruction."[82] The *Philadelphia Record* pointed out that, unlike *Kristallnacht,* "riots do not generally happen on a timetable."[83] Tongue in cheek, the *New York Times* observed that the rioters "worked with a precision that was a tribute to spontaneous demonstrations."[84]

The Response to *Kristallnacht*

Though the press may have offered differing explanations for the pogrom, there was little doubt about its revulsion at Germany. On this point the American reaction was "united as never before." The unanimity of press sentiment was so striking that it became the topic of many editorials. The press was described as being "nearly a unit in denunciation."[85] The United States had not been so aroused "since the Lusitania."[86]

If there remained any question about this feeling *Time,* which used the daily press as a major source for its own reports, noted that

> singular was the U.S. attitude in one respect: on a question of
> foreign affairs concerning which it seldom has much feeling, the

U.S. public had spontaneously expressed a strong national feeling.[87]

The question remained; Would the condemnations result in an official response? *Time* believed that public opinion, as exemplified by the press, had given Roosevelt "a mandate" which he would undoubtedly "translate into foreign policy." But the President, behaving in a characteristically cautious fashion, decided to wait in order to assess the nature of this mandate. Immediately after the pogrom, when first queried about events in Germany, he declined to comment and suggested to reporters that they "better handle that through the State Department."[88] Five days later, when the depth of public outrage was evident, not only did he comment but he broke a number of precedents in order to do so. He recalled Ambassador Wilson for consultation and, ignoring State Department suggestions that a written statement be sent to Germany, he read a presidential statement at his press conference. Moreover, contrary to established procedure, Roosevelt allowed himself to be quoted. This change in protocol was understood by reporters present to be indicative of the President's seriousness about the matter. To further strengthen the impact of his announcement, he used forceful and unambiguous language.

> The news of the past few days from Germany has deeply shocked public opinion in the U.S. Such news from any part of the world would inevitably produce a similar profound reaction among American people in every part of the nation. I myself could scarcely believe that such things could occur in a twentieth century civilization. With a view to having a first-hand picture of the situation in Germany I asked the Secretary of State to order our Ambassador in Berlin to return at once for report and consultation.[89]

Wilson's recall met with great approval. The *New York Times* believed it "difficult to conceive of a more forceful expression of this country's displeasure short of severing diplomatic relations." *Newsweek* considered it "remarkable." A West Virginia paper believed the President "spoke for America," and the *Philadelphia Inquirer* assured Roosevelt that the American people stood solidly behind him.[90] The State Department was surprised by the press's enthusiasm. The Chief of the Division of European Affairs of the State Department, Pierrepont Moffat, noted in his diary that "the press played it [the recall] up even more than we anticipated." The Department made a concerted effort to diminish the significance of the move by insisting that Wilson had planned to return to the United States anyway and that his hasty departure was not connected with *Kristallnacht.* [91]

But even as the press was "playing up" the recall, there was an underlying cautiousness in much of its praise. The initial shock of the pogrom had hardly begun to wear off and already some of the press was expressing a fear that the United States was on the verge of becoming entangled in European political affairs. The *New York Sun* acknowledged that the President "no doubt wish[ed] to record in some unmistakable manner this nation's deep concern and displeasure," but it reminded him of the "impropriety of interfering in the domestic affairs of a friendly power."[92] Many newspapers were pleased that Wilson's return was not irrevocable and did not entail a severing of diplomatic relations, and that it expressed American disapproval without direct American involvement.[93] The *New York Herald Tribune* was expressing a strongly felt American sentiment when it reminded the President that, while they strongly approved of his action, the American people had "no desire to go to war with Germany."[94] A few papers questioned the recall. The *St. Louis Globe Democrat,* for example, wondered "what such action would achieve other than to increase pressure on the helpless Jews." But even Roosevelt's most persistent critic, the *Chicago Tribune,* believed the President's decision and American feelings of revulsion were justified, though it too warned against engaging in threats and denunciation.[95]

A few liberal journals took issue with the recall because it was *too* limited. They were joined by a few other papers and journals in calling for action, not just the rhetoric of action, on behalf of persecuted Jews.[96] They complained that the recall was a symbolic gesture which failed to pressure the Germans to rectify their ways, and that something more "concrete" was needed.[97] The *Binghamton Sun* argued that "indignation should mean action," and wondered whether the United States was only "indignant enough to pass resolutions."[98]

What most of these critics wanted was not just a recall, but liberalization of refugee immigration. They tried to counter anti-immigration arguments by demonstrating that refugees, many of whom were not in the job market, were an asset, not a burden, bringing with them expertise previously lacking in America and freeing the country from dependence on foreign imports.[99]*

Some papers, while not fervent advocates of liberalization, did urge the United States to at least give "serious" consideration to some form of liberalization, though the liberalization that they advocated was highly proscribed. It generally consisted of support for Roosevelt's decision to permit the twelve to fifteen thousand German visitors here on visitors' visas to remain and to call for the entry of a limited number of gifted and "brainy" immigrants such as Einstein and Freud.[100] At best these papers advocated "temporary and careful modification of the immigration laws for the period of the pogrom."[101] What all these liberal critics failed to recognize was that just as the Evian conference had been designed to serve as a rebuke to Hitler, this recall was intended to demonstrate American disapproval, and not to render a material blow to Germany or even to aid the Jews.

Even as these critics called for more action, there were other voices which cautioned against changing the laws. The *Christian Science Monitor* rejected suggestions for changing immigration laws and counseled that the best protest was prayer.[102]** The *Christian Century* held that despite the fact that it was the Nazis' "inexorable purpose to annihilate the Jewish population of Germany," it was "highly inadvisable to let down our immigration barriers." Doing so would create "evils as great as those which it was designed to cure." Liberalization would exacerbate the already severe economic and social problems plaguing America. The *Cincinnati Times Star* even opposed the President's decision to allow Germans in the U.S. to remain on visitors' visas until places became available to them on the regular quota. The *Binghamton Press* and the *Tulsa World,* in rather inflammatory gestures, were among the papers

---

* These arguments about the benefit offered by immigrants could not, however, dispel a popular image of refugees pushing Americans out of work. During this period rumors were circulating in a number of cities, including New York, that certain department stores, some of which were owned by Jews, were firing their employees in order to hire refugees. Despite repeated denials by the stores, these rumors prevailed. They became so widespread that at one point several stores, including Bloomingdale's and Macy's, placed newspaper ads denying that they were hiring refugees.

** This suggestion, although of little succor to the victims, was less frivolous than it might initially appear. Christian Scientists maintain that prayer can "decisively shape the course of events."[103]

which cautioned their readers that there was a plan afoot to bring all Jews to this country.[104]

Despite these critical voices, the recall was an astute political response. In view of the realities of the moment, more extreme action might have met with opposition. Polls taken in November 1938 shortly after *Kristallnacht* demonstrated that Americans were adamantly opposed to any changes in refugee legislation.[105] In April 1939 they repudiated the idea of their country's serving as a haven for the persecuted by a margin of ten to one.[106] The anti-immigration mood was reflected in and reinforced by the editorials of most of the nation's major dailies and magazines, which cautioned against lowering the bars against entry to this land. The *New York Times* observed that no real answer to immigration problems was to be found in the gradual absorption of refugees through enlarged quotas. It argued that "the United States . . . cannot be expected to perform today . . . the historic service it has previously performed."[107]

This popular conviction that America could no longer serve as a home for huddled masses yearning to breathe free was not the only factor that Roosevelt seems to have taken into account when he decided to recall Wilson. He was politically vulnerable during the latter part of 1938, particularly in relation to foreign affairs. He had faced strong opposition to his attempts to increase armament production and had to lobby assiduously against concerted efforts to strengthen the Neutrality Act.*

Gallup polls from the period indicate that Americans regarded maintaining neutrality as the "most important" problem facing them.[108] A politically conservative Congress had been elected, and Roosevelt knew that his policies, foreign and domestic, faced opposition. In light of his political situation, Roosevelt's recall of Wilson was balanced. It went slightly beyond the public's— but not the press's—desire for an emphatic response but did not appear to draw the country into the ever intensifying crisis. The recall struck out at the perpetrators but virtually ignored the victims, and it was precisely because of its restrained and limited

---

* Existing laws, passed between 1935 and 1937, governed every aspect of American foreign relations with other states and were designed to prevent the United States from being lured into a conflict. In January 1938 an extraordinary presidential appeal had been needed to prevent the House from passing the Ludlow Amendment, which would have required a national referendum before the country could go to war. The amendment was defeated by the slim margin of twenty-four votes.

nature that it won press approval. Had Roosevelt chosen to offer concrete aid to the victims, that would have been opposed.

The combined voices of those papers and journals supporting some liberalization of immigration—however limited and strictly policed—could not counter the overwhelming weight of public and press opinion that adamantly opposed any relaxation of quotas. This was to remain a virtual constant in press opinion except for one brief period in the following spring when the ones to be rescued were children.

If Not Here, Where?

Since Wilson's recall was considered a sufficient American response and the quota system was treated as virtually immutable, press interest was sparked by proposals for resettlement of Jews in other areas. Frequently mentioned alternatives included British Guiana, Tanganyika, Kenya, Northern Rhodesia, and "someplace" in the vast territorial expanse of the British Empire. *Time* let Walter Lippmann, whom it described as America's "most statesmanly Jewish pundit," speak for it. Lippmann's strong influence on the press of the nation was reflected in the fact that various papers approvingly echoed his views and cited him as their authority. *Time* cited his argument that nothing could be done for the persecuted Jews, except possibly to find them refuge in Africa. *Time*'s implication was clear: if Lippmann, the Jew, believed America should not liberalize its quota system, then could *Time* or anyone else, Jew or non-Jew, be faulted for thinking likewise? (After a five-year silence regarding the persecution of the Jews, Lippmann devoted two of his syndicated columns to Europe's "over-population" problem. Without specifically referring to Jews, he contended that Europe had to be "relieved" of a million people each year. It was the surplus population which was the cause of European upheavals.)[109]

The discussion of where refugees should be allowed to settle after *Kristallnacht* prompted interesting role reversals on the part of prominent Americans. Herbert Hoover, the overseer of refugee rescue and aid during World War I, argued that "America cannot open its doors in the face of our own unemployment and suffering. Sanctuary must be found elsewhere." In striking contrast, Henry Ford, the industrial magnate whose newspaper, the *Dearborn Inde-*

pendent, had published the *Protocols of the Elders of Zion,* called for the immediate entry of Jewish refugees into America.[110] Ultimately it was Hoover, not Ford, who correctly reflected public sentiments, sentiments the press consistently reinforced.

Most of the press recognized that the willingness of some European countries to accept a few refugees would "scarcely make a dent in the evacuation program." Relatively unpopulated areas of the world were cited as offering the most feasible alternative. By suggesting that "colonial" areas be found, the press was able to avoid the question of whether America should admit these souls. The *Springfield Republican* argued that "since the best parts of our globe are already pre-empted, it would be necessary, in the main, to fall back upon 'marginal' lands, which are available precisely because they are not very desirable." Although some recognized that trying to settle a highly educated urban population in an area populated primarily by cacti, jungles, and wild animals was an impractical solution, they contended that the situation was so desperate that measures that "heretofore may have seemed visionary" now had to be discussed seriously.[111] In general, however, most of the press shied away from discussing the merits of specific areas and simply stressed the need to provide refuge somewhere—other than here. The most frequent suggestion was that Britain, anxious to win support for its rearmament program and foreign policy and responsible for *Kristallnacht* because of its timidity at Munich, should find an isle of refuge in its vast empire.[112]

* * *

The events of 1938 hardened America's feelings about Germany and its program of persecution. As Ambassador Dieckhoff noted shortly before returning to Germany, even those who had been "restrained" were now "violent and bitter." But no sooner had editorial boards passionately condemned Germany and voiced their horror than they also urged caution and restraint.

Reporters on the scene now were cautioning more strongly than ever against dismissing as rhetoric any Nazi threat against the Jews no matter how extreme. Otto Tolischus warned readers in a front-page *New York Times* story against ignoring the "seriousness" of "lurid" Nazi predictions such as those contained in the official Gestapo paper, *Das Schwarze Korps,* that if the Jews were not evacuated from Germany at once, they would be "starved into crime" and "exterminate[d] with 'fire and sword.' "[113] Although Tolischus was not predicting the Final Solution, he, along with a few others, did recognize that organized Jewish life in Germany was at an end. Though the editorial boards and policy makers now recognized more than they had before the seriousness of Nazi threats, they did not recommend dramatic changes in American policy. In fact they cautioned against them because the most efficacious and speedy solution would have necessitated ignoring two prevailing American sentiments: the necessity to maintain strict neutrality and even stricter bars to increased immigration.

The press's attitude fit squarely within the political climate of this country. It is best described by the phrase used to characterize the mood at Evian: "yes but." Yes, the American press was outraged at Germany's behavior, but nonetheless it was convinced that it must remain out of European affairs. Yes, the refugees' situation was distressing, but there was little America could do. It certainly could not throw open the gates of this land. The American press extended its heart but not its hands.

=== 5 ===

Barring the Gates to Children and Refugee Ships

Suffer the Little Children: The Wagner-Rogers Bill

The one significant break in American editorial opposition to alteration of existing refugee legislation occurred in 1939, when Senator Robert Wagner of New York and Representative Edith Nourse Rogers of Massachusetts introduced a bipartisan bill to permit the entry of 20,000 German children under fourteen years of age. The children, who would enter over two years time, would be admitted in addition to the German quota.

This was not the first immigration bill introduced in 1939. Senator Robert Reynolds of North Carolina and Representative Joe Starnes of Alabama proposed a cluster of bills which would have limited immigrants to 10 percent of the quota and halted immigration for a decade or until unemployment fell to 3 million. At the other, more liberal end of the spectrum was a resolution introduced by Representative Emanuel Celler of New York proposing that those who were refugees "because of race or religious beliefs, or liable on that account to criminal persecution, summary or arbitrary treatment, social or economic discrimination," be admitted outside the quota.[1] All these proposals died in committee.

When Wagner and Rogers introduced their proposal to admit the children, they won immediate overwhelming editorial support. More than eighty-five newspapers from thirty-six states supported it, among them twenty-six from the south, a region that ardently favored immigration restriction. The bill's sponsors placed over ninety editorials in favor of the measure in the *Congressional Record.*[2] There was no question but that the suffering of little children touched the hearts of editors and publishers in a manner that their parents' suffering had not. However, widespread editorial support of the bill was not a sign of a weakening of America's resolutely anti-immigration stance. If anything, it reflected the inflexibility of that resolve. Supporters of the bill generally agreed that the United States could not and should not "be asked to succor all the victims of race prejudice. . . . But the children are a special case."[3]

> It is impossible to offer sanctuary in this country to all refugees, however urgent their need. It would dishonor our traditions of humanity and freedom, however, to refuse the small measure of help contemplated by the Wagner resolution.[4]

The wisdom of existing policy was not questioned; the bill was perceived of by the press as a one-time exception to the rule. Readers were assured that Wagner-Rogers was not a "precedent for breaking down the immigration laws."[5] As was the case each time this topic came up, the economic repercussions of immigration were debated. Many editorials stressed that while there were legitimate economic grounds to bar refugees, the children would not enter the job market for a number of years and only a small number would enter in any one year.

> We can no longer offer refuge to the oppressed of all nations and all ages. . . . But the objections to letting down the bars to men and women of working age do not apply to children.[6]

The *Miami Herald* adopted a unique and revealingly honest position. An opponent of "too much" immigration, it dismissed the economic objections to immigration as "extraordinary foolishness," noting that immigrants did not take jobs but, because they were consumers, created them and therefore were an economic asset, not a burden. The *Herald* admitted that the real roots of anti-immigration sentiment were "social and political."

America is right in admitting no more immigrants than can be adjusted to their new environment and *to our ways of thinking and carrying on.*

Despite these objections, the *Herald* supported the bill because the children were "young enough, given the right chance, to be 'Americanized' with quickness and ease." Although this particular editorial did not explicitly cite *Jewish* immigrants as incapable of adjusting to the new environment, its position was noticeably parallel to that of *The Christian Century* which had reverted to its practice of blaming Jews when it argued after *Kristallnacht* that admitting Jewish immigrants would only "exacerbate America's Jewish problem."[7]

Although few papers or magazines were as explicit as *The Christian Century* in explaining their objections to increased immigration, the fact that Jewish children would be the ones admitted proved to be a significant obstacle. Though most opponents of the bill did not rely on overtly antisemitic arguments, *The Nation* observed that "a subtle and effective argument is the *sotto voce* contention that this is a Jewish bill." Despite Wagner's and Rogers's assurances to the contrary, the opponents claimed that all the children who were to be admitted were Jewish. The press was obviously aware of this charge, and numerous editorials justified their support of the measure by assuring readers that the children would include Jews *and* "Aryans."[8]

When the bill was first introduced, the press was confident that "general approval" was bound to come.[9]

There is a rumor that the plan will be opposed. We don't believe it. This is a land which professes admiration and even reverence for the source of the saying: "Suffer the little children to come unto me."[10]

Despite overwhelming editorial support, the rumor proved correct. Opponents amassed a broad-based coalition which argued that American children were in need and therefore charity must "begin at home."[11] Ultimately they succeeded in having the bill amended so that, instead of providing 20,000 additional places for children, it reserved 20,000 existing places for them, resulting in a stiffening and not a relaxation of the quota system. Its sponsors prudently allowed it to die in committee.

The opponents prevailed because Americans still wanted to bar the gates of this country. A January 1939 Gallup poll found

66 percent opposed to the plan to allow "10,000 refugee children from Germany to be brought into this country and taken care of in American homes."[12] The poll did not even suggest that the children were to be allowed to enter outside the quota restrictions. Had this been mentioned in the question, the opposition of those polled might have been even stronger. In late May 1939 the *Cincinnati Post* polled 1,000 women, mainly housewives, and found 77 percent were against the entry of children outside the quota limits while only 21.4 percent approved.[13] A *Fortune* magazine survey taken in April 1939 found that nearly 85 percent of the non-Jews polled were adamantly against any change in immigration quotas.[14]

Even though the bill was supported by a substantial segment of the national press, its supporters were unable to counter the opponents' charge that it was a step toward liberalization of the immigration system. For the American public no argument, even the suffering of little children, could justify such a change. The press's fight for the passage of the bill marked one of the few times that it vigorously moved out "ahead" of the public. The bill failed because the most eloquently worded and compelling arguments could not surmount the strength of public opinion, which remained firmly fixed against the admission of refugees to this land.

The Saddest Ship Afloat: The Saga of the *St. Louis*

In June 1939, as America prepared an elaborate welcome for the King and Queen of England, another group of transatlantic passengers found a very different greeting extended to them. During the first two weeks in June the saga of the passengers on the Hamburg-American Line's SS *St. Louis* was the subject of much press attention. It was prominently featured in many American papers. On six different occasions during the first eight days of June articles regarding the ship appeared on the front page of the *New York Times*. Other papers accorded it similar attention.[15]

The ship's passengers, who all held official Cuban landing certificates which they had bought from the Hamburg-American Line, won the press's sympathy. Most were on waiting lists for entry into the United States and planned to remain in Cuba until they could be included in the quota allocation. Some of the passengers would probably have been allowed to enter within a few months, while others would have had to wait a few years. Shortly before the ship sailed from Hamburg, Cuban President Federico Laredo Bru had signed a decree invalidating the type of landing certificates held by the passengers. The certificates for which the passengers had paid approximately 150 dollars were now useless. When the ship reached Havana, the passengers were not allowed off the ship. The Cuban government claimed that the certificates had been obtained illegally and that it was not obligated to honor them. The ship remained docked in the Havana harbor as the most trying part of its voyage commenced.

Predictably all the editorials which discussed the voyage decried the "sickening spectacle" Germany had created and blamed it for ridding itself "of thousands . . . whose only offense is racial."[16] But Germany was not alone in being condemned by the press. Major publications including the *Philadelphia Record,* the *New York Herald Tribune,* the *Memphis Commercial Appeal,* and the *Pittsburgh Post Gazette* all held Cuba responsible.[17] These papers believed that since the passengers had obtained entry permits issued by Cuban officials, the "blame for their present plight . . . seems to rest squarely on the shoulders of the Cuban government" and it was "under a moral obligation to undo the blunder by letting these innocent victims land."[18] The *Richmond Times Dispatch* considered this a case not of error, but of "graft." It cited Walter Winchell, who argued that the plight of the passengers was not the result of a failure to touch Cuban hearts—it was "a failure of touching Cuban palms. And we don't mean trees."[19]

But there were papers which demurred and justified the Cuban decision. They argued that Cuba's fear of a deluge of refugees and its economic problems rendered its decision to turn away the vessel "understandable."[20] A few papers not only exonerated Cuba but blamed the passengers. Once again, Jews were held responsible for having brought these troubles on themselves. The *Seattle Times* was emphatic about this.

> Cuba had not invited them; had not even been asked if they would be received as residents; and harsh as it may seem, Cuba's President Bru perhaps had no alternative but to deny them admission.[21]

Equally critical of the passengers was the *Columbia* (South Carolina) *State,* which wondered how the refugees could have been so careless about ascertaining whether and where they would be allowed to land? They had, it seems, only "provisional permits" from Cuba "to land as travelers en route to the United States, where they hoped to gain admission later." What ground is there for such hope? And just what does the word "later" imply to Cuba?[22]

Few papers were as callous as the *Christian Science Monitor,* which castigated Jewish refugees in general for being so selective about their destinations.

Most Jews apparently have no taste for the pioneering necessary in remote and undeveloped areas and do not take readily to some plans made in their behalf. While this is understandable, they may remember that other races have carved homes out of wilderness to escape oppression.[23]

The *Christian Science Monitor* ignored both the pioneering accomplishments of the Jewish settlers in Palestine and the fact that there were few, if any, "wilderness" countries which had offered Jewish refugees a place to "escape oppression." Britain had found no suitable place in its vast empire, and countries with large undeveloped areas, such as Australia, had made it clear that they were not desirous of "importing a Jewish problem."

As the saga continued, most editorials turned from trying to fix the blame to disposition of the problem. The suggestions offered were no different from those made at the time of Evian and *Kristallnacht:* find some "uncivilized" and "unexplored" part of the world to dispose of this human cargo. Despite the fact that these suggestions had been made since the *Anschluss* and no suitable area had been found, most of the press continued to believe that "in a broad world 25,000 miles in diameter there is room somewhere for these people." The places cited were the same as had been suggested during the past year: "British Guiana, Dutch Guiana, North Rhodesia, Dominican Republic, and the Philippines." Some papers were not so specific and simply suggested "someplace in Africa."[24] Typically the *St. Louis Post Dispatch,* which condemned the ship's fate as a "high crime of civilization," believed that a site surely could be found in the British Empire or in South America, but not in the United States, which had already "done better than most."[25] Papers noted that finding an "unoccupied" territory depended on "rapid, organized action by the humanitarian governments." It had been a year since Evian and eight months since *Kristallnacht.* Nothing had come of the attempt to find an alternative site, and in the interim, most nations had grown less, not more, inclined to accept those cast out of Germany.[26] But the suggestions were made nonetheless.

A few papers felt an "uneasy sense of guilt" about the attempt to affix blame on someone else by assuming, in the words of the *Baltimore Sun,* a "holier than thou" attitude toward Cuba.[27] As the ship steamed back to Germany (the European countries which eventually offered asylum had not yet announced that they would do so), the *New York Times* went so far as to decry the "sorry welcome" the ship had received in this hemisphere and to express discomfort with America's behavior.

> Off our shores she was attended by a helpful Coast Guard vessel alert to pick up any passengers who plunged overboard and thrust them back on the St. Louis again. The refugees could even see the shimmering towers of Miami . . . the battlements of another forbidden city.

Though the *New York Times* was ill at ease with the United States' behavior, it made no suggestion that anything concrete be done. Instead it reasoned that it was "useless now to discuss what might have been done," since the ship was on its way back.[28] It ignored the fact that the passengers, who at this point were thought to be returning to Germany, could have landed in Europe and boarded another ship back to Cuba if the United States had assured Cuba that they would eventually be admitted. But American officials refused to make any accommodations in order to aid the passengers. The *only* action taken by the American government was the dispatch of a Coast Guard cutter when the ship was close to the shore of Miami. The cutter's assignment was to apprehend any passengers who might jump overboard in an attempt to swim ashore and return them to the ship.

The *Greensboro* (North Carolina) *Press,* which had previously supported the admission of refugees, also condemned the world's response. "Humanity," the paper sadly noted, had doomed these passengers to "continued mistreatment by the gestapo and the storm troopers."[29] But this willingness to acknowledge implicitly some degree of American complicity in the problem was the exception and not the rule.

So too a few papers broke with the majority of dailies and argued that admitting the passengers would not set a "precedent," but would be an ad hoc gesture.[30] If the United States rejected them, then it certainly could not blame Cuba for "acting in a similar fashion in accordance with its conception of its own interests."[31] The fact that a number of papers were willing to countenance a limited change in immigration regulations appears to have been the result of the release at this time of a Quaker-sponsored report demonstrating that the imagined refugee "flood" which anti-immigrationists repeatedly claimed was inundating this country was but a trickle which had no adverse effect on the economy.[32] The report was cited by the *Boston Globe* and some other papers as proof that "wild stories, unrelated to the facts, have been passed around regarding the supposed influx of immigrants to the United States. Cold figures do not support the theories of street corner gossips."[33]

But the report could not effect a change in the prevailing attitude that "the United States has already provided a refuge for more of these European immigrants than any other major country" and was simply "incapable of supplying a solution. There is no hope for refuge here."[34] Editors repeatedly stressed that there was a limit "beyond which no nation may go."[35] Fears that here again was Pandora's box were expressed: One such "influx" is sure to be "followed by other ship loads." Letting this one dock would set a most "dangerous precedent."[36] Another argument that had been heard before was that trying to aid Jews would be an incentive to the Germans to subject them to even worse treatment. In this case it might prompt Germany to "dump its Jewish population upon other nations without regard for any international law or regulation."[37]

One cannot totally discount these fears. There seemed to be "hundreds of thousands of Central Europeans, both Jews and Christians, who [had] no place to go."[38] While the *St. Louis* was meandering aimlessly off American shores, other ships were plying the Atlantic with their cargo of "Jewish refugees." It was easy to get the impression that these ships were the vanguard of a flotilla of refugee vessels.[39] Word came from Mexico that 104 Jewish refugees had been refused entry, and from Paraguay and Argentina that 200 Jewish refugees aboard the *Cap Orte, Monte Oliva,* and *Mendoza* were turned away. The wire services reported that Costa Rica was preparing to deport twenty Jewish refugees.[40] During the previous year Italy had instituted antisemitic legislation. Everywhere doors were either slamming shut or Jews were being urged to leave.[41] Germany was then releasing Jews who had been arrested after *Kristallnacht*. They were told to depart at once or face arrest. A deluge of refugees appeared ready to flood the world.

* * *

The same papers which had supported the entry of 20,000 children but a few weeks earlier opposed the entry of these 900 voyagers on the *St. Louis*. Even those that had approved of the President's decision to allow 15,000 visitors to remain here on temporary visas did not advocate that the *St. Louis* be allowed to dock in Miami. As the situation grew more severe and the flood of Jewish refugees seeking a haven increased in size, the press advocated that the gates to this land be more firmly secured. Again the press offered its genuine sympathy to these victims of a fanatic regime. What it did not offer were concrete and viable suggestions to resolve the plight of those aboard what the *New York Times* described as the "saddest ship afloat."

The press reaction to the *Anschluss*, Evian, *Kristallnacht*, Wagner-Rogers, and the voyage of the SS *St. Louis* was indicative of the resolve behind America's anti-immigrant sentiment. But more than that, the reaction demonstrated the degree to which the American public's reaction to the persecution of European Jewry was tempered by other concerns. Whether a particular course of action—attending the Olympics, boycotting Germany, admitting refugees, or aiding children—was accepted or rejected depended on how it affected other American priorities. Would it compromise our neutrality, change the ethnic and social composition of our nation, force us to take a stand, drag us into war, or, after December 1941, deflect us from the war effort? Rarely, if ever, particularly during the prewar period, can America's inaction be attributed primarily to a lack of information or knowledge. It was not a question of ignorance, but a matter of priorities, and aiding persecuted Jews was never one of them.

6

Fifth-Column Fears

Long before it seemed even mildly likely that the United States would be drawn into a European conflagration, Americans believed that Hitler was preparing a network of spies in their midst. Eventually the fear that Germany was creating a "Trojan horse" in the United States grew to the proportions of a spy mania. By 1941 it had so engulfed America that Justice Department and FBI officials, who had initially counseled extreme vigilance, now urged citizens to refrain from trying to find spies lurking in thousands of dimly lit corners.[1]

The press was largely responsible for reinforcing the public's fear of a Trojan horse—or as it was often called, fifth column— of spies. Perusal of popular journals and newspapers from the 1930s and 1940s reveals a sustained sensational interest in Reich-controlled activities. Though the press vacillated as to whether Hitler was a "slick politician or a madman," it was convinced that "America had something to fear from Hitlerism."[2] Ironically, sometimes the press seemed convinced that America had more to fear from Hitler than did Germany.

Appearance Versus Reality

Germany had espionage and propaganda objectives in the United States and worked hard to achieve them. There were pro-Nazi spies and groups with pro-Nazi sentiments in this country. But they never constituted a network with the scope and power that the press attributed to them.[3] That, however, was irrelevant because the bombastic activities of American Nazis and the threat of alien spies made good copy. Intrigue and danger, militaristic training and secret pledges of allegiance to a foreign power captured the attention of the press. In the public's eyes the steady stream of media coverage elevated pro-Nazi groups from the rather inconsequential menace they were to a significant threat to American security. The reading public had an almost "insatiable interest" in them and devoured anything written on the topic.[4] John Roy Carlson's *Under Cover: My Four Years in the Nazi Underworld of America* went through twenty-one printings within six months of publication.[5] But it was not only the threat from organized groups which was the object of press attention. Individual spies— particularly those disguised as refugees—were also depicted as an ever present danger to this nation's security.

During the early 1930s most of press attention was focused on the Friends of New Germany (FONG). FONG was created in 1933 after the dissolution of the American branch of the Nazi Party.[6] Though its membership never rose above 6,000, it was generally portrayed as a powerful entity posing a serious threat to the United States.[7] The *Los Angeles Examiner* reported that Germany was maintaining storm troops in this country in the "guise of a [FONG] sports group."[8] According to the *Chicago Daily News,* "young Germans who have come to this country since the world war and many of [whom] are not citizens" were engaged in establishing a network of "clandestine" Nazi strongholds. The *Boston American* charged that Nazi emissaries were organizing "storm troop" clubs in order to "enlist [a] big shock army" which would "Hitlerize the United States."[9] The *New York Post* put Americans on alert: "should all these Nazi groups ever pool their energies . . . not merely Jews but the entire structure of the American Republic will be imperiled."[10]

Press reports of FONG's induction of 5,000 new members, of loyalty oaths and parades in swastika-bedecked uniforms, so aroused American hostility that German officials stationed in the United States urged Berlin to use its influence to curtail their activities insofar as it could and to demonstrate that they had no official relationship with Nazi Germany. A Foreign Ministry edict in the fall of 1935 ordered all German nationals residing in the United States to resign from FONG and any other organization which engaged in political activities.[11] Contrary to German expectations, this directive convinced much of the public and the press that FONG and similar groups *were* under Berlin's control.

In 1936, in the wake of the edict forcing German nationals to resign, FONG reorganized and reemerged as the Amerika-deutscher Volksbund. The size of the Bund, which was led by German-born Fritz Julius Kuhn, would rise to about 25,000.[12] Its growth was facilitated by the increase in German propaganda in the United States and a rising isolationist sentiment. The Bund succeeded in garnering even more press attention than FONG. Press estimates of the Bund's size varied, and some were way above the mark. Kuhn's private claims of a membership of between 180,000 and 230,000 were cited by *The Saturday Evening Post* as "much nearer the truth" in 1939 than his 1937 reports to the federal government that the membership was less than 9000.[13] Writers describing the Bund's members used the terms "thug," "social misfit," and "Nazi" almost without differentiation. They were depicted as "beer drinking bullies, scum from the lowest level of society."[14]

But it was Kuhn's apparent connections abroad which really mesmerized the press. A flurry of press comment followed his brief meeting with Hitler during the Olympics. Photographs of the two Nazis appeared in numerous papers along with Kuhn's claim that he took his orders directly from the Führer.[15] The influential *Literary Digest* described Kuhn as "more than friendly with Hitler."[16] As a result, Dieckhoff strengthened his warnings to Berlin about the damage press reports on the Bund were causing Germany. Kuhn's February 1938 visit to Germany and his subsequent claim to have received "specific directions" from Goebbels and Goering regarding Bund activities strengthened the public's perception of the group as an organization marching in locked step with Germany. Typical of the press reaction was an article in *Look* entitled "Hitler Speaks and the Bund Obeys."[17]

The press was fed more sensational information during the

1938 House Un-American Activities Committee hearings. In fact
a great deal of the attention given this topic by the press was
generated by such hearings and reports issued by members of
Congress, Martin Dies in particular. Other attention was generated
by federal investigations and trials of suspected spies. These hearings and trials were designed to win press attention and generate
public support for government counterespionage activities. A
United States Attorney in charge of prosecuting a group of suspected spies told his staff that the trial would go forward even
if their case was not as strong as they might have wished because
"the important point is that the American public must be made
aware of the existence of this spy plot, and impressed with . . .
the fact that it is imperative that we have an efficient counterespionage service." A "news-hungry" public awaited press coverage of this phenomenon and was not disappointed. During these
hearings and trials Nazism was presented as a dangerous influence
in American life. Charges were made at the hearings and repeated
in the press that large numbers of Germans were "spying for
Germany." The Bund was accused of organizing and conducting
much of the spying, but the fear that the Bund was serving as a
major spy network was really unfounded. The main spying and
propaganda activities that took place in America were not conducted through the Bund, but through isolationist circles. Isolationists were better equipped to achieve German objectives of
keeping America out of the war than were any of the pro-Nazi
groups in the United States.[18]

The Bund hastened its own demise when it catapulted itself
onto the front pages and into the editorial columns of this nation's
newspapers with a rally in Madison Square Garden in February
1939.[19] An audience of 22,000 gave the Bund the appearance
of being a real threat. Although the rally was intended to place
a pro-American slant on Bund activities, it galvanized public opinion against the organization. After this, press coverage of the
Bund and other fascist organizations became more frequent and
even more hostile. The *New York Times* called the Bund the "best
argument against itself." In a lengthy analysis of American fascist
groups *The Saturday Evening Post* reported that they were continuing to "prosper and spread" and warned that in addition to the
Bund there existed in America a network of "more authentically
American groups." These "star-spangled *Kamaraden*" were ready
to join the Bund at the barricades when "the time came."[20]

A Nation of Spy Hunters

When Western Europe fell before the Nazi blitzkreig, Americans became even more convinced that the Nazis were using internal spy networks to achieve their military objectives. At the same time a Congressional committee began to issue its findings about the "fifth column peril" facing America.[21] The public's mood was grim. It did not want to go to war but it needed to find someone to "fight." It needed an enemy to pursue. William Leutchenberg notes that "unable to agree on what to do about the enemy without, the nation hunted fifth-columnists within."[22] The press served as a front-line combatant in this conflagration as even the President proved susceptible to this sentiment. In May 1940, when Hitler was completing his conquest of Western Europe, Roosevelt told a group of Cabinet members and Congressional leaders, "Of course we have got this fifth column thing, which is . . . widespread through the country," and warned them "to be pretty darned careful."[23]

An article by J. Edgar Hoover in *American Magazine* typified the stories which appeared on the fifth column. In boldface type the editors alerted readers to the "tremendous import" of the message contained therein:

> Factories sabotaged . . . ships burned . . . machines smashed . . . trains wrecked. . . . In a war of utter ruthlessness the Fifth Column is on the march. . . . Saboteurs are striking at America. This article by the Chief of the G-men is . . . couched in cautious language. But if you read between the lines you will get its tremendous import.[24]

Those not capable of reading "between the lines" found it easier to grasp the "tremendous import" thanks to a series of subsequent articles in the magazine on the same topic that charged that "aliens" by the thousands were being "coerced into joining the Nazi network" in America. They controlled radio stations which broadcast special messages to spies and had instructions on how to foment a "revolution" in America when the time was right. One of the articles was an exposé entitled "Hitler's Slave Spies in America" relating how a "blitzkreig of blackmail is forcing hundreds of our foreign-born residents into the Nazi fifth column" where they created a "vast system of espionage, built on threats, robbery and reprisals."[25]

In the summer and fall of 1940 the *New York World Telegram, Pittsburgh Press, New York Post,* and *New York Journal American* were among the papers which ran series of articles detailing how the "fifth column [was] rapidly gaining power" and "swing[ing] into high gear."[26] There were other syndicated series including one by Bruce Catton which described the "incredible" German propaganda operations which were functioning on "a large scale all across America."[27]

There were some attempts to diffuse the panic by poking fun at the American propensity to see "five columns" everywhere. Walter C. Frame, writing in *America,* counseled in September 1940 that "hunting for Hitlers can be a mania." Edmond Taylor, also writing in *America,* warned that in France it was fear of "imaginary enemies and inability to see real ones [which] helped destroy the nation."[28] Some commentators declared fifth-column stories to be the "counterparts in this war of the atrocity stories in the last war."[29] The climate of fear became so pervasive that even J. Edgar Hoover, who in his 1940 *American Magazine* article counseled extreme vigilance against fifth columnists, reversed his position in 1941 and warned against "cooked-up hysteria" and "ugly schemes of vigilantes and fearmongers." The FBI was then receiving 300 complaints a day regarding "suspected un-American activity." Hoover decried the formation of vigilante groups to "combat fifth columnists, shoot down parachutists [and] investigate foreign-born citizens."[30]

The November 1940 issue of *McCall's* described how Americans' "passionate preoccupation" with fifth-column activities was producing a nation of spy hunters. Department of Justice officials complained that one of their hardest jobs was "demobilizing amateur sleuths and deflating hysteria." According to a report prepared by the Department for the Attorney General, the American press was paying more attention to the fifth column than to news of the war. The report contended that "if the fifth column in the United States had hired a million highpowered publicity men to create hysteria . . . they could not have managed better."[31]

This wave of panic about spies in America's midst had various repercussions. By July 1940, 71 percent of the respondents to a Roper poll believed Germany had already started to organize a fifth column in this country. By this point the phrase "fifth column," the *New York World Telegram* claimed, had reached "giant proportions in the consciousness of the United States."[32]

American Antisemitism: A Rising Tide

Americans were hostile to these pro-German groups' espousal of fascism and Nazism but were not immune to their antisemitic preachings. Various organizations' and individuals' depiction of the Jew as a universally unwanted burden struck a responsive chord in the American public. The American Institute of Public Opinion found that the Detroit-based radio priest Father Charles Coughlin had amassed a substantial listening audience. His radio show, which regularly broadcast attacks on Jews, including material which had originated in Nazi Germany but which Coughlin did not identify as such, had an estimated audience of 15 million, of whom 3.5 million were regular listeners. A majority of the listeners approved of his violently antisemitic message.

Regular listeners approving	67 percent
Occasional listeners approving	51 percent

The columnist Heywood Broun noted that the Jew served many Americans as a convenient "whipping boy." The preachings of the Nazis on one side and the Bundists and Coughlinites on the other convinced many Americans that their antipathy toward Jews was justified. Surveys taken from 1940 through 1946 show that Jews were almost consistently seen as a greater menace to the welfare of the United States than were any other national, religious, or racial group. In June 1944, with the war in Europe and in Japan still raging, 24 percent of those responding to a poll believed Jews a "threat," while only 6 percent considered the Germans to be one and 9 percent believed this of the Japanese. (Despite their antipathy toward Jews, Americans strongly disapproved of the Nazis' treatment of them. In the wake of *Kristallnacht* 94 percent of those polled disapproved of German persecution of Jews. However, an even higher percent, 97 percent, disapproved of German ill treatment of Catholics.)[33]

Refugees or Spies?

The greatest and most immediate consequence of the focus by the press on spies lurking in America was its effect on attitudes toward refugees.[34] Although Germany undoubtedly attempted to create a climate in America sympathetic to it and to implant spies, there is little evidence—and there was even less at the time— that refugees, particularly Jewish refugees, were involved. Nonetheless the conviction spread that a cadre of spies could be found within refugee circles. Feature stories about the role of the alien spy appeared in major American papers and magazines. Charges made in the daily and periodical press were repeated in Congress. Despite the efforts of liberal journals such as *The Nation*, the charges gained greater currency as 1940 progressed.[35]

The fall of Europe was attributed to its having been betrayed by those to whom it had offered refuge. An article in the *New York Herald Tribune* claimed that forty-two Nazi agents had been recruited from among " 'half' Jews" and 'quarter' Jews" from Germany who had been promised an "Aryan" passport for their work.[36] Samuel Lubell, writing in *The Saturday Evening Post*, charged that Nazi agents disguised as refugees had permeated Europe and America as spies. He described a Gestapo school where spies were taught to "speak Yiddish, to read Hebrew, pray," and even submitted to circumcision to make their disguise complete.[37] According to these articles, America too was now in danger. In June 1940 *Life* published a pictorial record of Nazi activities in Asia and the Americas which, the magazine claimed, was proof that there were "signs of Nazi fifth columns everywhere."[38]

Westbrook Pegler claimed that Norway, a country which had been the object of great sympathy in America, had been stabbed in the back by the German refugees it had befriended.[39] Edwin James, writing in the *New York Times*, reported that Norway had fallen as a result of a fifth column composed of Germans who had been brought to the country as orphans after World War I. Other papers warned of the "alien traitors" who like "termites" were "boring from within." The *Springfield* (Illinois) *Journal* observed that America "may avoid going to war, but war's backwash is surely coming to America." When Germany suggested that it might be willing to release "racial and political refugees" from

Europe, a number of papers immediately suggested that this was a way for the Germans to infiltrate the United States with spies.[40]

Respected figures repeated the claims of the press. The American Ambassador to France, William Bullitt, argued in the summer of 1940 that France had been defeated as a result of its lax immigration policy.

> The French had been more hospitable than are even we Americans to refugees from Germany. More than one-half the spies captured doing actual military spy work against the French army were refugees from Germany. Do you believe that there are no Nazi and Communist agents of this sort in America?[41]

The refugees bore the direct consequences of this hysteria about a fifth column. A "faulty immigration policy" was blamed by public and press for the threat facing America.[42] Charges that spies had been found among the refugees were made by Democratic Senator Robert R. Reynolds of North Carolina, an archfoe of immigration liberalization. Reynolds warned that the United States was in danger of an "attack by the enemy from within." In New York, District Attorney Thomas E. Dewey launched an investigation to "spotlight" fifth-column "treachery." In Washington the House required the fingerprinting of all aliens over fourteen years old.[43]

The most important step in this sequence of antirefugee measures was a June 1941 ruling by the State Department that refugees who had close relatives in Germany or German-occupied territories could not enter the United States. The ruling was issued after a hearing by the House Un-American Activities Committee in May 1941 at which it had been claimed that no one could be released from a Nazi concentration camp without signing a "pledge that he would serve the gestapo." The State Department announced that this decision was being taken in order to halt an already existing flood of spies disguised as refugees. It charged that there was such a flood despite the fact that a few months earlier only twelve out of a thousand people requesting visas had been found to be persons "whose presence would be prejudicial to the best interests of the United States." In addition, the State Department's announcement was ambiguous; it was not clear whether refugees had already committed acts of espionage or had merely been coerced into agreeing to act as agents in the United States.[44]

Most papers declared that the decision was, in the words of the *New York Herald Tribune,* "readily understandable." The *Philadelphia Bulletin* was somewhat more hesitant, both because of the lack of substantiating evidence for the State Department's claim and because the vast majority of those who had fled countries occupied by Germany had "the genuineness of their status [as refugees] attested." It too, however, declared the measure essential for "our national protection."[45] Another paper that was more tentative in its report of the ruling was the *New York Journal American.* It noted that the action had been taken because "alien refugees *may* be subject to pressure through threats against their kin."[46]

The *Philadelphia Record* chose a different approach. It stressed the severe repercussions of the ruling on the refugees:

U.S. VISA CURB NEW TRAGEDY
FOR AMERICANS' FOREIGN KIN[47]

The article described the measure as a "severe blow to hundreds of refugees." It depicted the "tragic portion" and "desperate" situation of all refugees but particularly those who had already begun their "trek to safety" and now found themselves stranded. The *Record*'s coverage was unique. Most of the press ignored the human ramifications of the ruling and subscribed to the "refugee equals spy" attitude.[48]

The liberal press argued that refugees made unlikely candidates for spies because their dress, language, and mannerisms attracted attention. It claimed that to identify refugees as Nazi agents was to yield to German designs. Part of the German objective was to "dump" Jews abroad in order to create confusion and consternation in enemy lands. *The Nation* and *The New Republic* emerged, predictably, as the staunchest defenders of the refugees. They took strong issue with the State Department's story that refugees were serving as spies. *The Nation* challenged the State Department to "cite a single instance of the coerced espionage."[49] No evidence substantiating the charges was ever provided. *The New Republic* believed the ruling to be simply a means of "persecuting the refugee." It claimed, as had the liberal New York daily *PM,* that prominent Nazis found few obstacles in their way when they applied for admission to the United States, while "bars have now been raised making it almost impossible for political refugees to get out of Europe at all." *PM* accurately blamed the policy on Assistant Secretary of State Breckinridge Long.[50]

The State Department ruling, coupled with other administrative obstacles, turned the flow of refugees who had entered in the wake of *Kristallnacht* into a mere trickle by the late fall of 1941. The fears of fifth columnists had been generated by the press, radio, newsreels, movies, books, churches, and patriotic groups. Had it not been for the often hysterical preoccupation of the press with spies in the nation's midst, it is doubtful whether 71 percent of those polled in July 1940 by Roper would have answered in the affirmative when asked whether they believed a spy network posed a significant threat. But this campaign against the fifth column also fortified American support for the destroyer-bases arrangement and the Lend-Lease Act. It made it easier for Roosevelt to prepare the country for what increasingly appeared to be an inevitable conflict with Germany. The President was determined to strengthen the antagonism of Americans toward the Reich and their readiness to aid the Reich's enemies.[51]

German officials stationed in Washington recognized this and tried to alert Berlin to the fact that American fears of spies and sabotage would benefit the President's efforts to cultivate interventionist sentiment. Both the German Ambassador, Hans Dieckhoff, and the Chargé d'Affaires, Hans Thomsen, warned Berlin that Bund activities and German efforts to create a network of sympathizers in America were sure to bring America into action on the side of our enemies and of destroying the last vestiges of sympathy for Germany."[52] Thomsen was right. As a result of the American feeling that Hitler had designs on America and might invade this continent once he conquered Britain, public opinion favored aiding that beleaguered country. By 1941 polls showed that 85 to 90 percent of the American public was willing to aid England, though close to 80 percent still opposed American entry into the war.[53]

The panic which was spread regarding spies in America's midst solidified anti-Nazi sentiment, but it also strengthened the barriers that were placed in the path of refugees desperate to escape the lengthening Nazi grasp. It helped bar the way to those for whom a refuge meant the difference between life and death.

PART II

THE FINAL SOLUTION

Newspapers are read at the breakfast and dinner tables. God's great gift to man is appetite. Put nothing in the paper that will destroy it.

W. R. Nelson, publisher of the *Kansas City Star*

Confirmation of the news is a sacrament. . . . There's an old saying in Chicago journalism . . . "You say your mother loves you. Check it out."

John Chancellor

7

Deportation to Annihilation:
The First Reports

One of the central questions in any discussion of the Allied reaction to the Holocaust is when those not directly involved in perpetrating the Final Solution became aware of the fact that Nazi antisemitism had progressed from brutal but haphazard persecution to a systematic program of murder.[1] It is strange, in some respects, that this should be such a matter of debate, for during the war there were official Allied pronouncements confirming that an extermination program was underway. As shall be demonstrated in the following pages, a surprisingly large amount of information was known and publicized despite the fact that the death camps were beyond the view of the press. Various details were, of course, missing; sometimes the number of victims was exaggerated and sometimes it was underestimated, and the size and specific function of particular death camps were not publicly revealed until relatively late.[2] Nevertheless, considering that there were no reporters on the scene and that the Nazis wished to camouflage what was going on, a fairly accurate picture of the situation was available first to government officials and then to the public, long before the end of the war. Often it was not believed. In order to understand how this was so, it is critical that we ask not *when* news was available but *how* it was made available.

Barriers to Belief

In considering the issue of knowledge of the Final Solution, it is important to remember that the Nazis treated the mass murder program quite differently from their other antisemitic campaigns. Until the mass murder program began, relatively few attempts were made to hide what was being done to the Jews. Reporters were witness to the April 1933 boycott, the July 1935 riots, the Nuremberg Laws, the brutalities inflicted on Austrian Jews in March 1938, and *Kristallnacht,* a modern-day pogrom conducted in public view. They witnessed Jews being rounded up in various parts of the Reich.[3] Even the deportation of thousands of Jews from Berlin, which was carried out "swiftly, efficiently and with as much secrecy" as possible, in the words of United Press, was witnessed by reporters.*

While the antisemitic actions which preceded the Final Solution were committed openly, the mass murder program was not. The Germans did more than try to keep things secret; they released all sorts of information designed to obfuscate. In trying to prevent the news of the murder program's existence from reaching the outside world, the Nazis used varied means of deception to convince the victims and those who witnessed the deportations that "resettlement" was the German objective. Victims were told they were being relocated, sent to work camps, "resettled." Though these explanations may not have always been believed in their entirety, they did inject a note of confusion into the situation. When the deportations from Germany were at their height, official German sources assured American reporters that they were military measures dictated by "economic requirements of the war" and denied that Jews in Berlin were being dispossessed of their dwellings or taken to concentration camps.

---

* In an interview Percy Knauth, who worked for the *Chicago Tribune* and then for the *New York Times* and also broadcast from Berlin for CBS when William Shirer was away, related how he watched Jews being rounded up on the streets of Berlin. The first time he came upon such a roundup, which was taking place near where he lived, he asked a policeman what was going on. The policeman matter-of-factly told him, "These are Jews. They are being sent away to be resettled."[4]

It is interesting to consider how such a denial was handled by two different papers. The *New York Times* quoted the Nazi claims but immediately shed doubt on them by noting that the official Nazi Party newspaper carried numerous announcements of auctions of furniture, household goods, and other property confiscated from Jews. Similar sales were also scheduled to take place in Frankfurt, Mannheim, and Breslau. In contrast, the *Washington Star* simply reported the German denials and added that "because this is a war measure no details are available."[5]

There were other obstacles, some of which were so formidable that even when the news managed to escape the perpetrators' grip, it still did not reach the bystanders. Historical precedent lessened the credibility of this news. During World War I similar "atrocity stories" had been circulated and proven false. Americans were intent on not falling prey, once again, to such "propaganda." Each side accused the other of atrocities, and within two and a half weeks after the beginning of the war, *Time* magazine was dubbing this or that report "the 'atrocity' story of the week." Atrocity charges were linked by much of the American press with each side's attempts to both sway neutral opinion in its favor and fire up the homefront. Typical of the attitude of some of the press toward Allied reports of atrocities was one paper's reaction to the March 1940 publication of the Polish emigré government's report that the Nazis had murdered numerous civilians, desecrated churches, and terrorized entire villages. One editorial reminded Americans that after World War I "a great many of the atrocity stories which were so well attested and so strenuously told, so indignantly believed and so commonly repeated, were found to be absolute fakes."[6]

The tendency to dismiss the reports of horrors was strengthened by America's desire to remain neutral. An isolationist American public, particularly one inclined to believe that Britain would stop at little to get us to join the Allied side, felt justified in dismissing these reports as British creations. The press was "distrustful" of both sides and unanimous, at least at the outset, in endorsing neutrality. Americans abhorred National Socialism, but as one contemporary commentator pointed out, "Tory England was an ideal for which Americans were hardly prepared to die." Furthermore, England had for so long dismissed Nazi persecution and racial policies as "an internal matter" and treated them as irrelevant in the formulation of foreign policy that now it was difficult to use these same policies as effective propaganda.[7] But the English did try to use them for propaganda purposes. At the end of October 1939 they released a White Paper on the tortures occurring in Nazi concentration camps. In a foreword to the report the British government explained why it had not released this information, some of which had been in its hands since *Kristallnacht*, earlier. It wanted to avoid doing "anything to embitter the relations between the two countries."[8]

If Tory England was an ideal not worth dying for, then the Soviet Union was an ideal which many Americans believed was not even worth preserving. Stalinist Russia was known for its brutality and for the "blood-purge." When Russia began to release reports accusing Germany of atrocities after June 1941, they were greeted skeptically by many Americans. When Germany and Russia each accused the other of mass murder, it was a case, according to the *Dayton* (Ohio) *News,* of the "pot and the kettle." While there were papers which believed that Hitler was "in a class by himself among modern dictators [for] not even Stalin practices racial persecution," there were others which believed that both Hitler *and* Stalin had records "written in crimson." The Germans attempted to make use of the American contempt for Stalin and took American reporters to the Russian front to show them corpses which were "allegedly" Ukrainians and Poles who had been murdered by Russian soldiers. They were not entirely successful in convincing American reporters, and, according to Fred Oeschner of the United Press, the correspondents refused to "leave out those little words 'alleged,' 'claimed,' or 'asserted' or to make flat statements instead of attributing them to the German guides." The Germans did have some success with some papers including the Hearst papers, which as late as November 1941 believed that the Russians were behaving worse than the Nazis and condemned the unprecedented "destruction wrought" by them. The Hearst papers declared that the "pillage and plunder conducted in Russian-occupied Poland has no counterpart among the many ravished lands of western and northern Europe, where ruthless carnage and savage despolition [sic] are not novelties."[9]*

---

* The Hearst papers' defense of Nazi Germany was not new. During the 1930s it had printed many pieces which tended to show fascism and Nazism in a positive light, including columns by Goering, the Nazi ideologist Alfred Rosenberg, and Mussolini. One of the most persistent critics of Hearst's record was veteran journalist George Seldes, who in his publication *In Fact* repeatedly attacked

These sentiments about Russians posed yet another obstacle to the news of the Final Solution. Anything that came from Moscow prior to Pearl Harbor and America's entry into the war was considered tainted information, particularly by Americans who believed communism a greater threat to the United States than Nazism. Even after that date, when Russia became America's ally, its accusations were still met with some skepticism.

The fact that this news was coming from behind enemy lines further complicated its dissemination. Couriers were reluctant to allow themselves to be quoted by name because some who were in the underground intended to return to German-occupied Europe or feared for the lives of their relatives. Accounts attributed to known neutral sources were difficult to obtain. When reporters could cite a "reliable" source, they hastened to do so but often without actually using the source's name. Such was the case in the November 10, 1941, edition of the *New York Journal American*. Alfred Tyrnauer, who for ten years had been head of Hearst's International News Service (INS) bureau in Vienna, reported that the Nazis were planning "mass pogroms" and the "total expropriation of Jewish property" in all Nazi-controlled countries. He stressed that his information came from "absolutely reliable" unnamed "diplomatic quarters."[11]

The news was not a secret, but it faced so many obstacles that it was almost more rational to dismiss it as untrustworthy than to accept it as true. And this is what the press often did. Some reports were never verified enough to assuage the doubts of skeptical reporters and editors. Some editors simply did not even consider plausible accounts of horrors that came from their reporters in the field. The skepticism which greeted these reports was reflected in the way the vast majority of American papers treated the news. They printed it but placed it in obscure places, an action which not only attested to their own ambivalence about the veracity of the news but also created another barrier between information and public understanding and belief. There were even

---

Hearst for his profascism and his antisemitism.[10] Ironically, by 1943 the Hearst papers had become one of the strongest advocates outside the ranks of the liberal press of Allied action on behalf of Jews. The Hearst papers carried numerous editorials in support of the demands of Peter Bergson and his followers, a small band of activists who conducted some controversial publicity-oriented activities on behalf of European Jews.

occasions when reporters injected into their reports their own doubts about the reliability of the information they were transmitting. This happened particularly when they related news of massacres, mass murder, and gas chambers. Sigrid Schultz complained about the Nazi tendency to brand any report of killings or brutalities as an "untrue atrocity story, reminiscent of the propaganda campaigns of World War I." They knew, Schultz observed, that anything labeled propaganda was bound to be disbelieved in America. Until Pearl Harbor many people in the United States read the reports of Nazi atrocities as if they were detective or horror stories, causing some gooseflesh but not to be taken too seriously. Even after Pearl Harbor there were those, including many reporters wary of being duped, who rejected these "tales." Richard C. Hottelet, who worked for United Press during this period, recently observed in an interview that "sophisticated" people, including many such as himself, who were ardent foes of the Nazis, rejected these stories as creations of "self-serving" parties.[12]

It must also be remembered that there was other news of far more central interest and "importance" than what was being done to Jews. A major conflagration was underway, and at times it threatened to involve the world. As soon as Germany crossed the Polish border, news of the persecution of European Jewry began to be crowded out of the press by news of the war. Editorials admitted that the "desperate plight of the civilians" was obscured as a result of the attention paid by the press to the "dramatic news of the mighty clashes between the military forces."[13] As the war progressed—particularly once America entered—the public was understandably far more interested in the entire orbit of war news than it was in reports on the treatment of one particular group, however outrageous that treatment. Ironically, after September 1939 the importance the press accorded the story of the Jews' persecution diminished even further despite the fact that the treatment being meted out to them increased in severity.

As the war engulfed ever growing numbers of people, the press subsumed Nazi antisemitic policy under the rubric of general wartime suffering. It soon became evident that millions of innocent civilians would experience terrible privations. Some would suffer because their homes had become battlefields, while others would be forced into slave labor and deported to far-off places. The press correctly recognized that Nazi brutality toward conquered people was severe and that many peoples, particularly those in Eastern Europe, faced an awful fate. For much of the war the press treated the Jews as one of those peoples, one among many. This approach to the Jews' plight reflected the way the press had often treated Nazi antisemitism in the past. As long as it failed to grasp that antisemitism was fundamental and central to Nazi ideology, it would not catch the signs of approaching deliberate annihilation and would not treat wartime persecution of the Jews as something different and distinct from the Germans' atrocious treatment of a multitude of other noncombatants. In this regard the press was simply replicating—consciously or not—the entrenched policy of the Allied leadership. The identity of the victims was universalized by the State Department and the British Foreign Office. Allied leaders always referred to "oppressed political" minorities or refugees; sometimes they added the adjective "racial." With a few exceptions, Allied officials steadfastly refused to refer to Jews as subjects of particularly harsh treatment. Jews were victims, but so were a multitude of others. While it was generally recognized that they might be the first to suffer, whatever happened to them was likely, according to the way the Allies disseminated the information, to happen to many other peoples.[14]

Another complex, almost paradoxical situation may have also helped push this news of intensifying persecution and, ultimately, of annihilation into the inner recesses of the paper. As the years passed and the persecution of European Jewry became a familiar topic, many papers increasingly tended to place it within the inner recesses of the paper, treating it as well-known or "old" news, even though they still did not really believe the news.

Ultimately the most formidable obstacle to the spreading and acceptance of news of the Final Solution was the nature of the information itself. People are naturally inclined to doubt the fantastic and the unprecedented, especially when the story told is an atrocity tale. Had the Germans chosen to enslave and oppress the Jews but not to annihilate them, there would have been fewer doubts about what they were doing. Given the German record since 1933 of brutalities and persecution, people might have eventually believed this news. But because the Nazis chose to do the unprecedented, the reports of their actions were most likely to be rejected as inaccurate. The extreme nature of the news fostered doubts in the minds of victim and bystander. The systematic annihilation of an entire people seemed beyond the realm of the possible. It certainly was beyond the realm of the believable. Both the means of murder—gas—and the size of the victim population—many millions—reinforced the natural barriers of incredulity. In a certain respect these were healthy doubts—the mind's rebellion against believing that human beings were capable of sinking to such levels of depravity—but they made it easier for the perpetrators to camouflage their plans.

In sum, Americans who depended on the media for their information were presented with a confused and confusing picture, a picture with many correct but unclear or incomplete details. The way in which the information was relayed enabled many people to categorize it as unverified rumors spread by unreliable sources. The suffering of Jews was often reported as the suffering of Poles, Russians, French, Dutch, and other national groups. The area in Poland to which many of the Jews were being transported was off limits to foreign reporters. But most of all, the idea of an entire people being murdered in gas chambers was unprecedented.

As shall be demonstrated in the pages that follow, all these barriers to belief resulted in a paradoxical situation: on occasion the Allied press did a better job of suppressing or casting doubt upon the news of the Final Solution than did the Nazis.

Misery Wholesale

Within a few weeks after the beginning of hostilities in Europe in September 1939, press reports indicated that the Nazis were intensifying their drive against the Jews. On September 11 Otto Tolischus, who visited the Polish front, noted that the Germans were blaming the resistance they met on the Jews. There were almost immediate reports of a planned "purge" of Jews in Poland and the creation of a "Jewish reserve" there. Early in the fall the *New York Times* reported that the deportation of Jews was "extending" throughout the German Protectorate and in a detailed page 3 report described the Jews as the "worst sufferers" among the various peoples who were being forcibly moved by the Germans. On November 1, a news summary by the foreign editor of the *San Francisco Chronicle* carried the headline

THOUSANDS OF JEWS IN A NEW
EXODUS FROM VIENNA TO POLAND

According to the article "no one seems to know" what their fate
would be, but since they were allowed to take virtually nothing
with them, if they did not find work, they were "expected to
starve." A similarly ominous article appeared on page 3 of the
Los Angeles Times. [15] By December 1939 reporters in Germany were
transmitting "official information" on the "forced migration [of
Jews] into a huge concentration camp in what was formerly Poland." Viennese Jews were being expelled at the rate of 2,000 a
week so that on March 1, 1940, Vienna would be free of Jews.
Over 150,000 Jews from Bohemia and Moravia were about to
be deported, as were the Jews of Teschen and other parts of
German-occupied territory. *The New Republic* described the "human suffering involved [as] . . . beyond the compass of the
imagination."[16]

It was not long before reports of the establishment of ghettos
and death from disease and starvation were also to be found in
the press. Within a few months after the start of the war, the
Vatican, the Polish government in exile, and the British government released reports on Nazi brutality, particularly in concentration camps. By this time stories of the horrors of the German
camps were generally accepted by the press. In fact, even before
the war general acceptance had begun. In April 1939 *Time* observed that "too many alumni have emerged from concentration
camps with the same story to leave any further doubt that sadism
and brutality are part & parcel of the concentration camp routine."
In August 1939, when the Munich *Illustrated Press* released pictures
depicting what the Germans claimed were the conditions in the
concentration camps, *Life* dismissed the pictures and the story
which accompanied them as a "whitewash." According to the magazine, conditions in the camps, German claims to the contrary
notwithstanding, were so awful that they seemed like an "incredible nightmare invented by malicious lunatics." When the British
released their White Paper on the situation in the camps, the
New York Times observed in an editorial that the "essential truth
of the sickening story" had "long since been established." In
the fall of 1939 *Christian Century,* which had demonstrated and
would continue to demonstrate an almost sardonic attitude toward
stories of atrocities, found its doubts giving way "as report follows

report." The abundant similar reports were too compelling to deny *totally,* though it was possible to argue, as we shall see, that things were not *as* bad as reported. At the beginning of 1940, when the Nazis ejected American and other diplomatic personnel from Poland, some papers began to wonder what forms of "dreadful oppression" the Germans wanted to hide.[17]

According to Sigrid Schultz, "the war had barely started" when reporters began hearing reports of "German atrocities in invaded countries." Schultz discovered an easy method to gather information about what was taking place on the eastern front.

> All one had to do was to go to one of the waiting rooms of the railroad stations in eastern Berlin and listen to Black Guards [SS] arriving from or leaving for the front. They seemed to enjoy describing how they had locked Poles and Jews into cellars and then thrown hand grenades through windows left open for the purpose.[18]

Even Jews who were not subjected to deportation were living in what Fred Oeschner of United Press described as "complete hopelessness." By the outbreak of the war Jews in Germany had been

> barred from all profession and trades . . . forbidden to enter restaurants, theaters, cinemas, museums, bathing beaches or any other place of recreation. . . . in the winter, gangs of elderly men and women without proper clothing, shoes or gloves could be seen shoveling snow in subzero temperatures in the streets of German cities. The Jews were given no ration cards for clothing and no permits to buy shoes.[19]

But not everyone was convinced. There were still a few papers which tried to dismiss stories of extreme suffering and atrocities as just a device to discredit the other side. They warned that any attempt to use them would be "abortive" because their "history is not good." This was rarely the picture depicted by Berlin correspondents, but on occasion some among them simply ignored the Jews' situation or painted it in a benign if not benevolent light. Such was the case when *Life*'s Berlin correspondent, William D. Bayles, sent the magazine a series of detailed letters on conditions in Germany. In his sole reference to Jews he said that those Jews who had been forced to sell their businesses in the wake of *Kristallnacht* "came out on top." Even though they had only received one-third the face value of their property, according to Bayles they were now "mostly out of the country or at least have the money safely put away," while the "Aryans" who bought their establishments "are now facing bankruptcy." Bayles wrote the letter in which he said this in November 1939 at the same time that other reporters were describing the severe suffering and destitute condition of German Jews. Bayles ignored the severity of their situation until six weeks later. Crossing the border from Germany into the Netherlands Bayles witnessed—and in an article described—how his fellow passengers who were Jews were physically and verbally abused by German guards and Gestapo agents: at the border men, women, and children were herded into a "windowless shed, without heat, ventilation, toilets or water," and were required to remain there for twenty-four hours.[20]

By early 1940 the news had become grimmer. In March the *Chicago Tribune* reported that a news "leak" out of Poland indicated that Polish Jews would be forbidden to emigrate, that Jews in camps would not be allowed to leave for countries controlled by the Reich, and that "gradually all Jews are being massed in the Lublin area, the most desolate region in former Poland." Also, American embassy officials in Berlin told the State Department of the progressively harsher regulations being imposed upon German Jews. They were particularly concerned when in early 1940 Jews from areas of the "old Reich" began to be deported. Embassy officials feared that this "presaged the general removal of Jews to Poland" from significant areas of the Reich. Assistant Secretary of State A. A. Berle, in a memorandum to the Secretary of State, described the deportations as "brutal in the extreme" and recommended that the Department register a protest either by sending a note to the Germans or issuing a press statement.[21]

News of this sort prompted some unknowingly prophetic observations, including one by the *Buffalo Courier Express* which described the Nazis as waging two wars, a conventional one against Britain and France and "one of the basest, most brutal and vicious wars in human history. . . . the war of extermination against the Jewish people of Germany." The *Newark Star Ledger* also offered a frighteningly accurate prediction: five and a half million Jews were in "distress," and many were "doomed to perish."[22]

These papers now understood that many Jews would die as a result of the conditions which they were being forced to endure. But even though they used the terms "extermination," "annihilation," and "doomed to perish," they could not and did not know the full extent of the horror that would soon engulf European Jews. During the entire period of Nazi rule these terms were used to mean different things. During the first years of Nazi rule, when Hitler and his followers threatened that the Jewish community would be "exterminated with fire and sword," the press generally understood this to mean that the Jewish community as a functioning part of German society would be destroyed: synagogues would no longer exist, Jewish institutions would be disbanded, Jews would be unable to obtain decent jobs that provided a living wage, many Jews would leave the Reich because of the intolerable situation there, and those who remained would eventually die off as a result of extreme poverty and difficult conditions.

This was what Edgar Ansel Mowrer meant in 1933 when he described the aim of the Nazis' "barbarous campaign" against the Jews as the "extermination, permanent subjection or voluntary departure of the Jews from Germany." He knew conditions would be terrible, but he was not predicting the Final Solution; for there was no way he—or any other reporter—could have been prescient enough to know that "extermination" would come to mean a systematic program of annihilation.* As the situation worsened, "extermination" was used in its literal sense: Many would die. But there was a difference in saying that many would die as a

---

* Scholars debate when Hitler decided on a program of annihilation of the Jews. Some, e.g., Lucy Dawidowicz, have argued that it was something he planned to do long before he came to power. Others, e.g., Yehuda Bauer, contend that annihilation was not decided on until all other options, such as forcing Jews to emigrate to other countries, were no longer feasible because of the Nazi conquest of most of the European continent, particularly European Russia. In this debate the question arises, What was the meaning of "extermination" when it was used by Hitler and his cohorts in the 1930s and early 1940s? The first group argues that as early as 1933 it meant the physical annihilation of the Jews. Others believe that it was initially used to mean a virtually *Judenrein* Reich in which those Jews who remained would be reduced to modern-day helots and would generally die premature deaths because of the terrible conditions in which they lived. From the perspective of this study what the Nazis meant prior to June 1941 when they used the term "extermination" is less important than how the term was understood and could have been understood by bystanders in general and the press in particular. None of the reporters, even those who were the most intensely hostile to Germany and Hitler, interpreted the term or themselves used the term prior to 1942 as meaning the systematic and planned physical annihilation of European Jews. It would, in fact have been surprising if they had interpreted it in this fashion. They could not have been expected to know what would follow. It was an unprecedented program that even the most vehement anti-Nazi could not have imagined possible. Those who today claim that the world should have recognized from the outset in 1933 that the Final Solution was in the offing are using historical hindsight, a tool that was obviously not available to contemporary observers.[23]

result of extreme deprivation or even murder and acknowledging that millions, almost the entire Jewish population of Europe, would die in systematic massacres and in death factories established specifically to kill them.

A similar interpretation of the terms "annihilation" and "wiped out" was applied in an article entitled "The Annihilation of German Jewry" by the Berlin correspondent of the British journal *The Spectator*, who described how as a result of the "ruthless" deportations, the entire Reich and the annexed Polish provinces would be "completely 'Jew-free' and Judaism will be completely wiped out." In 1941, shortly after his return from Europe, H. R. Knickerbocker went a step further in his use of these terms. He predicted that while "perhaps five or six million Jews . . . will ultimately perish" at Nazi hands, they would not be murdered but condemned to a "slow death." Hitler would not "kill them all at once" because he enjoyed watching them suffer, needed their labor power, and did not want to "outrage what there is left of world opinion."[24] During this period the press used such terms as "extermination" and "perish" to signify the "slow death" of a community, its institutions, and ultimately its people. No one could imagine even in 1941 that it would soon take on an even more diabolical meaning.

Between the fall of 1940 and the winter of 1941 antisemitic regulations were imposed in all Nazi controlled areas. In October 1940 Marshall Petain, chief of state of Vichy France, announced that Nuremberg-like decrees would also go into effect in unoccupied France. Foreign Jews could now be interned in special camps by local prefects, and Algerian Jews lost their French citizenship. The decrees were widely reported in the press; *Time* typically described them as "so un-French, so very German in accent that the outside world found it hard to believe they came from the mouth of an old fighter for France . . . Petain."[25]

By 1941 the press accepted Nazi persecution of the Jews as a "truism" and an "incontestable fact." Reporters on the scene recognized that "despite the war," Germany was intent on continuing to "press its persecutions of the Jews both in the Reich and in German dominated Europe." An exclusive report in *PM*, the liberal New York daily, suggested that the "best policy for a Jew in Poland today is neither to be seen nor heard." Reporters recognized that the treatment of the Jews had been standardized so that it followed a similar pattern in every city.[26] In March 1941 an Associated Press story delineated the specific steps entailed in that pattern: first Jews were "barred from professions and public office," then they were prevented or "discouraged from mixing with other people," finally they were driven from their businesses, "made to show distinguishing badges and . . . made to dwell in ghetto-like districts." It could be expected that wherever German forces were in control, Jews would be "segregated" in "hermetically sealed ghettos." Those Jews not yet deported from the Reich itself received, according to the *New York Herald Tribune,* "war work but little else." They could not purchase clothing or fuel, were barred from parks and main streets and forbidden to have social contacts with "Aryan Germans." A story in the February 15 issue of *Illustrated* magazine described the future for the "over a million Jews" who had been confined in Polish ghettos as a "gradual doom." Ghettoization was "but a first step towards their annihilation," which would result from "illness . . . lack of water and living conditions not adequate for cattle." In March the *Christian Science Monitor* printed a map of the Warsaw ghetto and described the segregation of the Jews as reminiscent of "the Middle Ages." The article carried a stark headline:

JEWS HAVE NO CHANCE in NAZIS' 'NEW ORDER'[27]

In early April a reporter for *The Saturday Evening Post* visited Warsaw's ghetto, which he described as a "Forbidden City" cut off completely from "the teeming life around it." The high-ranking Nazi leader who accompanied him claimed that the Jews preferred to live in the ghetto rather than be dispersed all over the city. This was "confirmed," the author observed somewhat skeptically, by Jews who "lived before last November in comfortable surroundings . . . and had been free to circulate anywhere in Warsaw . . . [who] now live in a crowded room . . . and can leave only on those rare occasions when they obtain special permission." Nonetheless, they insisted that they "like the new arrangement better" because of the "peace of mind" it afforded them. The editors, obviously fearful that readers might accept this at face value, appended a cautionary note to the beginning of the article. In a conquered country, they warned, "only the conquerors may speak freely to a reporter"; it was, therefore, necessary to "read between the lines."[28]

In mid-June a reporter for *PM* returned from fifty-four days in the Reich to write that Jews in Germany were forced to work for a pitiful wage which was insufficient to allow for even minimal subsistence. Those who somehow had enough funds to purchase food found that by the time they were allowed to shop—Jews could only enter stores after four in the afternoon—most of the shelves were empty. The reporter categorized life for Jews in the Warsaw ghetto as beyond "human endurance." It was worse than bombing; "bombing at least gets it over with in a hurry."[29]

But the imposition by Vichy in June 1941 of what the *New York Herald Tribune* described in its headline as a "final drastic decree" seemed to shock the press more than anything which preceded it. When such news had come from Poland, it was accepted somewhat matter-of-factly. When it came from France, this was not so at all, even though what was done in France was not as severe as in Poland. What had become normal behavior in Germany and Nazi-controlled lands seemed particularly out of place in France. Editorials in papers throughout the United States condemned France's "collaboration" in passing new laws which were a severe extension of those that had been issued the previous fall and essentially put Jews—foreign and French—"outside the law." Now local prefects could send a Jew to a concentration camp for "any reason whatever," and individuals could be interned on the "mere suspicion" of being Jews. When conditions in some of the French concentration camps were publicized in the American and British press, the French, sensitive to this criticism, ordered that they be improved. These improvements were more cosmetic than substantive, and the escalating French war against the Jews continued virtually unabated.[30]

As the commencement of the mass murder of European Jews neared, the press had enough information to indicate that many of them were doomed to die from disease, starvation, exposure torture and slave labor. Soon they would also have enough information to know that many were being massacred. But their own nagging doubts and those of their editors back home permeated the writing and publication of the news so that the American public would still have cause to disbelieve.[31]

The Beginning of the *Endlösung*

On June 22, 1941, German armored units rolled across the border into Russian territory, including that area of Poland previously occupied by Russia. In the wake of the Wehrmacht's military advance there began another assault of a vastly different nature. The special units in charge of this attack, the *Einsatzgruppen* (Action Groups), conducted a series of "sweeps" against Jews between the summer of 1941 and late 1942. Together they left well over 1 million Jews dead. This, the first step in the actual murder of European Jewry, lacked any of the technological "advances" subsequently instituted in the death camps. The Nazis' dissatisfaction with the "inefficient" *modus operandi* of the *Einsatzgruppen* led them to seek a different mode of annihilation: death camps and gas chambers.

Although the Nazis tried to keep the news of these mobile killing units from the outside world, reports of their existence filtered through enemy lines fairly rapidly. The main sources of information were *Einsatzgruppen* members and soldiers who had participated in or witnessed the massacres. In addition, German civilian personnel who were present transmitted this information back to Germany.[32] As early as August 1941 reports of massacres began to appear in the press. By the fall of 1941 news of the killing was widespread enough to have reached some foreign journalists. When they were brought by the Germans on a tour of German-occupied Russia, they told Nazi officials that they were fully aware of the massacres. But they remained cautious, and the reports they transmitted back to the states were often suffused with doubt and incredulity.

On August 8 AP described the massacre of hundreds of Lvov civilians as an "orgy of murder and rape . . . directed mainly at members of trade unions, workers in public services . . . [and] factory employees." A note of skepticism was injected into the report with the comment that its source was "communiques based in part on *purported* stories of persons *said* to have escaped." The doubts of the AP may have been exacerbated by the fact that the report of the "orgy" had been released by the Russians. The *New York Post* treated reports of mass deaths far more factually. In a lengthy and detailed article it told of a Polish White Paper on the "atrocities" committed by the Nazis during the first eighteen months of their rule. The story was, the *Post* observed, supported by over 200 items of source material, including "scores of affidavits from escaped eyewitnesses," and told of over 70,000 civilian executions in Poland. Neither of these two reports specified Jews as being among the victims, but other reports soon did.[33]

On October 26 the *New York Times* carried news of the slaying of 15,000 Jews in Galicia. Details on the "massacres of thousands of Jews deported from Hungary to Galicia and the machine-gunning of more thousands of Galician Jews" by German and Ukrainian soldiers were based on letters reaching Hungary from Galicia and on eyewitness accounts of officers who had been present. According to this news report, those who had not been "massacred" were living in conditions of "widespread" poverty and hunger. On November 13 the *New York Journal American* published a page 1 (on page 2 in another edition) story on the massacre of Jews in Odessa, where the toll was reportedly 25,000. At the end of the month the same paper carried a report which had come from Moscow on the massacre of 52,000 men, women, and children in Kiev on page 2.[34]

Although by the fall of 1941 news of the slaying of Jews had begun to appear, the press generally focused far more attention on Jewish life in Germany and German-occupied Western Europe, very naturally concentrating on what it could see—and in the fall of 1941 it could see quite a bit. In early September, after what the embassy in Berlin described as an "absence of some months," the Jewish question was "put very prominently back in the public eye" by the Gestapo decree requiring all Jews in Germany and Bohemia and Moravia above the age of six to wear a yellow star. By the end of the month the embassy and the press were correctly predicting that "more radical measures to segregate Jews in Germany" were in the offing.[35]

During the months of October and November the news reported was consistently distressing. Throughout the Reich and Western Europe Jews were being arrested, ordered to wear identifying tags, denied their possessions, forced to work at the most menial jobs, and evicted from their homes.[36] The most ominous news came in mid-October with the beginning of what United Press described as the "severest anti-Jewish drive in three years." According to Fred Oeschner, UP bureau chief in Berlin, the first wave of deportations had been somewhat "makeshift," but "there was nothing halfhearted" about this second wave. From various cities in Western Europe as well as the Reich—including Berlin, where many reporters were stationed—came reports that thousands of Jews "were being dispatched on short notice to ghettos in Poland." According to United Press, 1,000 or more Jews were being moved every night from Berlin to Poland for incarceration in ghettos and camps. Various reporters, including two from

United Press, witnessed how Jews were loaded on trains which then moved eastward. AP reported that a ghetto had been established in Lvov and that 450 Jews had died in Mauthausen, the camp in Austria. Whereas many people in Germany had not yet heard about the mass killings on the Russian front, there was virtually no one in Berlin who, according to Oeschner, "did not have some idea of what was going on." There was no doubt that foreign correspondents and diplomats stationed in the major cities in Europe knew that Jews by the thousands were being deported.[37] Unlike the massacres, which were "purported" and undocumented, these other incidents were witnessed by American reporters stationed in German-occupied Europe. The *Chicago Tribune* condemned the deportations as a "new savagery."[38]

Through the fall of 1941, reports from various parts of the Reich described the desperate situation. In the wake of the decree that all Jews had to wear a yellow star, a Stockholm paper reported that 200 Jews had committed suicide. Louis Lochner reported that there was "a new wave of antisemitism" in Berlin. Jews had been barred from grocers' lists and could not buy vegetables, fruit, sweets, canned milk, and many other products. Synagogues were being closed, and all Jewish households due to be evacuated had been ordered to fill out an inventory of all their possessions.[39] The Jews of Hanover were reported to be living in "cemeteries on the outskirts of the city" because their homes had been requisitioned. Everywhere Jews were described as being "hungry and without adequate shelter." The *Chicago Tribune* termed the regulations placed on the remnants of Berlin Jewry a "tribute to the diabolical ingenuity of the Hitler gang."[40] United Press, relying on what it described as "usually reliable sources," claimed that "a sentence to a concentration camp was the standard punishment" for violation of the decree that Jews must wear a yellow star. Children's laxity was punished by incarceration of the parents.[41] A Free Press News Service correspondent in Bern, Frank Brutto, in a lengthy survey of the conditions facing Jews in Europe, reported that 4,000 Yugoslavian Jews had been left without food and water on an island off the Dalmatian coast. Within a week, Brutto reported, 1,000 were dead.[42]

The press did not have to depend on reliable but unnamed sources; it could look directly to the Nazis for information. This had been the case before the war began and continued thereafter. With the exception of the details regarding the death camps and mobile killing units, much of the information reported by the press came from Nazis spokesmen and newspapers. In October 1939 a Nazi "authorized source" had told the press that Hitler was contemplating a "Jewish reservation" in Poland. In March 1940 the *New York Times* described the manner in which 80,000 Jews in Cracow were "gradually being pushed back to the ghetto, . . . cut off from practically all connections with . . . the [outside] world . . . thrown entirely on their own resources." At the end of the article, which painted a dismal picture of life under these conditions, the reporter stated that "this is the picture furnished by the official Government General organ" and then, as a means of insinuating that things might even be worse, noted that direct contact was forbidden and therefore the "full scope" was unknown. In August 1940 Associated Press reported that according to *Schwarze Korps*, the official "mouthpiece of Hitler's Elite Guard," a Jew-free Europe was the Nazi aim.[43] In the fall of 1941 German newspapers kept the public informed of at least some of the deportations. The Cologne newspaper *Kölnische Zeitung* reported that all the Jews in Luxembourg had been transported eastward.[44]

But officially the Nazis still denied that anything akin to mass murder was underway. Some papers used statistics released by German sources to shed doubt on the Nazi denials of persecution. In April 1940 the *Buffalo Courier Express* called attention to the jubilant "boasting" of the Scientific Institute of the German Labor Front that the number of Jews in Germany had been reduced by two-thirds since 1933. From a biological perspective, the Institute reported, "the Jewish population in Germany is 'already dead' because only about 10 per cent of the men and 7 per cent of the women are of an age at which they can have children." The *Courier Express* asked why the Institute report failed to indicate how much of the decrease in population was "due to emigration and how much to death by slow torture in Nazi concentration camps." The paper denigrated those who branded news of Nazi atrocities as "propaganda," because the most "imaginative of anti-Nazi propagandists" could not produce "indictments more damning than those which the Nazis have returned against themselves." A similar Nazi indictment "against themselves" was offered in November 1941 when Hans Frank, governor of the *General gouvernement*, that part of the Polish interior in which most Jews were concentrated, told the press that "Jews [who] leave Polish ghettoes" would be shot.[45]

The Treatment of the News

Using space allotment and page placement as measures of importance, it is clear that even though much of this news came either from German sources or from eyewitness accounts, its relative news value was not always considered high. While certain reports were prominently placed in the major dailies, often news of significant value was relegated to the depths of the paper. The *New York Times* carried the reports of "massive arrests" of Jews in Vichy in a twenty-six-line article on page 18 and the announcement that Jews over the age of six had to wear a star on page 14. The *New York Journal American* placed the announcement of German Jews' loss of all citizenship and residency rights and further confiscation of their property on page 30.[46] The story of a Nazi edict which, in the words of the *New York Journal American,* "enslave[d] Jews" was on page 8 of that paper and on page 15 of the *New York World Telegram.* [47] The *Chicago Tribune* placed the news that Jews were forbidden to use the telephone "even for [a] doctor" on the very bottom of page 10. News of an official decree that any Jews caught outside the ghetto which was the "sole living space alloted" to them would be summarily killed was carried on page 5 of the *Tribune* in a twelve-line story.[48] The imposition of "rigid antisemitic laws" in Norway was reported by the *New York Journal American* on page 32. The death of 450 Dutch Jews in Mauthausen concentration camp appeared in the *Baltimore Sun* in a thirteen-line article at the bottom of page 10. *New York Times* editors placed a warning by twenty-six leaders of the Russian Jewish community that if Hitler was not defeated, "wholesale extermination would be the lot of all Jews" on page 5 at the bottom of the page. It ran Slovakia's decision to "oust" its Jewish people and send them to "concentration centers" on page 18 and Jewish leaders' predictions that Jews in Poland faced "extinction" as a result of ghetto conditions on page 28. The story of 200 Jewish suicides in Berlin in the wake of the imposition of laws regarding the wearing of the yellow star was on page 8 of the paper.[49]

Not all the reports were placed this deep inside the paper. Though they were rarely accorded space on page 1, a number appeared in fairly prominent positions. The *New York Herald Tribune* story on the "herding" of Russian Jews into ghettos was on page 3, as was the report of new restrictions on German Jews' ability to earn a living. Economic restrictions on Vichy Jews and the promise of a "Jew-free Reich" by April 1, 1942; were on page 4 of the *Herald Tribune*.[50]

One of the few times that a number of major dailies—including the *New York Journal American, New York Herald Tribune, St. Louis Post Dispatch,* and *San Francisco Chronicle*—found a story worthy of page 1 was in early November 1941 when the Reverend Bernard Lichtenberg, dean of St. Hedwig's Roman Catholic Cathedral in Berlin, was arrested for praying for the Jews. The *Boston Globe* devoted an editorial to Lichtenberg's "revolt." Not all papers thought it so important. The *Chicago Tribune* placed it on page 16 and devoted only twenty-four lines to it.[51] The attention paid to Lichtenberg by most of the major papers can, of course, be explained by the locale from which he voiced his protest: Berlin. But generally during these years, whenever the Pope or other leading Christian religious leaders spoke out on the Jews' behalf or decried the suffering of civilian populations, their comments garnered more attention than a similar story coming from a Jewish or, sometimes, even a government source. This attention may be attributed to the fact that a Christian was protesting what was being done to the Jews and also to the relative rarity of such protests by prominent Christian leaders. Sometimes even Christian protests could not penetrate editorial barriers. In 1944 the prominent publisher and newsman Oswald Garrison Villard complained about the way the *New York Times* handled a resolution passed by 500 Christian ministers and laymen denouncing the "systematic Nazi destruction of the Jewish people." Villard said that

> it was news and it was eminently fit to print but it was given only a few lines by the *Times* and buried inconspicuously on page seven. A similar happening [on another occasion] was carefully interred on page seventeen.

Villard attributed this to the paper's "unfortunate trait" of trying to avoid appearing as "a vigorous defender" of the Jews.[52]*

By the end of October 1941 Louis Lochner was reporting that the total elimination of Jews from European life was "fixed German policy" and that Hitler's 1939 promise to render the Reich free of Jews was being realized. Nazi-like policies had been

---

* For additional discussion of *New York Times* policy on matters relating to Jews, see Chapter 8.

instituted in Roumania, and several times a week transports "start eastward with Jews from the Rhineland and Westphalia, Berlin, Prague or Vienna." The deportees' fate upon reaching the east was, Lochner observed with a note of real foreboding, unknown. That it would be extremely difficult was accepted without question.[53] Relying on reports such as those dispatched by Lochner, the *Springfield News Sun* predicted that the Nazis have "ominous plans for them [the Jews] when the time comes."[54] A similar sense of foreboding—but not surprise—was evidenced by Frank Brutto of the Free Press News Service when he observed that "Nazi blueprints of the new order have no provision in them for the Jew except ghettos, exile, proscription. Adolf Hitler has more than said it. . . . Nearly everyday, somewhere, new action is taken against them."[55] That "ghettos, exile, proscription" awaited the Jews there was little question. The process of segregation was being carried out on a systematic basis. Antisemitism had, it was noted, "inevitably followed close behind the German armies." No one disputed this conclusion. Early in November 1941 the Associated Press reported that the Jewish residents of Lvov had been ordered to move into a ghetto within the month.[56]

In late November reports of deportations were augmented with additional stories regarding massacres and tortures. The *New York Herald Tribune* chronicled the treatment of the Jews in occupied parts of Russia. Regarding the deportations it had no doubts: "According to reliable reports" which were subject to a "careful check," 20,000 Jews had been "deported" to the Pinsk marshes. It quoted from a poignant letter sent by a Jewish woman in Vienna to her relatives immediately prior to her deportation: "everything is too late now. We bid you farewell, trusting that we shall see you again in the course of our life. Please take care of our children and tell them to accept things as they are." But although by now the paper had received enough news to convince it that the reports of deportations and severe deprivation were reliable, when it came to discussing the massacres the *Herald Tribune* took a more restrained and skeptical stance. Using a reportorial style that would become virtually standard for stories on the mass murder of Jews, the paper distanced itself from the information and became the neutral transmitter. In the final paragraph of the news story it added, almost as an afterthought, that "some reports received here from Central Europe *speak* of massacres of Jews by Germans in the occupied part of Russia." The number of Jews killed in

Kiev *"has been put* as high as 52,000."[57] Apparently, the news of massacres was open to question, though the reports of brutality and slave labor were not, even though they came from similar sources.

By this time there were some news stories regarding the death of multitudes which were not skeptical in tone, but they were the minority. In December 1941, writing in the *New York Sun,* the columnist George Sokolsky singled out the Jews when he described the Nazis' "efficient process of murder." He predicted that by the end of the war half of the 8 million Jews under Nazi control might well be dead.[58] Even the *New York Herald Tribune,* which had demonstrated a lack of complete faith in the news of massacres, observed in an editorial at the beginning of December that the reports of mistreatment of Jews were no longer news— what was news was the "sheer mass" of those who had died. The fate reserved for the Jews was described by the *New York Herald Tribune* as "worse than a status of serfdom—it is nothing less than systematic extermination."[59] The Hearst papers described what the Nazis were doing as the "attempted extermination of an ancient and cultured race."[60] In a lengthy story which covered almost an entire page, the *Christian Science Monitor* noted that the "only purpose behind the ruthless treatment [of the Jews] appears to be the complete extermination of the race." What was being spoken of was no longer just the destruction of institutions and organized communal life. "Extermination" now meant the death of multitudes as a result of living "destitute and helpless" in the ghettos of Poland and the wastelands of the Ukraine.[61] Jewish leaders also recognized the increased severity of the situation. Dr. Henry Shoskes, a prominent Polish Jew who had come to the United States at the beginning of the war, explained to reporters in 1942 that the Nazis created conditions in the ghettos which were so severe that Jews were "doomed to annihilation."[62] By early 1942 it was clear that Jews would die not only because of terrible conditions but also as a result of massacres. But what the press did not yet know—and could not yet know—was that annihilation would not be haphazard but that this killing would culminate in a systematic program using "modern" scientific methods and whose victims would include millions of Jews from every corner of the European continent.

While the ultimate meaning of "extermination" would not be fully divulged until the latter half of 1942, journalists, particularly those in Germany, were increasingly cognizant of the changing nature of the situation. Information was available from too many sources to be easily denied. By early summer additional evidence would be available to prove that "extermination" had to be interpreted in its most terrible sense, that what was happening was even worse than had been previously imagined, and that the Nazis were no longer just persecuting the Jews or allowing them to die of starvation, but were murdering them. Despite the fact that these accounts of a systematic program of intentional and deliberate annihilation had been preceded by so much other information, they would find particularly formidable barriers in their path.

8

Official Confirmation

In late spring 1942, the American correspondents who had been in Germany at the time of Pearl Harbor were exchanged for Axis nationals stranded in the United States. These reporters returned to the United States with additional details on the mass murders which had occurred in Poland and Russia. Their descriptions of events were explicit and graphic. Glen Stadler, UP correspondent in Germany, described what had happened to Jews in Latvia, Estonia, and Lithuania as an "open hunt." Some of the reporters estimated that more than 400,000 had already been killed by Hitler's *"new order,"* including "upward of 100,000 [Jews who] met death in Baltic states alone, and more than double that many [who] have been executed in Western Russia."[1] Joseph Grigg, also of UP, believed that the number of Jewish victims had reached 200,000.

> Thousands lie in unmarked graves, many in mass graves they were forced to dig before the firing squads of S.S. [*Schützstaffel* or Defense Corps] troops cut them down.... One of the biggest known mass slaughters occurred in Latvia in the summer of 1941

when, responsible Nazi sources admitted, 56,000 men, women and children were killed by S.S. troops and Latvian irregulars. This slaughter went on for days. There was even an official German newsreel of squads shooting Jews in the streets of Riga. . . . In Lithuania about 30,000 Jews, according to most reliable estimates, were killed by special "cleanup" squads brought from Poland with the knowledge and approval of the German civil administration. The entire Jewish population of many towns and villages was driven into the country, forced to dig graves and then machine gunned. In one city alone, more than 8,000 were killed. . . . The slaughter in Poland was horrible, with 80,000 killed . . . a high percentage of [them were] Jews. The mass grave technique was used there too. . . . One German rifleman boasted to correspondents that he had killed thirty seven in one night, picking them off as a hunter does rabbits. Rumanians were even less reticent in boasting of their slaughters of Jews.

The repatriated reporters did not just describe how Jews had been killed, but some made it clear that they understood Hitler's plans for the Jews. Grigg noted that when the war broke out, Hitler had declared that it would result in the destruction of the Jews, and *"those of us who lived in Germany know that he and his agents have done everything to make the prophecy come true."*[2]

In addition to these news reports many of the correspondents immediately published accounts of their experiences, discussing not only their experiences in Germany but also what the Germans were doing to the Jews. They worked on the books during the six months they were "imprisoned." One of the most detailed accounts was published by United Press correspondent Frederick Oeschner, who believed that the full number of Jews "slaughtered by Nazi execution squads between the outbreak of war and spring, 1942" would never be precisely known but estimated that it was at least 200,000. Wallace Duel of the *Chicago Daily News* described the mass graves and the bonfires which were built in order to dispose of the bodies. Louis Lochner, whose account did not refer to the mass murder, did describe the deportations and said they constituted one of the "darkest blots on the Nazi escutcheon."[3]

As part of an extensive series on his experiences in Germany, this veteran AP reporter graphically told how "Hitler [was] still tightening screws on Jews in all lands where Nazis rule." The treatment meted out was "more severe than even that specified in [the] Nuremberg laws." Those Jews who had not yet been deported to Poland in "the most primitive" conditions discovered that the "plain fact is that the Jew stands beyond the pale of any law." According to Lochner, anything the Nazis wished to do to the Jews could be done. He made a point of noting that "decent" Germans were appalled by these reports and did whatever they could to ease the Jews' situation, including very seriously risking their own safety.[4] Though Lochner stressed the severity of the conditions facing Jews both when he was released and again in September, when he was interviewed by CBS radio, he did not make specific mention of an extermination or mass murder program.[5]

An American citizen who had been caught in Poland when America entered the war was also released with the reporters. In a widely syndicated INS series he acknowledged that Polish suffering was great, but "whatever is suffered by the general population in Poland it is not as bad as the fate of those poor unfortunates who live in the Jewish ghettos."[6]

Meanwhile additional ominous signs appeared on the horizon. Several articles in the press indicated an increasingly frightening situation. On June 13 Goebbels's threat to carry out "mass extermination of Jews in reprisal for the Allied air bombings" was reported by the press.[7] A few days later the *Los Angeles Times* carried a report on the slaying of 25,000 Jews in Latvia. That same day the *New York Journal American* reprinted a story from the *London Evening Standard* which reported that escapees arriving from Vilna had said that the toll of Jews slain there had reached 60,000. The *New York Times* also reported this news but in a way that contrasted sharply with the *London Evening Standard*'s report. According to the *Standard,* the source of the news was "a man who was in Vilna up to May 24 and himself saw much of the mass murder." The *New York Times* described him as a man "who *said* he was in Vilna until May 24." The *New York Times* then added the following paragraph. "The Polish refugee's story of the Vilna massacre, of which he *said* he was an eyewitness, is impossible to confirm now."[8] Thus the *New York Times* established yet another barrier between itself and the news, shedding doubt on its authoritative nature. But this kind of treatment of the news was not unique to the *New York Times,* as would become abundantly clear during the next few months.

Polish Confirmation and Press Reaction

In June of 1942 the Polish authorities in London released a report they had received from Poland which confirmed that the Germans were murdering Jews throughout Poland. It described the "system" of killings which was "applied everywhere." This information had been transmitted to London at the end of May by the Polish Jewish socialist organization, the Bund. The Bund report depicted how many of the massacres were conducted:

> Men, fourteen to sixty years old, were driven to a single place— a square or a cemetery, where they were slaughtered or shot by machine guns or killed by hand grenades. They had to dig their own graves. Children in orphanages, inmates in old-age homes, the sick in hospitals were shot, women were killed in the streets. In many towns the Jews were carried off to "an unknown destination" and killed in adjacent woods.

According to the report the Jewish death toll in Poland had reached 700,000. The number of dead in Rovno was said to be 15,000, in Vilna 50,000 and in Slonim 9,000. Sealed railway cars with 25,000 people in them had left Lublin and virtually "disappeared without a trace." But this report contained two other even more important and startling revelations. It told of death by gassings at Chelmno and estimated that on the "average" 1,000 people a day had been killed between November 1941 and March 1942 in gas chambers which could accommodate ninety people at a time. Of greatest significance was its revelation that these murders were part of a coordinated plan to murder the Jewish people. The opening line of the report stressed this point: "From the day the Russo-German war broke out, the Germans embarked on the physical annihilation of the Jewish population on Polish soil." The report then laid out the grim but accurate description of what had happened. (Though the plan only mentioned 700,000 victims, by this time the toll was in the vicinity of 2 million.)[9]

On June 2 the essence of the report was broadcast on the BBC. Toward the end of the month, after press conferences by members of the Polish government in exile's National Council, it was picked up by the British press. On June 29 the World Jewish Congress sponsored a news conference at which Sidney S. Silverman, a member of the British Parliament, and Ignacy

Schwarzbart, a member of the Polish National Council, told of the murder of Jews in Pinsk, Bialystok, Slonim, Rovno, Lvov, and dozens of other places. Schwarzbart spoke of the gassings at Chelmno and raised the estimated death toll to over 1 million.

These revelations constituted a watershed in the dissemination of information regarding the Final Solution. Here were the first public reports of gassing and the first reference to a systematic continent-wide program of murder. Moreover, the news now had the official imprimatur of the London-based Polish government in exile and of British officials, members of Parliament, and the BBC. This was the first step in the transformation of the news from rumor to officially confirmed fact. It was becoming more difficult, though certainly not impossible, to dismiss this story as having *no* basis in truth. Details continued to make their way out of Europe in the months and years that followed. Yet while the secret of the war against the Jews had begun to seep through the Nazi fog, it was difficult for it to break through barriers in the Allied world. The American press did not ease its path. It did not highlight this news and often omitted from its reports key pieces of information or burdened them with various disclaimers.

It is instructive to contrast the coverage of the American press with that of the British press. In Britain the story was treated in a direct and forceful style. The *Daily Telegraph and Morning Post* made the Bund report a main news item on the principal inside news page. The boldface headline read

GERMANS MURDER 700,000
JEWS IN POLAND

TRAVELLING GAS CHAMBERS

An even greater number of papers responded to the June 29 press conference. The *London Times:*

MASSACRE OF JEWS—OVER 1,000,000 DEAD SINCE THE WAR
BEGAN

Daily Mail:

GREATEST POGROM—ONE MILLION JEWS DIE

Manchester Guardian:

JEWISH WAR VICTIMS
More than a Million Dead

Daily Telegraph:

MORE THAN 1,000,000 JEWS KILLED IN EUROPE

Even some Canadian papers carried extensive accounts and explicit headlines. The *Montreal Daily Star:*

"NAZI SLAUGHTERHOUSE"—GERMANS MASSACRE MILLION
JEWS IN EXTERMINATION DRIVE
Appalling Conditions Reported From
Hitler-Dominated Countries[10]

The American reaction was far more muted. Behaving in a way that would become almost a hallmark of American press treatment of news of Nazi mass murders, papers placed the various stories on inner pages and allotted them but a few lines. Consequently, readers were left free to accept this news as valid or to dismiss it as unverified information in which the paper had little faith. The latter conclusion would have been easy to draw from the way the *New York Times* described the Polish escapee from Vilna, as mentioned above, or its decision to relegate the Polish government in exile's June announcement to seventeen lines at the bottom of page 5. The easily missed article noted that 700,000 had been slain through a variety of methods, but completely ignored the revelation that this was part of a program of systematic slaughter. The news of the June 29 conference was placed in the lower half of page 7 and failed to mention that Silverman or Schwarzbart, both of whom were members of official governmental bodies—one British and one Polish—had been present at the conference. Instead the announcement of the death of 1 million was attributed to nameless "spokesmen for the World Jewish Congress."[11] The *Los Angeles Times* used an AP report that omitted most of the details and simply stated that the British Section of the World Jewish Congress estimated "that more than one million Jews have been killed or died as the result of ill treatment." The two-paragraph, thirteen-line article, printed on page 3, carried the following headline:

NAZIS KILL MILLION
JEWS, SAYS SURVEY

The *Atlanta Constitution* ran the same two-paragraph AP report under a headline indicating a little more faith in the story than the *Los Angeles Times*:

1,000,000 JEWS KILLED
BY NAZI TREATMENT

The *Miami Herald* placed the story on page 2 but allotted it only twelve lines. The *New York World Telegram* ran a twenty-three-line story on page 4 which mentioned neither Schwarzbart's nor Silverman's participation in the news conference. But it did note that the death toll resulted from the Nazis' long-standing pronouncement that "physical extermination of the Jew must from now on be the aim of Germany and her allies." According to this article the Poles had said that *probably* 700,000 Jews had been killed in Poland and Lithuania, 125,000 in Rumania, 200,000 in Russia and 100,000 in the rest of Europe.[12] A similarly ambivalent attitude was demonstrated by the *Chicago Tribune*, which placed the story on page 6 and allocated a total of eleven lines to it. No mention was made of Silverman, and the deaths were attributed to "ill treatment."[13]

We might ask—and perhaps readers at the time wondered too—why the editors placed news of this magnitude on the inner pages and accorded it so little space. If they believed the news, then it should have been given more attention, and if they did not believe, then why were the stories printed at all? Part of the explanation may be found in the headline which the *New York Journal American* placed over its page 1 eight-line article which neither mentioned an extermination "policy" nor provided any death tolls for the various countries involved:

JEWS LIST *THEIR* DEAD AT MILLION[14]

This was a *Jewish* story, worthy of reporting, but not worthy of complete trust because Jews were "interested parties."*

* Even Jews could not quite bring themselves to believe this news. *The Jewish Frontier,* upon hearing of the news of a Final Solution, printed a portion of the report in small type in its back pages. This was an action which Marie Syrkin, who was a member of the editorial board, subsequently described as

CBS radio, which had provided sparse coverage of the persecution of the Jews, included news of the press conference in its June 29 New York news broadcast. It was the first discussion of the Jews' situation on CBS radio since May 23, when John Daly reported on fear of forest fires in Norway, conscription of Poles by the Germans, Germany's conquest of Sweden, and then added that "the Nazi oppression has even been extended to Jews in Holland. And the Jews have been ordered to display the star of David on their clothing. And that's the world today." On the 29th of June, Quincy Howe informed CBS listeners that

> A horrifying reminder of what this war means to certain non-combatants comes from the World Jewish Congress in London today. It is now estimated that the Germans have massacred more than one million Jews in Europe since the war began. That's about one sixth of the Jewish population in the Old World. Moreover, those Jews who survive lead a subhuman existence on a fraction of the already short rations to which the rest of the population of Europe is reduced. The Jewish population of Germany has declined from 600,000 to 100,000 since Hitler took power. Sweden, Switzerland and Portugal are the only countries in continental Europe where Jews still possess human rights. In the Pacific war zones the Japanese suffered another defeat at American hands. . . .

Though this broadcast offered more information than most other reports, there was still no mention of a systematic extermination program.[16]

There were some exceptions to this general pattern. The *New York Herald Tribune* devoted significant attention to this story, placing an eighty-two-line article on page 1 and running a headline which both accurately reflected the contents of the article and made it clear that things could still get worse:

NAZI SLAUGHTER OF MILLION JEWS SO FAR CHARGED;
World Congress Leaders Tell London of Systematic
Massacre over Europe[17]

---

an "imbecility." Within a few weeks the editorial board's doubts had vanished and it published a black-bordered special issue of the magazine devoted wholly to the massacre of the Jews of Europe. Syrkin cites this as revealing the change in comprehension between summer and fall 1942.[15]

Though the story acknowledged that what was taking place was part of a systematic program, it failed to mention the gas chambers at Chelmno and reports of poisonous gas in use in other parts of Poland. These facts may still have been too fantastic for the editors to accept.

The *St. Louis Post Dispatch* placed the story of the Polish government in exile's June 26 announcement on the front page of its news section in the far-right column. This article, one of the more detailed to appear on the topic, was written by David M. Nichol, a reporter in London. He said estimates were that 700,000 Jews had already died: "disease and starvation are allowed to operate to the fullest extent. Where these methods are considered insufficient or slow, massacre tactics often are substituted, . . . sources say." Both the headline and the story itself stressed something that many other papers simply ignored: poison gas was being used to kill Jews. Though the article spoke of ninety being killed "at a time," the headline made it sound as if only ninety had been killed. Neither the article nor the headline mentioned that the report estimated that 1,000 people a day were dying in this fashion.

NAZIS REPORTED
KILLING POLISH
JEWS WITH GAS

90 Said to Have
Been Herded Into
Chamber for Mass
Execution.

Despite this lacuna the article treated the news in far greater detail than did most of the other major dailies. Nichol was unable to believe that this killing did not have some ulterior purpose, and he surmised that these gas chambers were being used "perhaps [for] testing lethal weapons which may sometime find more general use." It is significant that Nichol noted that the charges of killing with gas "find grim confirmation" in the reports which had emerged from the Reich regarding the euthanasia program for people "incurably ill or mentally defective."[18] By citing this precedent for murder by gas, the article may well have pierced readers' fog of disbelief and made the news more credible. At least it offered a historical precedent to those willing to accept it.

Over the next few days various stories appeared concerning the massacres. On July 2 a one-column article on page 6 of the *New York Times* discussed the Bund report's revelation that gas chambers were being used and that massacres were frequent. In addition to noting that 25,000 had been taken from Lublin and that "nothing has been heard of them since," it listed other slaughter sites:

> At Lwow 35,000 were slain, at Stanislawow, 15,000; at Tarnopol 5,000; at Zioctrow 2,000; at Brezanzany only 1,700 were left of 18,000. The massacre still continues in Lwow.

The article concluded by quoting what was probably the most ominous sentence in the report, "Whoever wins, all Jews will be murdered." Even though the paper strengthened the credibility of the report by observing that the information in it was "supported by information received by other Jewish circles here and also by the Polish Government," the *New York Times* felt obliged to include a disclaimer. Apparently not believing that 700,000 people could be massacred, it informed readers that this figure "probably includes many who died of maltreatment in concentration camps, of starvation in ghettos or of unbearable conditions of forced labor." The value the *Times* placed on this news was also evident in its decision to run the story of Governor Lehman's donation of his tennis shoes to the scrap rubber drive on the top of page 1 and the Bund report on page 6. Furthermore, the headline highlighted a relatively minor aspect of the story, namely that the Polish underground had called for retribution, and made it appear that this was the main thrust of the article.

ALLIES ARE URGED TO EXECUTE NAZIS

Report On Slaughter Of Jews In Poland
Asks Like Treatment for Germans

Curb on Reich Sought

'Only Way To Save Millions From Certain Destruction,'
Says the Appeal[19]

One week later, on July 9, the paper reported that according to the Polish underground 3 million Poles and Jews had become victims of the Nazis. Over 500,000 had been sent to Germany as forced labor, while 200,000 Poles and 300,000 Jews were "murdered outright" by the Nazis. This excluded those who died of "starvation and disease." The Vice Premier of the Polish government in exile "fully corroborated the information." Approximately three-quarters of the way down the 125-line article, brief mention was made of the fact that Poles had refused to accept certain governmental and administrative posts offered them by the Germans. Though this was a relatively minor aspect of the story, it was the point the *New York Times* featured in the headline:

POLES SPURN POSTS UNDER NAZI REGIME

Cooperation Bid Falls Upon Deaf Ears,
Document from Underground Leaders Says

ARDENT PLEA TO ALLIES

Report Read in London Puts Germany's Toll of Victims at
3,000,000 Mark

On July 23 the *New York Times* printed a small story regarding 120,000 Jews who had been sent to Poland, where 53,000 had been killed. Reference was also made to 17,000 Austrians who had been murdered since the war began. The headline ignored the 53,000.

Says Nazis Slew 17,000

Austrian-American League, Inc., Reports Toll Since Invasion

The *New York Times* may have placed the smaller more plausible number in the headline because it came from a non-Jewish source, while the 53,000 came from a Jewish source.[20] This was not the only time the paper behaved in this fashion. Many times during this period, whenever the *New York Times* reported the deaths of non-Jewish civilians, it paid them more attention than it did the deaths of Jews, even though the number of non-Jewish victims was far smaller. On May 5 a page 1 story reported on the shooting of seventy-two Dutch anti-Nazis. In an editorial the paper strongly decried their deaths along with those of fifty-five at Lille, France, and eighteen in Oslo. Two days later a page 7 story told of forty killed in France in retaliation for the derailment of a German train. On May 24 a page 5 headline proclaimed

NAZIS' EXECUTIONS PUT AT 97 IN WEEK

Eight days later the following headline appeared on page 4:

18 MORE CZECHS EXECUTED BY NAZIS

Charged with Link to Attack on Heydrich,
Who Is Said to Approach Crisis

Total Slain is Now 81
Two Families at Bruenn Are Reported Among the
44 Persons Killed Saturday[21]

When the paper printed the story on the BBC broadcast concerning the death of 700,000 Jews, it ran it at the end of a series of other short stories concerning Nazi atrocities. Among the stories which *preceded* the BBC report was the news of the shooting of five Poles for striking Germans and the slaying of 800 Czechs in punishment for the Nazi leader Reinhard Heydrich's murder. The figure of 800 is exceptional: rarely did these stories deal with more than a hundred deaths; often the toll was far less. Nonetheless they were accorded more space and prominence than much larger death tolls. It is possible that the *New York Times* believed the death of non-Jewish civilians, particularly in reprisal for "anti-Nazi" behavior, to be something new and different and therefore especially worthy of readers' attention, whereas the death of Jews was no longer a novel event.

There is yet another explanation which must be considered in the case of the *New York Times*. The paper, particularly during the period of the 1930s and 1940s, was anxious not to appear "too Jewish." As Gay Talese, who once worked for the paper, observed, "the *New York Times* does not wish to be thought of as a 'Jewish newspaper' . . . and [therefore] it will bend over backwards to prove this . . . forcing itself at times into unnatural positions, contorted by compromise." David Halberstam, in *The Powers That Be*, offers a similar analysis of the paper's behavior regarding Jews.*

---

* Though some of the correspondents who were stationed in Berlin believe that the *New York Times* was interested in news regarding the Jews, there is much evidence to support Talese, Halberstam, and Oswald Garrison Villard's (see page 155) argument. Certainly it did not want its editorial staff and management to appear "too Jewish." Halberstam, who worked for the paper, relates

The *New York Times* was—and in many quarters still is—considered America's "newspaper of record," and in a poll taken during the period, accredited Washington correspondents by a vote of more than five to one judged it to be the nation's most reliable, comprehensive, and fair paper. Had the *Times* reacted with less equanimity, it is possible that other American papers would have followed suit.[23]

There is also another explanation for the attention the *New York Times*, as well as some other papers, paid to the reports of the reprisal killing of non-Jews: source credibility in editors' eyes. The information regarding such killings generally came from official German sources. In mid-June 1942 the Germans announced that they had killed 480 civilians in Lidice, in reprisal for the murder of the Nazi leader Reinhard Heydrich, Deputy Reich Protector of Bohemia and Moravia. In a front-page story the *New York Times* described the Germans as having "blot[ted] out" the Bohemian village. This, the *New York Herald Tribune* observed, was not the product of the

> terrified imagination of a refugee or [the] invention of an angry propagandist. It is the official announcement of the Nazi radio. A foolish German emperor, in an oratorical indiscretion, once told his soldiers to act like Huns. This is the formal statement of a government that it has actually done so.[24]

A similar judgment about source credibility may have been

---

in *The Powers That Be* that when Rollo Ogden, the editorial-page editor, died in 1937, Arthur Krock assumed that he would be given the job. It was given instead to John Finley. When Krock went to Arthur Sulzberger, the publisher, to complain, he explained that "it's a Jewish paper and we have a number of Jewish reporters working for us. But in all the years I've been here we have never put a Jew in the showcase." When Krock explained that only his father had been Jewish and therefore, according to Jewish law, he was not a Jew, Sulzberger responded, "Arthur, how do you know all that if you aren't Jewish?" When Krock became head of the paper's Washington bureau, he himself was known as someone who did not want Jewish reporters assigned to him. When one of his friends at the paper told him that given his record at the bureau some people thought he was an antisemite, Krock replied, "Maybe I am." Sulzberger was part of a group of Jewish leaders who went to Roosevelt in 1939 to try to persuade him *not* to appoint Felix Frankfurter to the Supreme Court because it might generate antisemitism. Given Sulzberger's aversion to Jewish editors and executives and desire that the paper not sound "too Jewish", it is quite logical to argue that the paper's treatment of this news was influenced, at least in part, by the fact that it concerned Jews.[22]

what led the *Chicago Tribune* to allot a front-page banner headline to the murder of 258 Jews by the SS but to relegate the news of the death of 1 million to eleven lines in the bottom half of page 6. The front-page headline, which stretched across most of the upper half of the page, read:

HITLER GUARDS STAGE NEW POGROM; KILL 258;
MASSACRED BY BERLIN GESTAPO IN 'BOMB PLOT';
Families Herded for Deportation.

Although the story was not the formal statement of a government, it came from "various trustworthy sources" in Berlin who had access to officials in the SS and the Propaganda Ministry. Two days later the *Chicago Daily Tribune* devoted nine lines on the lower half of page 6 to the report by the Federation of Jewish Relief Organizations that 25,000 Latvian Jews had been slain during the German invasion the previous summer. *This* news came not from the perpetrators or other "trustworthy" sources, but from the victims. Consequently it was less credible. The *New York Times* also ran the story of the execution of the 258 on page 1. Two days later it placed the report of the massacre of thousands in Vilna on page 6. It put the story of the BBC report on the death of 700,000 Jews on page 5 at the end of a string of other short articles concerning a variety of war matters.[25]

In addition to its being the word of the perpetrators, there is yet another explanation for why news released by the Germans was treated as more credible than news released by the Jews or by the Polish government in exile. The number of victims, while not small, was entirely within the realm of "reason." In contrast, the tolls given by Polish and Jewish organizations could be dismissed as too immense to be plausible. A million was a hard number to fathom, particularly a million victims not killed in the line of duty, but slaughtered in cold blood. A toll of 258 or even 800, while certainly tragic, was within most people's grasp. These were numbers with which they were conversant. Ironically, the larger the proportions of the tragedy, the less believable the story became.

Incidentally, in the case of the story of the 258, the accusations of the perpetrators were greeted with skepticism. *New York Times* reporter George Axelson, who cabled this story from Stockholm, did not doubt that 258 Jews "were put to death by the S.S."

However, he questioned the Nazi claim that the victims had planted bombs on the premises of an anti-Bolshevist exhibit because it seemed impossible that Jews who had to wear "the conspicuous Star of David on their clothing and are ruled off *Unter den Linden* and streets of central Berlin generally" could have obtained the bombs and then successfully placed them in the exhibit. Despite the Gestapo's claims to have "unquestionable proof," Axelson was skeptical, particularly because the five bombs were discovered prior to being detonated.[26]

The pattern of subdued, almost repressed treatment of much of the news of the Final Solution continued even as the pace and scope of the news increased. At the end of July, news of the plans to wipe out the Warsaw ghetto reached the west. In light of the previous reports of mass murder there was good reason to believe that the 600,000 Jews in Warsaw were about to face a fate similar to what had befallen the Jews of Vilna, Lvov, Latvia, eastern Galicia, and other parts of Poland and Russia. In the *New York Times* a UP release carried the following headline:

YUGOSLAVS DRIVING
AXIS FROM BOSNIA

Guerrillas Rout Italians and
Cause State of Siege in
Zagreb, London Hears

New Warsaw Curbs Due

Nazis Said to Plan Wiping Out
of 600,000 in Ghetto—17
Condemned in Bulgaria

Not only did readers have to reach the final section of this rather lengthy headline to find reference to the news of the fate which awaited the inhabitants of the ghetto, but they had to read through to the 79th line of a 121-line story to learn that the "Nazi authorities in Poland are planning to 'exterminate' the entire Warsaw ghetto whose population is estimated at 600,000 Jews." Although the report of the "despair and suicides [which] had swept the Warsaw ghetto" when the new deportations from the ghetto began was attributed to "reliable reports from the Continent," it was placed on page 7 as part of an array of other stories regarding the war. The page placement and the juxtaposition of the threat to 600,000 with the condemnation of 17 seemed to reflect this continued ambivalence about both the importance and the reliability of the news.[27]

The *Toronto Globe* adopted a markedly different approach. It ran the story on the Warsaw ghetto as a separate news story with the following headline:

GESTAPO PLANS TO EXTERMINATE ALL JEWS IN WARSAW GHETTO

According to Polish spokesmen quoted in the article, "two train loads of Jews have departed toward their doom without anything further being heard from them."[28] *Newsweek,* which ignored the Polish government in exile announcement but ran the story on the deportations from the ghetto, followed suit. According to the magazine Jews were now being taken from the Warsaw ghetto and relocated "600 miles farther east." Instead of speculating about what "relocation" might really mean, it simply noted that "two trainloads of Jews had already vanished into black Limbo."[29] The British-based news agency Reuters was far more explicit regarding the "passengers" destination. "Two trainloads have left. It is feared that when they arrive they will be murdered." Then, as if to further validate these fears, the Reuters dispatch went on to state that "near Lodzimieres in Eastern Poland there is a common grave, a mile long, of thousands of massacred Jews."[30]

Over the course of July and August additional such stories appeared in the press. Most of the major American dailies handled them in a similar way, showing remarkable restraint, given the nature of the news. It was almost never on the front page. Commonly found on pages 3 through 10, often it was allotted a few lines, and rarely was it given a bold headline. On July 26, a month after the announcement by the Polish government in exile that "deportation" to the east meant death for Jews, the *Chicago Tribune* reported that the Nazis would shortly begin deporting all Dutch Jews between the ages of eighteen and forty. This story ran on page 9. In late July the Polish government in exile released details concerning the execution of 200,000 Jews and a quarter of a million Poles. The *New York World Telegram* story on the announcement omitted mention of Jews as victims and was placed on page 22 next to an article about a doctor who hypnotized himself into making a parachute jump. The two articles were accorded exactly the same amount of space.[31]

Sometimes the press was so restrained that it simply ignored the Jews' fate. A *Los Angeles Times* editorial in August discussed the condition of the civilian population in occupied countries. It cited UP estimates that the total number of civilian victims was 400,000 and the number of "hostages" in the millions. No mention was made of the Jews and what was happening to them. Even when it reported on the "Stop Hitler" rallies held in several United States cities during the summer, much of the press ignored the fact that they were, in the words of the organizers, a protest against the "extermination of Jews. . . . [by] forced labor, in concentration camps or as victims of experiment in poison gas factories." Instead the rallies were described in nonspecific terms, e.g., as "rallies to protest against the barbaric treatment that is the lot of oppressed people in Nazi occupied countries." Often no mention was made of Jews, gas chambers, or a program for mass murder. The *New York Herald Tribune* covered the New York rally in a way that almost totally obscured its objective. It virtually ignored that the rally had been called because of events in Europe. Both the headline and the article focused on the fact that Governor Lehman was "hissed" when he spoke out against a separate Jewish army.* CBS, NBC, and Mutual radio broadcasts failed to cover the gatherings.[32]

Given the press ambivalence about the news, it is not surprising that there was little discussion of whether anything might be done to prevent further deaths. But during this particular period serious discussion of rescue had to face another obstacle as well. There was a common perception that the Allies were "not winning the war." Editorials, news stories, and columns bemoaned the dire military situation. The *Christian Science Monitor* complained that it was so precarious that Allied officials were "withholding bad news." Walter Lippmann decried the "cult of incompetence" that characterized Allied war efforts. The gravity of the situation was reinforced by setbacks in Russia, North Africa, and the Pacific. News of deportations from France and massacres and the death

---

* Jewish groups, particularly those which were Zionist in orientation wanted to establish a Jewish unit that would be under Allied command. The British strongly opposed the idea because they feared that the existence of such a force would be used to further the drive for a Jewish state.

of multitudes in Eastern Europe had to compete with headlines proclaiming

NAZIS SMASH AT MOSCOW
Russ Retreat All Along Line

The Germans were pushing toward the Caucusus; Stalingrad was on the verge of collapse. The German advance into Russia seemed unstoppable. Western Europe was firmly in Nazi control. The North African coast was in German hands. The Japanese were winning key Pacific battles. American military installations at Guadalcanal were under heavy bombardment. In late September a *Los Angeles Times* front-page headline proclaimed

WAR DECLARED BEING LOST[33]

Even those optimists who believed victory would come eventually had to acknowledge that a long pitched battle lay ahead.[34] Anyone who might have argued for rescue of Jews found the moral imperative of the argument significantly vitiated by the military situation. Thus those who could not or did not want to believe discounted the news as implausible, while those who believed and wanted concerted rescue efforts could not demand them when the military prognosis seemed so bleak.

Rationalizing the Deportations

As we have seen, ever since the Nazis had begun to persecute Jews, the American press had felt compelled to offer rational explanations of the events to its readers. It continued to do so even as the news of massacres and deportations reached the west. This inclination to find a rational explanation was so compelling that at times the press accepted information released by the Nazis—designed to camouflage the Final Solution—at face value. Deportations, the Nazis announced and the press reported, were necessary in order to provide homes for "bombed out Aryans." The denial of the right of Jews to emigrate was explained by Nazis and the press as due to the Reich's labor shortage.[35] On certain occasions when the Nazis made their intentions clear, the press refused to accept the implications of what was being said because it seemed too fantastic to believe. When Goebbels announced that the "Jews had started the war" and would "pay for every dead soldier," the *Chicago Tribune* responded by explaining that the deportations and persecution were "nothing but" a means of giving Germans who had lost fathers and sons in Russia and were "facing the privations of another war winter the spectacle of a few unfortunate people whose sufferings make their own seem bearable by comparison."[36] The *Springfield* (Ohio) *News Sun* also believed that the persecution of the Jews was a diversion aimed at keeping

> the German people from overmuch brooding on the hardships imposed by an order holding guns preferable to butter. Except some scapegoat were offered they might have put the blame for low living standards where it belonged. Nazi propagandists nominated the Jew.

Because the blitzkrieg had bogged down as the German assault on Russia was stalled, the Nazis intensified the drive against their "helpless old scapegoat, the Jews."[37]

American newspaper readers were told that Jews were being deported to the Ukraine to serve in work battalions and help with the harvesting of crops, that Jews in France, Belgium, and Holland were being deported because they had been "conscripted for work in Germany," and that the deportations were taking place because "some Jews tried to escape into neighboring countries." When 27,000 Jews in France were "rounded up" and sent to concentration camps at the end of July 1942, AP interpreted the move as a measure to increase "pressure on the French to supply the Nazi war industry with more skilled workers."[38] Even the *Manchester Guardian,* which had resolutely publicized the fate of European Jewry since the Nazi rise to power, fell prey to rationalizing. In late August 1942, two months after the release of the Polish government in exile report, the paper observed in an editorial that "the deportation of Jews to Poland means that Jews' muscles are needed for the German war effort."[39]

That there was a tendency during the initial years of the war to explain the deportations in this fashion is understandable; it was logical to do so. As has been pointed out, it was difficult to comprehend that antisemitism was not a means to an end, but an end in itself. It is harder to condone the continuation of this tendency to rationalize once word of the Final Solution was released. In August 1942 an article in the *Christian Science Monitor* on the deportations of Jews from France, Berlin, Finland, Slovakia, and Croatia acknowledged that Jews were being killed. In fact it considered it impossible to "escape the conviction that the Nazis are endeavoring to exterminate the Jews of Europe in the shortest possible time." The situation was more "desperate now than it had ever been." But then the paper went on to explain *why* this was happening. Not only did the Germans need a "scapegoat to justify the increased demands that are being made on the German people," but they wanted to isolate Jews from the invading Allied armies. The Germans feared that the Jews would be "a dangerous partisan threat" when the time came for the Allied attack and would rush to the Allies' aid.[40] Similarly, the London-based *Economist* hypothesized that Himmler may have feared the "enormous influence which the ghettoes could exercise upon the whole Polish underground movement at a moment critical for the Germans," and therefore decided to "apply more drastic measures. . . . [in the form of] the mass murder of tens of thousands."[41] UP explained that the Germans had deported millions of Jews and others in order to rid "potentially troublesome areas [of] . . . potential leaders and paralyze further resistance," to "weaken the help available to an Allied second front army," and to "provide slave labor for Nazi war factories and for construction gangs on fortifications."[42] This kind of explanation turned the murdering of Jews into a tactical imperative.

Of course the press was not alone in its failure to accept what was truly underway. Government officials and a great portion of the American public shared its doubts. When reports of a plan to massacre Jews reached Allied hands, some British officials dismissed them as "sob stuff." They argued that the reports of mass murder were exaggerated by Jews "who have spoilt their case by laying it on too thick for years."[43]

As the months passed and the deportations continued, press reports did not question the fact that to be a Jew in Nazi-occupied Europe was to live under the shadow of death. Typically, Paul Ghali, writing in the *St. Louis Post Dispatch,* described the conflict raging in Switzerland over the policy of expelling Jewish refugees who had crossed the border illegally. To Ghali, as well as the other reporters stationed in neutral countries in Europe, it was obvious that "turning back these refugees . . . will probably mean their death" *because of the conditions they would face.* Similarly, in an editorial on August 29, the *New York Times* condemned the deportation of 25,000 Jews from France. The paper described them as "serfs, destined to hard labor and the scantiest food and shelter after they have been deported to eastern Europe," but the editorial made no mention of another fate they were destined to face: murder.[44] There was no doubt that being a Jew meant living in conditions of disease, starvation, hard labor, all of which resulted in premature death. But what the press could not see or acknowledge was that Jews were now dying by the hundreds of thousands as the result of a policy more calculated and terrible in breadth and precision. And long after the Final Solution had been repeatedly confirmed and verified, explanations—sometimes of the most macabre sort—were being offered. Some of these explanations came from German sources, others from the Allies themselves. In February 1944 a number of papers reported the Dutch government's claim that Dutch Jews had been killed "so that more food will be available for Germans." In July of that year the *New York Times* related suspicions among the Allies "that the wholesale killing of Jews is just another Nazi method of opening peace negotiations."[45]

There were, of course, papers which understood the Nazis' motivations and were able to make the leap of imagination necessary in order to understand what was happening. In August 1942, when both the *Christian Science Monitor* and the *Economist* were offering tactical reasons to explain why the Nazis were killing Jews, a *London Times* editorial noted that while much of the uprooting of populations could be explained as German desire to denude "troublesome areas of most of their menfolk [and] . . . potential leaders" in order to "paralyze resistance," this was not what was happening to the Jews. When 20,000 Jews were deported from France, "strategic considerations [could] scarcely be involved." Those transfers had no military rationale but were proof of the "Nazi determination to purge western Europe of all its Jews." Most important, the paper recognized something which much of the American press would never really grasp:

> Hitler had always treated the complete segregation, if not extermination, of the Jews as the foundation of the "new order."[46]

The treatment in the American press of the news of dire conditions facing European Jewry—the fact that the press did not ignore the reports of deportations and even death but devoted little prominent space to them and often added disclaimers and qualifiers—reflected the chasm that existed between information and knowledge. It was a chasm that many editors and journalists would not be able to bridge until well after the Final Solution had reached its end.[47]

Allied Confirmation

Two weeks before the end of 1942 the Allied governments themselves confirmed the existence of a program for the annihilation of European Jewry. Nonetheless, press treatment of it did not substantially change. There was a momentary flurry of interest which rapidly faded. Allied confirmation was preceded, in late November and December of 1942, by important revelations that, as usual, were often greeted guardedly by editors and generally confined to the inner recesses of most papers.

Late in November 1942 Rabbi Stephen S. Wise, in his capacity as chairman of the World Jewish Congress, announced that 2 million Jews in occupied Europe had been slain in an "extermination campaign." According to Wise, Hitler had ordered the murder of all Jews in Nazi-ruled Europe; the Jewish population of Warsaw had been reduced from a half million to 100,000; 80 percent of the Jews in Europe had been transferred to Poland, where they were destined for death, and the Nazis were using their corpses for "war vital commodities as soap fats and fertilizers." Wise, anxious to allay any doubts about the reliability of his announcements, stressed that his sources had been "confirmed by the State Department." In addition to State Department confirmation, Wise said that a representative of the President had returned from Europe to tell Wise that the "worst you have thought is true."*

The press's handling of Wise's announcement provides some important insights into its treatment of the news of the Final

---

* Some of this information of Wise's, such as that corpses were being used for soap fats, was incorrect, as were his claims that the Nazis were killing their victims by injecting air bubbles into their veins. In this fashion one Nazi physician could supposedly "handle more than 100 men an hour." Actually a far more efficient method was already in use: lethal gas. His figures on the number dead were also far too low. Wise's information came from the report which was sent from Geneva by the World Jewish Congress representative there, Gerhard Riegner.[48]

Solution. Some of the major dailies—including the *Dallas News, Denver Post, Miami Herald, New York Herald Tribune, Los Angeles Examiner,* and *St. Louis Post Dispatch*—ran news of Wise's announcement on their front pages. Most, however, placed it on their inside pages. The *Los Angeles Times* carried it on page 2, the *San Francisco Examiner* on page 5, the *New York Journal American, New York World Telegram,* and *Baltimore Sun* on page 3, the *Chicago Tribune* on page 4, the *Washington Post* on page 6, the *Christian Science Monitor* on page 7, and the *New York Times* on page 10. The *Atlanta Constitution* put it on page 20 with the want ads and the train schedules, while the *Kansas City Star* and the *New Orleans Times Picayune* did not carry it at all. CBS, NBC, and Mutual radio broadcasts also ignored Wise's announcement.[49]

Despite Wise's contention that the State Department and the White House had authenticated his information, most major papers treated this as a story released by a Jewish source and an interested party. It was the "outcry of the victims themselves," an *ex parte* statement and consequently less trustworthy than those that came from disinterested parties.[50] Even the Jewish Agency, the official representative of the Palestinian Jewish community, considered non-Jewish eyewitnesses more credible than Jewish ones. In 1943 the Jewish Agency's Geneva office relayed to the State Department information it had received concerning the deportation and murder of the Jews from two people whom it pointedly described as "reliable eye-witnesses (*Aryans*)."[51]

The AP wire service report on Wise's announcement, which was used by most of the dailies, was skeptical about Wise's claims to have State Department confirmation. Wise was described as "*asserting* that he was authorized to disclose details by the State Department," recounting "atrocities which he *claimed* had been confirmed," and telling a story which was "*reportedly* confirmed" by the State Department. The headlines accompanying the article in most major dailies naturally adopted a similar approach. Wise was identified as the source, and the State Department's role was virtually ignored. The *Chicago Tribune:*

2 Million Jews Slain by Nazis, Dr. Wise Avers

Washington Post:

2 Million Jews Slain, Rabbi Wise Asserts

New York Herald Tribune:

> Wise Says Hitler Has Ordered 4,000,000 Jews Slain in 1942

Baltimore Sun:

> Jewish Extermination Drive Laid to Hitler by Dr. Wise

New York Journal American:

> Wise to Reveal Nazis' Program to Kill Jews

Los Angeles Examiner:

> Two Million Jews Slain, Wise Says[52]

The *New York Times* was one of the few major papers whose headline not only referred to the State Department but treated Wise's assertions with a degree of certitude:

> Wise Gets Confirmations
> ———————————
> Checks with State Department On Nazis' "Extermination Campaign"

Though the *Times* headline mentioned the State Department, the story was run on page 10 as an addendum to an article on the murder of 250,000 Polish Jews—an article based on information released by the Polish government in exile in London. The New York daily *PM*, which had a distinctively liberal editorial policy and was in the forefront of the few papers and journals calling for an activist rescue policy, ran a headline and a series of stories which contrasted sharply with those of other papers. The cover of the paper, which related what news was to be found on the inner pages, carried the following headline in boldface print:

> HITLER SPEEDS UP MURDER OF JEWS

Inside the headline read

> HITLER ORDERS MURDER OF ALL EUROPE'S JEWS

On the following day *PM* carried stories based on State Department documents which Wise released to the press:

This is Fascism: How Nazis
Slaughtered 24,000 Jews in Latvia[53]

Throughout this period *PM* publicized this news directly and forcefully. Its handling of these reports contrasted markedly with that of most other dailies.

The State Department, in a series of off-the-record conversations with press representatives, had distanced itself from Wise. In response to queries as to whether it had confirmed the information, all that J. McDermot, chief of the State Department's Division of Current Information, would say was that Rabbi Wise had visited the Department "in connection with certain material in which he was interested" and he was given this material. Even this was told to the press "in confidence and not for publication." According to McDermot, the only thing the Department had done was "facilitate the efforts of [Wise's] Committee in getting at the truth." He would neither confirm information nor answer any questions on the matter. Instead correspondents were directed to pose "all questions concerning this material to Rabbi Wise."[54] R. Borden Reams, who was in charge of Jewish affairs for the European Division of the State Department, pressured Wise, though unsuccessfully, to "avoid any implications" that the State Department was the source of "documentary proof of these stories."[55] It is not surprising, therefore, that the AP dispatch and the various headlines reflected some ambiguity.

Yet while the State Department's attitude and the fact that Wise was an interested party may have prompted the press to treat his statements in a circumspect fashion, the press often failed to highlight news from other sources. At the same time that Wise made his announcement, the Polish government in exile informed the press that the Nazis had ordered the extermination of half the Jews of Poland by the end of the year and that Jews were being rounded up and either massacred on the spot by an SS "special battalion" characterized by its "utter ruthlessness and inhumanity" or transported to "special camps at Treblinka, Belzec and Sobibor" where the "so-called settlers are mass-murdered." The *New York Journal American* carried this story on page 2; the *Washington Post* placed it on page 6 and the *New York Times* on page 10. The next day Ignacy Schwarzbart amplified this report and said that a million Jews had already been killed. The *New York Times* headline was graphic:

SLAIN POLISH JEWS PUT AT A MILLION

One-third of Number in Whole Country Said to Have Been Put to Death by Nazis,

Abattoir for Deportees

Mass Electrocutions, Killing by Injection of Air Bubbles Described in Reports

The story described Poland as "a mass grave." Jews from all over Europe were being transported to the Warsaw ghetto, where they were separated into two groups, "able bodied young and [the rest] . . . who are dispatched eastward to meet sure death." The article, which included a country-by-country delineation of the Jewish population prior to September 1939 and the population as of the end of 1942, appeared on page 16 next to a report on a truckload of coffee which had been hijacked in New Jersey.[56]

On the 26th of November Jewish leaders announced that an international day of mourning would be held and Jews the world over would join in prayer, mourning, and fasting. One of the objectives of the day was to "win the support of the Christian world so that its leaders may intervene and protest the horrible treatment of Jews in Hitler's Europe." The *Washington Post* placed the announcement regarding the day of mourning on the comic page next to a column on contract bridge. The day of mourning itself, however, received fairly sustained coverage in most newspapers.[57] The day also prompted editorial comment in the *Atlanta Constitution, Los Angeles Times,* and *New York Times.* The *New York Times* observed that the "homicidal mania of the Nazis has reached its peak, according to evidence in the hands of the State Department."[58] But no daily even considered whether any action was feasible.

Although the press may have had its doubts about some of Wise's claims, no paper or journal attacked Wise as did *The Christian Century.* It described his accusations as "unpleasantly reminiscent of the 'cadaver factory' lie which was one of the propaganda triumphs of the First World War" and wondered, even if Wise's reports were true, "whether any good purpose" was served by making such announcements. Two weeks later, when the Allied governments confirmed the existence of a program for the systematic annihilation of European Jewry, *The Christian Century* did not acknowledge that it had attacked Wise unfairly and that the Allies were now confirming exactly that which it had previously denounced Wise for making public. Its editorial on the declaration essentially ignored the tragedy and instead praised the "calm tone" of the pronouncement, which demonstrated a "cold determination not to expend in vain outcry one unit of emotional energy." According to *The Christian Century,* the right response was "a few straight words to say that it has been entered in the books, and then redoubled action on the . . . fronts." Even after the Allied statement corroborated Wise's announcement, *The Christian Century* still claimed that the State Department "did not support Dr. Wise's contention."[59]

The Christian Century's ambivalent response to Jewish suffering continued over the next two years. On a number of occasions in 1943 it unequivocally condemned the Nazis for murdering the Jews and even justified action at the time of the April 1943 Bermuda conference on rescuing refugees to "press . . . home on the British, American and Russian governments [the] demand that something shall be done." In September 1943 it observed that European Jewry was in a "desperate plight." But a year later, in September 1944, in spite of the fact that it had acknowledged the mass murders and that the Allies had done so as well, *The Christian Century* cited the reports of the "alleged killing" at a camp near Lublin of "1,500,000 persons" and pointed out that the "parallel between this story and the 'corpse factory' atrocity tale of the First World War is too striking to be overlooked." On another occasion an article attacked the motives and tactics of some of those who called for concerted action on behalf of the Jews.[60]

On December 8, 1942, a delegation of Jewish leaders went to the White House to present the President with a memorandum on the massacres and murders of European Jews. When they left the meeting, Wise, speaking for the group, said that the President was "shocked" at the revelations. There really was no reason for shock. The President had been informed of the massacres on a number of different occasions and had sent a message about them to a meeting held earlier that year in Madison Square Garden. It is possible that Wise used the term "shock" to connote outrage and not surprise. Consequently, Wise's statement to the press may have misrepresented what occurred at the meeting. According to the notes taken by one of the participants, Roosevelt did not express shock or surprise, but rather acknowledged that the

> government of the United States is very well acquainted with most of the facts you are now bringing to our attention. Unfortunately we have received confirmation from many sources. Representatives of the United States government in Switzerland and other neutral countries have given us proof that confirms the horrors discussed by you.[61]

AP's description of the twenty-page summary report Wise's group gave the President also conveyed the impression that this was a revelation for Roosevelt. The report was described as having "revealed for the first time that Hitler has officially ordered that all Jews in central Europe be 'annihilated' by the end of this year." Press coverage of the meeting with Roosevelt was not extensive. For example, the *New York Times* placed it on page 20—news about the President usually appeared in a far more prominent place—but did mention that 2 million had died and 5 million more faced extinction. *PM*, differing again from other papers, reprinted the report which the delegation gave to the President.[62]

Then, on December 17, the eleven Allied nations simultaneously issued their confirmation and condemnation of Hitler's "bestial policy of cold blooded extermination." This statement was the official imprimatur that had been awaited. Yet while the *New York Times* finally found something on this topic worthy of page 1—this was the only Holocaust-related story to appear on page 1 of the *Times* during the critical period of June through December 1942—in many other papers this statement received even less attention than had been given Wise's announcement. The *San Francisco Examiner* put it on page 3 and the *Los Angeles Times* on page 4. The *Washington Post* relegated it to page 10, the *Los Angeles Examiner* to page 16, the *New York Herald Tribune* to page 17, the *New York World Telegram* to page 28. The *St. Louis Post Dispatch* put this story next to the picture of a local woman who had just returned from fourteen months of service as an army nurse in Alaska. The *Atlanta Constitution* put the story in the lower half of page 2 and only allocated three paragraphs to it, focusing primarily on how punishment would be meted out "not later than the end of the war."[63]

Two days later the London-based Inter-Allied Information Committee released a report describing the German persecution of the Jews as "horror which numbs the mind" and calling Poland "one vast center for murdering Jews by mass shootings, electrocutions and lethal gas poisoning." The press covered this story in the same restrained fashion it had adhered to since Wise's November announcement. Once again the same pattern of page placement was evident. The *Los Angeles Times* put the story on page 2, the *Washington Post* on page 8, the *St. Louis Post Dispatch* on page 9, the *Los Angeles Examiner* on page 22, the *New York Times* on page 23, and the *New York Herald Tribune* on page 30. The *Chicago Tribune,* which used a headline saying that Poland had become a "Jewish abattoir," put the story on page 18 next to a marriage announcement. Even now that it was clear that "deportation to the east" meant murder, the news did not evoke any more interest or excitement than it had before, when it might have meant only relocation. A few days after the Inter-Allied report, the *Chicago Tribune* placed news of Dutch Jews getting "ready for deportation" to the camp at Westerbrook from which they were to be "deported to eastern Europe" on page 7 next to the weather forecast.[64]

By the time *Newsweek* referred to the Allied announcement, ten days after it had been made, it had been reduced to an item of little importance. The magazine briefly mentioned the Allied statement at the end of a page 46 article on the deportation of Oslo's 1,300 Jews, whom it described as a segment of the 2 million who had been deported and killed, "according to some Jewish sources." Despite the Allied confirmation, for *Newsweek* news of the Final Solution was still a *Jewish* story: not only was it about Jews, but it was news that came primarily from Jews. *Time's* reference to the Allied statement was also brief. With but a few exceptions most major magazines did not even mention the Allied declaration. In February 1943 *American Mercury* published an article by Ben Hecht entitled "The Extermination of the Jews." In specific and detailed language he described how the Nazis were murdering Jews. That same month *Reader's Digest* published a condensation of Hecht's article.[65]

Edward R. Murrow was one of the few journalists who acknowledged the transformation in thinking about the European situation necessitated by the information released since the end of November. On December 13, five days *before* the Allied declaration, he summed up the change on a CBS broadcast.

What is happening is this: Millions of human beings, most of
them Jews, are being gathered up with ruthless efficiency and
murdered. . . . The phrase "concentration camps" is obsolete,
as out of date as "economic sanctions" or "nonrecognition."
It is now possible to speak only of extermination camps.[66]

Another exception was the *Christian Science Monitor,* which once
again adopted a uniquely balanced approach. First, it dismissed
any suggestions that stories of the "slaughtering of 'non-Aryans'
. . . [were] simply a convenient substitute for the atrocity stories
of World War One." The stories were coming from "too many
sources and too continuously" to be called atrocity stories. But
then it expressed concern that in the aftermath of the war the
"peoples that the Nazis have so cruelly wronged" would take
out their wrath on Germans who were "innocent of anything worse
than passivity under Nazism."[67] It seemed to be a strange time
and place—particularly since no victory was in the offing—to worry
that Jews and other persecuted people would engage in a vendetta
against the Germans.

Old News

Between Wise's initial announcement and the Allied confirmation
three weeks later, reports of a murder program had come from
Polish leaders, church leaders in England, members of Parliament,
the British press, and Jews from Palestine who had been released
by the Germans in a prisoner exchange. Jewish leaders had visited
Roosevelt. A nationwide day of mourning had been held. The
Archbishop of Canterbury had called for rescue action. Yet as
is the case with most "shocking" news, the impact of these revelations was temporary.

Even before the Allied announcement an editorial in the *Atlanta
Constitution* explained the public's muted reaction to revelations
such as those made by Wise regarding the massacre of the Jews.
It had simply "gotten used to . . . the atrocities. . . . [Therefore]
horrors which blanched the cheek a few years ago are today accepted with a passing word of sympathy." The *Atlanta Constitution*
demonstrated the truth of its words in its own treatment of the
news. The December 17 announcement, though on page 2, was
brief and denuded of detail on the killings or the death toll up
to that point. On December 28 it put Wise's call to the Allies

to "implement their protest with action" on the lower half of page 16, the obituary page.[68]

What the press failed to acknowledge was that this news was different. While the news of the Jews' persecution was a decade old and the news that thousands of Jews and non-Jews were subjected to inhumane conditions was almost three years old, the fact that the Jews were being *systematically* annihilated—or, as one British journal put it, "in plain English put to death"—was a revelation. The *London Times* stressed this point. Though many of the individual pieces of information had already been known for quite a while, only when they were "accumulated from all the occupied countries . . . [was] the plan seen as a whole."[69]

The American press's treatment of this news was strangely cyclical. It had long thought of the story as unconfirmed rumor or the pleading of special interests. Therefore it reported the news but maintained a skeptical disinterest and treated the information in a circumspect fashion. One of the ways it did so was by relegating it to obscure corners of the paper. Then, once the news—all of it together—was confirmed, the press treated it as an old story, news it had, in the words of the *Atlanta Constitution,* "gotten used to" and "merely something to be expected from Nazidom."

The British Response

It is instructive once again to contrast the British reaction with the American one. The news of a Nazi program to annihilate the Jews had a profound impact in Britain, which was beset, according to the Archbishop of Canterbury, by a "burning indignation." Religious and political leaders repeatedly spoke out during this period and refused to let the matter rest. This reaction was the result, in part, of the way the British press treated the topic. On December 4 the *London Times,* the flagship of the British press and a paper which eschewed fanfare, published an article with a direct and chilling headline:

NAZI WAR ON JEWS

DELIBERATE PLAN FOR EXTERMINATION

In it the paper cited "evidence from Berlin and from Poland itself" which gave the "bleakest possible picture." It left "no doubt that the German authorities are dealing with Polish Jews more drastically and more savagely than ever before." According to the article, London had known for several weeks that "the worst of Hitler's threats was being literally applied." There were no disclaimers or riders. The *London Times* article elicited a prompt call from the Archbishop of Canterbury for immediate action. He argued in a letter to the paper that at the very least Britain "might offer to receive here any Jews who are able to escape the clutches of the Nazis."[70]*

On the same day that the Archbishop's letter appeared in the *Times,* the *Manchester Guardian* urged the Allies to issue a joint statement "putting on record their knowledge, and the proofs, of this annihilation policy" and formally indicating that these were "war crimes for which retribution will most surely be exacted." For the next few weeks the British press, led by these two prominent papers, kept a spotlight on the issue and demanded that something be done. The *Manchester Guardian* also called on Britain to "lend all aid to the rescue of such Jews as somehow get away." On December 8 it argued that it was incumbent on the Allies to "find ways to do more than mourn." The *Guardian* recommended that the BBC spread the facts and that a program to aid escaping refugees be established. Two days later the *Guardian* reiterated its call for "practical steps" to be taken in response to the "massacre of the Jews." It urged that a United Nations conference be convened and that a policy to help Jews reach neutral countries be instituted. Other British papers repeated this demand for action. On December 7 the *Times* described the terror being inflicted on Jews as a "European pogrom" which had been "carefully prepared." It had become apparent to the *London Times* that for many Jews "transportation means death."[72]

British officials soon began to react to this public discussion of the tragedy occurring in Europe. On the following day the British Foreign Secretary, Anthony Eden, sent a draft resolution to American Ambassador John Winant and reminded him that

---

* The reason why commanding religious and political personalities in the United Kingdom reacted in such a profound manner is something that remains to be analyzed. The British were aware of the "striking difference between the intensive propaganda campaign regarding Hitler's Jewish victims carried on here and the apparently negligible publicity in the United States."[71]

there was in England "growing public interest in this question and it is therefore desirable to make our attitude known at the earliest possible moment." The *London Times* article was considered noteworthy enough by Winant to be included in a telegram he sent to the Secretary of State on December 7.[73] On December 12 the *London Times,* even while acknowledging that a "prerequisite of real help is victory," urged that concern be "not so much with retribution as with aid." At the same time that the American press was still treating this news with faint skepticism and equanimity, if not lassitude, the British press had no doubts that it was true and that action was both necessary and possible.[74]

During December the British press "call for action" was echoed by religious and political leaders as well as members of Parliament from all parties. The Bishop of Chichester, one of the most influential Anglican Church leaders, urged that a rescue program be adopted and all steps be taken to grant Jews "temporary refuge."[75] The Archbishop of York spoke in the House of Lords on the "appalling outrages" against Jews in Poland and called for retribution against those who are "ordering these massacres" and against the "thousands of underlings who appear to be joyfully and gladly carrying out these crimes." The *London Times* believed the Archbishop to have given expression to the "immediate feeling that must be uppermost in every heart."[76]

While this sentiment may have been uppermost in the hearts of many—though certainly not every heart—in London, the same could not be said of the United States and particularly of its press. The American press may have been as horrified as the British press—though in view of its treatment of the news this does not seem likely—but unlike its counterparts on the other side of the Atlantic it accepted, almost without question, the official claim that rescue could only come with victory. During the month of December the same American editorials which unequivocally decried the Jews' fate unequivocally accepted the proposition that nothing could be done. The *New York Times* bemoaned the "world's helplessness to stop the horror while the war is going on" and believed that Jews' lives would only "be accounted for at the time of reckoning," i.e., victory, and no sooner. In its editorial condemning Nazi "savagery," the *Los Angeles Times* did not even raise the possibility that rescue action was possible. The most the *New York World Telegram* would support was the creation of an Allied commission to identify the guilty so that *after* the war they could be punished.[77] As has already been shown, *The Christian Century* believed that neither kinetic nor emotional energy should be expended on this issue.

Dorothy Thompson was one of the few journalists to strongly advocate action. In her column of December 22 she called what was being done to the Jews "complete extermination" and described the victims as 5 million "human beings who, after being removed from western and central Europe to the east are being poisoned, shot, gassed, and starved to death." She tried to organize an appeal to the German people from Americans of German background and from American Protestants. She proposed that a group of German-Americans visit the White House and ask the President to broadcast a direct appeal to the German people. None of her plans, with the exception of a full-page ad in the form of a "Christmas Declaration" which appeared in ten major metropolitan dailies, ever came to fruition. The ad was signed by fifty prominent Americans of German ancestry, including Babe Ruth, William Shirer, and Reinhold Niebuhr. The declaration did garner attention and was broadcast by the Office of War Information to Europe and to U.S. armed forces. In order to be able to place the ad, Thompson not only had to tone down the references to Jews but had to appeal to the American Jewish Congress to help defray the expenses.[78]

A few American newspapers and journals pressed for immediate action. The *New York Post* declared it "good, but not good enough" for the Allies to denounce the extermination and promise to "deal out 'retribution' " after the war. They needed to find a "serious plan" capable of stopping the killing and rescuing those in danger. *The Nation* and *The New Republic* both argued that the Jews of occupied Europe could do with "a little less pity and a little more help." These lonely editorial voices asked America to respond to the moral imperative of action and not to watch with indifference while the "spiritual and physical crucifixion of the Jews" proceeds apace.[79] Their requests proved as futile as their voices were few.

Official Doubts

In analyzing the American press reaction, one cannot ignore the degree to which government officials, particularly those in the

State Department, were staunchly opposed to publicizing this issue. From late summer 1942, when reports regarding the Final Solution began to arrive from Switzerland, Department personnel debated not only whether the charges of a plan to exterminate the Jews were true, but, if they were, whether they should be publicized. The general sentiment was that in view of the "fantastic nature of the allegations" it was better not to do so. Department officials balked at transmitting the information to Jewish representatives, such as Rabbi Wise, who might release it to the press.[80] During this time both the United States and Britain followed a policy of using horror propaganda sparingly.[81] Late in October 1942 Drew Pearson described in his syndicated column the debate among government officials regarding the release of the stories. Those who opposed publication argued

> that the atrocity stories of the last war were largely invented, and . . . left the public disillusioned; thus the people might now react unfavorably and charge the Government with pulling the same tricks.[82]

Allied officials also opposed publicity because they feared, or so they claimed, that the non-Jewish population of Europe would, upon learning of Nazi brutality, become so paralyzed with fright that it would terminate all its resistance efforts. It does not seem to make much sense for officials to have argued that Americans would dismiss the stories as fabrications but Europeans would accept them without reservation. This may have simply been an excuse not to release the information.

There were Department bureaucrats who argued that the reports were the product of Jewish publicity tactics and the government should in no way provide its imprimatur. When the first reports of a mass murder program reached the State Department's Division of European Affairs, it opposed release of the information because of the "impossibility of our being of any assistance." Division officials debated whether to "pass or suppress" it.[83] But for pressure from external sources, both the British Foreign Office and the State Department would have probably suppressed the information long past December 1942. One of the most ardent opponents of confirmation was R. B. Reams, the specialist on Jewish issues for the State Department's Division of European Affairs, who repeatedly stated his "grave doubts in regard to the desirability or advisability of issuing a statement." In December 1942 he was still telling those who inquired that the reports of mass murder were "to the best of my knowledge . . . as yet unconfirmed." On the day before Wise and the delegation of other representatives of the Jewish community were scheduled to visit the President in order to discuss the annihilation of the Jews, Reams argued that it was necessary for Wise "to call off, or at least to tone down, the present world-wide publicity campaign concerning 'mass murders.' " When Congressman Hamilton Fish of New York called him to obtain details on Wise's press release, Reams informed him that the reports are still "unconfirmed." On December 15, the eve of the Allied statement, he told an official from the Latin American Section that the reports about the murder of the Jews were still not confirmed. When it became clear that he would not be able to prevent the Allies from issuing a statement, Reams tried to weaken the proposed text and to add various disclaimers to it which would shed doubt upon the existence of the Final Solution.[84]

It had long been the State Department's policy to avoid public denunciation of massacres against Jews. In 1941 Franklin Mott Gunther, American Minister in Roumania, wrote to Washington regarding "oppressive and cruel measures employed against the Jews." Jews were being "massacred," "executed," and treated with "indescribable horror." Gunther suggested a variety of steps Washington could take, all of which were ignored by the State Department.[85]

There were other American officials who did not share their colleagues' reservations or spend their energies trying to keep their government from becoming involved in this issue. In October 1942 Paul C. Squire, the American Consul in Geneva, received a signed sworn affidavit from Paul Guggenheim, a professor of international law in Geneva, attesting to the existence of an order by Hitler "demanding the extermination of the Jews." Squire expressed his faith in the professor's "integrity, reliability and sincerity" and leaned in favor of publicizing Guggenheim's information. Squire lamented the "futile search . . . in order to find somewhere the Good Samaritan" who might help "relieve the tragic situation."[86]

John Winant, the American Ambassador to Britain, also was among those officials who supported publicizing the news. On the same day that Reams was urging the Department to distance itself from Wise and the reports of mass murder, Winant urged Washington to join with the British and Russians "in protesting against German terrorism and to make clear that punishment will be meted out to those responsible for Jewish atrocities."[87]

While most American State Department officials were trying to distance themselves from the news of the Final Solution, the British Foreign Office chose a different *modus operandi.* After initially following a policy marked by great reserve and telling the BBC to "soft pedal" the news of atrocities, it decided that it was "particularly important . . . to continue telling the Poles that we know about the suffering of the Jews" and to seize the opportunity to publicize British anger. Among the reasons for this turnabout was combined pressure from Jewish organizations, the Polish government in exile, members of Parliament, and the press. Press attention stimulated other British religious and political leaders to speak out on the matter. Faced with articles and editorials in the *London Times,* the *Manchester Guardian,* and a myriad of other papers; the appeals from commanding personalities such as William Temple, the Archbishop of Canterbury; threats from members of Parliament to publicly confront the government on this matter by asking pointed questions regarding Allied behavior and the possibility that there would be even stronger demands for action, the British began to push the Americans to participate in a joint Allied statement.[88] The British press alone could not have prompted the government to respond, but it clearly was a critical factor in arousing the interest and concern of both the public at large and opinion makers within the ranks of the public.

Once the statement was released, State Department officials tried to downplay its significance. Two days after the declaration, a cable was sent by the Department to Costa Rica stating that "there had been no confirmation of the reported order from other sources (except from a Jewish leader in Geneva)." Despite a claim by the *Baltimore Sun* that Roosevelt and the State Department have tried to keep the American public fully informed regarding the atrocities, when it came to the Final Solution this was *not* American policy. As Walter Laqueur has observed, the Department wanted to "have nothing to do with the content of the [Allied] message."[89] In fact, it really wanted to have nothing at all to do with publicizing any information regarding the Final Solution.

Why were officials so opposed to confirming the news? Why

did they claim to be unconvinced as to its veracity? Once they acknowledged that the Nazis were engaged in the systematic anni- hilation of the Jews, they knew that they would have to contend with rescue demands and, if they did not heed these requests, with charges that they were being laggard in their efforts. Their fears were justified, for this was precisely what happened. Both Washington and London now had to stave off increasingly strident requests for action from various Jewish and non-Jewish groups.[90] In July 1943 Foreign Office officials were still complaining about Polish and particularly Jewish groups' use of these stories to "stoke us up" and force the government to "waste a disproportionate amount of . . . time in dealing with wailing Jews." State Depart- ment officials felt similarly.[91]

Yet, though London and Washington, to a lesser degree, were beset with requests for rescue, they were ultimately able to dodge the issue—thanks, in part, to the press. The British government had a task here because of the pressure of the press and prominent personalities. Washington did not face this problem. By paying relatively little attention to what was happening to Europe's Jews and accepting the proposition that rescue would and could only come with victory, the American press as well as leading political and religious figures eased Washington's dilemma of having to do something, or at least appear to do something. On those occa- sions when British and American officials felt compelled to give the appearance of action—as they did in December 1942 and would again at Bermuda in April 1943—the press readily accepted their claims that they were genuinely trying to resolve the issue. Satisfied that all that could be done was being done, the press reported news of the Final Solution but did not pursue it with any urgency. In fact, it hardly pursued it at all. When it transmitted the information, it did so in a confused, skeptical, and obfuscated fashion. Mostly, there was an air of lassitude about the way it covered this story. On those few instances when the press focused on the issue, as the British press did in December 1942, public opinion and eventually the government responded.

9

Reluctant Rescuers

As 1943 unfolded, the German resolve to expedite the destruction of those Jews who remained alive seemed to grow stronger. Information emerged from all over Eastern Europe which served to confirm that the program to finally murder all the Jews was well underway. Ghettos which had once been full were now said to be mysteriously empty. Deportations were taking place in Western Europe, including Holland, Belgium, and France. There was even a report of a Nazi order to "starve" the Jews as a means of killing them. According to the *New York Times* mid-February had been set as the date for the "total liquidation of the Jewish problem" in France.[1] AP reported that Polish Jews had been confined to fifty-five different ghettos where they were "awaiting extermination."[2] The February 27 edition of *Collier's* printed a first-hand description of life in the Warsaw ghetto. Written by Tosha Bialer, who had been in the ghetto until the previous summer, the article was accompanied by pictures of those whom the magazine described as "starving people" and "homeless, hungry children."

The Nazi leadership seemed remarkably more candid about

its plans. According to a BBC broadcast, recorded in the United States by CBS, March 31 had been set as the day on which Berlin was to be completely Jew-free. Six thousand Jews would be deported daily in order to achieve that goal. Dr. Robert Ley, the Reich Labor Minister, reaffirmed Hitler's policy of extermination, and in light of the revelations and confirmations of the previous months no longer could his words be understood figuratively.

> No one in Germany is to speak any longer of the Jews as the chosen people. The Jew has been chosen but for destruction.[3]

Reports released by the Polish government in exile and the World Jewish Congress in mid-February painted an even bleaker picture of conditions in Europe. The World Jewish Congress charged on February 14 that the Germans had issued orders to "speed and intensify the extermination by massacre and starvation of the Jews remaining in occupied Europe." The *Washington Post* and *Los Angeles Times* considered this news worthy of pages 2 and 3 respectively; the *New York World Telegram* carried it on page 13, the *Atlanta Constitution* on page 18, and the *New York Times* on page 37.[4]

Additional information released in March indicated that the situation was becoming more desperate. The American Jewish Congress estimated that "two out of every seven Jews [have been] liquidated by the Nazi 'new order.' " In a lengthy article published on March 4 the *Christian Science Monitor* vigorously pointed out that Germany did not deny the estimate that 2 million Jews had been killed; in fact "Germany does not even deny that the extermination of the Jews is carried out according to a meticulously arranged plan." The article analyzed what was known about the fate of the Jewish population in each of the seventeen countries which the Nazis had conquered. It ended with the concise observation that the "deportees either starve while under way in sealed cattle cars or are killed after their arrival at one of the extermination centers that were established in Lithuania and Poland."[5]

That same day an Overseas News Agency dispatch from Stockholm reported that Himmler had issued a circular indicating that the Third Reich "seriously intends to annihilate all the Jews in Europe." The circular announced that Poles were to be taken to "educative labor camps" and then transferred to other places of incarceration, while Jews "are to be transferred to the next state police station for further dealing." The absence, the news report observed, of "any supplementary instructions would indicate strongly that in most instances 'further dealing' means execution."[6] On March 20 the Polish government in exile released news that the liquidation of the Warsaw ghetto was "being speeded up." This information was preceded by an AP dispatch saying that as a result of "fighting" which had occurred during the "forced removal" of Jews from the ghetto, fifty Germans had been killed. On March 21 a number of papers carried a brief AP report that the entire Jewish population of five Polish towns, approximately 35,000 Jews, had been killed.[7]

Though this news painted a frightening picture, most of these stories were paid insignificant attention by the press. If they were to be found in a paper, they were usually relegated to a few small paragraphs tucked away somewhere unobtrusively. However, by the beginning of March the attitude of some of the American press had begun to change. This change was a response, in part, to activities sponsored by various segments of the American Jewish community. For a short period of time in 1943 American Jewry managed to focus the attention of the press on the situation of European Jewry and, of even greater importance, prompted some papers to ask whether rescue through victory was the only alternative.

The March Rallies: The Possibility of Rescue

On March 1st a massive rally was held at New York's Madison Square Garden. It was addressed by Governor Thomas E. Dewey, New York City Mayor Fiorello La Guardia, AFL President William Green, and many other prominent personalities. The rally's theme was "Stop Hitler's decimation of the Jews now." Rescue could not wait until victory. Press estimates of the number of people who listened to the speeches over a public address system set up in the street because the 22,000-seat Garden was filled were as high as 50,000. The rally, which was sponsored by the American Jewish Congress, AFL, CIO, Church Peace Union, Free World Association, and a number of other Jewish and non-Jewish groups, received wide press attention. Newspapers from all over the country and magazines, including *Time* and *Newsweek*, commented on it and described it as the largest gathering of its kind ever held in the United States.[8] Stephen Wise, aware of the press's importance, tried to capitalize on the attention the rally generated by writing to editors of various newspapers in order to get them to publicize its proposals. Similar rallies were held throughout the United States in a variety of different cities.[9]

Even before the rally the question of rescue had been publicly raised by a small group of Palestinian Jews led by a man named Peter Bergson. Members of the Irgun, one of the secret Jewish armies in Palestine, they came to the United States to raise funds to support Irgun activities, including helping Jewish refugees break through the British blockade of Palestine. When news of the destruction of European Jewry began to be publicized, they turned their energies to that issue. From the outset they used the mass media effectively. Among their earliest activities was the publication on February 16, 1943, of a full-page ad in which they claimed that Roumania would not kill 70,000 Jews if it were paid 50 dollars a head. Though the principal demand of the ad, written by Ben Hecht, was the establishment of an Allied intergovernmental committee to "formulate ways and means of stopping this wholesale slaughter of human beings," it was the idea of ransoming Roumanian Jewry which captured people's attention. This was due in no small measure to the headline above the ad:

FOR SALE to Humanity
70,000 Jews
Guaranteed Human Beings at $50 a Piece

No sooner had the ad appeared than the established Jewish organizations accused the group of activities that bordered on "fraud" for making it sound as if a 50-dollar contribution to them could save a Roumanian Jew. The Bergsonites ignored the criticism and less than a week later published another ad signed by Senator Edwin C. Johnson of Colorado demanding Allied action on the Roumanian proposal. Both these ads appeared in a number of different papers.[10]

In addition to their effective use of these dramatic full-page ads, they sponsored a star-laden pageant entitled "We Will Never Die." Produced by Billy Rose, written by Ben Hecht, starring Paul Muni and Edward G. Robinson, directed by Moss Hart, with the NBC orchestra playing music composed for the pageant by Kurt Weill, the March 9 premier in New York City drew over 40,000. A second showing was hastily scheduled when 50,000 people descended on the Garden for tickets that, in the words of the organizers, "weren't there." Many people waited outside in the vain hope that a third performance would take place. The pageant was produced in five other American cities—Boston, Philadelphia, Chicago, Washington, and Hollywood. It generated press coverage wherever it was shown and was ultimately seen by over 100,000 Americans including Supreme Court justices, Cabinet members, 300 congressmen and senators, diplomats, and Eleanor Roosevelt, who in her newspaper column, "My Day," described it as

> one of the most impressive and moving pageants I have ever seen. No one who heard each group come forward and give the story of what had happened to it at the hands of a ruthless German military, will ever forget those haunting words: "Remember us."

The First Lady was obviously deeply moved by the performance, but not enough to suggest publicly that any action was possible.[11]

As the protest meetings gathered steam, some papers, led by the *New York Times,* became willing at least to consider the proposition made at the gatherings: something should and could be done *prior* to the end of the war. The *Times,* which in December had declared the world "helpless" to do anything, dramatically changed its stance and on March 3 called for the United States to "set a good example . . . in the interests of humanity" by revising "the chilly formalism of its immigration regulations." That same day *New York Times* columnist Anne O'Hare McCormick, in one of the strongest columns to appear on the topic, called upon the Christian community "to do the utmost to rescue the Jews remaining in Europe." Transcending the narrow confines of perceiving this as something of concern only to Jews, she declared the Jew the "symbol of what this war is about." The *New York Herald Tribune* also devoted an editorial to this topic on the 3rd. Entitled "They Will Never Die," it called attention to the pageant scheduled for the 9th and described it as a means of consecrating "the memory of men, women and children killed, not in combat, but in cold blood." Though the *New York Herald Tribune* was not yet willing to recommend a rescue program, it would do so shortly. The *Nation, New York Post,* and *New York Sun* were among the other publications which called for action based on the proposals adopted at the Madison Square Garden rally. Also on March 3, Acting Secretary of State Sumner Welles was asked at a press conference how the United States planned to aid those caught in the Nazi vise. The *New York Times* reporter at the conference described the question as being asked "in the light of the mass meeting" which had been held two days earlier. It was only after Welles was asked the question that the State Department released to the press a note, sent by Secretary of State Hull to the British on February 25, suggesting that the two countries convene a conference on the "refugee problem."[12]

Obviously, as the date on the note indicates, the conference proposal preceded the rally. However, the rally and the subsequent pageant energized the press and other prominent personalities into asking whether it was really true that nothing could be done. The more they asked, the more politicians and bureaucrats recognized the growing political danger of appearing to do nothing. For the first time American political leaders began to sense that there was a potential political liability in inaction, hence their release of the note.

When Hull's memorandum to the British, which contained suggestions for the "preliminary exploration" of the idea of holding a conference, was given to the press on March 3, the matter had already been under discussion for a few months at British instigation. The British, who had been the ones pressing America to act, accused Washington of publicizing the proposal in order to make "it appear that this [the American] Government had taken the initiative whereas the British Government had actually done so." Sumner Welles, responding to the British argued that they wanted the impression to be created that [Britain] was the great outstanding champion of the Jewish people and the sole defender of the rights of freedom of religion and individual liberty and that it was being held back in its desire to undertake practical steps to protect the Jews in Europe . . . by the unwillingness of this Government." In a strange reversal of their behavior in November and December 1942, the two governments were tripping over each other in their attempts to appear as the one with the better record in "assisting Jewish refugees."[13]

Various papers, including the *Christian Science Monitor, New York Times, Los Angeles Times, New York Herald Tribune, Miami Herald, New York World Telegram, Cleveland Plain Dealer,* and *Philadelphia Bulletin,* began to raise the question of action. *Christian Century,* which three months earlier had been pleased that no excess energy was being expended on this matter, now berated the British Parliament and American officials who had competed in December "to see who could express the most indignation at the Nazis' despicable treatment of the Jews" but done "nothing." The only devices to which they had resorted were "oratorical." The following week *Christian Century* returned to the same theme and suggested that the United States, "which is shouting to high heaven about its manpower shortage," might even consider taking in—"at least temporarily—some of the hunted ones." The Catholic publication *America,* citing the Archbishop of Westminster's message to the March 1 rally, called for "immediate action [and] . . . relief of every possible kind." *American Mercury, Reader's Digest, Christian Science Monitor,* and the *Los Angeles Times* all ran articles by Ben Hecht decrying the American willingness to stand by silently. "Humanity has done almost nothing. Its indignation has been small. . . . It has shuddered and taken matters for granted." In a column on the editorial page of the *Los Angeles Times,* Hecht attributed the Germans' success in murdering 2 million Jews who had neither "guns or sticks with which to defend themselves" not to German skill, but to humanity's willingness to stick its "skull into a fog. Its nerve endings are apparently dead."[14]

Even *Newsweek,* which had not paid too much attention to the issue, commented that Hitler's recent prediction that the war would end with the " 'extinction of Jewry in Europe' . . . sounded more like a promise than a threat and to a large extent is already in the process of being carried out."[15] The *Christian Science Monitor,* demonstrating a greater sense of urgency than it ever had before, argued that none of the various plans will be of any "avail for Europe's Jewish population unless some step is taken now." Yet, still unwilling to abandon its balanced approach, it observed that there "are other refugees who need consideration, but the Jews *seem* to be in the most danger, and therefore *perhaps* call for more immediate attention."[16]

On March 9 the Senate adopted a resolution which condemned the "atrocities inflicted upon the civilian population in the Nazi-occupied countries, and especially the mass-murder of Jewish men, women and children," and called for an immediate end to this "inexcusable slaughter." But neither the Senate nor the House, which adopted the same resolution on March 18, proposed any steps or concrete action to be taken to aid those in duress.[17] In fact the resolutions attracted little press attention. The *New York*

Times devoted a few paragraphs on page 12 to the Senate's action, and when the House subsequently passed its resolution, the *Times* put the three-paragraph story on page 11.[18]

The American indifference to rescue contrasts sharply with the mood of the British Parliament, many of whose members had been demanding since December that their government tell them whether the "claims of humanity come before your quota restrictions." Between the December declaration by the Allied governments and the end of March, the Archbishops of Canterbury, York, and Wales publicly demanded on a number of occasions in the "name of the whole Anglical Episcopate" that the British government provide a sanctuary. Parliamentary calls for rescue were so persistent that Foreign Minister Anthony Eden complained to the Cabinet on February 22 that "it was becoming difficult" to satisfy the Parliament's demands to know what was being done.[19] Richard Law, the Parliamentary Undersecretary for Foreign Affairs, who would eventually be appointed to head the British delegation to Bermuda, warned the State Department in February that "public opinion in Great Britain has been rising to such a degree that the British Government can no longer remain dead [sic] to it." According to Law, the British government found it unable to delay any longer "some reply to the persistent demands to know what it is doing to help the Jews."[20]

The British press continued to pursue this issue with greater persistence than its American counterparts.[21] Particularly noteworthy was the *Manchester Guardian's* observation on February 16 that the report released by the British Section of the World Jewish Congress on the Nazi determination to speed up the annihilation of the Jews "confirms many of the details" which had previously been provided by the paper. For the *Manchester Guardian* the integrity of this news was not compromised by its source, a Jewish group.[22]

Even after London and Washington made public their plans to discuss the issue, English leaders continued to press for greater action. On March 24, when the Archbishop of Canterbury rose in the House of Lords to urge that the rescue of European Jews be expedited and that Jewish children in Bulgaria be transferred to Palestine, he was greeted with cheers. The House of Commons called an all-party conference which sent a message to Eden stressing the extreme urgency of the situation. It gave its strong support for immediate and generous action, compatible with the requirements of military operations, to provide help and temporary asylum for refugees.[23]

The only things comparable in this country were the rallies and pageants and the willingness of some papers to raise the issue of rescue. And these did make their impression. On March 23 the Secretary of State wrote to the President and cited the Madison Square Garden gathering and others like it as indicative of the "intense and widespread feeling on this subject" among "Jewish . . . [and] other elements of our population" and the need, therefore, for some response.[24] When Eden conferred with Hull in Washington at the end of March, it was clear that from a political perspective further delay was intolerable. Finally, over three months after the December declaration and close to nine months after the first news of a systematic plan for the annihilation of the Jews had reached London, Britain and America prepared to convene a conference to seek ways to resolve the plight of the "refugees."

The Bermuda Conference

In truth, the conference organizers were far less concerned with the plight of these identityless refugees than they were with their own plight: the intensifying demands from the press and leading religious and political personalities that something be done. This was a gathering—Henry Feingold has aptly described it as a "mock conference for surplus people"—which had a written and an unwritten goal. While the official purpose was to seek a means to rescue refugees, the unofficial but primary purpose was to placate public opinion. There is no question but that Bermuda was designed not to effect rescue, but to impress upon the world that all that could be done was being done. The press would serve as an important tool in Washington's and London's attempts to make this impression.

In their lengthy exchange of notes prior to the meeting, State Department and Foreign Office officials anticipated that they would be able to quell "public anxiety" over this issue by demonstrating that the two governments were concerned enough to "examine the problem and its possible solutions." British and American officials agreed that a meeting would be useful to demonstrate "the practical limitations" faced by the Allies despite "their intense sympathy for the victims of Germany's policy."[25] Their goal was to "let the . . . people and the world know [the Allies'] record in assisting Jewish refugees," and not to devise new and dramatic methods of rescue. Long before the conference was publicly announced, both governments privately acknowledged that if the "main result" of the gathering would be only to "elicit full statements" on what was already being done and the difficulties in trying to doing more, "this in itself would be of great value."[26]

In order to quell public anxiety, British and American officials knew that it was mandatory that they not only strictly control the information released to the press, but that they try to mold the perceptions of the press regarding what could be anticipated from the gathering. Both the British and Americans recognized that if public expectations were high and the conference accomplished nothing concrete, the propaganda costs would be great. And expectations were high. When the conference opened, the *New York Times, New York Herald Tribune,* and *New York World Telegram* all expressed the conviction that something could and should be done. The *New York Times* argued that even though "nothing, not even the desperate plight of the refugees," could interfere with the war, measures "can be devised that go beyond palliatives which appear to be designed to assuage the conscience of the reluctant rescuers rather than to aid the victims." The *New York Herald Tribune* observed that days of mourning and pious expressions of sympathy were pointless unless they were "also [a] dynamic stimulus to action." The *New York World Telegram* declared that the "time for 'exploratory' conferences, verbal denunciations and promises of future punishment is past."[27]

In addition to these calls for action, the conference also had to contend with a deep-seated skepticism. Freda Kirchwey, publisher of *The Nation* and an outspoken critic of the State Department's rescue policy, deprecated the "modest step" of a conference even before it began and reminded readers that this meeting was not called "because our government felt impelled to do something about the greatest crime committed in our generation," but because of the public pressure as exemplified by the March rallies. Nonetheless, she urged, "let's have the conference," and let the "restrained and practical" proposals adopted at the Madison Square Garden rally on March 1 serve as guidelines.[28]

Washington and London, well aware of both the high expectations and the skepticism, did not want to risk exacerbating the very situation that Bermuda had been designed to resolve. In the days prior to the opening of the meeting, whenever officials met with reporters they repeatedly stressed certain themes which then appeared in all the news stories about the meeting: Bermuda was a first step, it was exploratory, and therefore not much should be expected from it; there were tremendous problems which made previctory rescue virtually impossible despite the Allies' best intentions; and—lest they be accused of shirking their responsibility—America and Britain had already done a great deal for the refugee victims of Nazi Germany. On the eve of the meeting an unnamed "high authority" told the press that a total of 600,000 European political refugees had been "permitted to enter the United States since Hitler came to power ten years ago." Kingsbury Smith, INS correspondent in Washington, observed that this was "one of the main reasons why further mass movements of European refugees to this country in the near future will be opposed" at Bermuda.[29] An AP dispatch on the conference observed that the United States, which was "beginning to feel the pinch of wartime shortages, is sheltering more than 500,000 refugees" from German controlled countries.[30] The message was clear: the problem was great but the United States had done its share and more. The British stressed the same theme. Richard Law told the press that "it would be extremely difficult to find any place in the British Empire for victims of Axis persecution." Again and again readers were told that refugee aid was "linked to victory in war" and therefore substantial relief was "not possible now."[31]

The prominent journalist Raymond Clapper reiterated the official line regarding the conference and described it as "largely an exploratory affair" from which few concrete decisions could be expected. At best it might recommend a program for "future consideration." He even echoed what we now know were some American and British officials' deepest fears: that Germany would decide not to kill multitudes of Jews, but to release them. In 1943 British officials expressed their fears to the State Department that Germany might "change over from a policy of extermination to one of extrusion and aim as they did before the war at embarrassing other countries by flooding them with alien immigrants." In 1944 both British and American officials worried that "Germans might play the card of offering an unmanageable number of refugees to the United Nations." Clapper expressed this same concern. If Germany were to offer to free refugees, this would, he argued, have to be turned down because "no move of that kind [would be made] from humanitarian motives, but only for military reasons that would benefit Germany." This would be a way for Germany to unload its "excess population on the Allies."[32]

E. Berg Holt, the *Christian Science Monitor's* special correspondent in London, also expressed these fears that Germany might actually free some Jews.

> Supposing the Axis were to allow them to be transported to the Coast, how would the United Nations find ships to take them away? Where would they take them? How would they feed them?

Since the Allies could neither move nor care for this "excess population," such an offer by the Axis would have to be rejected.[33] When British Foreign Secretary Anthony Eden was in Washington in March 1943 right before Bermuda, Secretary of State Hull raised the issue of rescuing the 60,000 to 70,000 Jews in Bulgaria who were threatened with death unless they could be rescued quickly. Eden responded, according to Harry Hopkins's summary of the meeting, that the Allies should be very cautious about acting.

> If we do that, then the Jews of the world will be wanting us to make similar offers in Poland and Germany. Hitler might take us up on any such offer and there simply are not enough ships and means of transportation in the world to handle them.[34]

Because Bermuda was a military controlled area, access to the island was extremely difficult. Even if the proponents of various rescue proposals had been able to get to Bermuda, they would not have been allowed to present their ideas to the delegates. This was not fortuitous, but had been carefully planned by the organizers. Breckinridge Long, who was in charge of the arrangements for the American delegation, was particularly adamant on this point. He refused a last-minute British request that representatives of the English Jewish community be allowed to attend. No one who might raise embarrassing questions or stymie the public relations goals of the conference was to be present. When Jewish and non-Jewish groups criticized this decision, the State Department denied that Bermuda was being held, in the words of CIO President Phillip Murray, "behind closed doors."[35] But the Department's denials could not alter the fact that the doors *were* closed—the meeting was on an island in a military area into which entry was completely controlled—and with good reason. Officials correctly feared that if the true nature of the proceedings was known, the criticism would be even more severe.

Surprisingly few papers were critical about being barred. No groups or individuals—other than the delegates—could monitor the proceedings, and the officials and experts accompanying the delegation were absolutely forbidden to talk to the press, but most reporters and editorial boards did not question these limiting conditions. In contrast, the press as a whole was vehemently critical of the efforts made to bar it from covering the United Nations Food Conference at Hot Springs, Arkansas, convened by Roosevelt and to be held shortly after Bermuda. Typical was Raymond Moley of the *Chicago Journal of Commerce* syndicate, who devoted two columns to the Hot Springs meeting. He argued that "access by the press to public officials" was a right.[36] The president of the American Association of Newspaper Editors decried the limits that were to be placed on the press at the food gathering as a "dangerous precedent." The *New York Times* discussed the controversy on its front page, and the Senate held an "extraordinary" closed session of the Foreign Relations and Agriculture committees to discuss the grievances of protesting journalists.[37] Because of journalists' protests Hot Springs was eventually opened to the press.

Few journalists had any protests about the arrangements at Bermuda because while their access to delegates and substantive information was extremely limited, they were not *totally* barred from Bermuda. One columnist who did complain was the *Christian Science Monitor's* Roscoe Drummond. He wrote that the reason Bermuda had been chosen was that it was

> nicely secluded from the press and radio . . . in a theater of war. . . . The lack of transportation means that the Administration has only to crook its finger in the direction of the War Department to prevent all correspondents from going to Bermuda.

In contrast to Drummond's complaint, Raymond Clapper praised the conveners of Bermuda for *not* attempting to implement secrecy arrangements. He visited Bermuda right before the conference began and dismissed the charge being voiced by Jewish groups and the liberal press that it was being held at an "isolated island" as invalid. He then described the half-hour horse-and-buggy ride necessary for any member of the press corps to reach the meeting site! He also claimed that the delegates were accessible to the press. Clapper's views were diametrically opposed to Congressman Emanuel Celler's contention that Bermuda was being held under "hermetically sealed" conditions, or a *Christian Science Monitor* staff correspondent's comments during the conference that the delegates were "exceptionally guarded in [their] occasional statements to the press." At the conference's end the same correspondent noted that reporters had only been allowed to interview delegates on "rare occasions and most of what they said was 'off the record.' . . . In no sense was the press encouraged" in its attempts to cover this gathering. But these complaints about the conference's inaccessibility were the exception to the rule.[38]

Every time officials met with the press they elaborated on the tremendous problems facing them. The tenor of press comment throughout Bermuda reflected this. Headlines referred to "hurdles" and "problems" faced by the conferees. Anyone who read the wire service reports from Bermuda would have learned virtually nothing about what could be done and much about why the refugee problem was "insoluble at present." While even Bermuda's critics would not have taken issue with the contention that "winning the war [was] more essential than any other action for relief of oppressed peoples," they argued that there were certain things that could be done even while the war was underway.[39] Some of the proposals which were either not considered at Bermuda or hastily rejected as not feasible included sending food to the victims; using neutral Portuguese and Spanish ships or empty American ships which had deposited men or material in Europe to transport Jews to a safe haven—including America; increasing the number of refugees allowed to enter the United States; changing Britain's Palestine policy so that Jewish refugees could enter; and negotiating with satellite Axis countries regarding release of their Jews. Since it was becoming increasingly clear that the Allies would win the war, many people believed that the Axis satellites would have been anxious to win favor with the Allies and might have considered releasing Jews as a means of doing so.

One of the major "hurdles" facing those who wanted Bermuda to accomplish something concrete was that there still was a deep-seated anti-immigration feeling in this country. While Bermuda was in session, *Editorial Research Reports* predicted that it was "doubtful" whether Congress could be convinced "to make any sweeping change in immigration statutes to admit large numbers of European refugees." At the last minute Congress had added an addendum to a bill to permit the "importation of aliens for agricultural work." The addendum, which stipulated that these aliens had to be " 'native-born residents' of North, South or Central America, or adjacent islands," was added, it was explained on the floor, in order to bar the entry of "European refugees in the guise of farm laborers."[40]

Even by the time the conference opened, the press was already ambivalent about how important this gathering was. While the *New York Times, New York Herald Tribune,* and *Christian Science Monitor* carried the story on the front page, the *San Francisco Chronicle* placed it on page 6, the *New York Journal American* on page 4, the *Chicago Tribune* on page 8, the *San Francisco Examiner* on page 10, and the *Los Angeles Times* on page 11.[41]

On the same day that the delegates began their deliberations, the Inter-Allied Information Committee in London released a report replete with what Eric Hawkins, *New York Herald Tribune* bureau member, described as "sickening details of torture, massacre and butchery carried out by the Germans." According to the report, one-eighth of the Jewish people had been killed and 5 million faced the peril of death. The article, which was on the front page of the *New York Herald Tribune* along with the AP dispatch on Bermuda, bore a bold five-line headline:

> REPORT TELLS OF NAZI ANNIHILATION
> OF 2,000,000 JEWS IN EUROPE
> ———————
> Inter-Allied Committee, in Passover Document,
> Tells of Butchery of Eighth of Jewish Peoples
> and Peril of Death Facing 5,000,000 More

In contrast, the *New York Times* devoted twenty-three lines to the report, which it placed on page 11 as an addendum to the Bermuda story. The *New York Journal American* devoted twenty-five lines on page 4.[42] Most other papers simply ignored the report.

After the opening day most of the reports on Bermuda in the major dailies were but a few paragraphs long and were to be found in fairly out-of-the-way corners of the paper. Reporters had little to tell except that the conferees faced "great limitations" in the action they could take, that any substantial programs or "large scale rescue" was "out of the question," and that solutions were "unlikely." Delegates claimed that progress had been made, though what that progress was remained a mystery. While Alexander Uhl of the liberal daily *PM* dismissed the official claims that the meeting was "getting to the heart of the problem," other papers, including the *St. Louis Post Dispatch, Christian Science Monitor, Chicago Tribune, San Francisco Chronicle,* and even the *New York Times,* believed progress was being made.[43] On April 22 the *Monitor* carried a picture of the delegates entitled "Envoys of Hope" and this headline:

Bermuda Parley Draws
Pattern for Refugee Aid

The *St. Louis Post Dispatch* also gave readers a feeling of progress:

Refugee Conferees'
Plan Taking Shape[44]

As the conference proceeded, both London and Washington knew that the delegates would be "under heavy pressure to disclose" the conference's recommendations after it was over. In order to avert what the Secretary of State described in a telegram to Bermuda as the "adverse press and public criticism which may follow the withholding of information," delegates told the press that nothing could be said because "Hitler will, if possible distort to his own purposes efforts of the conference." The delegates' silence was also explained as resulting from "anxiety lest premature publicity nullify the proposed steps." In his telegram to the conference, Hull explained that he would not have raised the issue of the public's disappointment if information was withheld at the end of the meeting "were it not considered of real importance from the point of view of public relations not only for the delegation but for the Department itself."

The British were equally sensitive to how Bermuda and Allied government actions might appear to the public. They agreed that a small number of refugees be removed from Spain to North Africa so that neutral Spain would not be blocked as an escape route. Their main impetus for considering the transfer of these refugees out of Spain was that if they did not do this, world "public opinion" would conclude that there was no "serious endeavor to deal with the refugee problem." Toward the end of the conference the chairman of the American delegation, Harold W. Dodds, fearful of public reaction to the conference, cabled Long urging that the British proposal for the removal of Jewish refugees from Spain to a camp somewhere in North Africa be seriously considered. It was important that this be done because this would "impress public opinion as matching British measures which otherwise will monopolize attention." The only concrete result of Bermuda was the transfer—over a year after Bermuda ended—of 630 refugees to a North African camp.[45]

Long after the meeting's conclusion, whenever the lack of concrete results was mentioned, the official explanation continued to be that "the most strategic work of the conference could not be made public for security reasons."[46] In the short run, whether for lack of information or just loss of interest in the issue, when the conference ended the *New York Herald Tribune,* which had placed the story regarding its opening on page 1, ran the story on page 8. The *New York Times,* which had also placed the opening story on page 1, carried this news on page 9. The *New York World Telegram* put it on page 27. Other papers followed suit.[47]

If the framers of the Bermuda conference intended to "pull off a propaganda coup," they did not meet with total success: critics charged that Bermuda was designed to quiet public criticism, not save lives. While the gathering was still underway, Ida Landau, the Overseas News Agency representative at Bermuda, described it as "floundering in its own futility" as the delegates "pursue their deliberations in an attitude of doleful defeatism." She suggested that they might "better go home" where they could make a "better contribution to the war effort by puttering in their victory gardens."[48] Freda Kirchwey considered Bermuda a "farce" devoted to formulation of excuses for the failure of Britain and America to "do anything effective." It was an "excuse for inaction."[49] Congressman Emanuel Celler condemned the meeting as a "puppet show" in which even the "strings were visible."[50] He believed that his prediction that Bermuda would "labor and bring forth a mouse" was justified.[51] Even the *Christian Science Monitor* expressed some disappointment in Bermuda, which it described as "essentially a political meeting," and noted the absence of those most familiar with the refugees' situation—the representatives of refugee relief agencies such as the Red Cross, the American Friends Service Committee, and the Joint Distribution Committee. Even the final press communiqué, the *Christian Science Monitor* wryly noted, "said as little as it was possible to say in 300 words."[52]

The *New York Herald Tribune* believed that Bermuda had been characterized by a false compassion. This was an "empty sentiment" because it neither eased the lot of those already suffering nor "avert[ed] any like suffering." The *New York Post* demanded that the unallocated immigrant quotas for that year be used for refugees. The *Boston Globe* described the news on Bermuda's accomplishments as "not encouraging." It called upon the British Foreign Office and American State Department to recognize the "rescue of victims of Hitlerism [as] one of the things for which the people of the United Nations are fighting." Celler termed the conference a "blooming fiasco." *The New Republic* declared it "simply not true" that nothing could be done for the Jews until Hitler was defeated.[53]

The Jewish community was in the forefront of the ranks of the critics. After the conference Wise called the meeting a "tragic disappointment," and the Bergson group placed full-page ads condemning Allied inaction. One ad stretched across six columns of the *New York Times* and carried the following headline:

TO 5,000,000 JEWS IN THE NAZI DEATH-TRAP BERMUDA WAS
A "CRUEL MOCKERY"

Both the "mainstream" and Bergson factions had proposed different rescue alternatives, including revision of American immigration laws, permission for "a reasonable number of victims" to enter England, immediate consideration of havens in British territories, revision of Latin American regulations which made it difficult for Jews to enter the countries there, the opening of Palestine, the creation of something like the "Nansen" passport system which had been in operation after World War I for refugees and stateless people, and the establishment of an intergovernmental agency with "full authority . . . to save the remaining millions of Jewish people."[54]

The most sustained press criticism came from PM and its foreign news editor, Alexander Uhl. Even before the conference opened, *PM* found it a cause for disappointment because it was exploratory, no Jewish organizations were invited, it was being held in a place which was inaccessible to the press, and it had been too long delayed in getting started. When the conference organizers claimed that even the most general information had to be kept from the press because it might be of use to the Germans or "embarrass negotiations with other countries," Uhl observed, "it is unlikely that the Conference will pull anything out of its hat that will embarrass anyone."[55] After the meeting, on May 2, Uhl accused the State Department of not being interested in "getting too deeply involved in this refugee problem."[56] His final word on the meeting came on May 9: "Never was there a conference with so many good reasons, so eloquently and patriotically presented, to do so little." Moreover, Uhl recognized that those who criticized or asked the delegates embarrassing questions were on the defensive. "You had the strange feeling that . . . somehow you weren't being a very good American."[57]

Not all the articles on the gathering's close were so pessimistic. The *New York Times* headline offered a different impression:

HOPEFUL HINT ENDS
BERMUDA SESSIONS

Communique Says Substantial
Number of Refugees May
Obtain Relief as Result[58]

The *Chicago Tribune* was also convinced that the conference had accomplished its goals. Its page 1 headline left little doubt:

End Refugee Parley;
Agree on Aid Plans[59]

Although the conference met with criticism, it succeeded in at least temporarily lessening the "considerable pressure" of demands for action. As the months passed, fewer editorials calling for rescue appeared in the press, and the general clamor for action was no longer as audible. After the first flurry of criticism about the absence of results, the press accepted with little more comment the official explanation that nothing could be done until victory. There were those who perceived of Bermuda as a "valuable contribution towards post-war planning and a lasting peace," while others simply were convinced that all that could be done was being done.[60] In June staunch anti-immigrationist Breckinridge Long observed that the "refugee question has calmed down. The pressure groups have temporarily withdrawn from the assertion of pressure."[61] Though the Jewish community and long-time critics like *The New Republic, The Nation, PM,* and the *New York Post* were not silenced, the press in general seemed satisfied by the official explanations given. Most newspapers and other periodicals did not question Britain or America's commitment to rescue. It would be over six months before Washington would be compelled to act and establish the War Refugee Board. By then the tragedy would have reached far greater proportions.

The terrible futility which characterized Bermuda was graphically illustrated by two headlines that appeared next to each other in the April 20 issue of the *New York Journal American:*

Rescue Far Off For Axis	2 Million Jews Slain
Victims, Parley Fears	By Nazis

A similar juxtaposition was to be found on the front page of the *New York Herald Tribune:*

Victory Called Vital to	Report Tells of Nazi
Solving Refugee Relief	Annihilation of 2,000,000 Jews in
	Europe[62]

The annihilation was proceeding with unbridled ferocity; the details were emerging. But rescue was "far off."

On April 22 a small article appeared on the front page of the *New York Times.* Though there was little this conference could have done to aid the particular group of Jews involved, their plight was a consequence of the kind of futility which was at the heart of Bermuda:

SECRET POLISH RADIO ASKS AID, CUT OFF

Stockholm, Sweden, April 21—The secret Polish radio appealed for help tonight in a broadcast from Poland and then suddenly the station went dead. The broadcast, as heard here, said: "The last 35,000 Jews in the ghetto at Warsaw have been condemned to execution. Warsaw again is echoing to musketry volleys.

"The people are murdered. Women and children defend themselves with their naked arms.

"Save us . . ."[63]

This sudden front-page attention quickly faded, and the next day the story of the battle in the ghetto was on page 9, despite the fact that it described how the Nazis were forced to use tanks against the ghetto fighters and noted that the battle was reported to be costing many German lives. Two weeks later a report that the battle had been going on for seventeen days as Jews "fighting against annihilation" had "converted their homes into forts" was contained in 29 lines on page 7. Even the reported toll of 60 Nazis killed during the uprising was on page 6. Whereas other reports of resistance usually generated excitement and attention, this story did not.[64]

A year later on the anniversary of the uprising the *New York Times* devoted an editorial to the Warsaw ghetto uprising. In it it spoke of the "profound respect" due the ghetto fighters, who "set for the rest of us an example of courage that history can scarcely match." It seems strange that the paper, which now found them such an "inspiration," did not pay too much attention while the battle was underway.[65]

═══ 10 ═══

Witness to the Persecution

As 1943 drew to a close and 1944 began, an Allied victory grew increasingly certain. At the same time that the Nazi assault on Europe was losing momentum, the campaign against the Jews proceeded with even greater ferocity. Leland Harrison, the American Consul in Bern, Switzerland, wrote to the State Department that the German commitment to "total warfare has not pushed doctrine [of antisemitism] aside," but instead "renewed emphasis [is] placed" on it.[1]

Articles in the American press firmly indicated that the pace of the Final Solution had not abated.[2] Jewish communities that had previously seemed fairly secure were now reported to be in great danger. The reports of ghettoization and deportations were accompanied by stories of Jewish communities which had disappeared in their entirety. Some communities—Danish Jewry, most notably—were miraculously rescued, but generally communities were reported by the press to be either "virtually wiped out," as in Greece, or on the verge of destruction. The Jewish community of Rome, which had survived for so long despite the fact that Italy was Germany's chief ally, now faced deportation. Norway's Jews were reported to have been rounded up and sent to Germany.[3] Jewish and non-Jewish sources spoke of a death toll even higher than had been previously imagined. Repatriated Americans who had been held in German prison camps returned in March 1944 with "harrowing stories" about the "systematic elimination of Jews in Prague and the use of Czech Jews as guinea pigs to test the strength of Skoda's poison gas."[4] As the Russians began to regain territory occupied by the Germans, eyewitnesses provided additional reports on massacres, such as those in Kiev.

Though the news of the Final Solution was more devastating and more certain than ever before, the major dailies—including the *New York Times, New York Herald Tribune, New York World Telegram, New York Journal American, Atlanta Constitution, Christian Science Monitor, Chicago Tribune, Dallas News, Los Angeles Times, Los Angeles Examiner, Miami Herald, San Francisco Chronicle, San Francisco Examiner, Seattle Times, St. Louis Post Dispatch, Washington Post,* and *Washington Star* among many others—continued to ignore the news or give it cursory coverage at best. Though the *New York Times* provided more coverage than most papers, it too was quite sparing in the space and attention it allotted to this news. On February 11, 1944, the final two paragraphs of a page 5 *New York Times* article on Greece's civil war mentioned that "according to reliable information" all Salonika's Jews had been "wiped out." On February 12 a twenty-nine-line article at the very bottom of page 6 reported that a Jewish fugitive from a Nazi camp had described an "execution mill" in Poland and told how he had witnessed trains packed with Jews leave the camp for eastern Poland and the site of the crematorium in the morning and return in the evening empty.[5] Five days later an article on page 9 relayed the Polish government in exile's charges that the Nazis were carrying out the "complete extermination of all Jewish children in Poland."[6] On February 18 the *Times* devoted thirty-two lines on page 7 to a UP report that Holland's 180,000 Jews had been "completely wiped out." This article ran beneath a long somewhat humorous story about how a sleeping American sergeant had been awakened by the King and Queen of England.[7]

In early March the Jewish National Committee in Poland estimated that within a few weeks no more than 50,000 Jews would remain in Poland. "In our last moment before death, the remnants of Polish Jewry appeal for help to the whole world." The *New*

York Times devoted sixteen lines to their appeal and attached it to a page 4 story on the budget granted to the Intergovernmental Committee on Refugees. That same day a lengthy story on page 1 was devoted to gangster Louis Lepke's attempts to delay his execution.[8] On March 14 the Polish Telegraph Agency reported on the "wholesale killings in Lwow" and described how a "continual stream of Poles and Jews [were delivered] to the execution grounds." This thirty-five-line article appeared on page 14.[9] Even when the news came from the paper's own reporters, its policy was not perceptibly different. On March 5 a *New York Times* reporter with the Russian forces in the Ukraine provided a description of the application of German antisemitic policy with "horrifying precision" throughout the Ukraine. The article appeared on page 6 of the paper, while page 1 carried a report on how even Monte Carlo was beginning to feel the pinch of wartime austerity. Its "war boom spree" was over, and now British whisky, Havana cigars, American cigarettes, and whipped cream would all be harder to obtain.[10]

There was a real contradiction between the *New York Times* policy of page placement and its declared editorial policy. At the same time that the paper was carrying the story of the Final Solution in small articles on inner pages, on its editorial page it proclaimed the "need to keep reminding ourselves" that "the cold-blooded extermination" of the Jews was taking place.[11] Obviously, for the *Times* a few short lines on pages 4, 6, and 14 were reminders enough. A careful reader of the paper might well have seen many of these articles, but many probably did not. But the way the *New York Times* treated a particular story did not just determine the number of *Times* readers who saw it. The *New York Times* is considered "the gatekeeper of the American press." Many American papers take their cues from it; i.e., when it stresses a story, other papers are likely to do likewise. Conversely, if the *Times* ignores something, this too sends a message to other papers. In addition various dailies subscribe to the *New York Times* foreign wire service and reprint important stories from the paper. Only rarely were stories concerning the Jews treated in a way that would have prompted other papers to think them significant or worthy of reprinting. When the *New York Times*'s record is compared with that of other dailies, many of which almost totally ignored the story, it can be said to be relatively good. If, however, one compares the *New York Times* coverage with its editorial declaration of the need to continuously "remind" Americans of what was taking place or its claim to be the "newspaper of record," then it was a failure.*

Hungary: A "Living Hell"

In March 1944 the situation of approximately 1 million Hungarian Jews suddenly took a dramatic turn for the worse. The Nazis installed a puppet government in Budapest, and it was clear that one of its first activities would be to clamp down on the Jews. Even before the occupation of Hungary was completed, columnist Paul Winkler, writing in the *Washington Post,* predicted that Hungarian Jews could anticipate the imposition of the "same ruthless treatment meted out to their co-religionists in other countries." The *Christian Science Monitor* matter-of-factly noted that once the Germans assumed control of civil rule, the Jews in Hungary "may expect to suffer."[13]

The news of these developments in Hungary was particularly disturbing because it was especially difficult to deny. It came after "reliably" confirmed reports of a similar nature had come from many other parts of Europe; the story of the Final Solution was now more than two years old and hard to dismiss as a fabrication. Second, information also came from neutral diplomats stationed in Hungary who were known to be quite sympathetic to the Hungarian government. Their confirmation in the spring of 1944 of the Hungarian government's plans to murder this community of over 1 million was, therefore, authoritative. In contrast to Jewish groups, who would later be described as "having an ax to grind," or even refugee agencies or governments in exile, which were also considered interested parties, these diplomats could not be accused of telling lies in order to incite hostility against the Hungarians. Third, it was clear that the Axis would soon be defeated. With the end of the conflagration in sight, it was particularly hard to fathom—especially for those in the ranks of the press who did not grasp the idea of a war against the Jews as separate and apart from the conventional war—why the Germans were destroy-

---

* One of the reasons the *New York Times* had a "better" record than other papers was that during the war, when newsprint was rationed, it chose to emphasize news, while some of its major competitors, the *New York Herald Tribune* most prominent among them, chose to emphasize advertising.[12]

ing this community. Even as portions of Europe were on the verge of being liberated, the Jews of Hungary were on the verge of destruction. Finally, Hungary had been one of the few European countries in which Jews had been relatively secure until March 19, the date on which the Nazis established the puppet government in Budapest. But despite all these factors the press continued to treat this news as, at best, a "war sidelight."[14]

By early spring of 1944 the situation in Hungary was rapidly deteriorating. In mid-April Winkler noted that the speed with which the Germans were imposing restrictions on the Jews indicated that should they be faced with defeat, they "intended to leave no Jews alive behind them." For Hungarian Jews the "sentence of death has been passed." Even the euphemism long used by the Nazis to obscure what they were doing no longer served its purpose. When the Hungarian government announced its intention to build "special baths," *New York Times* reporter Joseph Levy told his readers that these "baths are in reality huge gas chambers arranged for mass murder, like those inaugurated in Poland."[15] (Actually the Hungarian government never built the "special baths," but deported the Jews to Poland, where they were murdered.)

Now little was left open to speculation. One of the most striking aspects of this terrible saga is that at each stage in the process of the destruction of Hungarian Jewry, the news of what had happened *and of what would next occur* was available to the press, but many papers chose not to make it available to their readers. Once again, with the exception of the liberal *PM,* the *New York Times* can be said to have had the best record. But as I have noted, "best" is a relative term. On May 4 a page 11 article reported that Hungary had liquidated over half the remaining Jewish businesses. On May 10 an article on page 5 described how Jews in Hungary were "living in fear of imminent annihilation, from which there seems to be no escape."[16] On May 18, Levy reported that the initial steps in the destruction of Hungarian Jewry had been completed. "The first act in the program of mass extermination of Jews in Hungary is over, and 80,000 Jews of the Carpathian provinces have already disappeared. They have been sent to murder camps in Poland." Levy, whose dispatches on this topic were among the most detailed and frightening to appear in the press, offered those who read page 5 of the paper a sobering prognosis. "Unless drastic measures are taken immediately to put an end to the Hungarian government's brutality 1,000,000 Hungarian Jews are doomed." That same day page 1 of the paper reported that New York County's Republican Committee had chosen to honor its leader by making "Yankee Dewey Dandy" its theme song. On June 2 the *Times* reported that the deadline for Budapest Jews to move into the ghettos had passed. It described the "ruthlessness" and the "confusion and terror" which prevailed and conveyed the news that "suicides apparently have been numerous" in thirty-six lines in the middle of page 6.[17]

An equally bleak picture of the Hungarian Jews' situation was offered readers of the *Christian Science Monitor* by its staff correspondent J. Emlyn Williams. According to him, sixty-five concentration camps had been established "to which Jews have been herded prior to transport to the execution camps of Poland." "Confusion and terror" were said to reign within the community as the date of their deportation from Budapest drew near. On July 2 a twenty-line page 12 dispatch in the *New York Times* noted that the "final stage in the tragedy of Hungarian Jews" had begun. According to the article, which was based on "authoritative information," 400,000 Hungarian Jews had already been dispatched to a death camp in Poland called Auschwitz, and 350,000 more were expected to be put to death there by July 24.[18] On July 13 the *New York Times* predicted that a group of 2,500 Hungarian Jews who had been taken from Hungary "will arrive in the Auschwitz and Birkenau camps by this week-end, . . . [where] railroad sidings have been constructed directly to the gassing halls in both establishments to expedite matters."[19] Despite the terrible and definitive nature of this information it was appended to a short article on how Hungarian children were being moved out of Budapest so that they would not be endangered by Allied bombs, an article whose headline gave no hint it contained information regarding death camps and gassing halls:

BUDAPEST CHILDREN ORDERED EVACUATED
Clearing of All Industrial Areas Planned to Escape Bombs[20]

The Press Considers the Possibility of Rescue

While the way the press handled the news did not change in the face of the Hungarian crisis, the editorial policy of many papers did change somewhat during this period. Beginning in the summer of 1943 and throughout the Hungarian crisis, growing numbers of papers began to argue that the Allies were at least partially culpable for their failure to rescue. This changing editorial policy was partially the result of the activities of the Bergson group and the mainline American Jewish Conference. They proposed rescue programs which called for opening Palestine to all Jews who could reach it, encouraging neutral countries to aid Jewish refugees, strong warnings to the Axis and its satellites that they would be punished for crimes against Jews or for preventing the escape of Jews, and establishing an intergovernmental agency to expand the work of rescuing Jews.[21] The active editorial support of the *New York Herald Tribune,* all the Hearst papers, the *New York Post, The New Republic* and even *The Christian Century,* among others, for rescue programs was indicative of growing discomfort with the lack of an Allied response to the persecution of the Jews.[22] The Bergson group was particularly successful in mobilizing this support. It placed full-page ads in various journals and papers, including the *New York Times, Los Angeles Times, Washington Post, New Republic,* and *Nation,* accusing the Allies of "cowardice" in failing to rescue the Jews. One ad carried this boldface headline:

HOW WELL
ARE YOU
SLEEPING?
Is There Something You Could Have Done to Save
Millions of Innocent People—Men, Women,
and Children—from Torture and Death?[23]

In mid-August, after meeting with Peter Bergson, Eleanor Roosevelt devoted her column "My Day" to the tragic plight of the Jews. Adhering to the official Allied line of "rescue through victory," she did not recommend that anything specific be done to aid the victims. One of the most substantial publications on the question of rescue was a fifteen-page special section of *The New Republic* which appeared on August 30, 1943, and was entitled "The Jews of Europe: How to Help Them." *The New Republic* argued that responsibility for the crimes against the Jews fell not only on the perpetrators but "on the whole of humanity . . . [including] the Allied States," which had failed to take any "concrete action for the purpose of curtailing this crime."[24] Bergson established ties with the publisher William Randolph Hearst. The Hearst chain became and remained active supporters of rescue activities, particularly those proposed by the Bergson group. On various occasions Hearst exhorted Americans to "Remember . . . THIS IS NOT A JEWISH PROBLEM. It is a HUMAN PROBLEM." Though few Americans and even fewer publishers and editors of major American dailies ever perceived of the issue in these explicit terms, increasing numbers of dailies were slowly beginning to recognize that it was "up to the Allies" to do something.[25]*

The burgeoning demand for action was intensified in November 1943 by a resolution introduced by Senator Guy M. Gillette and Representative Will Rogers, Jr., calling for the establishment of a commission to effect a plan to rescue European Jewry "from extinction." Over twelve major dailies, including the *Washington Star, Washington Post, New York Herald Tribune,* and *Christian Science Monitor,* supported it.[27] When Assistant Secretary of State Breckinridge Long testified in secret before the House Committee on Foreign Affairs, he argued that a commission was unnecessary and defended the State Department's record on rescue. He incorrectly told the assembled congressmen that 580,000 refugees had been admitted to the United States since 1933. He also claimed that the Intergovernmental Committee on Refugees established at Evian had been revitalized at Bermuda and given a mandate to take all action necessary for rescue. In truth it did not even have an office in the United States and, contrary to his claims, was not authorized to negotiate with the Axis countries, something that was mandatory in order to effect rescue plans. On December 17 the London headquarters of the Intergovernmental Committee

---

* Not all of the Bergson activities were a success from the perspective of media coverage. In October 1943 the Bergson group organized a visit of 500 American rabbis to Washington. The visit was essentially a failure. Not only did the President rearrange his schedule so that he could leave the capital early and avoid meeting them, but most of the press, with the exception of the local papers, ignored the visit. Even when the visit was mentioned in the press, sometimes its main purpose was ignored. This was the case in *Time* magazine, which was the only magazine to mention the pilgrimage. It totally ignored the question of rescue and made it sound as if the rabbis had come to Washington just to discuss the opening of Palestine to Jewish settlement. *Time* did contrast the "diplomatically minimal" reception the rabbis received with the "full red carpet treatment" accorded that same week to Prince Faisal of Saudi Arabia.[26]

described Long's remarks as "absolutely incorrect." But Congress and the press accepted his claims, particularly about the immigration figures, at face value just as they had accepted similar claims at the time of Bermuda. The *New York Times* was so impressed that it broke with its usual practice of placing news regarding Jews on inner pages and ran the story on Long's immigration figures in the upper half of the front page. The anti-immigration *Chicago Tribune,* a staunch foe of liberalizing immigration policies, charged that the quotas were being ignored.[28]

Long's claim that the United States had done everything possible to rescue Jews, which at first pacified the politicians and the press, ultimately evoked a storm of controversy. His figures were highly inflated, as Jewish and non-Jewish sources quickly demonstrated. Earl Harrison, United States Commissioner of Immigration and Naturalization, said his department had admitted about 279,000 persons as immigrant aliens and only a portion of those could be considered refugees. Jewish rescue organizations also countered Long's claims. Long was forced to amend his testimony. The figure of 580,000 included all the visas that *could have* been distributed to immigrants from all the countries under Hitler's control, he now said. Congressman Celler immediately accused Long of creating the bottleneck in the granting of visas and described him as shedding "crocodile tears" for the Jews. The liberal press now began to take Long to task.[29] *The New Republic* and *The Nation,* both of which had been advocates of a more liberal immigration policy for a long time, attacked Long for being duplicitous and accused him of acting in a "deceptive" and "hypocritical" fashion. On December 20 *PM* published a feature article entitled "Justice Department's Immigration Figures Knock Long's Testimony into a Crocked Hat." The *New York Post* described Long's testimony as "false and distorted." Ten days after the release of Long's testimony eight prominent Christian clergymen sent Congress a statement strongly urging the creation of a special commission to rescue the Jews, the very action which Long so strongly opposed. The Hearst papers used the occasion to offer another editorial in favor of a rescue commission.[30]

The confusion regarding the entire American record was reflected in an article by David Anderson, *New York Times* staff correspondent in London. In it he analyzed how many refugees various countries had admitted. In relation to the United States he observed that the precise number it had admitted was unknown, "or at least it [the number claimed] is not accepted as sufficiently reliable to stand up under close scrutiny."[31]

In mid-January the growing pressure on the White House for action was brought to a head by Secretary of the Treasury Henry Morgenthau's memorandum to Roosevelt on the State Department's dismal rescue record. Roosevelt, well aware of the rising demand for rescue, particularly in the Congress, which stood ready to pass a resolution calling for a rescue commission, established the War Refugee Board with the mandate to effect the "immediate rescue" from the Nazis of as many of Europe's persecuted "minorities" as possible.[32]

The establishment of the War Refugee Board was greeted by the press with kudos and with cynicism. A number of commentators castigated the Allied nations for not having done enough to assist Jews in escaping the Nazis. *The New Republic* was, as might have been expected, still quite dubious about the seriousness of the Allied commitment to rescue, since there was no sign that "either the United States or Great Britain is prepared to let down the bars and permit immigration." Even more cynical was Edgar Ansel Mowrer, syndicated columnist with the Press Alliance, who had been one of the first American reporters expelled from Germany in 1933. His column in the *New York Post* questioned the President's sudden urgency in establishing the Board in light of the fact that during the past years "tens of thousands of Jews" who might have been rescued were not because "the President gave no lead, Congress was of two minds, [and] State Department officials ruthlessly 'weeded out' applicants." Even after Bermuda, a place chosen "for inaccessibility to the press," where government officials promised to do something "nothing much happened." Then "suddenly" on January 22 the President established a War Refugee Board to effect "immediate rescue." Mowrer had no doubt why, after years of delay, "the President demanded almost feverish speed"—1944 was an election year.[33]

The Hearst papers were pleased that the Board had been established but believed its mandate was "too vague and too general." Even papers such as the *Washington Post* began to show a change in editorial policy. In the past it had simply ignored news of the persecution of European Jewry and had vehemently charged the

Bergson group with engaging in fraudulent activities. Pleased that the Board had been set up, the *Post* nonetheless accused America of having been "laggard in this humanitarian duty." Maybe it could not stop the massacres, but it could, the *Post* argued, "set up centers where the rescued can go."[34]*

But the War Refugee Board and its director, John Pehle, quickly began to quiet some of the critics. By mid-March a 190-line article in the *Washington Post* on the War Refugee Board's activities carried a boldface headline which proclaimed the new organization's success:

RESCUING REFUGEES AND IN TIME!
New Board Is Striving to Get
Victims Out of Europe 'In Mass'

According to *Washington Post* reporter Emily Towe, Pehle did not speak "in generalities" when it came to rescuing Jews. He was convinced that the War Refugee Board had been formed to "act right now," and that, Towe observed in amazement, was "just what the Board is doing." Even *The New Republic* had abandoned much of its cynicism and described the War Refugee Board's work as marking the "first time" since the beginning of the war that the United States was making a "genuine effort" to rescue Jews.[36] But just as the War Refugee Board was beginning to move into action, the news from Europe indicated that the situation in Hungary had taken a turn for the worse. Press demands for Allied action now became even more intense.

Free Ports: A "Repulsive" Notion

Within three days of the German occupation of Hungary in March 1944, Roosevelt issued a warning that those who took part in

* The publisher of the *Washington Post*, Eugene Meyer, was adamantly opposed to any special demands for the rescue of Jews. In fact, in a private letter he wrote to U.S. Solicitor General Fowler Harper in response to the attacks in the *Post* on Bergson and his followers, he claimed that the calls for rescue of Jews constituted "harassment" of the President who was trying to win the war. Meyer concluded his letter by arguing that he did not feel "it is necessary for any pressure group, however well meaning, to devote its time and money to the business of 'molding American opinion' on this subject."

Meyer, a Jew, never identified with the Jewish community. His rejection of his Jewish heritage was so complete that once, when his daughter Kay Graham was asked by some classmates at Vassar what it was like to be a Jew, she could not respond because no one had ever told her she was one.[35]

the annihilation of European Jewry would not "go unpunished." Describing the "wholesale systematic murder of the Jews" as one of the "blackest crimes of all history," he promised that "all who knowingly take part in the deportation of Jews to their death . . . are equally guilty with the executioner." Roosevelt's statement was prominently reported by many papers in the country. The *Los Angeles Times, New York Times, Christian Science Monitor,* and *New York Herald Tribune* were among those papers which placed it on the front page.[37] But the cynicism about the American record which had been growing during the preceding months also greeted the President's remarks. While the *New York Times* approved of his statement, it reminded readers that the United States and its allies had to also bear part of the responsibility because they had not done all they could to provide "havens of refuge." In an editorial on the refugee situation which was even stronger than the one it had published at the time of Bermuda, the paper declared that providing these havens and the "means for maintenance and support" for those facing death was "*as* important as the winning of a battle." Another expression of discomfort with the American record appeared in the *Baltimore Sun,* which challenged Roosevelt to go "beyond exhortations and threats" and "a generalized sympathy" for persecuted Jews and be more specific regarding our rescue policy.[38*] The *New Republic,* one of the most fervent advocates of rescue, was also skeptical: "one hopes that the President's message may do some good, but it is hard to be optimistic about it."[40]

But it was a proposal made in the beginning of April by Samuel Grafton, a syndicated columnist for the *New York Post,* which galvanized the press's discomfort with America's rescue record. Aroused by developments in Hungary, Grafton proposed the creation of "free ports for refugees" in which Jews could be temporarily placed until a decision was made about their future. A country could establish a free port without obligating itself to permanently

---

* The President's statement was general and lacked specific suggestions. His close personal adviser, Samuel Rosenman, was a Jew and was quite concerned about drawing too much attention to the Jews. He claimed that this could stir up antisemitism in America and convinced Roosevelt to eliminate some of his direct references to Jews and to avoid focusing on the Final Solution. The original draft, which Rosenman insisted Roosevelt change, had already been approved by Secretary of the Treasury Morgenthau, Undersecretary of State Edward R. Stettinius, and Assistant Secretary of War John McCloy.[39]

admit the people housed there. Grafton argued that the plan was necessary because of the strong opposition toward allowing refugees to immigrate. It was a proposal born out of desperation, one that treated refugees as unwanted guests at best and pariahs at worst.[41] This idea, which had been suggested earlier by German refugees, had been discussed previously by the War Refugee Board staff but opposed by the State Department and others in the administration.[42]

The proposal won strong press support. The Hearst chain, *New York Herald Tribune, New York Post, Christian Science Monitor, Boston Globe, Washington Post, New Republic, Nation, Commonweal,* and even *The Christian Century* all favored it. It also found a strong backer in the *New York Times,* which dismissed the two most frequent objections to it—that the free ports would be nothing more than concentration camps for refugees and that refugees, once admitted to the country, would find a way of staying there.[43] (In fact the one such haven that came into being in the United States, at Fort Oswego, New York, did become a modified concentration camp, in that entry and exit from it were strictly controlled, and most of those interned there did remain in this country.)

But the press's support for the plan did not indicate a shift in its long-standing opposition to liberalizing American immigration laws. In fact, one of the reasons many papers were willing to support it was that it did not signal a change in the law. Typical of this sentiment was the attitude of the *Christian Century,* which favored the free port notion precisely because it could save lives without affecting America's immigration system "at all."[44] There were also opponents of the plan in the ranks of the press, though many did not vocalize their opposition until some refugees actually arrived. Among those who vehemently spoke out against the idea from the outset was the syndicated columnist Westbrook Pegler, who warned that Roosevelt would use the plan to bring in "many thousands" of undesirable people.[45]

Not surprisingly, the strongest and most outspoken support for the idea came from the liberal press and journals, which had long been critical of America's immigration policy. But even as they praised the idea, they did not ignore the basic anti-immigrant sentiment which made such a plan necessary. *The New Republic* approved but called attention to the basic hostility toward refugees implicit in the plan:

Build a few concentration camps along the eastern seaboard [and] put the refugees into them with the understanding that they are to see no more of America than this, and will be sent somewhere else when the war is over.[46]

The liberal Catholic publication *Commonweal* supported the free port idea but also condemned American immigration policy for its lack of "liberality or charity." Well aware of the reasons why such a plan appealed to many Americans, it sadly noted that "Grafton calls his plan 'repulsive,' " adding, "We could not get anyone to try the nobler ones."[47]

There was strong public support for the creation of free ports. A Gallup poll taken a few days after the publication of Grafton's column, which appeared in forty-one newspapers with a combined circulation of over 4 million, found the proposal had a 70 percent approval rate. That espousal of saving refugees, particularly without changing America's immigration policy, may have become a politically advantageous position was further suggested by a rumor then circulating that Thomas E. Dewey, governor of New York and a contender for the Republican presidential nomination, was about to announce his own plan for harboring 100,000 refugees until war's end.[48]

As the Hungarian situation grew more dire, public and press pressure for the plan increased. At the end of May Senator Guy Gillette sought Senate approval for a resolution urging Roosevelt to create centers for "temporary detention and care" of refugee Jews and other victims of Nazi persecution.[49] In an editorial in May the *New York Times* again castigated the Allies by arguing that the tragedy in Hungary was "in part the fault of the United Nations, who did not offer them [Hungarian Jews] adequate places of refuge." It was during that same week that *Christian Century*, apparently struck by the desperation of the Hungarian situation, came out in support of the free port plan.[50]

Meanwhile the War Refugee Board, aware of the importance of press support to get the measure accepted, was quietly pushing Jewish organizations to conduct a campaign to win approval for the plan from the press and radio commentators. Liberal journalists such as Max Lerner and I. F. Stone also worked to win press support for the plan. On June 1—in the wake of the news that a portion of Hungarian Jews had already been deported—Stone addressed a letter "to fellow newspapermen and to editors the country over." Published in that week's edition of *The Nation*, the letter argued that it was the press which could make the difference between a program that would die stillborn and one that would save lives. "A few sneering editorials" mocking Roosevelt's refusal to act could well effect a change in the White House's attitude.[51]

After increased public pressure, threats from some House members that hearings would be conducted on a rescue bill if no action was taken, and questions from reporters at his press conference, the President announced his support of the idea. But, in a move which *Newsweek* accurately described as leaving matters in a "confused state," he expressed his opposition to calling the refugee havens "free ports" and, more important, to establishing any of them "in this country." In light of his statement, *The Nation* wondered just how sincere the President was about his putative support of this program. The *New York Post* dismissed his statement as too indefinite and wondered how, if this country refused to establish them, "can we ask other countries to set up havens?" At his next press conference, when asked to elaborate on his remarks and clear up the confusion, Roosevelt said that the government was considering using abandoned army bases to house refugees. Finally on June 9 the President told the press that 1,000 refugees and "that is all" would be brought to this country. The *Washington Post* described admitting 1,000 as "but a drop in the bucket compared with the needs."[52]

In early August the 1,000 refugees, who were to be housed at the army base at Fort Oswego, arrived from southern Italy, where they had reached the safety of Allied territory. They were the only refugees brought here under this much-hailed program. Roosevelt, wary of arousing the anti-immigrationists, made it clear that he had no intention of expanding on this plan. As David Wyman points out, these 1,000 refugees arrived in this country at a time when immigration quotas were 91 percent unfilled. During the preceding year Sweden, a country about one-twentieth the size of America, had admitted 8,000 Danish Jews. Despite the paucity of the American response, the arrival of these refugees captured the front page in a way that the destruction of millions never had. By focusing attention on rescue, the press made it appear as if America was at long last forcefully responding to the terrible situation in Europe. In truth its action was a gesture, a gesture that was, in the words of I. F. Stone, "a bargain-counter flourish in humanitarianism."[53]

Auschwitz and Birkenau: The Truth Emerges

In June of 1944—as the Allies opened a second front and Hungary's Jewish community reached its final days—details about a place called Auschwitz began to be revealed to the world.* The description of Auschwitz was based on an extensive eyewitness report transmitted by four young Jews and a Polish major who had escaped from the camp there. After a long circuitous passage their information reached Geneva in mid-June. On the basis of their testimony it was firmly established that Auschwitz was not a labor camp or slave town with crematoria or even gas chambers attached. It was a place whose primary purpose was to serve as a killing center, a "model" killing center whose efficiency surpassed all others.

There had been previous reports on Auschwitz, and Birkenau as well—some had even mentioned gas chambers—but none had attracted much attention. On March 22 the *Washington Post* devoted twenty lines on page 2 and the *New York Herald Tribune* devoted twenty-three lines to a summary of a "lengthy report" issued by the Polish government in exile. According to the dispatch, the Nazis had built gas chambers and crematoria at "a concentration camp at Oswiecim, southwest of Krakow," which could "dispose of ten thousand bodies a day."[54]** On June 4 the *New York Times* reported on page 6 that a young Pole who had been in Auschwitz and escaped when transferred to a camp in Germany had described the Auschwitz and Birkenau gas chambers. He related how in 1942 "trainload after trainload of Jews were shipped to camps for execution."[55] On June 16 the *New York World Telegram* and on June 17 the *Los Angeles Times* carried small UP dispatches on the execution of 3,000 Jews in gas chambers during the preceding March. The thirteen lines on page 3

---

* Birkenau was a satellite of Auschwitz which Himmler ordered built in 1942 when it became apparent that the facilities at Auschwitz would not be sufficient for the task that lay ahead. For all intents and purposes the two were really one camp.

** Auschwitz is the German name for Oswiecim.

devoted to this topic by the *Los Angeles Times* included somewhat garbled information on how these Jews had been moved from Birkenau to Terezin and "executed in gas chambers." (The transfer had been from Terezin to Birkenau.) The *New York World Telegram* avoided this problem by cutting the dispatch back to ten lines and dropping all references to the place of execution.[56]

On June 20 the *New York Times* devoted twenty-two lines in the middle of page 5 to the news that 7,000 Czech Jews had been "dragged to gas chambers in the notorious German concentration camps at Birkenau and Oswiecim," where they were "killed en masse." That same day an even shorter Reuters dispatch on the 7,000 appeared in the *Washington Times Herald.* On June 25 the *New York Times* reported that "new mass executions" by gas had taken place at Auschwitz in recent weeks. The news was contained in thirty-three lines on page 5 of the paper.[57]

It was during the first ten days of July that the real extent of the horror that had been perpetrated in this place was reported by the press, but treated with great equanimity if not disinterest. When the same news based on the same eyewitness report was released four months later by the War Refugee Board and not, as was the case in June and July, by refugee organizations or governments in exile, it shocked the press in a way that it had not been shocked since *Kristallnacht.* Then dozens of papers published articles and editorials on the news.[58] One of the reasons the War Refugee Board report may have had more impact was that it contained the complete report on Auschwitz. The earlier version had only been an eight-page summary. Nonetheless, the information released to the press in the summer contained the most critical information regarding Auschwitz and clearly indicated the scope of the tragedy taking place there.

The *New York Times, Christian Science Monitor, Los Angeles Times, Washington Times Herald, Seattle Times, Washington Star, Kansas City Star,* and *PM* were among those papers which, during the first ten days of July, reported the details of this killing center. The reports varied in length and detail—though most tended to be short—but all included one basic piece of information: between April 1942 and April 1944, when the eyewitnesses escaped, approximately 1.5 to 1.7 million Jews had been killed at Auschwitz and its satellite camp Birkenau. Most papers cited the Swiss-based European relief agencies, the International Church Movement Ecumenical Refugee Commission, and the Fluchtingshilfe as their source for this information.[59]

As was so often the case during this period, of all the major dailies the *New York Times* had the most extensive information, but despite the magnitude of the horror, it was never on the front page. On July 3 the paper provided its readers with a list of the number of Jews "eradicated" in these camps, "excluding hundreds of thousands slain elsewhere." There neatly listed midway down the center column of page 3 were the grim statistics:

Poland	900,000
Netherlands	100,000
Greece	45,000
France	150,000
Belgium	50,000
Germany	60,000
Yugoslavia, Italy, and Norway	50,000
Bohemia, Moravia, and Austria	30,000
Slovakia	30,000
Foreign Jews from various camps in Poland	300,000

To this number, the *New York Times* reporter noted, "must now be added Hungary's Jews. About 30 percent of the 400,000 there have been slain or have died en route to Upper Silesia [Auschwitz]." The article described how prisoners were "ordered to strip for bathing" and then taken to rooms into which "cyanide gas" was released. Death came in three to five minutes, after which the bodies were burned.[60]

The *Christian Science Monitor* and the *Washington Evening Star* carried slightly abbreviated versions of the *New York Times* report, while the *Los Angeles Times* and the *Washington Times Herald* carried highly truncated ones. The AP dispatch, used by most of the dailies which reported this news, was based on the *New York Times* story. The *Los Angeles Times* placed the report on page 5. The article referred to the number of victims as being between 1.5 and 1.75 million, but the headline cited the smaller figure of 1.5 million. It made no mention of gas chambers and claimed that the Jews were killed by being given a shot of phenol "near the heart."[61] The *Washington Times Herald*'s ten-line report stated that between 1.5 and 1.75 million Jews had been "put to death by gas or other methods." The headline over the story made no reference to a precise number and identified all the Jews killed as Polish:

REPORTS SLAUGHTER OF POLISH JEWS[62]

The *New York Times* continued to pursue this story, but in its own restrained fashion. On page 6 of the July 6 edition of the paper, reporter Daniel Brigham described how the information on Auschwitz had been obtained and verified. Brigham noted that if Hungarian Jews had been included in the toll of those killed, it "would lie somewhere around the 2,000,000 mark." But, he noted, those who died en route to the camp were not "to be pitied," for those who survived had to endure a "living hell."[63]

On the same day twenty lines on page 3 in the *New York Herald Tribune* were devoted to the news that the 100,000 Hungarian Jews who had been deported on May 15 were now being "put to death in gas chambers at Oswiecim." On July 7 the *Washington Post* devoted twenty-four lines to the news that Poland had become a Jewish "abbatoir."[64]

Once again the *Christian Science Monitor* chose to treat the story of European Jewry in a unique way. It certainly did not ignore the tragedy. On July 3 and again on July 9 the paper mentioned the death toll at Auschwitz and the fate of Hungarian Jews. But on July 6, while the *New York Times, New York Herald Tribune,* and *PM* were describing the method of killing, the *Christian Science Monitor* ran a lengthy page 1 exclusive on what had happened to the Jews of Roumania. The story contended that the "burden of persecution" had fallen mainly on the poor Jews of Roumania, while the rich managed to retain "a large measure of their wealth . . . and even some political influence." These "wealthy upper-crust" Jews were mainly intent on "safeguarding their wealth," though they did send some clothes to those Jews who had been deported to Transnistria, the Roumanian-controlled area between the Dniester and Bug rivers. This aid amounted to "no more than a drop in the limitless . . . sorrow," but, the reporter surmised, it may have "helped to save a few individual lives and salve more consciences." According to the *Christian Science Monitor* reporter, these Jews had found the means to continue to run their businesses and enterprises even under an antisemitic regime.

This story began on page 1 and covered almost 40 percent of a subsequent page, while the shorter article on the toll of 1.75 million appeared on page 7.[65]

Continuing with this theme, a month later in an article on the Hungarian situation the *Christian Science Monitor* reported that "32 members of the wealthiest Hungarian Jewish business families" had arrived in Portugal in a special German aircraft with forged entry visas. According to the article, a *Christian Science Monitor* exclusive, this group had been taken from Budapest to Stuttgart in a special train and then flown to Lisbon "while less happily-situated Jews in Hungary were reportedly being deported by the thousands to the notorious Nazi 'extermination camp' at Oswiecim in Poland." *The Christian Century* treated the story similarly.[66]

* * *

By late summer 1944 even those papers which had paid some attention to the Hungarian story had generally abandoned it. First, though, in July and August there was brief but limited interest in an offer by the Hungarians to release some Jews. Most papers never seriously considered the offer and generally dismissed it out of hand.[67] When it seemed increasingly certain that the deportations from Hungary would be completed and that over 200,000 Jews still in Budapest were in imminent danger, there was a last flurry of calls for rescue. The *New York Times* proposed that Hungarian cities and towns be retaliated against if the "murders do not stop." Anne O'Hare McCormick, the *New York Times* columnist, attacked those who argued that Hungarian Jews' fate was "hopeless." She believed that since the Nazis stood on the brink of defeat, they and their allies would be more inclined to abandon this policy, particularly if they knew its ramifications. There had to be serious and sustained "protests [and] demands" that rescue be initiated not just to save Jews "from death . . . but to save ourselves from ignominy."[68]

The Nation proposed that temporary asylum be provided refugees in neutral countries and that Palestine be opened to Jewish immigration.[69] *The New Republic* suggested that the United States and Britain give these "unhappy victims" the protection of American or British citizenship.[70] Alexander Uhl, *PM*'s foreign editor, called for rescue efforts to be mounted through neutral countries and for the British to facilitate immigration to Palestine.[71] Paul Winkler, columnist for the *Washington Post*, suggested the creation of Allied-backed "visas for somewhere," which would serve as guarantees that the Allies would ensure that the refugee reached some safe haven. This, he argued, would encourage neutral countries bordering on Nazi-controlled lands to admit more Jews, and would aid more Jews than just those who might reach free ports.[72]

Jewish groups also called for action.[73] A massive rally was held in Madison Square Garden on July 31. Despite the heat, over 40,000 people attended. Those who could not find seats packed the surrounding streets. The rally was designed to pressure the government to act, but the press paid it and subsequent efforts only cursory attention. When President Roosevelt and Governor Dewey sent messages to the rally expressing their "abhorrence" of Nazi behavior, I. F. Stone suggested in *PM* that they were doing nothing more than indulging in a "sentimental gesture," since they condemned the Nazis but refused to actively support American efforts which would save lives. Rescue, Stone argued, was possible but neither Britain nor America was willing to "provide . . . a destination" for those who might be saved.[74]

Though the *New York Post, The Nation,* the *Washington Post,* the Hearst papers, and *The New Republic* all insisted that "no effort should be spared" in order to save those who faced deportation, there was desperation and futility in the air. This was exemplified by the attitude of *The New Republic,* one of the first journals in the United States to argue that rescue before victory was not only possible but a moral imperative. *The New Republic,* which exactly a year earlier had published an entire section on how to help the Jews of Europe, now admitted that it did not seem likely that much could be done and mused that in all likelihood the "delivery of Hungary's Jews will come through military liberation rather than evacuation."[75] To all intents and purposes the story of Hungarian Jewry was over and this passionate advocate of saving Jews seemed to know it. Despite the Allied condemnations and the press calls for action, little was accomplished by the Allies to save Hungary's Jews. They were dispatched to their death in the same manner that so many of their co-religionists had been murdered in the preceding years.

Even as some papers reported each step in the ghettoization, deportation, and murder of Hungarian Jews, the press in general was beginning to tell a much happier tale: the liberation of Europe. Though it would be a while before the guns were totally silenced and all those in danger—Jew and non-Jew—were safe, reporters were already beginning to discover that in most of the places liberated by Allied armies there were no Jews left. After returning from Minsk, Edmund Stevens of the *Christian Science Monitor* reported on CBS that there remained "only 25 or 30 Jews where there were once nearly 30,000." According to Stevens the "rest were in nearby ditches."[76] A Soviet writer returned from the liberated portions of Poland; he had "heard many groans and seen many tears in Poland but no groans or tears of Jews," for "there are no Jews in Poland."[77] When Rome was liberated, the Italian paper *Il Tempo* estimated that out of a prewar Jewish population in Rome of 11,000, 6,000 had "vanished." There were reported to be 5,000 Jews surviving in Germany out of a prewar population of 500,000, and 180 in Vienna out of a prewar total of 150,000. For those few Jews who had miraculously managed to survive, "life ha[d] been very cruel." In a dispatch from a liberated Paris, *New York Times* reporter Raymond Daniell wrote of the few surviving Jews in that city that "no where else . . . is the mark of Nazism so indelibly printed as it is on the faces of these folk." On August 30 a UP report in the *Washington Post* estimated that only fifteen of the approximately 50,000 Jews of prewar Pinsk were "alive today."[78]

One cannot attribute the paucity of press coverage on Hungarian Jews to skepticism. It may have been that by the summer of 1944 most journalists had simply tired of this story even though they had never really paid it much attention. It was a familiar tale, and its very familiarity rendered it unworthy of page 1 or even page 10. It is possible that if the press had raised a major outcry, nothing would have happened. The Allies were as intent on adhering to a policy of rescue through victory as the Nazis were intent on destroying the remnants of European Jewry before their defeat. They would soon begin the terrible death marches designed to keep surviving Jews from falling into the hands of the liberating forces. But the press does not decide how it will treat a story on the basis of whether attention to a topic will effect a change in policy. The press pays attention to those stories it considers significant. And even at this late date for much of the American press this news was still a minor "sidelight."

=== 11 ===

Against Belief

Since the onset of Nazi rule Americans had greeted almost all the news of Nazi Germany's persecution of the Jews skeptically. Inevitably, their first reaction was to question whether it was true. Before, during, and even *after* the war many Americans, including those associated with the press, refused to believe the news they heard.

The "Show Me" Syndrome

In September 1942 Vernon McKenzie, writing in *Journalism Quarterly,* decried Americans' tendency to dismiss all reports of atrocities as propaganda. He blamed an American "attitude of cynicism" which prompted many people to declare that they would "not be such simpletons that they would be fooled again" as they had been by the much publicized but false atrocity stories of World War I. In a January 1943 Gallup poll nearly 30 percent of those asked dismissed the news that 2 million Jews had been killed in Europe as just a rumor. Another 24 percent had no opinion on the question. Informal polls taken by the *Detroit Free Press* and the *New York Post* in 1943 found that a broad range of Americans did not believe the atrocity reports.[1]

Journalists who had been stationed in Germany were among those most distressed by the American refusal to believe that the Germans were engaging in physical persecution. In March 1943 William Shirer, writing in the *Washington Post,* castigated the public for thinking that the stories of the atrocities were untrue or had been magnified for "propaganda purposes." He attributed this attitude to a "silly sort of supercynicism and superskepticism" which persisted despite the fact that there was "no earthly reason" for people not to believe. These doubts were not, of course, a new phenomenon. When Shirer was a reporter in Berlin, "most of the Americans who visited Germany in the early Nazi days used to say: 'The Nazis can't really be as bad as you correspondents paint them.' " Shirer found the persistence of disbelief particularly inexplicable in light of the fact that the Nazis had themselves admitted the truth of some of the atrocities and that many others had been committed in public view.[2]

In April 1943 Dorothy Thompson, in her column "On the Record," decried the American conviction that atrocity stories were either "merely propaganda" or "greatly exaggerated."[3] In January 1944 Arthur Koestler also expressed his frustration that so many people refused to believe that the "grim stories of Nazi atrocities are true." Writing in the Sunday *New York Times Magazine,* Koestler cited public opinion polls in the United States in which nine out of ten average Americans dismissed the accusations against the Nazis as propaganda lies and flatly stated that they did not believe a word of them. How, he wondered, could Americans be convinced that this "nightmare" was reality? *The Christian Century* responded to Koestler by arguing that there really was no point in "screaming" about the atrocities against the Jews because this would only "emotionally exhaust" those who wanted to devote their energies *"after"* the war to "building peace." In another one of the magazine's long line of disparaging comments about the Jewish community, the article castigated "people who claim to be more aroused about this mass killing of Jews in Europe than the rest of us, . . . [and who] seem to want more committees." Koestler, the journal graciously acknowledged, was "too honest a person" to be among those who were the "screamers."[4]

Even members of the armed forces vigorously dismissed the accounts of horror. *Saturday Evening Post* editor Edgar Snow related how an American flyer who had just returned from bombing the German lines emphatically stated that "he didn't believe all that 'propaganda' about Nazi brutality." This soldier, who was typical of many of his colleagues, was convinced that it was "probably all lies" designed to convince Americans of the enemy's nefarious ways. Moreover, soldiers argued, there was no real difference between Axis and Allied forces. "They say they are fighting for an ideal and they are ready to die for it, and that's just what we're doing." A newspaperman who was serving in the armed forces wrote that the "boys" in uniform got "vastly more indignant about gasoline rationing than they do about the slaughter of civilians." Koestler, who had been lecturing to the troops since 1941, also found that the men in uniform didn't believe in "the mass graves of Poland; they have never heard of Lidice, Treblinka or Belzec. You can convince them for an hour, then they shake themselves, their mental self-defense begins to work and in a week the shrug of incredulity has returned like a reflex."[5]

This confusion regarding what was going on in Europe did not really dissipate with either the passage of time or the release of more information. In October 1944 Averell Harriman, American Ambassador to the Soviet Union, felt compelled to reassure the press that the reports of massacres and atrocities committed by the Germans and their supporters in Russian territory "have not been and cannot be exaggerated." Though a December 1944 Gallup poll revealed that 76 percent of those queried now believed that many people had been "murdered" in concentration camps, the estimates they gave of the number who had died indicated that they had not really grasped the scope of the tragedy. Furthermore, while more Americans were now willing to believe that many people had been killed, they generally did not believe in the existence of gas chambers and death camps.[6]

By the final weeks of the war increasing numbers of reporters and columnists were complaining about the public's unshakable doubts. In April 1945 *Washington Post* correspondent Edward Folliard observed that on the basis of his experiences with American forces, "where atrocities are concerned most Americans are skeptics . . . they have to be shown" to believe and most of them had apparently not yet seen enough.[7] Syndicated columnist Marquis Childs criticized Americans who "put down to 'propaganda' the latest reports of murder factories."[8] Paul Winkler described his frustration in trying to convey to the "ever-skeptical masses" the proof of "Teutonic bestiality." Henry J. Taylor of the *New York World Telegram* and the Scripps-Howard newspapers, declared it "incredible that there should be any doubt at home about the truth of the Nazis' wholesale atrocities," but there were. Taylor observed that "in the last war only a few of the German atrocity stories were true, yet most of them were believed. In this war the atrocity stories are true yet few seem to be believed."[9]

But doubts still persisted even at the very end of the war after American soldiers, reporters, editors, publishers, and members of Congress had seen camps and after the Army Signal Corps screened a movie on the atrocities in American theaters. In May 1945, upon his return from visiting the camps, Joseph Pulitzer, publisher and editor of the *St. Louis Post Dispatch,* wrote "A Report to the American People," in which he described Buchenwald and Dachau. He began this lengthy article by expressing his dismay at finding that there were still Americans who were saying, "this talk of atrocities is all propaganda." On May 5, 1945, *Editor & Publisher* recommended that all newspapers devote as much space as possible to pictures of Nazi atrocities. The magazine acknowledged that "for years all Americans" had found it difficult to believe the atrocity stories. But even after these stories had been verified by war correspondents, some Americans had "built up such immunity to what they call propaganda that they still refuse to believe it." Some of the soldiers who participated in the liberation of the camps took pictures of what they saw. When they returned to the United States, they found that people were impressed by the fact that the photographs were not "official" pictures taken by the Army Signal Corps, but were photos by an "amateur photographer in which there could be no doctoring of scenes and no faking of film." Other soldiers returned to find that even their own pictures did not convince people. "They said it's propaganda." One G.I. who was at Dachau told his parents what he saw "and they didn't know what the hell I was talkin' about." From that point on, he "rarely mentioned" his experience.[10]

There were critics who argued that the reports, photographs, and films detailing what had been found in the camps were being released in order to implant in the American public a feeling of vengeance. James Agee, writing in *The Nation* of May 19, 1945, attacked the films even though he had not seen them—he did not believe "it necessary" to do so. "Such propaganda"—even if true—was designed to make Americans equate all Germans with the few who perpetrated these crimes. Milton Mayer, in an article in *The Progressive,* went a step further than Agee. He not only argued against vengeance but questioned whether the films and reports could really be true. "There are to be sure fantastic discrepancies in the reports."[11]

This attitude was not unique to America. The English public was also difficult to convince. In the April 28, 1945, edition of the *New Statesman and Nation* an article decried the people "who don't believe, don't *even now* believe and say that this is merely a newspaper stunt, or is government propaganda." In mid-April 1945 BBC officials, well aware of listeners' inclination to dismiss any reports of atrocities as "propaganda," broadcast Edward R. Murrow's famous depiction of Buchenwald rather than that of their own BBC reporter. They did so because they believed that the British public, which held Murrow in high esteem, would not reject information broadcast by him as government-inspired atrocity tales.[12]

The Responsibility of the Press

Though a number of columnists and reporters complained about these doubts as the war neared its end, the fact is that the press bears a great measure of responsibility for the public's skepticism and ignorance of the scope of the wartime tragedy. The public's doubts were strengthened and possibly even created by the manner in which the media told the story. If the press did not help plant the seeds of doubt in readers' minds, it did little to eradicate them. In the pages that follow we shall examine how, as the war neared its end, editors and reporters tried to explain their treatment of the news.

During the war journalists frequently said that the news of deportations and executions did not come from eyewitnesses who could personally confirm what had happened and therefore, as journalists, they were obliged to treat it skeptically. This explanation is faulty because much of the information came from German statements, broadcasts, and newspapers. If anything, these sources would have been inclined to deny, not verify, the news.[13] Neutral sources also affirmed the reliability of the reports. Moreover, even when the press did encounter witnesses, it often dismissed what they had to say because they were not considered "reliable" or "impartial."

The victims themselves recognized the difficulty they faced in piercing the barriers of incredulity. A Polish underground courier who, in August 1944, reached London with news of the stepped-up pace of the slaughter of Hungarian Jews was shocked to find that despite the fact that he brought news from within Auschwitz itself, "nobody will believe." As late as 1944 eyewitness accounts—particularly those of victims—were not considered irrefutable evidence even if they came from independent sources and corroborated one another. The press often categorized them as prejudiced or exaggerated. At the end of the war Kenneth McCaleb, war editor of the *New York Daily Mirror,* admitted that whenever he had read about German atrocities, he had not taken them seriously because they had always come from " 'foreigners' who, many of us felt, had some ax to grind and must be exaggerat[ing]."[14]

Given this prejudicial feeling about witnesses, one would have expected that visits by journalists themselves to the massacre sites would have dissipated these doubts. But when the barriers to belief were strong enough, even a face-to-face encounter with the remains of a Nazi atrocity did not suffice to dispel doubts, as an incident in the fall of 1943 demonstrated. In October 1943, as German forces were beginning to retreat from Russian territory, Soviet officials brought a group of foreign reporters to Babi Yar, the ravine outside Kiev in which the Nazis had killed thousands of Jews. The Russians told the reporters that the Germans had massacred between 50,000 and 80,000 Kiev Jews in September 1941 and the total number of Jews of Kiev who had been killed might climb to over 100,000.

By this point the Nazi threat to "exterminate" the Jews should have been understood as a literal one. There was little reason, in light of the abundance of evidence, to deny that multitudes were being murdered as part of a planned program of annihilation. But despite all the detail there was a feeling among some correspondents, *New York Times* reporter Bill Lawrence most prominent among them, that the reports that Hitler and his followers had conducted a systematic extermination campaign were untrue. Lawrence did not doubt that Hitler had "treated the Jews badly, forcing many of them to flee to the sanctuaries of the West"; but even in October 1943—ten months after the Allied declaration confirming the Nazi policy of exterminating the Jews and six months after Bermuda—he could not believe that the Nazis had murdered "millions of Jews, Slavs, gypsies. . . . and those who might be mentally retarded."[15]

His skepticism permeated his story on Babi Yar. Though he acknowledged that there were no more Jews in Kiev, their whereabouts he simply dismissed as a "mystery." Lawrence's report surely left even the least skeptical reader unconvinced of the Babi Yar slayings.

> On the basis of what we saw, it is impossible for this correspondent to judge the truth or falsity of the story told to us. It is the *contention* of the authorities in Kiev that the Germans, with characteristic thoroughness, not only burned the bodies and clothing, but also crumbled the bones, and shot and burned the bodies of all prisoners of war participating in the burning, except for a handful that escaped.[16]

Equally skeptical about the reports of mass murder was Jerome Davis of Hearst's International News Service and the *Toronto Star.* Neither Lawrence nor Davis seemed able to accept the idea of a massacre, much less of a Final Solution.

Davis's and Lawrence's doubts would have been more understandable had their colleagues who visited the site with them manifested the same suspicions. But they drew markedly different conclusions. Bill Downs, who was Moscow correspondent for CBS and *Newsweek,* was convinced that one of the "most horrible tragedies in this Nazi era of atrocities occurred there." Henry Shapiro of United Press, Maurice Hindus, a special correspondent for the *St. Louis Post Dispatch,* and Paul Winterton of the BBC all described the flesh, human bones, hair, shoes, glass cases, and even gold bridgework they found in the dirt. Lawrence and Davis, who saw the same things the other reporters found, could not believe that they represented the remains of thousands. Though neither Lawrence nor Davis suggested it, it was obvious that they both believed that these items could have been placed in the sand by those who wished the reporters to believe that such things had happened there.[17]

Even meetings with eyewitnesses who had seen the action and participated in the burning of the bodies did little, if anything, to dispel Lawrence or Davis's skepticism. In fact, they seem to have reinforced it. Lawrence described the witnesses as men "who *said* they were Soviet soldiers who had been captured by the Germans and forced to take part in the disinterment and burning." Davis also described the men as "persons who *say* they were eyewitnesses."[18] In contrast, Shapiro described the same men as "three living witnesses of the German effort to exhume and burn every body in this charnel mass." The fact that they were both Red Army lieutenants and "like most of the victims in Babi Yar— Jews" seemed to render them less credible witnesses for Lawrence and Davis but not for Downs, Shapiro, and Hindus.[19] The Reuters Moscow correspondent also sent a straightforward report devoid of any skepticism in which he described how he had seen "the relics of giant funeral pyres in which the Germans . . . burned the remains of thousands of men, women, and children whom they had murdered."[20] In his report to the BBC Winterton relayed witnesses' accounts of how the ground moved after the pit had been filled in because many of the victims were still alive when they were buried.[21]

Lawrence's refusal to believe may explain why the *New York Times,* in contrast to a number of other papers, including the *St. Louis Post Dispatch, Los Angeles Times, Los Angeles Examiner,* and *New York Journal American,* ran the story on page 3 and not on page 1.[22] The *New York Journal American* not only ran Shapiro's story on page 1 but gave it a banner headline:

100,000 KIEV CIVILIANS KILLED BY NAZIS
Wholesale Massacre Revealed[23]

Despite subsequent reports further confirming the disappearance of the Jews from cities and towns throughout Europe, Lawrence maintained his "built in skepticism" for a long time. If someone such as Lawrence, a seasoned reporter for the most important and influential American newspaper and one who had the chance to visit the site and talk with witnesses, remained so riddled with doubt, it is not surprising that the American public, which depended on the press to bring it the news, tenaciously clung to its skepticism. As we shall see, Lawrence was far from alone. In fact many of those in the highest and most powerful echelons of his profession maintained their skepticism for another year and a half.[24]

It was not until ten months later, in August 1944, that Lawrence was willing to accept the validity of the charges against the Germans. It was his visit to Maidanek, one of the first death camps to be reached by the Russian forces, which finally erased his skepticism. Lawrence's report on this visit constituted more than just an extensive description of the camp and the horrors that took place there. It was also a *mea culpa* for what he now knew to be his unjustified doubts.

> Never have I been confronted with such complete evidence clearly establishing every allegation made by those investigating German crimes. After inspection of Maidanek, I am now prepared to believe any story of German atrocities, no matter how savage, cruel and depraved.[25]

Though Lawrence was at last willing to acknowledge that these stories were true, the *New York Times* apparently was convinced that many of its readers were not, and it took the unprecedented step of declaring its faith in one of its reporters. An editorial which appeared on the same day as Lawrence's description of Maidanek assured readers that he was "employed by this newspaper because he is known to be a thorough and accurate correspondent" and that therefore they could believe what he wrote. Lawrence, who eventually became the *New York Times* White House correspondent, before joining ABC, wrote in his autobiography that never "before or since have I seen the *Times* so describe one of its reporters."[26]

Other reporters who toured Maidanek with Lawrence had similar reactions. Associated Press staff member Daniel De Luce admitted that prior to the visit most of the other American and British correspondents in the group "could not even begin to imagine the proportions of its frightfulness."[27] Now they had no doubts.

Edgar Snow of the *Saturday Evening Post,* Richard Lauterbach of *Time* and *Life,* and Maurice Hindus of the *St. Louis Post Dispatch* and the *New York Herald Tribune* all found the storehouse for the personal possessions of the victims more "terrifying" than even the gas chambers and the crematorium. In them they found rooms filled with shoes—one for men's shoes and one for women's—kitchenware, clothes, books, pocketknives, and other items that the unsuspecting victims had brought with them to facilitate their "relocation."[28] Maidanek "suddenly became real" to Lauterbach when he stood on top of a "sea" of 820,000 pairs of shoes which had cascaded out of a warehouse. After viewing the camp *Newsweek*'s Moscow correspondent described those killed upon arrival as "relatively lucky."[29] In the introduction to his detailed description of this camp, Snow explained why he broke with his magazine's norm and wrote about a subject which was fully reported by the daily press. Maidanek was evidence of the way Nazi ideology enabled people to commit "crimes almost too monstrous for the human mind to accept."[30]

But even now not everyone was convinced. In what could by this time be described as an almost reflexive action, *The Christian Century* rejected the news and attacked those who relayed it. It chided American newspapers for giving the story the "big headline of the day," and claimed that the "parallel between this story and the 'corpse factory' atrocity tale" of World War I was "too striking to be overlooked." Neither the eyewitness journalist accounts nor the pictures of the gas chambers, the crematoria, the piles of bones and skeletons, the thousands of pairs of shoes, and the canisters of poison gas convinced this prominent journal that this report was not an atrocity story.[31]

Christian Century argued that its doubts were justified because the information came from the Russians, whom the journal did not trust. This lack of faith in the Russians had been exacerbated by Germany's announcement in April 1943 that it had discovered a mass grave containing the bodies of over 10,000 Poles, mainly officers, near Katyn forest, west of the Russian city of Smolensk. These officers, who had all been shot with their hands tied behind their backs, were believed to have been men who surrendered to the Russians in September 1939.[32] Though the London based Polish government in exile charged the Russians with murder, most of the American press—with the exception of a few papers and journals including *The Christian Century*—dismissed the German claim as an attempt to divide the Allies and arouse anti-Russian sentiment.

Christian Century further justified its dismissal of the Maidanek story by claiming that it was designed to divert attention from the Russian refusal to aid the Warsaw uprising of August 1944. The Russians, anxious to ensure that a communist government would rule postwar Poland, had purposely stalled their advance into Warsaw until the Germans had executed hundreds of thousands of Poles who had participated in the revolt. It was generally recognized in the west that the Russians wanted them killed because they believed that their loyalties were to the London based Polish government in exile and not to the Russian backed Polish Committee of National Liberation.[33]

Had the Russian released news of Maidanek been the only proof of German atrocities and had reporters not been brought to the site to inspect it and taken pictures of what they found, *Christian Century*'s doubts might have been more understandable. But given the human remains the reporters found at Maidanek and the preponderance of evidence which preceded it, much of which had not come from the Russians, such skepticism and derision of those who did believe seemed highly misplaced and possibly motivated by other sentiments.

Even this news of Maidanek and the eyewitness accounts by reputable American correspondents did not significantly change the way the American press treated this story: momentarily attention was paid, but all too quickly the news was forgotten. Though no other paper or journal was as skeptical as *The Christian Century*, few seemed inclined to abandon what had by now become an established pattern of relegating such news to positions of little importance. After a brief wave of interest, reports once again appeared in short articles on inner pages. But this pattern of deprecating the importance of the news regarding the Final Solution did not originate with the press. In fact the press was faithfully duplicating an Allied policy of obfuscation and camouflage.

Universalizing the Victims

Part of the responsibility for both American skepticism and the press's ambiguous treatment of this news can be traced directly to Allied opposition to publicizing reports of atrocities against Jewish victims. On many occasions when atrocities against Jews were discussed, the identity of the victims was universalized. In other words, Jews became Poles or Russians or innocent civilians.[34] American and British leaders had been intent on avoiding mention of Jews as the specific victims of Nazi hostility as early as 1938 at Evian, and their policy had not substantially changed since. The Allies argued that if they treated Jews as a separate entity, it would validate Nazi ideology. A truer explanation for this behavior was American and British fear that singling out the unique fate of the Jews would strengthen the demands of those who wanted the Allies to undertake specific rescue action on their behalf. The Americans worried that they might be asked to admit more Jewish refugees, and the British were concerned that pressure would be put upon them to open Palestine to Jews.

It therefore became Allied policy to refer to "political refugees" and not Jews, even when these refugees were clearly Jews. Rarely did any reporters or editorial board take note of this policy. One notable exception was *PM*'s Alexander Uhl, who angrily wrote during Bermuda that delegates were so anxious to avoid linking the rescue problem with Jews that it had been regarded as "almost improper to mention the word 'Jew' " at Bermuda despite the fact that there were, according to Uhl, "at least 2,000,000 whose very existence is threatened."[35]

Probably the most outrageous example of this explicit policy of ignoring the Jewish aspect of the tragedy occurred in Moscow in the fall of 1943. There Churchill, Roosevelt, and Stalin met and affixed their signature to what is known as the Moscow Declaration, which warned that

> Germans who take part in the wholesale shooting of *Italian* officers or in the execution of *French, Dutch, Belgian* or *Norwegian* hostages or of *Cretan* peasants, or who have shared in slaughters inflicted on the people of *Poland* or in the territories of the *Soviet Union* . . . will be brought back to the scene of their crimes and judged on the spot by the peoples whom they have outraged.

Nowhere in the declaration were Jews even obliquely mentioned, a phenomenon the press simply ignored. While there were some exceptions to this Allied policy, e.g., the December 1942 statement confirming the Nazi policy of exterminating the Jews, they were few. When declarations did contain references to Jews, as was the case in March 1944 when Roosevelt referred to the Hungarian situation, the President's advisers vigorously worked to ensure that they were not too prominently mentioned.[36]

This policy began to change somewhat when John Pehle and the War Refugee Board pushed for a different approach. But only quite late in the war did the Office of War Information officially take the "lead in getting out, and on official records, every pertinent fact regarding murder and mistreatment practiced by the Nazis." Prior to that it had avoided too frequent mention of atrocities, particularly those against Jews. The *War Information Guide*, a handbook prepared and distributed by the Office of War Information for government personnel and for "those outside groups which are cooperating with the government in giving the American people the full facts of war," instructed that atrocity stories were to be used to illustrate the enemy's "planned strategy and principles," and not just to incite hatred. Government officials determined that all information on atrocities which bore upon the "rulers and ruling parties in the countries with which we are at war should be publicized." Reports that simply inspired Americans to hate "all members of the races guilty of such action (i.e. Japanese)" were to be avoided.

There was, however, an even more stringent policy in operation regarding atrocities against Jews. The Office of War Information, working in tandem with the Administration, tried to severely limit any public attention paid to this story. Despite the fact that the Final Solution was the prime illustration of the enemy's "strategy and principles," the Office of War Information wanted it to be avoided by news agencies and not mentioned in war propaganda. Deputy Director of the Office of War Information Arthur Sweetser sent a memorandum to Leo Rosten, who was Deputy Director in charge of information on the enemy, on the "impending Nazi extermination of the Jews." In it he argued that the story of atrocities would be "confused and misleading if it appears to be simply affecting the Jewish people," and therefore news of the particular fate of the Jews should be contained and even suppressed. Consequently, when the news of German atrocities was publicized, the Jewish aspect was often eliminated.[37]

The press mirrored the official policy of omitting mention of Jews or incorporating them into the general suffering faced by many other national groups. Such was the case in 1943 when Charles E. Gratke, foreign editor of the *Christian Science Monitor*, who had served as the paper's Berlin correspondent in the 1930s, analyzed the first decade of Nazi rule. Here is Gratke on Nazi racial hatred:

> No one in 1933, hearing the vitriolic denunciations of the Poles, could escape the meaning of the Nazi doctrine of racial hatred. In the days when Hitler came to power, few Nazi insults were more potent than to call a man a "Pole." . . . And today, under the Gestapo heel, an entire race is being systematically decimated. . . . Millions—literally—of *Polish men and women* have paid in final anguish for the disbelief of the world.

Gratke had been in Germany during the Nazi takeover. He had heard bitter denunciations of the Jews and had witnessed the first steps in their disenfranchisement. His paper had reported various aspects of the Final Solution, albeit in a confused and ambiguous fashion. Moreover, his article appeared *after* the Allies had confirmed the existence of a plan to annihilate the Jews. Nonetheless, in his article no "Jew" was to be found in his discussion of either "racial superiority" or acts of persecution.[38]*

The *Christian Science Monitor* was, of course, not alone in this curious behavior. Another striking omission was evident in the January 1943 *Los Angeles Times* review of the preceding ten years, which it termed the "Black Decade." The review was largely based on information compiled by the Office of War Information. Although the April 1 boycott against German Jews was mentioned as one of the outstanding events of 1933, *Kristallnacht* was not referred to, nor was the news of the extermination program included in the listing for 1942, when the Allies had jointly confirmed the existence of a program to annihilate the Jewish people. The massacre of 2,000 Czechs and the destruction of Lidice and Levszaky in the aftermath of Heydrich's murder were included in the list of events.[40]

Even when war had virtually ended and the camps were being liberated, reporters continued to incorporate the fate of the Jews into that of all other national groups that had been incarcerated and murdered at the camps.[41] For example, Edgar Snow wrote that at Maidanek "Jews, Germans and other Europeans were all robbed in common and were all fed to the same ovens."[42] Other reports described the victims as "men, women and children of 22 nationalities"—some citing Jews as constituting "half" or "most" of the victims, others simply listing them along with Russians, Poles, Frenchmen, Italians, Czechs, Yugoslavs, Greeks, Belgians, Germans, and Dutchmen. *Time* correspondent Sidney Olsen, who accompanied the U.S. Seventh Army as it liberated

---

* Sometimes it was hard to discern whether a press reference to "Poles" included Jews or not. In January 1940 the *New York Times* had run two editorials on Nazi "horrors" in Poland. They decried the "bitter agony of the Poles" and the German attempt to "destroy the Polish spirit and disperse the Polish people," which was really an attempt to "exterminate a whole people." Did those threatened with extermination include Jews? The reader was left free to decide because Jews were not mentioned. Another editorial about the Poles observed that "no people in modern times has been subjected to such calculated brutality on such a large scale." The Nazi "bloodthirsty treatment of the Poles is enough to damn them beyond defense."[39] Here too it was unclear if "Poles" included Jews.

Dachau, described its inmates as "Russians, French, Yugoslavs, Italians, and Poles." In this camp, Olsen observed, were "the men of all nations whom Hitler's agents had picked out as prime opponents of Nazism; here were the very earliest of Nazi-haters. Here were German social democrats, Spanish survivors of the Spanish Civil War." But nowhere in his article was there a Jew.[43]*

This reaction was not simply indicative of reporters' failure to know the specific identity of the inmates or victims of a particular camp. It was indicative of something far more significant. Throughout the war the press had tended to ignore or minimize the specific fate of the Jews, and even now that correspondents were witnessing the grim results of the Final Solution, they could not grasp what they were seeing. None of the reporters who toured Maidanek—even those who mentioned Jews as among the victims—associated what they saw there with the Nazi plan to annihilate the Jewish people. It was as if they recognized that a battle against innocent civilians had occurred but did not understand what war it was part of. This failure to understand that Maidanek or any one of numerous other places reached by the Allies in the last months of the war was part of this particular larger picture, the plan of annihilation, is a reflection of the dissonant way the press treated the persecution of the Jews. Because most journalists had ignored and minimized the reports of atrocities against the Jews, when they saw the final outcome they found it difficult to admit to themselves—and to their readers—what they were witnessing.

Press inability to understand the all-encompassing nature of the event that Maidanek and other places like it represented would become painfully apparent in the final moments of the war when a group of America's most influential publishers and editors visited German concentration camps. On April 12, 1945, General Dwight Eisenhower visited one of the first concentration camps to be liberated by the Allies. In a letter to his wife Mamie, Eisenhower wrote that he "deliberately" visited the camp in order to be able to give *"first hand* evidence . . . if ever, in the future,

---

* One of the very few articles that made it quite clear who the victims at Maidanek were appeared in *Life:*

LUBLIN FUNERAL
Russians honor Jews whom Nazis
gassed and cremated in mass[44]

there develops a tendency to charge these allegations merely to propaganda."[45] He also decided that influential Americans who helped shape public opinion must do the same as a further way of forestalling any assertion that the story of Nazi brutality was just propaganda. At his suggestion Washington invited a group of American publishers and editors to see the German concentration camps which had been liberated by American forces. The group, which was selected by the War Department, included, among others, publishers and editors of the *New York Times, St. Louis Post Dispatch, Reader's Digest, Detroit Free Press, Los Angeles Times,* the Hearst papers, and the Scripps-Howard papers. The reports by these editors and publishers, who visited Buchenwald, Bergen-Belsen, and Dachau, as well as the reports by correspondents accompanying the Allied forces in the weeks before V-E Day, were widely featured in the press. Many were conspicuously placed on the front page.[46]

Now that these top members of the press corps were face to face with the victims, their doubts about the atrocity reports disappeared. But even now they were unable to grasp what the Final Solution had been. They did not seem to understand that the fate of the Jews had been unique in both ideology and scope. Their failure to comprehend the Jewish aspect of this entire tragedy was reflected in their description of the victims and explanation of why they were in the camps. Joseph Pulitzer, in an address to the Missouri Legislature upon his return, described the camps as full of *"political* prisoners" including "Jews, Poles, and Russians."[47] Malcolm Bingay, editor of the *Detroit Free Press,* explained that the prisoners he saw at camps were there because

they refused to accept the political philosophy of the Nazi party. . . .
First Jews and anti-Nazi Germans, then other brave souls who
refused to conform. [48]

These editors and publishers described the people they found in the camps as "prisoners whose only crime was that they disagreed or were suspected of disagreeing with the Nazi philosophy."[49] When twelve members of Congress returned from a visit to Dachau, Buchenwald, and Nordhausen at about the same time, they did the same and described the victims of the Nazis as those "who refused to accept the principles of Nazism or who opposed the saddling of the Nazi yoke on their countries."[50]

Jews were not in the camps for any of these reasons, and the press did not seem to understand that even now. While no one denied that Jews were mistreated and often were the most cruelly mistreated, journalists still seemed reluctant to admit that much of what they were seeing was part of a program to systematically wipe out an entire people. They had been unable to link Maidanek, Babi Yar, or the fact that in every place reached by the Allies the Jews were gone with the plan to destroy the Jewish people. So too they did not associate what they were now seeing in these camps, where most of the survivors were Jews, with the Final Solution. Once again the fate of the Jews was intermingled with that of the other victims. The way in which the issue was dealt with was typified by an official army report on Buchenwald which noted that all prisoners were treated brutally and "Jews were given even worse treatment than the others." It was the same theme that had been apparent in so many of the previous press reports: everyone suffered and the Jews probably a bit more than everyone else.

These visiting publishers, editors, and reporters seemed almost eager to impress on the American public that Jews had not been the only ones to be killed. The persistence of this theme in their reports raises the question of whether they believed or had been convinced by government and military officials that the public would be less aroused if it thought that only Jews had been mistreated. Jack Bell, war correspondent for the *Miami Herald,* acknowledged that Jews had been killed but hastened to point out that they were but one group among many.

> The murder of Jews was automatic, yes, but it was not only they who were tortured. Germans who opposed the Nazis, slaves from every nation in Europe, children and women, as well as men— all came, were beaten and worked until they could go on no longer—then they died of wounds, or starvation and their bodies were carted to crematories.[51]

The editors' report, issued in Paris on May 5, did the same. It described what happened in the camps and noted that "after the Jews, the most cruelly treated victims were the Russians and the Poles.[52] According to the Congressional delegation, Jews, Russians, and Poles were "treated with a greater degree of severity than other nationalities." Neither the editors nor the members of Congress were able to admit that though multitudes had been cruelly tortured and murdered, Jews alone had been singled out for total national annihilation.[53] This was something that should have been clear to them given their access to the news and the dispatches. But because they had ignored and avoided this story during the preceding years, they did not seem able to make the leap of imagination necessary in order to understand.

The *St. Louis Post Dispatch* took issue with the Congressional delegation for describing the victims as "intellectuals, political leaders and all others who would not embrace and support the Nazi philosophy and program." It pointed out that they were not the only ones to feel the Nazi wrath. Also destined for extermination were those "whose only offense was living." But then the paper went on to explain why the latter were killed:

> The purpose was not only to suppress opposition but also to slaughter conquered peoples so as to weaken their military potential.[54]

This may have correctly explained why the Nazis killed many of their victims. However, in the case of the Jews, the German rationale was entirely different. Jews were not killed in order to suppress opposition or weaken the military potential of the enemy. In fact Jews were killed even when this weakened the *Germans'* military potential or deflected the full capacity of their might from the war effort. The press may not yet have known about the slave factories which were closed down when the Jews who worked in them producing critically needed munitions, uniforms, and other war matériel were dispatched to their death. But it did know about the millions who had been killed in various death camps and should have been able to recognize the drain such a program imposed on the war effort.

When the camps were opened in the spring of 1945, the chaos of war and postwar confusion reigned supreme, making it extremely difficult to ascertain precise numbers and know what was being found in other places. But enough information had previously emerged to enable Allied journalists, had they been inclined, to see the larger picture. The Hearst papers were among the few that were willing to explicitly acknowledge that "the Jews of Europe have been the *principal victims* of this bestiality."[55] There were some reporters who understood that the philosophy which led to the destruction of the Jews was inherently different from that which resulted in the destruction of so many others.[56] For example, Paul Ghali, correspondent of the Chicago Daily News–

Post Dispatch News Service, recognized that Germany had won its war against the Jews.

> At least one point in Adolf Hitler's "Mein Kampf" program has been carried out thoroughly—the bestial extermination of European Jews. Of the total of eight million Jews living in Germany and German occupied countries before the war, 6,200,000 have died from either execution, cruel treatment or starvation.[57]

But such observations were exceptions to the rule. In most cases the particular fate of the Jews was incorporated into that of all of Europe's peoples.

Another example of confusion or myopia was the persistent appearance during the spring of 1945 of press reports describing the *concentration* camps, as opposed to the death camps such as Maidanek and Auschwitz, as sites where the worst atrocities were committed.* Gene Currivan of the *New York Times* described Buchenwald as "second only to . . . Dachau, near Munich, as the world's worst atrocity center."[58] Judy Barden, staff correspondent of the *New York Sun,* described Dachau as "evidence of the most horribly gruesome tortures yet to come to light from any German prison camp." Associated Press reporter Howard Cowan called Dachau the "most dreaded extermination camp."[59] As terrible as these places may have been, the death camps in the east were far worse. Though these reporters had not been there, enough detailed information had been given to the press to demonstrate the differences between the two kinds of camps. The War Refugee Board's detailed report on Auschwitz had been released in November 1944. A large group of journalists had visited Maidanek in August 1944. Their descriptions and photographs of the place had appeared in numerous papers and magazines. The camps visited in spring 1945 by war correspondents and publishers— e.g., Dachau, Bergen-Belsen, and Buchenwald—contained prisoners who had been transferred during the final stages of the war from Auschwitz and other death camps to camps in Germany. These prisoners were able to disabuse reporters of the notion that these were "the worst camps." And in certain cases they

---

* The death camps, i.e., those camps which contained gas chambers for the express purpose of killing victims, were in the east and were therefore liberated by the Russians. The camps liberated by the Americans and British were in Germany and Austria.

did. Helen Kirkpatrick, of the Chicago Daily News–Post Dispatch News Service, described Buchenwald not as one of the worst camps, but as

> the best camp of its kind in Germany, its inmates say. It was the rest camp of camps, with organized recreation. The worst camps were those at Auschwitz, in Silesia, and Lublin, Poland where many of Buchenwald's residents had been at one time or another.[60]

In his famous broadcast Edward R. Murrow did the same. Based on what he learned from various inmates who had been in other camps, he described Buchenwald not as the worst, but as "the best concentration camp in Germany." But Murrow and Kirkpatrick were exceptions. Most of their colleagues' reports simply ignored the death camps. During this period, when the discussion of the concentration camps and German atrocities was front-page news in many American papers, the death camps, particularly those established solely for murdering Jews, such as the ones at Treblinka, Chelmno, Sobibor, and Belzec, were rarely mentioned. While some of them had been destroyed by the Germans, reports about them had reached the west. Maidanek, which had been visited by American reporters, was conspicuous by its absence from the news reports on the camps. Auschwitz, whose function and physical plan had been described in great detail by the War Refugee Board report, was often not mentioned.

It is true that reporters concentrate on and tend to believe what they and their colleagues can see, and no report of other places which were worse could compare with witnessing these graphic horrors first hand. Some reporters who had seen a number of different camps understood that there were gradations of horror. Henry J. Taylor, a special writer for the Scripps-Howard newspapers, worried that "much of the unspeakable horrors in some of them [the camps] may be doubted when the better treatment in the other camps becomes widely known." By April 30 he had already been in eighteen different camps, including labor camps, prisoner-of-war camps, and "horror camps," in which the "brutality . . . [was] beyond dispute." Of these he found Bergen-Belsen "the largest and most terrible." In most cases even for reporters, whose task it is to piece together what they see with other information in order to give readers a coherent picture of a larger issue, only seeing constituted believing. They witnessed the remains of what had happened at Dachau, Bergen-Belsen, Ohrdruf, and Buchenwald, and in their minds and reports these places came to epitomize Nazi atrocities. Moreover, what reporters saw in these camps was so terrible that it was difficult to imagine—even if one read about it in a government report or a colleague's account—that anything could be worse. As Percy Knauth, who wrote the *Time* report on Buchenwald, observed, "this was the legend come to life before my eyes."[61]

Had this tendency to describe such camps as Buchenwald and Dachau as the "worst" of the camps prevailed only during this period of liberation, it would be less noteworthy. But for many years following the end of the war it persisted. Raul Hilberg describes this pattern as a "functional blindness" which obliterates both the particular character of the German action against the Jews and the particular identity of the victims.[62] The Final Solution and its victims, the Jews, lose their specific identity and become part of an all-encompassing program of Nazi persecution and the general mass of victims of this persecution. During the war this "blindness," when practiced by the Allied governments and emulated by the press, functioned as a means of forestalling demands for specific action to rescue Jews.

Responsibility for the confusion about the Jewish identity of the victims lies not only with the Americans and the British but with the Russians as well; they also practiced a policy of ignoring the distinctive antisemitic nature of German persecution. At first the Russians were not that inclined to avoid mention of the Jews as victims. In January 1942 they released a detailed account of "monstrous villainies, atrocities and outrages committed by the German authorities in the invaded Soviet territories." Jews were cited as one of a series of groups who had been persecuted, including Russians, Ukrainians, Letts, Armenians, and Uzbeks. In the report the victims at Babi Yar were described by Russian officials as "Ukrainians, Russians and Jews who showed their loyalty to the Soviet Government." The Jews who were killed, according to the report, were "unarmed helpless . . . toilers."[63] The truth was that these Jews were not killed because of their loyalty to the Soviets or because the Germans had a specific policy of killing "toilers." In this report—as in subsequent reports, in which the references to Jews were even more oblique—the Russians refrained from stating what they already knew to be true, namely that the Germans were methodically subjecting massive numbers of Jews to systematic executions because they were Jews.[64]

Even government observers in Washington, where a policy of not singling out Jews as victims was strongly adhered to throughout the war, were struck by the extent to which the Russians consciously ignored the Jewish aspect of the persecution.[65] When the representatives of the Soviet Atrocities Commission conducted the reporters through Maidanek, they described how on one day the Germans "annihilated 18,000 people—Poles, Jews, political prisoners and war prisoners."[66] Although many Soviet citizens who were not Jews had died in the course of the German advance, they had not been subjected to the systematic annihilation meted out to the Jews. It is not surprising that press coverage of this visit and other Russian news releases made it appear as if the Jews were simply one of the groups among the "thousands of civilians" who had been subjected to "abominable violence."[67]

Henry Shapiro, UP's correspondent in Moscow during this period, later described how the Russians progressively eliminated mention of Jews as victims. When he went to Babi Yar with other foreign correspondents in November 1943, there "was no question that this was a Jewish massacre and nothing else." When reporters were taken to Maidanek, the Soviets "minimized" the role of the Jews. By the time Auschwitz was liberated in 1945, Shapiro recognized that the Russian authorities were intent on seeing to it that "the Jewish role—both as victim and as Soviet hero—was to be forgotten."[68]

On occasion the Russians not only avoided mention of the Jews but actively censored reports that did mention them. Shortly after publication of his story on Maidanek, Bill Lawrence, the *New York Times* reporter in Moscow, received a cable from *New York Times* managing editor Edwin L. James, inquiring "why if most of the victims were Jewish, I had not said so." This was, Lawrence noted in his biography, his "first realization that the Russians had eliminated this from my story." When he confronted the Russian authorities and demanded to know why they had censored his story, he received what he described as a "rather lame and halting explanation . . . that some antisemites around the world might feel that if the victims were Jews, the murders were justified." (Though Lawrence attacked the Russians for such a "lame" explanation, the American War Department, the Office of War Information, and the U. S. Army used a similar excuse in November 1944 in order to try to suppress information about Auschwitz—see below, pages 265–67.)[69]*

The Russians continued with their practice of not singling out Jews even after the camps were liberated. One of the earliest Pravda dispatches on Auschwitz, liberated by the Red Army on January 27, 1945, described its inmates as "thousands of tortured people. . . . Russians, Poles, French, Yugoslavs and Czechs."[71] The Soviet Foreign Minister described those who had died at Auschwitz as "citizens of various European countries."[72] When the Soviet news agency Tass released its special bulletin on Auschwitz on May 7, 1945, it condemned the "most horrible crime against the peoples of Europe" which had been committed there. The bulletin, which was based on the official report of the Extraordinary State Commission, said those peoples included "citizens of Russia, Poland, France, Belgium, Holland, Czechoslovakia, Romania, Hungary, Yugoslavia and other countries."[73] Essentially this statement was correct. Of the approximately 4 million people killed at Auschwitz a minimum of 2 million were Jews.[74] All of them were citizens of various European countries, but they were killed as Jews.

Both the Allies and the American press repeatedly depicted Jewish victims simply as nationals of countries. This helped cloud the public's perceptions of the Nazi war against the Jews. The Final Solution was in and of itself difficult to accept. The skeptical and ambiguous treatment of it by the Allies and the inability of the press to break with this pattern served to reinforce public confusion, doubt, and disinterest. Also, at the same time that the Allies were universalizing the Jews' identity under the greater

---

* There were other Russian attempts to obscure the fact that Jews were the primary victims of the Nazis. In May 1944 a Soviet Extraordinary State Commission for investigation of German atrocities charged that over 102,000 people had been killed near Kovno, Poland, during the war. The commission quoted one witness: "I frequently saw how Ukrainians, Russians, Poles and Jews—Soviet citizens—were killed." The commission report, as described by AP, made it appear, once again, that Jews were simply one among many different groups of victims all of whom were united by one common characteristic, that they were Soviet citizens. A Soviet film on the Ukraine released in 1944 described Babi Yar as containing the bodies of Soviet "citizens" killed by the Nazis.[70]

whole of *all* victims of persecution, the Nazis were singling Jews out for increasingly severe treatment.*

The News About Auschwitz: An Eyewitness Account

The extent to which certain American officials were opposed to focusing on the murder of Jews was demonstrated in the fall of 1944 when John Pehle of the War Refugee Board received from American officials in Switzerland a full text of the eyewitness account of Auschwitz.[76] The report contained precise details on the number and national origins of the victims, the process of moving newly arrived victims from the freight trains to the gas chambers, the kinds of work done by the inmates, the physical plant of the camp, the physical dimensions of the barracks, gas chambers, and crematorium, and the way in which the "selections" for the gas chambers were conducted. The escapees who were the eyewitnesses had also witnessed the preparation of the camp for the "handling" of Hungarian Jewry.[77]

When Pehle received the report—he had previously only seen a summary—he did two things. First, he urged John McCloy, Assistant Secretary of War, to "give serious consideration to the possibility of destroying the execution chambers and crematoria in Birkenau through direct bombing action." McCloy rejected Pehle's request with the incorrect but familiar explanation that it would pose too great a risk to American bombers and would divert critically needed air power.[78] Pehle then decided to release the report to the press as a means of awakening public support for action.

Not since *Kristallnacht* had a story been so widely featured or prompted such extensive comment. Many papers carried it on the front page or in a prominent position elsewhere. The headlines alone encapsulated the press's horrified reaction.

---

* Even after the war, when the Allies had to deal with the survivors, they maintained the policy of treating Jews as nationals of the country they came from. To have done otherwise, they claimed, would have been to perpetuate Hitler's discriminatory policy. In one of the most painful historical ironies this meant that initially, German and Austrian Jews were treated as Germans and Austrians, i.e., enemy nationals.[75]

New York Herald Tribune:

U. S. CHARGES NAZIS TORTURED MILLIONS TO DEATH IN EUROPE

War Refugee Board Says 1,765,000 Jews Were
Killed by Gas in One Camp Alone; Witnesses' Testimony
Gives Details of the Atrocities[79]

Louisville Courier Journal:

THE INSIDE STORY OF MASS MURDERING BY NAZIS

Escapees Give Detailed Accounts of the Gassing and
Cremating of 1,765,000 Jews at Birkenau
FROM AN OFFICIAL PUBLICATION OF THE WAR REFUGEE BOARD[80]

Philadelphia Inquirer:

1,765,000 JEWS KILLED WITH GAS AT GERMAN CAMP[81]

New York Times:

U.S. BOARD BARES ATROCITY DETAILS TOLD BY WITNESSES AT POLISH CAMPS[82]

Washington Post:

TWO MILLION EXECUTED IN NAZI CAMPS

Gassing, Cremation Assembly-Line Methods Told by
War Refugee Board[83]

The Board appended a one-page preface attesting to its complete faith in the report's reliability. It stressed that all the information—both dates and death tolls—tallied with the "trustworthy yet fragmentary reports" previously received and therefore the eyewitness statements could be considered "entirely credible."[84] The *New York Herald Tribune* described the report as the "most shocking document ever issued by a United States government agency." Virtually every news story on the report emphasized not only that this was an eyewitness report but that it had been released by the War Refugee Board, an official government body, composed of "the three highest ranking Cabinet officials."[85]* This was, according to Ted Lewis of the *Washington Times Herald,* "the first American official stamp of truth to the myriad of eyewitness stories of the mass massacres in Poland." The *Louisville Courier Journal,* which devoted an entire page to excerpts from the report, observed in its article that "there is no longer any need to speculate on the mass murdering of millions of civilians." The amount of detailed informaion contained in the fifty-nine-page report made it difficult for anyone who had read it, one paper acknowledged, to dismiss it as "propaganda." Joseph Myler, who wrote the UP dispatch, opened his account with a quote from the report itself: "Those remaining, about 3,000, were immediately gassed and burned in the usual manner." This line, he noted, "varying but slightly, runs like a refrain" through the entire report.[86] The release of this report and the response it engendered are a prime example of the symbiotic relationship between the government and the press. When an official government agency reacted forcefully, the press followed suit. As we have seen, most of the time this symbiosis worked in the opposite direction and produced a dramatically different result: the news was ignored.

One of the few papers to inject an explicit note of skepticism into its report was the *Chicago Tribune,* which prefaced its news story with the observation that there have been numerous reports on German atrocities, "some of which have been verified." While previous reports had been accompanied by photographs, "no pictures were released to corroborate the atrocity story released today." The extensive detail was still not enough for the *Tribune,* it wanted pictures. It never mentioned to readers that Auschwitz, the subject of the report, was still in German hands and consequently no pictures were available.[87]

The War Refugee Board's release of this information should not be interpreted as a sign of a changing government policy. Two incidents demonstrate that Pehle was really acting on his own. Even after he sent the text of the full report on Auschwitz to the general press for release on November 26, 1944, some Administration officials tried to stop its publication. Pehle received a call from Office of War Information Director Elmer Davis, who was, according to Pehle, an "able journalist and a recognized liberal." Davis, who was angry about the publicity, pressured Pehle

---

* The Secretaries of State, the Treasury, and War.

"to call back the press release" because, he claimed, Americans would think it was propaganda.

> The public would not believe that such things were happening and as a result would be inclined to question the government's credibility on other information released concerning the war effort.[88]

But Pehle did not do so, and, contrary to Davis's expectations, the information was not dismissed as propaganda. It was, in fact, the government's imprimatur which made this story credible in the eyes of the press.

Equally as striking as Davis's attempt to suppress this news was the successful attempt by high-ranking army officers to prevent it from reaching the armed forces. On October 30 *Yank* magazine, published by the armed forces for their members, contacted the War Refugee Board and asked if it "dealt in German atrocity stories." A reporter for the magazine, Sgt. Richard Paul, had been assigned to prepare an article about German atrocities in order to "show our soldiers the nature of their enemy." Paul arranged to meet with Pehle to gather information for the story. At their meeting Pehle gave Paul a copy of the report for use by *Yank.*

A few days later Paul informed the War Refugee Board that the report would appear in the next issue of the magazine. But Paul's superiors intervened, told him that the story was "too Semitic," and instructed him to get a "less Jewish story" from the Board. Pehle's assistant at the War Refugee Board refused to give him one, and in her explanation she explicitly stated something neither the Allied governments nor the Allied press ever really made clear: most of the victims in the German death camps were Jews.*

Paul continued to try to win permission to publish his article, but he found that War Department and army officials had a "very negative attitude" toward what they described as a "hell of a hot story." Paul's superiors in the army and at *Yank* claimed that because of "latent antisemitism in the Army" they did not want to use the story. They argued, as did the Russians who had censored Lawrence's story and Samuel Rosenman, who censored

---

* Other peoples had suffered and many had died in the concentration and death camps; but no people had been as singled out as the Jews and none had lost such a large proportion of its population.

Roosevelt's, that to speak of atrocities against Jews would serve to increase world antipathy toward the Jews. Paul lost his fight and *Yank* never published the story.[89]

This was not a unique incident at *Yank*. Generally when the magazine discussed atrocities, it simply ignored those committed against Jews. On only a few occasions did it even mention Jews as *among* those killed. Its report on Lublin and Maidanek, for example, contained no reference to Jews. This may explain why as late as September 1944 there were army officers fighting in Europe who professed not to have heard anything about the concentration or death camps. What they did hear they dismissed as rumor.[90]

The release of the Auschwitz story erased many, though certainly not all, of the press's doubts. As would become clear at the end of the war, many publishers, editors, and seasoned reporters managed to ignore or repress this news. Others continued to hope that somehow it was an exaggeration. Only a face-to-face encounter with the evidence would convince them otherwise. At that point the struggle with this news would be transformed from one between belief and disbelief to one between knowledge and understanding.

Seeing and Trying to Believe

One of the most revealing aspects of the press reaction to the opening of the camps was the newspeople's almost uniform admission that only now were they convinced that the atrocity reports had not been exaggerated. Almost all reporters, publishers, and editors acknowledged that they had not believed the news that had been dispatched over the past years and had come to Europe "in a suspicious frame of mind." Their reaction sheds some light on the perplexing question of why they suppressed or ignored so much of this news. They had convinced themselves—in the face of much evidence to the contrary—that it was not true.

Joseph Pulitzer, the publisher and editor of the *St. Louis Post Dispatch,* anticipated that he would find that many of the reports which had reached the United States—including the descriptions of the horrors found in the camps—were "exaggerations, and largely propaganda," just like the accounts of the previous war.[91]

After visiting Buchenwald, he recognized that the reports that had appeared in the American press had been "understatements," not exaggerations. The *Los Angeles Times*'s Norman Chandler admitted that now that he had seen the camps, he knew that the reports which had appeared in the American press had not been exaggerations. "Exaggeration, in fact, would be difficult."[92] In a similar vein, Walker Stone, associate editor of the Scripps-Howard newspapers, said that only when he saw the camps did he know that nothing he had "read has been an overstatement."[93] Harold Denny, war correspondent for the *New York Times*, writing in the *New York Times Magazine*, acknowledged that his fellow reporters had the same reaction as did the publishers and editors. "Before our invasion of Germany, most of us had deprecated stories of these atrocities as touched up by propaganda."[94] Ben McKelway, editor of the *Washington Star*, summed up the editors' conclusions by quoting a G.I. they had encountered. "I always thought they were exaggerating to make us hate the Krauts. Now I know these things are true." Richard C. Hottelet noted forty years later that he, along with many of his journalistic colleagues, "knew the Nazis had to be defeated and we did not need these kind of stories to convince us of that." He, along with many of his colleagues, therefore assumed they must be at least partially untrue.[95]

Why these doubts? Given the abundance of information that had passed through these individuals' hands—whether they chose to print it or not—and given the information that had appeared in their own papers, how can one explain such skepticism? In the preceding pages we have explored some of the reasons the press itself offered to justify its failure to believe: its experience with World War I atrocity stories, the American fear of falling prey to propaganda, an Allied policy which hid rather than publicized information regarding Jewish atrocities, the absence of eyewitnesses, and the distrust of information that came from the Russians.

In addition, among the editors and reporters of the nation's newspapers and magazines were many Americans who had studied in Germany, were of German ancestry, had toured Germany, or had been prisoners of the Germans during the previous war. To them these tales of horror seemed implausible. After visiting Buchenwald, M. E. Walter, managing editor of the *Houston Chronicle*, recalled his experience as a prisoner of war in a German camp during World War I.

> By and large [I] had been treated well. The food was poor but so also was the food of the native population. Hence I was somewhat dubious of the [current] horror stories . . . wondering how much exaggeration was in them.[96]

Then also, America had been at war, and Americans, beset by many personal problems, worried about the fate of their friends and family in the armed forces. Convinced that war was the "ultimate atrocity" and any concomitant of war a related atrocity, they were not disposed to focus on the travail of one specific group. This was particularly so when the group in question, Jews, seemed always to be lamenting its fate despite the fact that millions of others were suffering. As Vernon McKenzie observed even before the worst of the news was released,

> Is there room in bewildered minds, obsessed by personal problems, to ponder about the fate of remote individuals?[97]

For many bystanders, including reporters, editors, and publishers, it may have been psychologically easier to deny the truth than to admit that one was not really moved to act at all.

There was also something peculiarly American in this reaction. Americans prided themselves on their skepticism. The *Baltimore Sun* tried to explain how, despite so much evidence, Americans had been able to reject the reports as untrue. "Atrocities? Americans, a sophisticated people, smiled at this idea. . . . When it came to atrocities, seeing, and seeing alone, would be believing, with most Americans." Kenneth McCaleb also believed the root of the problem was the American persona. "We are from Missouri. We have to be shown."[98]

But the press had been shown. It had been shown by reporters who had been stationed in Germany until 1942 and who had heard numerous reports including those of participants in the persecution of Jews. Sigrid Schultz, for example, sat in the train station listening to returning soldiers describe the massacres on the eastern front. In 1942 UP's Glen Stadler, who had just returned from Germany, described what was being done to the Jews as an "open hunt." By 1944 captured soldiers were confessing to atrocities that Harold Denny, the *New York Times* reporter assigned to the American First Army, called "so wantonly cruel that, without such confirmation, they might have been discounted as propagandist inventions."[99] Reporters had seen places such as Babi Yar, where the soil contained human remains, and Maidanek, where mass graves were visible. The American government had released a documented report on Auschwitz. Yet these editors, publishers, and reporters claimed not to believe what they heard.

The truth is that much of the press had not rejected as propaganda all that it heard, but it had erected barriers which enabled it to dismiss parts of it. It accepted a portion, often quite grudgingly, and rejected the rest as exaggeration. It adhered to a pattern which I have chosen to call "Yes but." At first it argued, *Yes, bad things may be happening but not as bad as reported.* Subsequently it was willing to acknowledge that *Yes, many Jews may be victims but not as many as claimed. Yes many may have died, but most probably died as a result of war-related privations and not as a result of having been murdered. Yes, many may have been killed but not in gas chambers. Yes, some Jews may have died in death camps, but so did many other people.*

As this sequence of events progressed, the press seemed willing to believe a bit more, but rarely was it willing to accept the full magnitude of the atrocities. This was as characteristic of the press's behavior in 1945 as it was in 1933. In 1933 it could not believe that Jews were being indiscriminately beaten up in the streets, and in 1945 it could not believe that they had been singled out to be murdered. When it came to atrocity reports, particularly those concerning the annihilation of the Jewish people, skepticism always tempered belief. By responding in such a fashion, the press obscured the true picture for itself and its readers.

What Raul Hilberg calls "functional blindness" also protected the press from the full impact of the news. Each time a report confirming some aspect of the Final Solution was released, the press treated it as if it were the *first* official confirmation. Previous reports and news stories were ignored. In December 1944 *Newsweek* claimed that the War Refugee Board's description of Auschwitz constituted the "first time" an American governmental agency had "officially backed up" charges made by Europeans of mass murder. But the United States government had backed up the charges two years earlier, in December 1942. A *Chicago Herald American* editorial in May 1945 claimed that only "recently" had America become aware of what was going on in Germany. *Life* made similar claims when the camps were opened.

> For 12 years since the Nazis seized power, Americans have heard charges of German brutality. Made skeptical by World War I "atrocity propaganda," many people refused to put much faith in stories about the inhuman Nazi treatment of prisoners. Last week Americans could no longer doubt stories of Nazi cruelty. *For the first time there was irrefutable evidence* as the advancing Allied armies captured camps filled with political prisoners and slave laborers, living and dead.[100]

Newsweek, Life, the *Chicago Herald American,* and a variety of other papers and magazines ignored the fact that over the past twelve years there had been a tremendous amount of "irrefutable evidence," evidence which they had dismissed as implausible and had placed in obscure corners of the paper or magazine so that readers either missed it or dismissed it. Almost without exception American journalists who visited the camps at the end of the war ignored that fact too.

But the reporters were, once again, emulating government behavior. In May 1945 U.S. Office of Strategic Services officials in Italy received the Auschwitz report, which nearly a year earlier had been released to the press and which had gotten tremendous press attention six months earlier when the War Refugee Board had released it in its entirety. Despite the publicity and attention it had already received Office of Strategic Services officials treated it as if it were a new revelation.[101]

A far more honest and accurate appraisal of the situation was offered by the Swiss paper *Basler Deutscheszeitung.* Despite the American and British "spontaneous wave of almost paralyzing disgust" at the atrocities "discovered" by the advancing Allied troops, in reality

> the world had known before of the atrocities in German concentration camps. . . . However, *the human mind did not wish to see these ugly and disturbing facts* although for 12 long years fellow men were systematically tortured and killed in cold cruelty.[102]

Had the American press been willing to build on the information which had been steadily emerging over the past twelve years, there would have been little reason for "surprise." But the press was never able to see the full picture, even when it had many, if not all, of the details in hand. It could not admit to itself or to its readers that these stories were the truth. Often, instead of explicitly rejecting the news as exaggerated, it simply put a critically important story on the comic page or next to the weather report. It put on blinders and erected all sorts of barriers which made it more rational for readers to disbelieve than to believe.

Epilogue: "Facts That Pass Belief"

We have seen how the reporters, editors, and publishers who visited the camps generally claimed that until that moment they had simply not believed that the stories were true. After their visits any vestiges of doubt had been eradicated. Now they knew such things could happen, but they could not fathom how. Their amazement had, in fact, only increased. In a front-page story in the *Baltimore Sun* Lee McCardell, the Sunpapers' war correspondent, voiced his confusion and disorientation after touring a camp.

> You had heard of such things in Nazi Germany. You had heard creditable witnesses describe just such scenes. But now that you were actually confronted with the horror of mass murder, you stared at the bodies and almost doubted your own eyes.
> "Good God!" you said aloud, "Good God!"
> Then you walked down around the corner of two barren, weatherbeaten, wooden barrack buildings. And there in a wooden shed, piled up like so much cordwood, were the naked bodies of more dead men than you cared to count.
> "Good God!" you repeated, "Good God!"

McCardell's reaction to what he found at this camp, Ohrdruf, which was far from the worst scene of German atrocities, was similar to that of the American major who first entered the camp:

> "I couldn't believe it even when I saw it," Major Scotti said, "I couldn't believe that I was there looking at such things."[103]*

A similar sense of overwhelming incredulity was expressed by Malcolm Bingay, who in addition to serving as editor of the *Detroit Free Press* was representing the Knight chain of papers on

---

* Ohrdruf was one of the camps to which the Germans had marched survivors of Auschwitz in mid-January 1945. Ohrdruf had been planned as a future army command center which was to be built by thousands of Jewish slave laborers.[104]

the press delegation that visited camps in April 1945. He related the terrible consternation that beset hardened and seasoned journalists who no longer doubted that the implausible had been committed:

> I have talked, . . . with endless numbers of war correspondents who have lived at the front throughout the war. Their stories do not differ and always there is a vast wonderment: How creatures, shaped like human beings, can do such things.
>
> Last night I talked with one of our correspondents, Jack Bell, one of the most worldly wise and experienced reporters I have ever known. . . . "Bing," he exploded with sudden vehemence, "it is the damndest, craziest, most insane thing that has ever happened to the world. You think you are awakening from a nightmare and then realize that you have not been sleeping. That what you see has actually happened—and is happening."

Though Bingay and his colleagues talked "far into the night" in their quest for some explanation, they ultimately concluded there was none, for this was the "maze of madness."[105]

Now that there was no longer room for doubt, various papers sought to explain to themselves as well as to their readers why they had been so filled with doubts. One theme was repeated in editorial after editorial. It was the same answer Bingay and his colleagues offered one another: this was a "maze of madness." The *New York Times* described the news of "the cold-blooded extermination of an unarmed people" as "facts that pass belief." Even before the camps were opened and the full horror known, the *Atlanta Constitution* argued that the "horror [was] too fantastic for belief."

> We know, logically, the stories of Nazi death camps, of wholesale slaughter of helpless captives are true, [but] . . . we cannot realize in our hearts they actually happened.[106]

This, the *Atlanta Constitution* claimed, was why "decent Americans"—its staff and editors included—had not believed. The *Washington Evening Star* wondered how could "the enormity of the thing be made to seem more than some wild nighmarish imagining?"[107]

The most outspoken skeptics were quick to use this line of reasoning to excuse their behavior. When the camps were opened,

The Christian Century, which had so often in the past deprecated both the reports of atrocities and those who reported them, sought to excuse—in words laden with pious contrition—its behavior by claiming that the fantastic nature of the news had compelled it to disbelieve.

> We have found it hard to believe that the reports from the Nazi concentration camps could be true. Almost desperately we have tried to think they must be widely exaggerated. Perhaps they were products of the fevered brains of prisoners who were out for revenge. Or perhaps they were just more atrocity-mongering, like the cadaver factory story of the last war. But such puny barricades cannot stand up against the terrible facts.[108]

This explanation, even when offered by *The Christian Century,* cannot be totally discounted. The magnitude of the horror *was* unfathomable. The tales of horror beggared the imagination. They were just "too inconceivably terrible."[109] This was certainly a critical factor in allowing the press to suspend belief. There were many failures in America's behavior during this period, and a failure of the imagination was one of them.

But there is a problem with explaining or excusing the press treatment of this news by relying on the fact that this was a story which was "beyond belief." While the unprecedented nature of this news made it easier, particularly at the outset, to discount the news, by the time of the Bermuda conference in 1943 and certainly by the time of the destruction of Hungarian Jewry in 1944 even the most dubious had good reason to know that terrible things were underway. Numerous eyewitness accounts which corroborated one another had been provided by independent sources. Towns, villages, and ghettos which had once housed millions now stood empty. The underground had transmitted documentation regarding the freight trains loaded with human cargo which rolled into the death camps on one day and rolled out shortly thereafter, only to be followed by other trains bearing a similar cargo. Where could these people be going? Where were the inhabitants of the towns and villages? Had they simply disappeared? There was only one possible answer to these questions. And most members of the press—when they stopped to consider the matter—knew it.

Given the amount of information which reached them, no responsible member of the press should have dismissed this news of the annihilation of a people as propaganda, and the fact is that few did. In the preceding pages we have seen numerous examples of papers and journals acknowledging that millions were being killed. By the latter stages of the war virtually every major American daily had acknowledged that many people, Jews in particular, were being murdered. They lamented what was happening, condemned the perpetrators, and then returned to their practice of burying the information.

There was, therefore, something disingenuous about the claims of reporters and editors at the end of the war not to have known until the camps were open. They may not have known just *how* bad things were, but they knew they were quite bad.* It seems as if these publishers, editors, and reporters protested a bit too much. Why their claims to have doubted? Why their protestations of ignorance? They may have instinctively known that in a situation such as this, doubts are far more easily explained than apathy; disbelief is more readily understood than dispassion. They could rationalize and justify their doubts, but they could not justify the equanimity with which they responded to the news of the tragedy. The American press may not have believed everything that was reported, but it certainly believed a great deal. And therein lies the real question regarding the press reaction to the persecution of European Jewry. Why, given what it did believe, did most of the press react so dispassionately?

The dispassion, if not indifference, of most of the press becomes all the more noteworthy when it is compared to the behavior of publications such as the *New York Post, The Nation, The New Republic, Commonweal,* and *PM* and journalists such as Dorothy Thompson, William Shirer, Arthur Koestler, Sigrid Schultz, Freda Kirchwey, I. F. Stone, Alexander Uhl, Max Lerner, Henry Shapiro, W. Randolph Hearst, and a few others. They were able to surmount the obstacles posed by World War I atrocity stories, absence of impartial eyewitnesses, German obfuscation, and the unprecedented nature of the tragedy. They had no more information than the rest of their colleagues. In fact, some of them depended on reports in other major dailies for their information. One cannot ignore the fact that many publications and a disproportionately

---

* Typically, in a pictorial essay on Palestine which appeared in 1943, *Life* matter-of-factly noted that of the 8 million Jews who had been in prewar Europe at least 3 million were "certainly dead."[110]

high number of the reporters were associated with politically liberal philosophy.* But this alone cannot explain their behavior. The real difference between these publications and journalists and the vast majority of the rest of the press is not between belief and disbelief, but between action and inaction, passion and equanimity. They not only believed what was being reported but refused to accept it as inevitable. They were convinced that the Allies could do something if they would stop behaving as if "the Jews were expendable."[112] They did not accept the position that nothing could be done and therefore there was no point in even talking about it.

There are those who are inclined to suggest that little was done because of contempt the Allies harbored for these particular victims because they were Jews. One is loath to accept that as true, but it must be acknowledged that many government officials, members of the press, and leaders of other religions behaved as if Jewish lives were a cheap commodity.[113] The government and the press reacted much more forcefully when non-Jewish lives were threatened. The Allies allowed food to be shipped through enemy lines to Axis-occupied Greece because the population was starving. They rejected requests from Jewish groups that the same be done for Jews in Eastern Europe. The Americans claimed that they had no means to transport Jews to safety at the same time that cargo ships were returning from Europe with empty holds.

---

* Hearst and his papers constituted a notable exception to this. There are those who attribute Hearst's strong stand on rescuing Jews as well as his outspoken support of a Jewish national home in Palestine to a desire to embarrass the British, whom he had loathed since the prewar years when he had been an isolationist and believed that the British were intent on involving America in the war.

It is also important to note that in many circles, particularly official government ones, liberal publications such as *The Nation*, *The New Republic*, and *PM* were neither popular nor considered representative of mainstream American views. Arno Mayer, who eventually became a member of the history department at Princeton, learned this in 1944 when he was a young soldier assigned to get information from German generals who had been captured and flown to Washington. The generals had served the Wehrmacht and the notorious Waffen SS on the eastern front. Mayer was told to learn as much as possible from them about the Red Army (America was already preparing for the Cold War). He was to "keep these fellows happy" by providing them with anything they might need, including liquor and newspapers. One day he brought them *The Nation* and *PM*. He was told by his commanding officers "in no uncertain terms" that in the future he could provide them with *Life*, the *New York Times*, and *Reader's Digest* but not "any of that other stuff."[111]

The press was far more outraged over Lidice and the killing of European resistance fighters than it was over any similar action against Jews. When Jewish fighters in Warsaw managed to hold the Germans at bay, most of the press simply ignored the fact.

A real antipathy toward Jews certainly affected the Allied response. While no one among the Allies or in the press wanted to see Jews killed, virtually no one was willing to advocate that steps be taken to try to stop the carnage. Many Allied officials in positions of power in London and Washington were tired of hearing about Jews and even more tired of being asked to do something about them even though there were steps that could have been taken. In 1942 British officials described eyewitness accounts of massacres as "familiar stuff. The Jews have spoilt their case by laying it on too thick for years past." In 1944 another official complained that "a disproportionate amount of the time of the [Foreign] Office is wasted dealing with these wailing Jews." In 1944 State Department officials warned Hull that the War Refugee Board should be restrained in its rescue efforts lest "Hitler take advantage of the offer to embarrass the United Nations at this time by proposing to deliver thousands of refugees."[114] The most efficacious thing for the Allies to do was to try to ignore the tragedy and make sure that those whose responsibility it was to disseminate information did the same. And the press, having convinced itself that there was nothing that could be done and having inured itself to the moral considerations of what was happening, followed suit. It was a cumulative and collective failure. The press was ultimately as culpable as the government.

There is, of course, no way of knowing whether anything would have been different if the press had actively pursued this story. The press did not have the power to stop the carnage or to rescue the victims. The Allies might have remained just as committed to inaction, even if they had been pressured by the press. But in a certain respect that is not the question one must ask. The question to be asked is did the press behave in a responsible fashion? Did it fulfill its mandate to its readers?

Many years ago Alexis de Tocqueville praised the press in large and populous nations such as America for its ability to unite people who share certain beliefs about an issue but, because they feel "insignificant and lost amid the crowd," cannot act alone. According to Tocqueville the press fulfills its highest purpose when it serves as a "beacon" to bring together people who otherwise might ineffectively seek each other "in darkness." Newspapers can bring them "together and . . . keep them united." If there were no newspapers or if newspapers failed to do their task, he observed, "there would be no common activity."[115] There is no way of knowing whether the American people would have ever been aroused enough to demand action to rescue Jews. But we can categorically state that most of the press refused to light its "beacon," making it virtually certain that there would be no public outcry and no "common activity" to try to succor this suffering people.

The press had access to a critically important and unprecedented story. Yet it reacted with equanimity and dispassion. In these pages I have analyzed and explained its skepticism; I find it much more difficult—if not impossible—to fully comprehend its indifference. That indifference may be a part of the history of the Holocaust which, despite the efforts of scores of historians, will remain unfathomable. We still cannot answer the question that Malcolm Bingay's colleagues asked one another as they saw the remains of the Nazis' work—"how creatures, shaped like human beings, can do such things." Nor can we explain how the world of bystanders—particularly those with access to the news—were able to treat this information with such apathy. Both the Final Solution and the bystanders' equanimity are beyond belief.

Today we do not doubt that millions of people can be massacred, systematically and methodically, or that millions more can bear witness and do nothing. Over the past forty years we have lost our innocence and have become inured not only to the escalating cycle of human horror but also to the human indifference. Then the news shocked and confounded us. Today similar news, whether it come from Biafra, Cambodia, Uganda, or any one of a number of other places, does not shock us and sometimes it does not even interest us. It has become an "old," all too familiar, and therefore relatively unexciting story.

Our reaction is among the more tragic legacies of the Final Solution. The inability of reports of extreme persecution and even mass murder in foreign lands to prompt us to act almost guarantees that the cycle of horror which was initiated by the Holocaust will continue.

NOTES

Key to Abbreviations

Abbreviations are used for three frequently cited sources after their first full citation in notes:

DGFP Documents on German Foreign Policy, published by the U.S. Government Printing Office, Washington

DS Department of State Decimal Files, in the National Archives, Washington

FRUS Foreign Relations of the United States: Diplomatic Papers, published by the U.S. Government Printing Office, Washington

Introduction

1. Thomas Jefferson to Edward Carrington, quoted in James E. Pollard, *The Presidents and the Press* (New York: Macmillan, 1947), pp. 52–53; Oscar Wilde, quoted in James Reston, *The Artillery of the Press: Its Influence on American Foreign Policy* (New York: Harper & Row, 1966), p. 43; Adlai Stevenson, quoted in Thomas Bailey, *The Art of Diplomacy* (New York: Appleton, 1968), p. 124.

2. Arthur Morse, *While Six Million Died: A Chronicle of American Apathy*

(New York: Random House, 1967); Henry Feingold, *The Politics of Rescue: The Roosevelt Administration and the Holocaust, 1938–1945* (New Brunswick: Rutgers University Press, 1970); David S. Wyman, *Paper Walls: America and the Refugee Crisis, 1938–1941* (Amherst: University of Massachusetts Press, 1968); David Wyman, *The Abandonment of the Jews: America and the Holocaust, 1941–1945* (New York: Pantheon Books, 1984); Saul Friedman, *No Haven for the Oppressed: United States Policy Towards Jewish Refugees, 1938–1945* (Detroit: Wayne State University Press, 1973); Monty Noam Penkower, *The Jews Were Expendable: Free World Diplomacy and the Holocaust* (Urbana: University of Illinois Press, 1983).

Recently additional attention has been devoted to the behavior of the organized Jewish community in research projects that are themselves somewhat controversial. Critics such as Lucy Dawidowicz have accused factions in the Jewish community of "revis[ing] the past for their own self-aggrandizement and unscrupulously distort-[ing] the historic record" in order to justify and legitimize their current political agenda. The appointment of a private, blue-ribbon Commission on the Holocaust under the chairmanship of Arthur J. Goldberg, former Associate Justice of the Supreme Court, which was charged with the task of "embark[ing] on a searing inquiry into the actions and attitudes of American Jews," aroused a great deal of controversy. Lucy Dawidowicz accurately described this charge as sounding like an "arraignment." Lucy Dawidowicz, "American Jewry and the Holocaust," *New York Times Magazine,* April 18, 1982, pp. 47–48, 101–114. See also Marie Syrkin, "American Jewry During the Holocaust," *Midstream,* October 1982, pp. 6–12. A few years ago Ariel Sharon, in an address to the Conference of Presidents of Major Jewish Organizations, accused the Jews of the free world of having remained silent during the war. Bernard Wasserstein, "The Myth of 'Jewish Silence,' " *Midstream,* August-September 1980, p. 10. Monty Noam Penkower, "In Dramatic Dissent: The Bergson Boys," *American Jewish History,* March 1981, pp. 281–309; David Wyman, "Letters to the Editor," *New York Times Magazine,* May 23, 1982, p. 94. Wyman's *The Abandonment of the Jews* offers the most piercing analysis of the American Jewish community's reaction.

3. Elmer Roper, *You and Your Leaders* (New York, Morrow, 1957), p. 71; Selig Adler, *Isolationist Impulse* (London, Abelard-Schuman, 1957), p. 279.

4. Gay Talese, *The Kingdom and the Power* (New York: Bantam Books, 1970), p. 1. One foreign policy official described the function of the press as giving those in government a "daily feel" of the public's reaction to events. Bernard C. Cohen, *The Press and Foreign Policy* (Princeton: Princeton University Press, 1963), pp. 233–234. The

fact that reporters see themselves as the public's agents in breaking down any barriers which might impede the free flow of news also enhances the press's importance in the foreign policy arena. Reston, p. 71; Theodore Peterson, "The Social Responsibility Theory of the Press," in Fred S. Siebert, Theodore Peterson, and Wilbur Schramm, *Four Theories of the Press* (Urbana: University of Illinois Press, 1956), p. 91; Cohen, p. 32; William O. Chittick, *State Department, Press and Pressure Groups: A Role Analysis* (New York: Wiley, 1970), p. 6; Bernard R. Berelson, Paul F. Lazarsfeld, and William N. McPhee, *Voting: A Study of Opinion Formation in a Presidential Campaign* (Chicago, 1954), pp. 93–115, and Elihu Katz and Paul Lazarsfeld, *Personal Influence: The Part Played by People in the Flow of Mass Communication* (Glencoe, Ill., 1955), chap. 14, and pp. 32–33, 325, as cited in Peter G. Filene, "On Method and Matter," chap. 1 in his *Americans and the Soviet Experience, 1917–1933* (Cambridge: Harvard University Press, 1967). Also see Filene pp. 1–7, for a discussion of some of the problems involved in analysis of mass media.

For an example of a veteran reporter's reaction to the barring of his colleagues from the battlefield see Drew Middleton, "Barring Reporters from the Battlefield," *New York Times Magazine,* February 5, 1984, pp. 36–37, 61ff. For an analysis of the political impact of television see Austin Ranney, *Channels of Power: The Impact of Television on American Politics* (New York, 1984), as cited in Ted Koppel, "The Myth of the Medium," *New Republic,* February 6, 1984, pp. 26–28; A. Lawrence Chickering, "The Media and the Message," *Commentary,* February 1984, pp. 79–80.

5. Cohen, p. 255; Reston, pp. 75–76.

6. Frederick Oeschner, *This Is the Enemy* (Boston: Little, Brown, 1942), p. 130.

7. W. Phillips Davison, "More than Diplomacy," in Lester Markel et al., *Public Opinion and Foreign Policy* (New York: Harper & Row, 1949), p. 132; Reston, pp. 69–71. Incidentally, because press criticism of government policy often tends to influence policy via an intellectual, political, and journalistic elite and not through the masses, the number of people who read a particular publication is often less important than *who* reads it.

8. Graham J. White, *FDR and the Press* (Chicago: University of Chicago Press, 1979), pp. 13, 22, 135; Raymond Clapper, *Watching the World* (New York: Whittlesey House, 1944), p. 51; Arthur Krock, *Memoirs* (New York: Funk & Wagnalls, 1970), p. 183; Reston, pp. 67–68; *Complete Presidential Press Conferences of Franklin D. Roosevelt,* introduction by Jonathan Daniels (New York: Da Capo Press, 1972); James

E. Pollard, "Franklin D. Roosevelt and the Press," *Journalism Quarterly*, vol. 22, no. 3 (September 1947), p. 201.

9. Reston, pp. 67–68.

10. The *Press Information Bulletins* are to be found in Franklin D. Roosevelt Papers, Franklin D. Roosevelt Library, Hyde Park, N.Y., White, pp. 79–81; James Reston, "The Number One Voice," in Markel, p. 70; Pollard, p. 200; H. V. Kaltenborn, *Fifty Fabulous Years* (New York: G. P. Putnam, 1950), p. 172.

11. Chittick, pp. 24–25.

12. For examples of German concerns regarding American press coverage see: Richard Sallet to the Ministry of Propaganda, August 3, 1934, no. 569, III A 3140, *Documents on German Foreign Policy* (hereafter cited as *DGFP*), series C, III (Washington: U.S. Government Printing Office, 1957), p. 1111; Luther, April 8, 1935, *DGFP*, series C, IV, pp. 23–29; *Investigation of Nazi Propaganda Activities and Investigation of Certain Other Propaganda Activities: Hearings Before the Special Committee on Un-American Activities, House of Representatives*, 73d Cong., 2d sess. (Washington: Government Printing Office, 1935); memorandum of a conversation between Ambassador Hugh Wilson and Joseph Goebbels, Berlin March 22, 1938, enclosed in a letter from Sumner Welles to President Roosevelt, April 22, 1938, Hugh Wilson folder, President's Secretary's File, Germany, FDRL, as cited in Sander Diamond, *The Nazi Movement in the United States, 1924–1941* (Ithaca: Cornell University Press, 1974), p. 36. For additional discussion of German attempts to sway American public opinion and press coverage, see Chapter 6.

13. Thomsen to Berlin, November 20, 1939, no. 684, *DGFP*, series D, VIII, p. 432, as quoted in Saul Friedlander, *Prelude to Downfall: Hitler and the United States, 1939–1941* (New York, Alfred E. Knopf, 1967), p. 56.

14. Reston, *Artillery*, p. 65; Friedlander, pp. 42–43, 52. For American attempts to influence the press see: Messersmith to Hull, March 25, 1933, DS 862.4016/496, as cited in Shlomo Shafir, "The Impact of the Jewish Crisis on American German Relations, 1933–1939," Ph.D. diss. (Ann Arbor: University Microfilms International, 1971), p. 77; Messersmith to Hull, March 31, 1933, *Foreign Relations of the United States: Diplomatic Papers* (hereafter cited as *FRUS*), 1933, vol. II (Washington: Government Printing Office, 1949), pp. 341, 346; telephone call between Phillips and Gordon, April 2, 1933, *FRUS*, 1933, vol. II, p. 346.

15. For contemporary discussion of the evolution of these two fields and bibliographies see Harold G. Lasswell, "Propaganda," *Encyclope-*

dia of the Social Sciences (New York, Macmillan, 1934), vol. 12, pp. 521–528; Leila A. Sussmann, "The Public Relations Movement in America," M.A. diss., University of Chicago, 1947; and Harwood L. Childs, ed., "Pressure Groups and Propaganda," *Annals of the American Academy of Political and Social Science,* 179 (May 1935)—all as cited in Michael Schudson, *Discovering the News: A Social History of American Newspapers* (New York: Basic Books, 1978), pp. 141, 211, n. 52.

16. In 1908 Congress stipulated in an appropriations bill that the government was to use no funds for "the preparation of any newspaper or magazine articles." In 1913, after investigating the public relations activities of federal agencies, Congress passed a law prohibiting the government's use of funds for "publicity experts." But the law was the last futile attempt to try to stop what would soon become an accepted government activity. Edward L. Bernays, *Propaganda* (New York: Liveright, 1928), p. 27; F. B. Marbut, *News from the Capital* (Carbondale: Southern Illinois University Press, 1971), pp. 192–196, all as cited in Schudson, p. 139, 141.

17. George Creel, *How We Advertised America* (New York: Harper & Row, 1920), p. 4; Harold D. Lasswell, *Propaganda Technique in the World War* (New York: Peter Smith, 1927), p. 20; and James R. Mock and Cedric Larson, *Words That Won the War* (Princeton: Princeton University Press, 1939)—all as cited in Schudson, p. 212.

18. J. Roth, *World War I: A Turning Point in Modern History* (New York: Knopf, 1967), p. 109.

19. Lasswell, "Propaganda," *Encyclopedia Britannica,* vol. 18, p. 582, as cited in Markel, p. 15.

20. Schudson, p. 142.

21. Ibid., pp. 156–57; Leo C. Rosten, *The Washington Correspondents* (New York: Harcourt, Brace, 1937), p. 351. For an argument in favor of objectivity see Walter Lippmann, *A Preface to Morals* (New York: Macmillan, 1929, reprinted ed., Time Incorporated, 1964), pp. 222–224.

22. Donald F. Drummond, *The Passing of American Neutrality, 1937–1941* (Ann Arbor: University of Michigan Press, 1955); William L. Langer and S. Everett Gleason, *The Challenge to Isolation, 1937–1940,* (New York: Council on Foreign Relations/Harper & Row, 1952).

23. Franklin Reid Gannon, *The British Press and Germany, 1936–1939* (London: Oxford, 1971), pp. 1–32; Harold Lavine and James Wechsler, *War Propaganda and the United States* (New Haven: Yale University Press, 1940), pp. 241–242.

24. Harrison Salisbury, *Without Fear or Favor: An Uncompromising Look at the New York Times* (New York: Times Books, 1980), p. xi.

25. Claud Cockburn, *In Time of Trouble,* as quoted in Gannon, p. xiv.

Chapter 1

1. Sackett to Hull, March 9, 1933, *FRUS,* 1933, vol. II, pp. 206–209. For examples of some of the early laws see "Law for the Restoration of the Regular Civil Service," *Reichsgesetzblatt,* 34, April 4, 1933, and "First Decree with Reference to the Law for the Restoration of the Regular Civil Service," *Reichsgesetzblatt,* 37, April 11, 1933; reprinted in *The Jews in Nazi Germany: The Factual Record of Their Persecution by the National Socialists* (New York: American Jewish Committee, 1933), pp. 1–2.

2. *The Jews in Nazi Germany,* p. 21. For typical examples of coverage which did not focus on Nazi antisemitism see *New York Herald Tribune,* March 1, 1933, p. 1, March 2, 1933, p. 1, and *New York Times,* March 6, 1933, p. 1.

3. H. R. Knickerbocker, *New York Evening Post,* April 15, 1933, as cited in *The Jews in Nazi Germany,* pp. 24–27.

4. *Pittsburgh Sun,* March 24, 1933; *Poughkeepsie News,* March 11, 1933; *Toledo Times,* March 23, 1933—all cited in *The Jews in Nazi Germany,* pp. 71–79.

5. *St. Louis "Times-Dispatch"* (sic), March 24, 1933, as cited in *The Jews in Nazi Germany,* p. 81; *Nashville Banner,* as cited in *Literary Digest,* April 8, 1933, p. 3; *New York Times,* April 2, 1933.

6. *Chicago Tribune,* March 1, 1933, p. 1, March 3, 1933, p. 4; *New York Times,* March 5, 1933, p. 20.

7. *New York Herald Tribune,* March 8, 1933, p. 22; *New York Times,* March 10, 1933, p. 1, March 15, 1933, p. 10, March 20, 1933, p. 1; *Los Angeles Times,* March 16, 1933, p. 10, March 20, 1933, p. 1; *Chicago Tribune,* March 20, 1933, p. 1.

8. *Toledo Times,* March 23, 1933, as cited in *The Jews in Nazi Germany,* p. 77.

9. *Los Angeles Times,* March 16, 1933, p. 10, March 26, 1933, p. 2, March 27, 1933, p. 1.

10. *New York Herald Tribune,* March 25, 1933, p. 1.

11. *New York Times,* March 13, 1933, p. 1. On March 9 in a page 1 story Birchall portrayed the situation in Germany as one in which Nazi extremists were committing a variety of actions against Jews, including the "boyish trick" of flying a swastika over a synagogue.

In one portion of the article he noted that the police had been ordered to investigate, and in another section he admitted that the police were under Nazi control. *New York Times,* March 9, 1933, pp. 1, 10.

12. *Los Angeles Times,* March 27, 1933, p. 1; *Christian Century,* April 5, 1933, p. 443.

13. Augusta (Maine) *Journal,* March 25, 1933.

14. *Columbus* (Ohio) *Journal,* March 24, 1933; Vernon McKenzie, "Atrocities in World War II: What We Can Believe," *Journalism Quarterly,* vol. XIX, (September 1942), pp. 268–276.

15. *Christian Science Monitor,* February 18, 1933, p. 3, March 16, 1933, p. 12, March 22, 1933, p. 5; Moshe Gottlieb, "The First of April Boycott and the Reaction of the American Jewish Community," *American Jewish Historical Society Quarterly,* vol. LVII (June 1968), p. 519.

16. *Christian Science Monitor,* March 24, 1933, p. 1; *New York Herald Tribune,* March 24, 1933, p. 2, March 25, 1933, p. 1; William L. Shirer, *20th Century Journey: A Memoir of a Life and the Times,* vol. II, *The Nightmare Years, 1930–1940* (Boston: Little, Brown, 1984), p. 187.

17. *Literary Digest,* April 8, 1933, p. 3.

18. Marion K. Sanders, *Dorothy Thompson: A Legend in Her Time* (Boston: Houghton Mifflin, 1973), p. 185; *New York Times,* May 12, 1933, p. 12.

19. *The Yellow Spot* (New York: Knight Publications, 1933), p. 33. Ernst Hanfstaengl, a graduate of Harvard, was appointed to head a press bureau which was designed to influence foreign correspondents in general and those from America in particular. His mother was a member of a prominent Back Bay Boston family, the Sedgwicks. Ernst Hanfstaengl, *Unheard Witness* (Philadelphia: Lippincott, 1957); *Christian Science Monitor,* March 24, 1933, p. 8; Gottlieb, "The First of April Boycott," p. 519.

20. Sigrid Schultz, *Germany Will Try It Again* (New York: Reynal & Hitchcock, 1944), p. 117.

21. *New York Times,* March 26, 1933, sec. IV, p. 1; *Time,* April 3, 1933, pp. 16–17; *Los Angeles Times,* March 11, 1933, sec. II, p. 9; *Nation,* December 27, 1933, p. 728.

22. Louis Lochner, *What About Germany?* (New York: Dodd, Mead, 1942), p. 286.

23. *New York Times,* June 24, 1933, p. 12.

24. Memo, Hull to Sackett, March 21, 1933, *FRUS,* 1933, vol. II; memorandum of press conference of Secretary of State, March 22, 1933, *FRUS,* 1933, vol. II, p. 328.

25. Memo, Gordon to Hull, March 30, 1933, *FRUS,* 1933, vol. II, p. 335.

26. *New York Times,* March 27, 1933, p. 1; *New York Herald Tribune,* March 27, 1933, p. 1; *Newsweek,* April 1, 1933, p. 5.

27. Telephone call between Gordon and Phillips, March 31, 1933, *FRUS,* 1933, vol. II, p. 342; Gordon to Hull, March 23, 1933, *FRUS,* 1933, vol. II, pp. 328–331; Gordon to Hull, March 26, 1933, DS 862.4016/ 116, as cited in Shlomo Shafir, "The Impact of the Jewish Crisis on American German Relations, 1933–1939, Ph.D. diss. (Ann Arbor: University Microfilms International, 1971), p. 54.

28. Shafir, p. 77; *New York Times,* March 27, 1933, p. 1.

29. Louis Lochner to Betty Lochner, November 12, 1933, Lochner Papers, Mass Communications History Center, State Historical Society of Wisconsin. A portion of Lochner's letters to his children who were students in the United States have been reprinted in "Round Robins from Berlin: Louis P. Lochner's Letters to His Children, 1932–1941," *Wisconsin Magazine of History,* vol. 50, no. 4 (Summer 1967), pp. 291–336; *Chicago Tribune,* January 28, 1936, p. 3.

30. *FRUS,* May 12, 1933, vol. II, p. 398.

31. Interview with C. Brooks Peters, February 12, 1985.

32. *New York Herald Tribune,* March 24, 1933, p. 2; *Chicago Tribune,* April 9, 1933, p. 4; Schultz, p. 187; Edgar Ansel Mowrer, *Triumph and Turmoil: A Personal History of Our Times* (New York: Weybright and Talley, 1968), p. 225.

33. *FRUS,* 1933, vol. II, pp. 403–406; Lilian Mowrer, *Journalist's Wife* (New York: Morrow, 1937), p. 307. For bungled attempts to get the *New York Evening Post* and *Philadelphia Public Ledger* to recall Knickerbocker, see *FRUS,* May 12, 1933, vol. II, pp. 400–401.

34. Shirer, p. 138; S. Miles Bouton, "A Peculiar People," in Robert Benjamin, ed., *The Inside Story by Members of the Overseas Press Club of America* (Englewood Cliffs, N.J.: Prentice-Hall, 1940), p. 116; interview with Howard K. Smith, February 27, 1985; *Saturday Evening Post,* June 2, 1934, p. 34; interview with Richard C. Hottelot, December 21, 1984.

35. Shirer, p. 551.

36. G. E. R. Gedye, "Vienna Waltz," in Hanson Baldwin and Shepard Stone, eds., *We Saw It Happen: The News Behind the News That's Fit to Print* (New York: Simon & Schuster, 1938), p. 68.

37. Louis Lochner, *Always the Unexpected: A Book of Reminiscences* (New York: Macmillan, 1956), p. 252; Lochner, *What About Germany?* p. 307.

38. Sigrid Schultz, "Hermann Goering's 'Dragon from Chicago,' " in David Brown and W. Richard Bruner, eds., *How I Got That Story* (New York: Dutton, 1967), p. 76.

39. Lochner, *What About Germany?* p. 303; Howard K. Smith, *Last Train from Berlin* (New York: Knopf, 1942), p. 48; interview with Percy Knauth, February 18, 1985; interview with C. Brooks Peters, February 12, 1985; transcript of recollections of Sigrid Schultz, Tribune Company Archives, tape 52A/000–745, part II, pp. 3–4, 14, Sigrid Schultz Collection, Mass Communications History Center of the State Historical Society of Wisconsin.

40. Shirer, p. 229; Edgar Mowrer, pp. 225–226; H. R. Knickerbocker, *Is Tomorrow Hitler's? 200 Questions on the Battle of Mankind* (New York: Reynal & Hitchcock, 1941), pp. 213–214.

41. Edgar Mowrer, pp. 216–217, 224; Lilian Mowrer, p. 275, 287.

42. *FRUS*, May 12, 1933, vol. II, p. 399; Shafir, p. 43.

43. *Manchester Guardian*, April 9, 1933 (reprinted in *New York Times*, April 9, 1933); *New York Times*, December 24, 1933, p. 1.

44. Edgar Mowrer, *Triumph*, pp. 216–217, 224; Lilian Mowrer, pp. 275, 287.

45. *FRUS*, March 31, 1933, vol. II, p. 340.

46. Hamilton Fish Armstrong, *Hitler's Reich: The First Phase* (New York: Macmillan, 1933), p. 19; Martha Dodd, *Through Embassy Eyes* (New York, Harcourt, Brace, 1939), p. 99; Hamilton Fish Armstrong, *Peace and Counterpeace: From Wilson to Hitler* (New York: Harper & Row, 1971), p. 530.

47. *Macon* (Georgia) *Telegraph*, May 25, 1933, as quoted in *The Jews in Nazi Germany*, pp. 20–21; Shafir, pp. 76–77.

48. *New York Times*, June 14, 1933, p. 4; *The Jews in Nazi Germany*, p. 16.

49. *New York Times*, May 29, 1933, p. 5; May 30, 1933, p. 14.

50. Edgar A. Mowrer, *Germany Puts the Clock Back* (New York: Morrow, 1933), pp. 230, 239; *Baltimore Sun*, August 1, 1935.

51. Lochner, *What About Germany?* p. 109; Frederick Oeschner, *This Is the Enemy* (Boston: Little, Brown, 1942), p. 56.

52. Dodd (White) to Hull, August 20, 1935, DS 862.4016, Decimal Files 1538, Department of State, National Archives, Washington, D.C. (hereafter DS and file numbers only).

53. *Chicago Tribune*, March 13, September 14, 1932, February 4, 1933, March 13, 1933, March 24, 1933, August 9, 1933, August 11, 1933, August 12, 1933 (reprinted in *Los Angeles Times*, August 23, 1933), August 24, 1933, May 14, 1934, July 31, 1934—all as cited in Jerome Edwards, *The Foreign Policy of Col. McCormick's Tribune, 1929–1941* (Reno: University of Nevada Press, 1971), pp. 66, 92–94. Joseph Gies, *The Colonel of Chicago* (New York: Dutton, 1979), pp. 130, 147; Schultz, *Germany Will Try It Again*, p. x; George Seldes, *Tell the Truth*

and Run, (New York: Greenberg, 1953), p. 114; transcript of recollections of Sigrid Schultz, part II, p. 9.

54. Margaret K. Norden, "American Editorial Response to the Rise of Adolf Hitler: A Preliminary Consideration," *American Jewish Historical Society Quarterly,* vol. LVII (October 1968), p. 293.

55. John Evelyn Wrench, *Geoffrey Dawson and Our Times,* as cited in Shirer, p. 206; Franklin Reid Gannon, *The British Press and Germany, 1936–1939* (London: Oxford, 1971), p. 121.

56. *New York Times,* August 26, 1934, p. 1, August 27, 1934, p. 8. The North American Newspaper Alliance, for which Thompson wrote her column, issued her own report on her expulsion on August 26, 1934. The report was front-page news in many American newspapers. According to Ambassador Dodd, the reasons for her expulsion lay in her interview with Hitler in 1932 and her reports in 1933 condemning Hitler's antisemitic campaign. Marian K. Sanders, *Dorothy Thompson: A Legend in Her Own Times* (Boston: Houghton Mifflin, 1973), pp. 167–168, 200; interview with William Shirer, December 19, 1984.

57. Enrique Hank Lopez, *Conversations with Katherine Anne Porter* (Boston: Little, Brown, 1969), pp. 175–176, 178, 180; Joan Givner, *Katherine Anne Porter: A Life* (New York: Simon & Schuster, 1982), pp. 259–263; Mary Anne Dolan, "Almost Since Chaucer with Miss Porter," *Washington Star,* May 11, 1975.

58. Shirer, pp. 189, 193; Edgar Mowrer, p. 225; Lochner, *What About Germany?* p. 100.

59. *Philadelphia Record,* March 28, 1933.

60. Edgar Mowrer, p. 224; John Gunther, *Inside Europe,* (New York: Harper & Brothers, 1937), p. 10.

61. *New York Times,* August 11, 1935, p. 4.

62. William E. Dodd, Jr., and Martha Dodd, eds., *Ambassador Dodd's Diary, 1933–1938* (New York: Harcourt, Brace, 1941), pp. 157, 248, 288–289.

63. Dodd to Hull, July 30, 1935, August 20, 1935. For a less critical evaluation of the Hitler regime by an American official, see the report of Military Attaché Truman Smith to the War Department, September 24, 1935, *Attaché Reports,* reprint 2657-B-780/4, as cited in Shafir, p. 506.

64. *New York Times,* August 4, 1935, p. 19.

65. Edgar Mowrer, *Triumph,* p. 233; Dodd and Dodd, pp. 99, 298.

66. *New York Times,* August 4, 1935, p. 19.

67. Smith, *Last Train from Berlin,* p. 9, Lilian Mowrer, pp. 288, 313; *Nation,* October 18, 1933, p. 433; Rhea Clyman, "The Story That Stopped Hitler," in Brown and Bruner, p. 58.

68. Another American Olympics visitor who would eventually become a virtual spokesman for Nazi Germany was Charles Lindbergh. When he met with reporters, he too lectured them on conditions in Germany. Shirer, pp. 232, 237; Martha Dodd, p. 99.

69. Howard K. Smith, who visited Germany when he was a student, was struck by American students' failure to grasp the true nature of Nazi Germany. Smith, *Last Train from Berlin,* p. 9.

70. Memo, Messersmith to Hull, March 25, 1935, DS 862.4016/496, as cited in Shafir, p. 76.

71. Schultz, *Germany Will Try It Again,* p. 97. The American Commercial Attaché in Berlin, Douglas Miller, revealed that the Nazis even insisted that contracts which Americans signed with German firms had to carry a printed clause to the effect that "this contract is made under National Socialist principles." Though those principles were never explicitly spelled out, American firms in Germany were often blackmailed into appointing Nazis to their boards and inviting Nazi delegations to the United States to "investigate whether the product was, in fact, Jewish." Douglas Miller, *You Can't Do Business with Hitler* (Boston: Little, Brown, 1941), pp. 88, 197–201.

72. During the winter Olympics Shirer, concerned about the way some American businessmen were responding to Nazism, arranged for them to have lunch with Miller. The "tycoons," Shirer recalled, "told *him* what the situation was in Nazi Germany. . . . Miller could scarcely get a word in." Shirer, p. 232.

73. *Business Week,* May 24, November 11, 1933, December 8, 1934, September 7, 1935, August 15, 1936, January 2, August 21, 1937, all as cited in Daniel Shepherd Day, "American Opinion of National Socialism, 1933–1937," Ph.D. diss., University of California at Los Angeles, 1958, pp. 112, 124; Harold C. Syrett, "The Business Press and American Neutrality, 1914–1917," *Mississippi Valley Historical Review,* vol. 32 (September 1945), pp. 215–230; Gabriel Kolko, "American Business and Germany, 1930–1941," *Western Political Quarterly,* December 1962, pp. 715ff.

74. Miller, p. 194. See Charles Higham, *Trading with the Enemy* (New York: Delacorte Press, 1983), for a discussion of American business connections with Nazi Germany. Higham demonstrates how American businesses continued to trade with Germany long after Pearl Harbor.

75. *Christian Science Monitor,* April 18, July 6, July 12, August 2, August 3, August 9, August 24, October 5, October 12, October 19, 1933.

76. *Newsweek,* July 29, 1933.

77. Armstrong, *Hitler's Reich,* pp. 11–12; *Los Angeles Times,* June 2, August 29, August 31, September 3, October 6, October 14, November 11, 1933; Martha Dodd, pp. 27–28.

78. *Chicago Tribune*, August 9, August 11, August 12, 1933 (reprinted in *Los Angeles Times*, August 23, August 24, and August 25, 1933); Edwards, pp. 93–94; Shafir, p. 33.

79. Transcript of recollections of Sigrid Schultz, part II, pp. 7–8.

80. *Christian Century*, August 16, 1933, pp. 1031–1033.

81. *Minneapolis Tribune*, July 31, 1935; *Rochester Democrat and Chronicle*, August 31, 1935; *Knoxville Journal*, August 8, 1935; *Grand Junction* (Colorado) *Sentinel*, October 28, 1935; *Harper's*, January 1935, p. 125; Armstrong, *Hitler's Reich*, p. 19.

82. *Philadelphia Record*, March 28, 1933; *New York Evening Post*, March 27, 1933.

83. *Philadelphia Ledger*, March 28, 1933; *Hartford Courant*, March 28, 1933.

84. *St. Louis Times Dispatch*, March 24, 1933, as cited in *The Jews in Nazi Germany*, pp. 81–82; *Columbus Journal*, March 24, 1933; *Toledo Times*, March 23, 1933.

85. *Collier's*, February 11, 1939, p. 12.

Chapter 2

1. *Saturday Evening Post*, June 2, 1934, p. 36.

2. *Kansas City Journal Post*, July 25, 1935; *Cleveland Plain Dealer*, July 21, 1935; *Davenport* (Iowa) *Times*, July 29, 1935; *Terre Haute Star*, July 22, 1935.

3. *Greensboro* (North Carolina) *News*, July 24, 1935; *Wilmington* (Delaware) *Journal*, July 24, 1935.

4. *Davenport* (Iowa) *Times*, July 29, 1935; *Birmingham* (Alabama) *Age Herald*, July 22, 1935; *Dallas News*, November 18, 1935.

5. *Houston Post*, as cited in *Literary Digest*, April 8, 1933; *Chicago Tribune*, March 13, September 14, 1932, February 4, March 13, March 24, 1933, May 14, July 31, 1934; *Cincinnati Enquirer*, November 18, 1935; Shlomo Shafir, "The Impact of the Jewish Crisis on American German Relations, 1933–1945," Ph.D. diss. (Ann Arbor: University Microfilms International, 1971), p. 33; Jerome Edwards, *The Foreign Policy of Colonel McCormick's Tribune, 1929–1941* (Reno: University of Nevada Press, 1971), pp. 92–94.

6. *Christian Science Monitor*, March 28, March 30, 1933; *New York Herald Tribune*, March 27, 1933, pp. 1, 5, April 1, 1933, p. 1; *New York Times*, March 27, 1933, p. 4, April 1, 1933, p. 1; *Literary Digest*, April 8, 1933, p. 3.

7. *Christian Science Monitor*, April 4, 1933. In its editorial comment of April 2, 1933, the *New York Times* used a tongue-in-cheek manner and diagnosed millions of Germans as "suffering from malign obses-

sions, painful hallucinations and nervous disorders of an alarming kind. . . . They forget entirely the impressions which their wild conduct may make upon others. If they hear protests and appeals from the outside world [to stop the terror and boycott], these only heighten their persecution mania." In his report from Germany, Frederick Birchall observed that the boycott had been limited to one day and said that "one would like to believe this to be a last-hour concession to the sober remonstrances of the few thinking Germans there seem to be left in this maelstrom of ultranationalist frenzy." This, however, Birchall contended, was not the case. "Instead it must be confessed that the [boycott] movement has been revealed . . . as a triumph of propaganda on a scale never before achieved here, even in wartime." As a result of the boycott and the preboycott propaganda, the German people had been incited to turn against the Jews. Hostility and hatred toward the Jews had increased significantly. Germans blamed Jews for spreading "atrocity" stories which maligned Germany. Furthermore, Birchall argued, by scaling down the boycott to one day and eliminating many of those who were initially to be boycotted, the government had achieved these ends but had avoided many adverse economic effects. In short, the propaganda objectives had been fulfilled at limited cost. *New York Times*, April 1, 1933. *FRUS*, 1933, vol. II, p. 333.

8. *Christian Science Monitor*, April 4, 1933. This was not the only time that the *Christian Science Monitor* directly accused Jews of bringing about their own misfortune. It also did so in 1939 when the SS *St. Louis* was meandering off the Cuban coast looking for a place to unload its Jewish refugee passengers (see Chapter 5). For background on the Christian Science movement see Erwin D. Canham, *Commitment to Freedom: The Story of the Christian Science Monitor* (Boston: Houghton Mifflin, 1958), p. 287, and Stephen Gottschalk, *The Emergence of Christian Science in American Religious Life* (Berkeley: University of California Press, 1973), pp. 273–274. There were prominent Social Gospel leaders who were extremely critical of Christian Science. Walter Rauschenbush described it as a "form of selfish spirituality which turned its back on the world." Rauschenbush, *A Theology for the Social Gospel*, p. 103, as cited in Gottschalk, pp. 260–261.

9. Ismar Schorsch, *Jewish Reactions to German Anti-Semitism, 1870–1914* (New York: Columbia University Press, 1972), pp. 169–170.

10. *Reformed Church Messenger*, April 6, 1933, August 24, 1933, pp. 9–11, September 7, 1933, pp. 8–9; *Lutheran Companion*, September 2, 1933, p. 1105; *Moody Bible Institute Monthly*, May 1933, p. 392; *King's Business*, June 1933, p. 171; *Sunday School Times*, December 9, 1933, p. 778, all as cited in Robert W. Ross *So It Was True* (Minneapolis: University of Minnesota Press, 1980), pp. 33–36.

11. These questions appeared in *The Christian Century* on April 26, 1933,

p. 574. The article, entitled "A Jew Protests Against Protesters," by Robert E. Asher, appeared April 12, 1933, pp. 492–444. For *The Christian Century*'s comments urging restraint regarding judging Germany's treatment of Jews, see April 5, 1933, p. 443. In light of *The Christian Century*'s eventual attitude toward Jewish immigration and the reports of mass murder, these early comments are instructive.

12. Walter Lippmann, "Today and Tomorrow," *Los Angeles Times*, May 19, 1933 (emphasis added). In 1943 George Seldes described Lippmann as one of the two most influential columnists in the United States. (The other, he said, was Westbrook Pegler.) Lippmann was considered by many of his colleagues to be the commentator with the greatest influence on "all men of intelligence." George Seldes, *Facts and Fascism* (New York: In Fact Inc., 1943), p. 233. *DGFP*, series C, *The Third Reich, First Phase*, I, *January-October 1933* (Washington: Government Printing Office, 1957), pp. 451–455.

13. David Halberstam, *The Powers That Be* (New York: Knopf, 1979), p. 370.

14. Ronald Steel, *Walter Lippmann and the American Century* (New York: Vintage Books, 1980), pp. 191–192, 331. Lippmann rejected an invitation to join the Jewish Academy of Arts and Sciences and later turned down an award from that organization. He explained that he made it an "invariable rule not to accept awards or membership in organizations which have a sectarian character." Steel, p. 619.

15. Henry Cantril, *Public Opinion* (Princeton: Princeton University Press, 1951), p. 381; Steel, p. 332.

16. *Harper's*, January 1935, p. 126.

17. *Columbus Dispatch*, April 16, 1933.

18. Roosevelt–General Nogues talk, January 17, 1943, *FRUS*, Casablanca Conference, pp. 608–609. Later the same day Roosevelt repeated this proposal in conversation with General Henri Giraud, of France, ibid., 609–612. Wasserstein notes that at least on one occasion Churchill had expressed similar views. A letter from James de Rothschild to Churchill on May 27, 1938, contained the following statement: "When you spoke with such sympathy last week at Cranborne about the Jewish situation in Germany, you mentioned that the number of Jews in the various professions and occupations had been, in the days before Hitler, very high in comparison with the proportion which Jews bore to the total population. The idea that this was so was fostered by Nazi propaganda, and has been widely accepted. I am enclosing an article which appeared in the *Manchester Guardian* of 3rd January 1936, which disproves this by official German statistics." Martin Gilbert, *Winston S. Churchill, Companion Vol.*

5, *The Coming of War* (London, 1979), as cited in Bernard Wasserstein, *Britain and the Jews of Europe, 1939–1945* (London: Institute of Jewish Affairs, 1979), pp. 207–208.

19. *Los Angeles Times*, March 21, March 25, March 30, April 6, 1933; *Columbus* (Ohio) *Journal*, March 24, 1933; *Youngstown* (Ohio) *Vindicator*, March 22, 1933; *New York Times*, March 9, 1933, pp. 1, 10.

20. *Los Angeles Times*, August 12, 1935, p. 2; *Canton* (Ohio) *Repository*, July 24, 1935; *Wilmington* (Delaware) *Journal*, July 24, 1935; *La Crosse* (Wisconsin) *Tribune*, July 23, 1935.

21. *Boston Post*, July 29, 1935.

22. *Boston Evening Transcript*, July 20, 1935; *Literary Digest*, August 3, 1935, p. 12.

23. A southern paper drew a revealing parallel between the Nazi Party and the Ku Klux Klan. Both organizations were founded, it claimed, by "men who were striving desperately to restore order from chaos. Their aims were good and they accomplished a great deal of good." Soon, however, they descended into "hoodlumism, mob tyranny and butchery." According to this theory, Nazi and KKK leaders had tried but been unable to restrain their followers from being swept up by the forces that they had rather innocently unleashed. *Winston-Salem* (North Carolina) *Journal*, July 23, 1935.

24. *Trenton Times Advertiser*, August 4, 1935; *New York Herald Tribune*, as cited in *Birmingham* (Alabama) *News*, July 20, 1935; *Dallas Times Herald*, July 17, 1935 (emphasis added); *Winston-Salem* (North Carolina) *Journal*, July 23, 1935; *New York Times*, February 21, March 1, August 20, 1935.

25. *Atlanta Constitution*, November 22, 1938; *Hamilton* (Ohio) *Journal News*, November 26, 1938.

26. *Newsweek*, July 27, 1935, p. 12; *New York Times*, July 20, 1935, p. 1.

27. *Baltimore Sun*, July 19, 1935; *Davenport* (Ohio) *Times*, July 20, 1935.

28. *New York Post*, July 17, 1935.

29. *Rochester* (New York) *Democrat and Chronicle*, July 22, 1935; *Utica* (New York) *Press*, July 19, 1935.

30. *Trenton* (New Jersey) *Star Gazette*, July 18, 1935; *Jersey City Journal*, July 19, 1935.

31. Memo, Dodd to Hull, July 17, 1935, *FRUS*, 1935, vol. II, p. 402–403; Shafir, p. 481.

32. William L. Shirer, *20th Century Journey*: vol. II, *The Nightmare Years, 1930–1940* (Boston: Little, Brown, 1984), p. 137; *Time*, July 29, 1935, p. 19; *Newsweek*, July 27, 1935, p. 12.

33. *Chicago Tribune*, March 13, March 24, 1933; *Christian Science Monitor*,

March 7, 1933, p. 12; *Los Angeles Times,* March 15, 1933, sec. II, p. 4.

34. *Christian Science Monitor* March 24, 1933, p. 1. Not all *Christian Science Monitor* reports were skewed in this direction. A few days later the *Christian Science Monitor* bureau in Berlin offered a less sanguine picture, one which contradicted Steele's optimistic assessment. The reporter acknowledged that while there was little active persecution, antisemitism continued in other forms. Newspaper articles attacked Jews. Propaganda designed to elicit hatred of Jews was to be found everywhere. Storm troopers on Berlin streets were to be seen selling pamphlets entitled "Jews demand Hitler's murder." *Christian Science Monitor,* March 27, 1933, pp. 1, 4.

35. *New York Times,* March 12, 1933, sec. IV, p. 4, July 10, 1933, pp. 1, 10; *Nation,* July 19, 1933, p. 59.

36. *St. Paul Dispatch, Detroit News, St. Louis Post Dispatch,* as cited in *Literary Digest,* April 8, 1933, p. 1.

37. During the same period an official rebuke was given to two towns where Jews had been forced to suffer a variety of indignities including pulling weeds out of a railway bed with their teeth. Goebbels's and Schmitt's comments coupled with the reprimand fostered a perception of evolving moderation in the treatment of Jews. However, the day after Schmitt's remarks were publicized, an unnamed "high ranking German official" made it clear that the Minister of the Economy's call for a hands-off policy did not represent any deviation from "Nazism's plan to rear a purely 'Aryan' State." *New York Times,* September 28, 1933, p. 1; September 29, 1933, pp. 10, 11, 18; *Newsweek,* October 7, 1933, p. 12.

38. Memo, Dodd to Hull, July 30, 1935, *FRUS,* 1935, vol. II, pp. 402–403; *New York Post,* July 31, 1935; *Birmingham* (Alabama) *Herald,* July 31, 1935; *Washington Star,* July 30, 1935.

39. *Philadelphia Ledger,* July 31, 1935; *Pittsfield* (Massachusetts) *Eagle,* July 30, 1935; *Louisville Courier Journal,* July 31, 1935; *Wheeling* (West Virginia) *Register,* July 31, 1935; *Memphis Commercial Appeal,* July 31, 1935; *Galveston* (Texas) *News,* July 31, 1935; *Davenport* (Ohio) *Democrat,* July 31, 1935; *Schenectady* (New York) *Gazetteer,* August 1, 1935; *Syracuse Herald,* July 31, 1935.

40. *Troy* (New York) *Record,* July 24, 1935; *Jackson* (Mississippi) *Patriot,* July 23, 1935; *Washington Post,* August 4, 1935.

41. *Brooklyn Eagle,* July 19, 1935; *Oakland* (California) *Tribune,* July 23, 1935; *Cleveland Plain Dealer,* July 21, 1935; *Syracuse Post Standard,* July 24, 1935.

42. *New York Times,* July 23, 1935, pp. 1, 18, July 24, 1935, p. 1.

43. Wallace R. Duel, *People Under Hitler* (New York: Harcourt, Brace, 1942), p. 4.

44. *Birmingham* (Alabama) *Herald*, July 31, 1935; *Mobile* (Alabama) *Press Register*, July 21, 1935; *Knickerbocker Press* (Albany, New York), July 20, 1935; memo, Dodd to Hull, July 30, 1935, *FRUS*, 1935, vol. II, pp. 402–403.

45. *Milwaukee Journal*, August 4, 1935.

46. *Baltimore Sun*, August 1, 1935; *New York Post*, July 31, 1935; *Washington Post*, August 4, 1935; *Chattanooga Times*, August 6, 1935.

47. Andrew Sharf, *The British Press and Jews Under Nazi Rule* (London: Oxford University Press, 1964), p. 27.

48. Hamilton Fish Armstrong, *Hitler's Reich: The First Phase* (New York: Macmillan, 1933), p. 55.

49. Streicher, whom Dodd described as the "greatest Jew baiter of all," warranted a lengthy dispatch from the embassy to the Secretary of State. On August 15, 1933, the *Stürmer* editor gave his "maiden speech" in Berlin before a crowd of 12,000 to 14,000. (A few thousand could not get into the hall and listened to the speech over radio in a nearby hall.) Berlin was home for at least one-third of the Jews still in Germany when Streicher gave his speech. According to the American embassy, Streicher's antisemitic harangue was "not without its significance." Dodd believed that it reflected a "new offensive against the Jews." He explained that incidents against Jews "involving physical violence are still occurring constantly but in a lessening degree; mental and spiritual persecution, on a 'legalized' basis, much more insidious and far-reaching, is supplanting it." Memo, Dodd to Hull, July 30, 1935, DS 862.4016/1514; memo, Dodd to Hull, August 20, 1935, DS 862.4016/1538; memo, Dodd to Hull, September 7, 1935, DS 862.4016/1550; *Newsweek*, August 24, 1935, p. 16.
    Those who interpreted the antisemitic outbreaks, including the riots, as simply a manifestation of tension between extremists and moderates found their position bolstered by the statements of Hjalmar Schacht. Schacht, who remained the American press's favorite German "moderate" until his ouster from power in 1939, criticized the extralegal actions of those such as the July rioters. However, he condoned legal antisemitism. When he was contrasted with someone like Streicher, it was easy to portray Schacht as a moderate. *Newsweek* praised him for his good courage and his willingness to criticize some of the antisemitic outbreaks. *Newsweek*, August 24, 1935. The *Cleveland News* went so far as to fret that he may have endangered himself by his outspoken comments. It cautioned him to be more judicious in his criticism. *Cleveland News*, August 20, 1935.
    It is true that Schacht was a far more appealing and moderate character than Streicher or Goebbels. However, he supported mea-

sures which would not have bloodied Jews in the street but would have forced them into a modern ghetto. Schacht's suggestions would have left Jews so economically deprived that they would have had to endure a living death. He advocated the slow and regulated institution of economic legislation against the Jews. He wished to avoid the foreign boycotts and financial disruptions which threatened to ensue each time there was an outbreak of violence. His position was predicated on financial calculations. He rarely differed with the basic antisemitic ideology of the party or its objective of eradicating the German Jewish community. In fact one of the most immediate results of the 1935 party rally at which the Nuremberg Laws were announced was a "stiffening of antisemitism" in Schact's domain. Among other things, he gave notice to officials in the Reichsbank who were married to Jewish women. Dodd to Hull, September 26, 1935, DS 862.4016/1561. See also Hjalmar Schacht, *My First Seventy-Six Years: The Autobiography of Hjalmar Schacht* (London: Allan Hacht, 1955), p. 347.

One of the few press voices to demur from the general praise of Schacht was the *New York Times*. Although prior to the riots it had described him as a moderating influence, subsequently it accused him of wryly playing two games at one time. On one hand, he was genuinely concerned about the repercussions of a foreign boycott; on the other hand, he was also trying to establish an alibi in the face of economic collapse. It was wrong, the *Times* argued, to call him a humanitarian when, although he might decry wanton public attacks on Jews, he did not object to private persecution as long as it did not result in foreign repercussions. *New York Times,* February 21, March 1, August 20, 1935.

Christian Century took a similar stance. Schacht's statements were for "foreign consumption, since if he had any convictions . . . he would have resigned long ago." More of a pragmatist than a moderate, Schacht emerged as a popular figure in the American press because he could be so favorably compared with the other unsavory characters at the helm of the Germany state. He represented the elite, educated "good German" from whom, Americans hoped, would come the sanity and rational thinking then absent in Germany. *Christian Century,* September 11, 1935.

50. Prior to the events of the latter half of 1935, particularly the riots and the Nuremberg decrees, there had even been some confusion in the ranks of the German Jewish community as to whether their future was to be in Germany or outside of it. The rate of emigration slowed down markedly. In the first year of the Hitler regime 50,000 Jews left the Reich. In 1934 only 25,000 departed, and in fact many who had left returned. Some of the returnees were placed in concen-

tration camps. As a result of what took place on July 15, 1935, and through November of that year, when the second set of laws governing Jewish rights of citizenship were issued, many leaders of the German Jewish community abandoned any hope for the survival of their community under Nazi rule. For expressions of pessimism on the part of German Jews, see Dodd to Hull, September 7, 1935, DS 862.4016/1550. See also Consul General Douglas Jenkins to Hull, November 4, 1935, *FRUS*, 1935, vol. II, pp. 292–293. For examples of the treatment of young German Jews who returned to their country from a foreign state, see memo, Consul General Samuel Honaker to Hull, August 23, 1935, DS 862.4016/1543. See also *American Jewish Year Book*, vol. 37, pp. 183–185, vol. 38, p. 320; Shafir, pp. 476–477.

Shortly after the riots, when rumors were rife about laws which would affect the status of the Jew in Germany, even the American embassy subscribed to the scapegoat explanation. It reported to Secretary of State Hull that "the tenets of the Party include making the Jew a scapegoat at a time when it is beset by serious internal difficulties. In this connection it is noticeable that even the lower class Germans have frequently been heard to express the view that intensive Jew-baiting is intended to divert attention from financial difficulties and domestic political opposition." Memo, White to Hull, August 20, 1935, DS 862.4016/1538.

51. *Literary Digest*, June 18, 1932, p. 19; Edgar Mowrer, *Germany Puts the Clock Back* (New York: Morrow, 1933), p. 239.

52. *Cleveland News*, September 17, 1935; *Cincinnati Enquirer*, September 18, 1935; *Boston Transcript*, September 16, 1935; *Macon* (Georgia) *Telegraph*, September 19, 1935; *Flint* (Michigan) *Journal*, September 19, 1935; *Pueblo Springs* (Colorado) *Gazetteer*, September 18, 1935; *Fort Worth* (Texas) *Star Telegraph*, September 19, 1935; *Memphis Commercial Appeal*, September 18, 1935; *Denver News*, September 21, 1935; *Newsweek*, September 21, 1935. Many papers which had not previously commented on Nazi persecution did so on the occasion of the Nuremburg Laws. Shirer, *Nightmare Years*, p. 226.

53. *New York Herald Tribune*, July 28, 1935; *New York Sun*, August 2, 1935; *Washington Post*, August 1, 1935; *Lynchburg* (Virginia) *News*, August 2, 1935; *Richmond Times Dispatch*, August 4, 1935; *Kenosha* (Wisconsin) *News*, September 9, 1935; *Easton* (Pennsylvania) *Express*, September 10, 1935.

54. *Newsweek*, September 21, 1935, p. 12.

55. *Los Angeles Times*, September 16, 1935. The headline in the *New York Herald Tribune* did make the ban on citizenship the lead item, but it referred to the change in flag twice:

NAZIS BAR JEWS AS CITIZENS,
MAKE SWASTIKA SOLE FLAG
IN REPLY TO N.Y. 'INSULT'

SUBSERVIENT REICHSTAG IN EXTRA SESSION
OUTLAWS MIXED MARRIAGES, PUTS JEWS BACK IN MIDDLE
AGES

Memel 'Tortures' Decried by Hitler

World Anti-Jewish Flag 'Insulted' by Semites in New York
Replaces the Reich Imperial Banner

New York Herald Tribune, September 16, 1935.

56. *Washington Herald,* September 16, 1935.

57. *New York Times,* September 16, 1935.

58. *Baltimore Sun,* September 16, 1935.

59. *Christian Science Monitor,* September 16, 1935, p. 10.

60. In another example of an obfuscated reaction to the news, the *Troy* (New York) *Record,* September 17, 1935, believed the most important part of the laws was the limits placed on Jewish children's education. "One might digest some of these proscriptions without gagging if it were not for the inhuman Asiatic practice recently embraced in Germany, of punishing children for fancied shortcomings of their ancestors." The *Record* decried punishing children whose parents "are *socially objectionable*" (emphasis added). The *Record*'s description of Jews as "socially objectionable" indicated failure to comprehend the demonic place Jews occupied in Nazi ideology. The paper compared their treatment with Stalinist treatment of middle-class children and concluded the lot of Russian children was more trying because they were denied any education, while the Nazis promised state aid for "separate Jewish taught schools." See also *Meridan* (Mississippi) *Star,* September 18, 1935; *Beaumont* (Texas) *Enterprise,* September 16, 1935; *Boston Transcript,* September 16, 1935.

61. *Cleveland News,* September 17, 1935.

62. *New York Times,* September 22, 1935.

63. *Christian Science Monitor,* October 17, 1935. See also Memo, Dodd to Hull, August 20, 1935, DS 862.4016/1538.

64. *Boston Transcript,* September 16, 1935.

65. Diplomatic dispatches from the period indicate that as a result of previously issued antisemitic legislation the status of the Jew was quite dire. See, for example, report by Ralph C. Busser, American Consul in Leipzig, July 22, 1935, DS 862.4016/1503; report by American Consul General in Stuttgart Samuel W. Honaker, August

23, 1935, DS 862.4016/1543; memo, Dodd to Hull, October 17, 1935, DS 862.4016/1568.

66. *Memphis Commercial Appeal,* September 18, 1935.

67. *New York Times,* September 1, 1935, p. 12. Memo, Chargé in Germany J. C. White to Hull, August 20, 1935, DS 862.4016/1538; Dodd to Hull, September 26, 1935, DS 862.4016/1561.

68. *Los Angeles Times,* September 18, 1935, sec. II, p. 4; *St. Louis Post Dispatch,* November 17, 1935; *Cincinnati Enquirer,* September 18, November 18, 1935.

69. *St. Louis Post Dispatch,* May 22, 1935; Margaret K. Norden, "American Editorial Response to the Rise of Adolf Hitler: A Preliminary Consideration," *American Jewish Historical Quarterly,* vol. 30 (October 1968), pp. 290–301.

70. Memo, Dodd to Hull, September 26, 1935, DS 862.4016/1561; memo, Dodd to Hull, October 31, 1935, DS 862.4016/1573; *Voelkischer Beobachter,* October 23, 1935, as cited in Eliahu Ben Elissar, *La Diplomatie du III Reich et les Juifs, 1933–1939* (Paris-Julliard, 1969), pp. 160–162.

Chapter 3

1. *New York Times,* May 29, 1933.

2. *New York Times,* June 8, 1933, p. 1.

3. Richard D. Mandell, *The Nazi Olympics* (New York: Ballantine Books, 1971), p. 78. The Amateur Athletic Union of the United States (AAU) was scheduled to meet in November 1933. At that meeting, in a near-unanimous vote, it agreed not to certify athletes for the Games unless Germany's position regarding Jewish athletes changed "in fact as well as in theory." The AAU stated that the German Olympic Committee had violated the ideals of the Olympic Games and of sports competition by depriving German Jews of the right to "prepare for and participate in" Olympic competition. *New York Times,* November 21, 1933, p. 1, November 22, 1933, p. 28; *Nation,* November 29, 1933, p. 607; *Literary Digest,* December 2, 1933, p. 22.

4. *Newsweek,* April 22, 1933, p. 13. On July 2, 1933, the Nazi Minister of Education announced that Jews would henceforth be excluded from youth, welfare, and gymnastic organizations and that use of the facilities of all athletic clubs would be denied to them. Later that month Jews were forbidden from serving as lifeguards in Breslau. Eventually all swimming resorts were closed to them. It was

not long before Jews who wished to train for the Games found the requisite playing fields and training camps off limits. Mandell, pp. 64–66; *New York Times*, November 28, 1933, p. 25.

5. Mandell, p. 81; Arthur Morse, *While Six Million Died: A Chronicle of American Apathy* (New York: Random House, 1967), p. 174; Eliahu Ben Elissar, *La Diplomatie du III Reich et les Juifs* (Paris: Julliard, 1969), pp. 167–170; Shlomo Shafir, "The Impact of the Jewish Crisis on American–German Relations, 1933–1939," pp. 581, 584–585; *New York Times*, November 27, 1935, p. 14.

6. *Literary Digest*, July 11, 1936, p. 35; *New York Times*, November 23, November 26, December 1, 1933, October 22, p. 1, October 23, 1935; *Grand Junction* (Colorado) *Sentinel*, October 29, 1935.

   Sherrill's resignation from his ambassadorial post had been "joyfully accepted" by the State Department. See entry for January 11, 1934, Phillips Diary, Phillips Papers, as quoted in Shafir, p. 584; memo of Sherrill's visit to Hitler in Munich on August 24, 1935, in Roosevelt Papers, President's Secretary's File, box 7, Franklin D. Roosevelt Library, Hyde Park, N.Y., Elissar, pp. 173–175; Morse, pp. 181–182; *New York Times*, September 27, 1934, p. 28.

7. Morse, p. 174; list of places forbidden to Jews is contained in Ambassador Dodd's dispatch, May 17, 1935, DS 862.4016/1457. From the middle of 1933 on, warnings had come from American embassy officials in Germany, particularly George Messersmith, to the effect that German promises could not be trusted regarding Jewish participation in the Games. Memo, Messersmith to Hull, June 17, 1933, DS 862.4016/1181, and November 28, 1933, DS 862.4063/01 Games 1, as cited in Shafir, p. 581.

8. *New York Times*, December 7, 1934, p. 31, August 2, 1935, p. 8.

9. William Johnson, *All That Glitters Is Not Gold* (New York: Putnam, 1972), p. 176.

10. Ibid.

11. *New York Times*, August 12, 1935, p. 1; memo, Dodd to Hull, December 10, 1935, DS 765.84/3007, as cited in Shafir, p. 587.

12. H. J. Resolution 381 opposing the expenditure of public funds on the Olympics was introduced by Emanuel Celler of New York on August 16, 1935. *Congressional Record*, 74th Cong., 1st sess., 1935, 79, part 12 (Washington: Government Printing Office, 1935), 13332; *New York Times*, August 16, 1935, p. 4.

13. *Springfield* (Massachusetts) *News*, July 27, 1935.

14. *Commonweal*, August 16, 1935; *Norfolk* (Virginia) *Pilot*, August 8, 1935.

15. *Norfolk Pilot*, August 24, 1935.

16. *New York World Telegram,* September 16, 1935; *Troy Record,* September 9, 1935; *East St. Louis Journal,* August 8, 1935; *Trenton Gazette,* August 10, 1935.

17. *New York World Telegram,* September 16, 1935.

18. *Boston Globe,* July 30, 1935.

19. *Trenton Gazette,* August 10, 1935.

20. *Springfield* (Illinois) *Journal,* August 11, 1935.

21. Johnson, pp. 175–176. *Allentown* (Pennsylvania) *Call,* September 8, 1935.

22. *Saturday Evening Post,* May 6, 1933, p. 71.

23. *Chicago Tribune,* July 5, 1936, p. 16.

24. *Des Moines Register,* November 5, 1935.

25. *Superior* (Wisconsin) *Telegram,* August 5, 1935; *Seattle Star,* August 7, 1935; *Lawrence* (Massachusetts) *Eagle,* August 1, 1935.

26. *Atlanta Constitution,* August 25, 1935.

27. *Milwaukee Herald,* September 10, 1935; *Christian Century,* August 7, 1935, p. 1007, August 14, 1935, p. 1028.

28. *New York Times* July 12, 1936. Memo, Dodd to Hull, January 30, 1936, DS 862.4016/1610; Messersmith to Hull, November 15, 1934, DS 862.4063/01. G. 57; Messersmith to Phillips, November 30, 1935, DS 862.00/3573; Messersmith to Geist, November 12, 1935, Frankfurter Papers, box 25, Library of Congress, Washington, D.C., as cited in Shafir, p. 587.

29. *Minneapolis Star,* August 8, 1935; *St. Joseph* (Missouri) *Gazette,* August 1, 1935. Bang was quoted in a "roundup" of sports writers' opinions in the *Knoxville Journal,* November 8, 1935.

30. *Lansing* (Michigan) *Journal,* August 7, 1935; *Wheeling* (West Virginia) *News Register,* September 10, 1935.

31. *Charleston* (South Carolina) *Post,* August 6, 1935; Morse, pp. 359–360; Henry L. Feingold, *The Politics of Rescue* (New York: Waldon Press, 1970), p. 257.

32. Mandell, pp. 68, 77–78.

33. Dodd to Hull, January 30, 1936, DS 862.4016/1610. See also *FRUS,* 1936, vol. II, p. 197.

34. *Charleston* (South Carolina) *Post,* August 6, 1935.

35. *Rochester Democrat and Chronicle,* October 23, 1935; *Albany Press,* November 1, 1935; *Charleston Post,* August 5, 1935; Memo, Dodd to Hull, October 31, 1935, DS 862.4016/1573.

36. *Los Angeles Times,* August 7, 1935.

37. *Los Angeles Times,* September 13, 1935.

38. *Mobile* (Alabama) *Register,* November 9, 1935.

39. *Literary Digest,* August 31, 1935.

40. *New York World Telegram,* February 17, February 19, 1936; Mandell, pp. 87–88; *Washington Post,* August 3, 1936, p. 7, August 5, 1936, p. 7.

41. *Los Angeles Times,* September 9, 1935.

42. William L. Shirer, *20th Century Journey: A Memoir of a Life and the Times,* vol. II, *The Nightmare Years, 1930–1940* (Boston: Little, Brown, 1984), p. 233; author's interview with William Shirer, December 19, 1984.

43. *New York Times,* October 22, November 4, 1935.

44. Compare the *New York Times* editorial of October 22, 1935, with that of *Christian Century* August 7, 1935. *Commonweal,* August 9, 1935; *Waterbury Evening Democrat,* August 30, 1935; *New York American,* October 7, October 17, 1935; *New York Evening Post,* October 22, 1935; *Amsterdam News,* August 23, 1935; *South Bend* (Indiana) *News Times,* September 26, 1935; *Troy* (New York) *Record,* September 9, 1935, as cited in Margaret K. Norden, "American Editorial Response to the Rise of Adolf Hitler: A Preliminary Consideration," *American Jewish Historical Quarterly,* vol. 30 (October 1968), p. 295. For additional expressions of opposition to the Games see *Patterson* (New Jersey) *Call,* October 11, 1935, *Wichita* (Kansas) *Beacon,* October 18, 1935, and *Dallas Times Herald,* October 19, 1935.

45. Moshe Gottlieb, "The American Controversy over the Olympic Games," *American Jewish Historical Quarterly,* vol. LXI (March 1972), p. 207; *New York Times,* October 1, October 22, 1935; *Los Angeles Times,* October 15, 1935; *Economic Bulletin,* November 1935, p. 6.

46. *Easton* (Pennsylvania) *Express,* October 24, 1935; *Boise* (Idaho) *Statesman,* October 23, 1935; *Worcester Post,* October 29, 1935. Sherrill to Louis Rittenberg, October 3, 1935, Felix M. Warburg Papers, box 331, American Jewish Archives, Cincinnati, Ohio; Shafir, p. 586; Gottlieb, pp. 188–189. For Brundage's comments see *Los Angeles Times,* December 10, 1935, January 26, 1936. *Wheeling* (West Virginia) *Register,* December 8, 1935; *New York Times,* July 16, 1936.

47. *Commonweal,* November 8, 1935, p. 40, and November 29, 1935; *Christian Century,* August 7, 1935, p. 1007, and August 14, 1935; *New York Times,* October 22, 1935.

48. *New York Times,* October 23, 1935; Committee on Fair Play in Sports, *Preserve the Olympic Ideal: A Statement Against American Participation in the Olympic Games in Berlin* (New York, 1935), pp. 31–32.

49. *Rochester* (New York) *Democrat and Chronicle,* August 31, 1935; *Los Angeles Times,* August 7, 1935; *Knoxville Journal,* November 8, 1935.

50. *Knoxville Journal,* November 8, 1935; *Time,* November 4, 1935, pp. 61–62; Mandell, pp. 77–78, 86–87; *Catholic World,* January 1936, p. 394.

51. *Christian Century,* August 7, 1935, p. 1007, August 14, 1935, August 28, 1935, p. 1075; *New York Times,* August 5, 1935, p. 7.

52. George Messersmith wrote to Julian Mack, the Federal Judge and Zionist leader, appealing for public opposition to participation. When Mack relayed Messersmith's sentiments to President Roosevelt, FDR described the American envoy as "one of the best men we have in the whole [Diplomatic] Service and I count greatly on his judgement." Memo, Mack to Roosevelt, December 2, 1935, and Roosevelt to Mack, December 4, 1935, in *Franklin D. Roosevelt and Foreign Affairs,* vol. III, (Cambridge: Harvard University Press, 1969), p. 111; Memo, Dodd to Hull, October 11, 1935, DS 862.4063/01 G. 49; Dodd to Hull, December 10, 1935, DS 765.84/3007; Messersmith to Hull, November 15, 1934, DS 862.4063/01 G. 57; Shafir, 587.

53. *New York Times,* November 18, November 27, 1935.

54. *Brooklyn Citizen,* November 27, 1935; Troy (New York) *Times Record,* November 27, 1935; *Washington Post,* November 23, 1935; *Philadelphia Record,* December 2, 1935; *Los Angeles Times,* December 8, 1935.

55. *Nation,* October 16, 1935, p. 426, October 23, 1935, p. 461. Approximately 150 editorials were examined regarding the Olympic Games. Two-thirds of these favored a boycott and one-third opposed one.

56. Gottlieb, pp. 208–209; *Los Angeles Times,* November 28, December 2, 1935; *New York Times,* September 22, December 7, December 9, 1935.

57. *Philadelphia Record,* December 10, 1935; *Washington Post,* December 10, 1935; *Hartford* (Connecticut) *Times,* December 10, 1935; *Indianapolis Star,* December 12, 1935; *Christian Science Monitor,* December 11, 1935.

58. *Wheeling* (West Virginia) *Register,* December 9, 1935.

59. *Philadelphia Record,* December 10, 1935.

60. *Los Angeles Times,* December 9, 1935.

61. *The Nation,* August 1, 1936, p. 124; *New York Times,* August 16, 1936; interview with William Shirer, December 19, 1984.

62. *Time,* August 10, 1936, p. 40; August 17, 1936, p. 37; August 24, 1936, pp. 56–58.

63. *Literary Digest,* July 11, August 29, 1936; *Los Angeles Times,* July 14, 1936.

64. *Chicago Tribune,* July 5, 1936; *Los Angeles Times,* July 5, 1936, sec. II, p. 11, July 18, 1936, p. 13; *Time,* August 10, 1936, p. 40; *New*

York Times, August 16, 1936. It is true that the more ostensibly anti-Jewish placards and newspapers did "disappear" for the duration of the Games. However, Streicher's antisemitic journal *Stürmer* not only appeared but had on its cover a cartoon occupying half a page showing a "degenerate and brutal person labeled 'Jew' staring with envy and hatred at a German looking victor crowned with laurel." At the bottom of the page in heavy black letters was the slogan "Jews are our Misfortune." The issue contained a special article directed at foreign visitors, with long series of quotes from dead and living foreign antisemites. *New York Times,* July 30, 1936; Mandell, p. 159.

No American paper seemed to have been as taken with the Games as the French Ambassador to Germany, who declared them "the apotheosis of Hitler and his Third Reich." André François-Poncet, *The Fateful Years: Memoirs of a French Ambassador in Berlin, 1931–1938* (New York, 1949), pp. 203–207; Robert Dallek, *Democrat and Diplomat: The Life of William E. Dodd* (New York: Oxford University Press, 1968), p. 288; Franklin Ried Gannon, *The British Press and Germany, 1936–1939* (London: Oxford, 1971), p. 102.

65. *Washington Post,* July 25, 1936; *Los Angeles Times,* July 27, 1936, sec. II, p. 9.

66. *Los Angeles Times,* July 27, 1936, sec. II, p. 9, August 2, 1936, p. 1 and sec. II, p. 11, August 4, 1936, sec. II, p. 4.

67. *Washington Post,* February 17, 1936; *New York Times,* August 14, 1936; *Los Angeles Times,* July 18, July 31, August 7, 1936. Gallico was then one of the highest paid and most respected sports writers in the country. When he covered the competition at Garmisch, he was about to leave sports writing to take up a career as a writer. Shirer, *Nightmare Years,* p. 235.

68. *Literary Digest,* July 11, 1936, p. 33.

69. *New York Times,* July 6, 1936, p. 14.

70. *Time,* February 17, 1936, p. 37; *New York Times,* July 12, July 18, July 31, 1936, August 1, 1936, p. 1, August 2, 1936, p. 1, August 16, 1936.

71. *New York Times,* August 3, 16, 1936.

72. *Washington Post,* July 30, 1936, sports section, p. 1.

73. *Los Angeles Times,* August 2, 1936, sports section, p. 1; William Shirer, *Berlin Diary,* (New York: Knopf, 1941), author's interview with William Shirer, December 19, 1984; Mandell, p. 108.

74. *Washington Post,* February 9, 1936, August 2, 1936, p. 7.

75. *Washington Post,* August 3, 1936, p. 7.

76. *Washington Post,* August 5, 1936, p. 7, August 6, 1936, p. 17, August 16, 1936, part B, p. 5; August 17, 1936, p. 7.

77. For treatment of Owens see: *Time,* August 17, 1936, p. 37; *Washington Post,* August 6, 1936, p. 1; *Washington Post,* July 31, 1936; *New York Times,* August 3, 1936, p. 1, August 4, 1936, p. 1; *Nation,* August 15, 1936, p. 185; *Literary Digest,* August 29, 1936, p. 33.

78. Wise to Brandeis, October 6, 1936, Brandeis Collection, roll 26, as quoted in Shafir, pp. 593–594. After the Games, Ambassador Dodd was far less sanguine than his boss, the President. He reported to Washington that the "Jewish population awaits with fear and trembling the termination of the Olympic period which has vouchsafed on them a certain respite against molestation." He doubted that the Nazis would be "quite so foolish" as to immediately resume their "spectacular" antisemitic activities and thereby "spoil the good impression" they had made on foreign opinion by the Games. Some of the press echoed Dodd's fears. Actually the Nazis waited a while before actively pursuing their antisemitic campaign. The Games marked the beginning of a slight pause in the persecution of the Jews. "Political Report of the Ambassador in Germany," *FRUS,* 1936, vol. II, August 19, 1936, p. 202. *Williamsport* (Pennsylvania) *Sun,* July 29, 1936.

79. Shirer, *Nightmare Years,* p. 232.

80. Interview with Howard K. Smith, February 27, 1985.

81. Mandell, p. 118.

Chapter 4

1. *New York Times,* March 23, April 3, 1938. Gedye's report of April 3 was cited by State Department official George Messersmith as a reliable description of what was happening in Vienna. It was, Messersmith wrote in a personal letter, "an unspeakably horrible situation." George Messersmith to Jacob Billikopf, April 4, 1938, American Jewish Archives, Cincinnati, Ohio. His article and the fact that he was ordered out of Austria by the Nazis for his reports were also mentioned by some papers in their editorials. See, for example, *San Jose Mercury Herald,* April 9, 1938.

2. For listing of editorials see the *Press Information Bulletin,* March 24 through April 14, 1938. *Bulletins* are to be found in Franklin D. Roosevelt Papers, Franklin D. Roosevelt Library, Hyde Park, N.Y.

3. Shlomo Shafir, "The Impact of the Jewish Crisis on American–Jewish Relations, 1933–1939," Ph.D. diss. (Ann Arbor: University Microfilms International, 1971), pp. 696–697; Dieckhoff to Foreign Ministry, March 22, 1938, *DGFP,* series D, I, pp. 696–697.

4. *Detroit Free Press*, March 23, 1938.

5. *Greensboro* (North Carolina) *Record*, March 24, 1938.

6. *Newsweek*, April 4, 1938, p. 11; *Miami Herald*, March 26, 1938; *Trenton* (New Jersey) *Gazette*, March 26, 1938.

7. *Trenton* (New Jersey) *Gazette*, March 26, 1938; *Mobile* (Alabama) *Register*, March 25, 1938.

8. *Newsweek*, April 4, 1938; *Lansing* (Michigan) *Journal*, March 27, 1938. For a detailed description of Freud's treatment by the Nazis, see Ernest Jones, *The Life and Work of Sigmund Freud* (New York, Basic Books, 1961), pp. 512–518.

9. *FRUS*, 1938, vol. I, pp. 740–741. "The Press Conferences of President Franklin D. Roosevelt," XI (March 25, 1938), 248–250; David S. Wyman, *Paper Walls: America and the Refugee Crisis, 1938–1941* (Amherst: University of Massachusetts Press, 1968), p. 43. The President announced that the conference would attempt to alleviate the situation of all political refugees, including those from Russia, Spain, and Italy, and not just Jews. This may have been an attempt to diffuse some of the criticism that he believed would be leveled at the plan for the conference. Roosevelt may have also reasoned that this broad approach was a way of winning the support of those who were concerned about Spanish or Russian refugees. At any rate it misfired. Certain papers cited it as a means of camouflaging the fact that these were mainly Jewish refugees, while others complained that it was a sign that the plan was but the beginning of a broad liberalization of immigration. Roosevelt Press Conference, March 25, 1938; *Chattanooga Times*, March 26, 1938; *Huntington* (West Virginia) *Advertiser*, March 25, 1938.

10. The German quota was not filled from 1930, when quotas were first instituted, until 1939. The allowance for Germany was 25,957; after the *Anschluss* it was combined with the Austrian quota for a total of 27,360. The following table shows the number of immigrants who entered under the German quota during the first five years of Nazi rule:

1933	1,445
1934	3,744
1935	5,532
1936	6,642
1937	11,536

See Louis Adamic, *America and the Refugees*, pp. 10–11, and Lewis and Marian Shibsby, "Status of the Refugee Under American Immigration Laws," *Annals*, CCIII, May 1939, 78ff., both cited in Henry L. Feingold, *The Politics of Rescue: The Roosevelt Administration and the Holocaust, 1938–1945* (New Brunswick: Rutgers University Press, 1970), p. 313, n. 39.

11. Achilles memorandum on refugee program under cover memo from Butler to Duggan and Drew November 15, 1938, DS 840.48 Ref./900 1/2, as cited in Shafir, p. 702.

12. *Paterson* (New Jersey) *News,* March 28, 1938; *El Paso Times,* March 27, 1938; *Portland Oregonian,* March 25, 1938.

13. *Time,* April 4, 1938, p. 12; *Memphis Commercial Appeal,* March 27, 1938; *Pasadena Star News,* March 26, 1938.

14. *Memphis Commercial Appeal,* March 27, 1938; *Dayton* (Ohio) *News,* March 29, 1938.

15. *Charleston* (South Carolina) *News and Courier,* March 29, 1938.

16. *FRUS,* 1938, vol. 1, pp. 740–741; *Birmingham Age Herald,* March 29, 1938; *Providence Journal,* March 28, 1938; *Paterson News,* March 28, 1938.

17. There were of course those who were not reassured by these stipulations. In addition, many papers were buoyed by their belief that through America's gates would come a stream of "brainy men," the Einsteins and Freuds, the "brilliant minds of the old world." *Augusta* (Georgia) *Chronicle,* March 27, 1938; *Memphis Commercial Appeal,* March 27, 1938; *Boston Globe,* March 28, 1938; *La Crosse* (Wisconsin) *Tribune,* March 30, 1938; *Cincinnati Enquirer,* March 30, 1938; *Jacksonville* (Florida) *Journal,* March 31, 1938; *Indianapolis News,* March 26, 1938.

18. *New Bedford* (Massachusetts) *Standard Times,* March 28, 1938; *Greenville* (South Carolina) *News,* March 27, 1938; *Butte* (Montana) *Post,* April 2, 1938; *Indianapolis News,* March 31, 1938.

19. Norman Bentwich, *Wanderer Between Two Worlds* (London: Kegan Paul, Trench, Trubner & Co., 1941), pp. 185–186; Shafir, p. 700.

20. *South Bend* (Indiana) *Tribune,* April 2, 1938; *Jacksonville* (Florida) *Journal,* March 31, 1938.

21. *Salem* (Oregon) *Journal,* March 30, 1938; *Time,* April 4, 1938, p. 12.

22. Roosevelt to Frankfurter March 26, 1938, as quoted in Shafir, pp. 705–706.

23. *Time,* April 4, 1938, pp. 11–12; *Newsweek,* April 4, 1938, pp. 10–11. Wyman interview with George L. Warren, former executive secretary of the President's Advisory Committee on Political Refugees, corroborates this view that the plan for the conference and the conference itself were part of the design to move America away from its strictly isolationist stance. See Wyman, pp. 44, 236, n. 2.

24. For delineation of groups which opposed the plan see Wyman, pp. 46–47; Shafir, pp. 715–716. *Jackson* (Michigan) *Citizen Patriot*, April 3, 1938.

25. *Binghamton Press*, March 26, 1938.

26. *Youngstown* (Ohio) *Vindicator*, March 26, 1938; *Milwaukee* (Wisconsin) *Journal*, March 30, 1938; *Missoula* (Montana) *Missoulian*, April 5, 1938.

27. *Milwaukee Journal*, March 28, 1938; *Ft. Wayne News Sentinel*, March 29, 1938.

28. *Milwaukee Journal*, March 30, 1938.

29. *Portland* (Oregon) *News Telegram*, March 30, 1938.

30. *Detroit News*, April 5, 1938.

31. *Christian Century*, November 30, 1938, pp. 1456–1459.

32. *Holyoke* (Massachusetts) *Trans–Telegram*, November 16, 1938.

33. *Newsweek*, June 27, 1938, p. 16. Proceedings of the Intergovernmental Committee, Evian, July 6–15, 1938, Verbatim Record of the Plenary Meetings of the Committee, Resolution and Reports, July 1938.

34. *New York Times*, July 6, 1938, p. 1; *Newsweek*, July 18, 1938, p. 13.

35. *Little Rock Gazette*, July 8, 1938.

36. *Lewiston* (Idaho) *Tribune*, July 7, 1938; *San Francisco Chronicle*, July 9, 1938; *New York Times*, July 6, 1938.

37. *Washington Post*, July 3, 1938; *Houston Chronicle*, July 7, 1938; *Providence* (Rhode Island) *Journal*, July 11, 1938; *Boston Herald*, July 13, 1938.

38. *New Orleans Times Picayune*, July 15, 1938; *Houston Chronicle*, July 7, 1938; *Chattanooga Times*, July 18, 1938.

39. *Salt Lake City Tribune*, July 8, 1938.

40. *Philadelphia Record*, July 17, 1938.

41. *Baltimore Sun*, July 16, 1938; *Boston Transcript*, July 18, 1938; *Cincinnati Enquirer*, July 18, 1938.

42. *Utica* (New York) *Observer Dispatch*, July 11, 1938; *El Paso Times*, July 8, 1938.

43. *Detroit Free Press*, July 11, 1938.

44. *Galveston Texas News*, July 9, 1938.

45. *Norfolk* (Virginia) *Pilot*, July 10, 1938; *Buffalo Courier Express*, July 14, 1938.

46. *Time*, July 18, 1938, p. 16; *New York Herald Tribune*, July 12, 1938.

47. *New York Times*, July 8, 1938.

48. *New Republic,* July 20, 1938, pp. 291–292.

49. *Richmond News Leader,* July 13, 1938.

50. *Philadelphia Record,* July 17, 1938.

51. *Newsweek,* July 18, 1938, p. 13.

52. *Washington Star,* July 13, 1938. See also *Washington Post,* July 10, 1935.

53. *New York Herald Tribune,* July 17, 1938; *New York Times,* July 14, 1938; *Boston Transcript,* July 9, 1938; *Houston Chronicle,* July 18, 1938; *Buffalo News,* July 18, 1938; *Newark Star Eagle,* July 22, 1938; *Albany Knickerbocker News,* July 11, 1938; *San Francisco Chronicle,* July 18, 1938.

54. *Fortune,* July 1938, pp. 80–82.

55. *Tulsa* (Oklahoma) *World,* July 15, 1938; *Erie* (Pennsylvania) *Dispatch Herald,* July 15, 1938; *Springfield* (Illinois) *Journal,* July 17, 1938.

56. *Los Angeles Examiner,* November 16, 1938; *San Francisco Chronicle,* November 16, 1938; *Seattle Post Intelligencer,* November 17, 1938.

57. *Newsweek,* June 27, 1938, p. 16; Lionel Kochan, *Pogrom, 10 November 1938* (London: Andre Deutsch, 1957), p. 127; *DGFP,* series D, IV, 1938, pp. 639–640.

58. *New York Times,* November 13, 1938; Bill Graves to Roosevelt, November 12, 1938, DS 862.4016/1826, as cited in Shafir, p. 819; Sander Diamond, "The *Kristallnacht* and the Reaction in America," *YIVO Annual of Jewish Social Science,* vol. XIV (1969), pp. 200–203.

59. For the sheer mass of comment see *Press Information Bulletin* for the period from November 10 to early December 1938.

60. *Newsweek,* November 21, 1938, p. 18; *Nation,* July 5, 1933, p. 2.

61. Kochan, p. 11.

62. *Knoxville Journal,* November 15, 1938; *Butte* (Montana) *Post,* November 23, 1938; *New Haven Journal Courier,* November 23, 1938; *Washington Times,* November 15, 1938.

63. *New York Daily News,* November 15, 1938, p. 27.

64. *Wilmington* (Delaware) *News,* November 13, 1938; *Newsweek,* November 21, 1938, p. 18; Kochan, p. 15.

65. *Dallas Times Herald,* November 16, 1938; *Denver News,* November 17, 1938; *Philadelphia Bulletin,* November 22, 1938; *Pittsburgh Press,* November 16, 1938; *Macon* (Georgia) *Telegraph and News,* November 20, 1938; *Portland* (Oregon) *Journal,* November 18, 1938.

66. *Virginian Pilot,* November 15, 1938; *Charleston* (West Virginia) *Gazette,* November 25, 1938; *Phoenix Republic,* November 19, 1938; *New York Evening Post,* November 17, 1938; *Philadelphia Record,* November 18, 1938; *San Antonio* (Texas) *Express,* November 23, 1938; *Schenectady Gazette,* November 25, 1938.

67. *Fort Worth Star Telegram,* November 19, 1938.

68. *Lynchburg* (Virginia) *News,* November 28, 1938; *Richmond News Leader,* November 22, 1938; *East St. Louis Journal,* November 21, 1938; *Binghamton* (New York) *Sun,* November 22, 1938; *Chester* (Pennsylvania) *Times,* November 20, 1938; *Troy* (New York) *Record,* November 22, 1938.

69. *Gary* (Indiana) *Post Tribune,* November 16, 1938; *Denver News,* November 23, 1938; *Waco* (Texas) *News Herald,* November 22, 1938; *Rapid City News Journal,* November 23, 1938; *Gadsden* (Alabama) *Times,* November 20, 1938; *Richmond News Leader,* November 22, 1938; *Houston Press,* November 17, 1938; *Ogden* (Vermont) *Standard Examiner,* November 24, 1938.

70. *New York Times,* November 16, 1938, p. 22.

71. *Cleveland Plain Dealer,* as cited in *New York Times,* November 12, 1938; *Nation,* January 7, 1939; *Rutland* (Vermont) *Herald,* November 24, 1938; *New Orleans Times Picayune,* November 16, 1938; *Paterson* (New Jersey) *News,* November 18, 1938; *Fort Worth* (Texas) *Star Telegram,* November 17, 1938; *Portland Oregonian,* November 17, 1938; *Canton* (Ohio) *Repository,* November 18, 1938; *St. Joseph* (Missouri) *Gazette,* November 18, 1938; *Tacoma* (Washington) *News Tribune,* November 26, 1938; *Pittsfield Berkshire Eagle,* November 19, 1938.

72. *St. Louis Post Dispatch,* November 25, 1938; *Baltimore Evening Sun,* November 14, 1938.

73. *New York Times,* November 14, 1938, p. 18; see also *Christian Science Monitor,* November 15, 1938, pp. 1, 5; *Cleveland Plain Dealer,* as quoted in *Los Angeles Times,* November 17, 1938, p. 4; *Nation,* January 7, 1939, pp. 33–35. This was also one of the major theses of Soviet reports regarding *Kristallnacht.* The attacks were, a *Pravda* editorial concluded, a "direct result of the hopeless position in which the Fascist dictatorship has found itself." *Pravda,* November 16, 1938, as cited in Kochan, p. 137.

74. *Saturday Evening Post,* April 22, 1939, p. 104.

75. Interview with Senator Alan Cranston, May 7, 1985.

76. *Staatzeitung und Herald,* as quoted in *Nineteenth Century,* January 1939, p. 120; *Contemporary Jewish Record,* January 1939, p. 42; *Springfield Republican,* as quoted in *New York Times,* November 12, 1938, p. 4; *Tampa Tribune,* November 15, 1938; *Helena* (Montana) *Independent,* November 15, 1938; *Hamilton* (Ohio) *Journal News,* November 19, 1938; *Springfield* (Illinois) *State Register,* November 20, 1938; *Huntington* (West Virginia) *Advertiser,* November 19, 1938; *Eugene* (Oregon) *News,* November 19, 1938.

77. Diamond, p. 36. Jan Ciechanowski, *Defeat in Victory* (New York: Doubleday, 1947), p. 119.

78. *Chattanooga* (Tennessee) *News,* November 15, 1938; *Chicago News,* November 19, 1938; *New York Herald Tribune,* November 13, 1938; *Trenton* (New Jersey) *Gazette,* November 19, 1938; *Durham* (North Carolina) *Herald,* November 21, 1938.

79. *Atlanta Constitution,* November 22, 1938; *Hamilton* (Ohio) *Journal News,* November 26, 1938.

80. Franklin Reid Gannon, *The British Press and Nazi Germany, 1936–1939* (London: Oxford, 1971), p. 228.

81. *Lincoln* (Nebraska) *Journal,* November 15, 1938.

82. *Time,* November 11, 1938, p. 19; *Newsweek,* November 21, 1938, pp. 17–18.

83. The *Philadelphia Record,* as cited in *Contemporary Jewish Record,* November 1939, p. 56, and January 1939, pp. 41–50. See also *Commonweal,* November 25, 1938, p. 113, and *Christian Century,* November 23, 1938, pp. 1422–1423.

84. *New York Times,* November 10, 1938, p. 1, November 11, 1938, p. 3; *New Republic,* November 23, 1938, p. 60; *Christian Science Monitor,* November 10, November 12, 1938.

85. *Louisville Times,* November 17, 1938; *Frederick* (Oklahoma) *Leader,* November 17, 1938; *Schenectady Union Star,* November 18, 1938; *Danville* (Virginia) *Register,* November 20, 1938; *Long Beach Press Telegram,* November 16, 1938.

86. *Ashville* (North Carolina) *Citizen,* November 16, 1938; *Roswell* (New Mexico) *Dispatch,* November 18, 1938; *Boston Transcript,* November 14, 1938.

87. *Time,* November 28, 1938, p. 10.

88. *Time,* November 21, 1938, pp. 18–19, November 28, 1938, pp. 10–11; *Newsweek,* December 12, 1938, p. 16; *New Republic,* December 21, 1938, p. 189; *Commonweal,* December 9, 1938, p. 177; Joseph Alsop and Robert Kintner, *American White Paper: The Story of American Diplomacy and the Second World War* (New York: Simon & Schuster, 1940), pp. 24–25; *Complete Presidential Press Conferences of Franklin D. Roosevelt,* introduction by Jonathan Daniels (New York: Da Capo Press, 1972), vol. XII, p. 224; Selig Adler, *Isolationist Impulse,* (New York: Abelard-Schuman, 1957), p. 279; Elmer Roper, *You and Your Leaders: Their Actions and Your Reactions, 1936–1956* (New York: Morrow, 1957), p. 71. Diamond, p. 205; Shafir, p. 829.

89. Not only did the President ignore the State Department's advice on the statement, but he did not adhere to the language of the statement that had been prepared for him by the Department. Immediately prior to delivering it to the press, he changed the wording. The proposed statement read as follows: "The news of

the past few days from Germany has shocked public opinion in the United States. Such news from any part of the world would inevitably produce a similar reaction among the American people. With a view to gaining a first hand picture of the situation in Germany I asked the Secretary of State to order our Ambassador in Berlin to come home for report and consultation." *Press Conferences of Roosevelt,* vol. XII, pp. 227–229. See also Cordell Hull, *The Memoirs of Cordell Hull* (New York: Macmillan, 1948) vol. I, pp. 24–25, 599; Shafir, pp. 828–829; Diamond, p. 205.

90. *New York Times,* November 16, 1938, p. 1; *Newsweek,* November 28, 1938, p. 11; *Philadelphia Inquirer,* November 16, 1938; *Huntington* (West Virginia) *Advertiser,* November 19, 1938.

91. There was no unanimity of opinion in the State Department regarding an American response. George Messersmith, the former Consul in Berlin, urged that Ambassador Wilson, who was due to visit in the near future anyway, be recalled "for consultation." Messersmith advocated this step because, among other things, he believed it would constitute a fitting response to American public opinion. Others in the State Department argued against removal of America's representative from Germany. Pierrepont Moffat objected to yielding to "pressure in favor of one particular population or group." He objected to Wilson's recall and counseled that some means be found of making a "gesture that would not . . . hurt us." See the Moffat Diary entries for October 29–30 and November 14 as quoted in Shafir, p. 825. It is true that Wilson was planning a visit to the United States, but he left earlier than was intended and was clearly summoned home by FDR in the wake of the pogrom. *New York Times,* November 15, 1938; *FRUS,* 1938, vol. II, pp. 402–403.

92. *New York Sun,* November 15, 1938; *Minneapolis Star,* November 19, 1938.

93. *Milwaukee Journal,* November 18, 1938; *Toledo* (Ohio) *Blade,* November 21, 1938; *Witchita* (Kansas) *Eagle,* November 19, 1938; *Indianapolis Star,* November 19, 1938; *Miami News,* November 21, 1938.

94. *New York Herald Tribune,* November 19, 1938, p. 10; *Fortune,* April 1939, p. 102; *New York Times,* November 15, 1938, p. 1, November 16, 1938, p. 4.

95. *St. Louis Globe Democrat,* as quoted in *New York Times,* November 12, 1938; *Chicago Tribune,* November 17, 1938.

96. *Nation,* July 6, 1940, pp. 4–5; *New Republic,* November 23, 1938, p. 60, November 30, 1938, p. 87, June 28, 1939, p. 197, April 28, 1941, pp. 592–594; *Commonweal,* November 24, 1938, p. 113; *Collier's,* December 31, 1938, p. 50. See also *Survey Graphic,* October

1940, pp. 524–526; *New York Daily News,* March 16, 1939, as quoted in *Admission of German Refugee Children: Joint Hearings Before a Subcommittee on Immigration, U.S. Senate, and Subcommittee on Immigration and Naturalization, House of Representatives,* 76th Cong., 1st sess., on S.J. Res. 64 and H.J. Res. 168, April 20–24, 1939, p. 31; *Forum,* November 1938, pp. 209–210. *Davenport* (Iowa) *Democrat,* November 22, 1939; *Denver News,* November 15, 1938; *Richmond News Leader,* November 16, 1938; *New York Daily News,* November 19, 1938; *Wichita* (Kansas) *Eagle,* November 18, 1938; *Hartford Courant,* November 15, 1938.

97. *Pittsburgh Press,* November 16, 1938.

98. *Binghamton Sun,* November 29, 1938; *South Bend* (Indiana) *News Times,* November 28, 1938; *Vicksburg* (Mississippi) *Herald,* November 29, 1938.

99. John R. Carlson, *Under Cover* (New York: Dutton, 1943), p. 66; *Philadelphia Evening Bulletin,* April 7, 1939, p. 3; Wyman, pp. 6–7; *Survey Graphic,* October 1940, p. 534ff; *Commonweal,* October 6, 1939, pp. 531–533, November 25, 1938, p. 11; *Current History,* May 1939, pp. 19–22; *New Republic,* July 20, 1938, pp. 291–292; *Time,* December 5, 1938, p. 18; Michael N. Dobkowski, *Politics of Indifference* (Washington: University Press of America, 1982), p. 286.

100. *Pittsburg Press,* November 16, 1938; *St. Joseph* (Missouri) *Gazette,* November 21, 1938; *Wilmington* (Delaware) *News,* November 21, 1938; *Kansas City Journal,* November 19, 1938; *Danville* (Virginia) *Register,* November 11, 1938; *Pasadena Star News,* November 15, 1938; *Lake Charleston* (Louisiana) *American Press,* November 18, 1938; *Huntington* (West Virginia) *Advertiser,* November 23, 1938; *South Bend* (Indiana) *News Times,* November 28, 1938; *Binghamton Sun,* November 29, 1938; *Dallas Dispatch,* November 28, 1938.

101. *Richmond* (Virginia) *News Leader,* November 14, 1938; *Toledo* (Ohio) *Times,* November 16, 1938; *Erie* (Pennsylvania) *Times,* November 21, 1938; *Springfield* (Ohio) *Sun,* November 22, 1938; *Madison* (Wisconsin) *Times,* November 26, 1938.

102. *Christian Science Monitor,* November 15, 1938, p. 1.

103. Mary Baker Eddy, the founder of the movement, requested that her followers pray at the time of the Russo-Japanese War and the Boxer Rebellion. According to her, this was the "greatest contribution they could make toward the peace of mankind." Stephen Gottschalk, *The Emergence of Christian Science in American Religious Life* (Berkeley: University of California Press, 1973), pp. 267–268.

104. *Christian Century,* November 30, 1938, pp. 1456–1459; *Cincinnati Times Star,* November 19, 1938; *Binghamton Press,* November 19, 1938; *Tulsa* (Oklahoma) *World,* November 18, 1938; *Oakland Tri-*

bune, November 22, 1938; *New Haven Journal Courier,* November 23, 1938; *Tampa* (Florida) *Tribune,* November 21, 1938; *Mobile* (Alabama) *Register,* November 19, 1938; *Akron* (Ohio) *Beacon Journal,* November 18, 1938; *Danville Register,* November 20, 1938; *Lewiston* (Indiana) *Tribune,* November 18, 1938; *Spokane Spokesman Review,* November 17, 1938.

105. Charles Stember, *Jews in the Mind of America* (New York: Basic Books, 1966), pp. 140, 145–148. Roosevelt was also careful about other aspects of his action. He reassured the press that those citizens of the Reich in the United States on visitors' visas who would be allowed to remain "were not all Jews by any means." *Press Conferences of Roosevelt,* vol. XII, pp. 238–241.

106. *Fortune,* July 1938, p. 80, April 1939, p. 102. A Gallup poll taken at the time revealed that 95 percent of the American public was opposed to American involvement in European affairs. William Langer and S. Everett Gleason, *The Challenge to Isolation* (New York: Harper, 1952), p. 36.

107. *New York Times,* November 16, 1938, p. 22.

108. Adler, pp. 270–273; *Public Opinion Quarterly,* October 1939, pp. 595–596; Langer and Gleason, pp. 14, 39, 51; *Public Opinion Quarterly,* October 1939, p. 599; DGFP, series D, IV, pp. 639–640.

109. *Time,* December 5, 1938, p. 18; Ronald Steel, *Walter Lippmann and the American Century* (New York: Vintage Books, 1980), p. 173. Lippmann failed even to mention antisemitism as a contributing factor to the creation of a refugee problem. Instead he attributed the situation to the fact that there were "too many shop keepers, professional men, artists and intellectuals." All of which were code words for Jews. *Los Angeles Times,* November 13, 1938; *Birmingham Age Herald,* November 19, 1938; *Bethlehem* (Pennsylvania) *Globe Times,* November 19, 1938; *Cincinnati Times Star,* November 19, 1938; *Brockton Enterprise and Times,* November 18, 1938; *Charleston* (West Virginia) *Gazette,* November 24, 1938.

110. *National Jewish Monthly,* January 1939, p. 156; Herbert Hoover, *Further Addresses upon the American Road* (New York: Scribner, 1940), p. 244.

111. *Springfield Republican,* as cited in *Contemporary Jewish Record,* January 1939, pp. 41–50; *Christian Science Monitor,* November 16, 1938; *Time,* November 28, 1938, p. 11; *New Republic,* November 30, 1938, p. 87; *Newsweek,* November 28, 1938, pp. 13–14, December 12, 1938, pp. 16–17; *Atlantic Monthly,* December 1938, p. 77; *Christian Century,* December 7, 1938, p. 1485.

112. *Washington News,* November 17, 1938; *Camden* (New Jersey) *Courier,* November 18, 1938; *Knoxville* (Tennessee) *News Sentinel,* November

16, 1938; *Pittsburgh Press,* November 17, 1938; *Houston Chronicle,* November 18, 1938; *El Paso Herald Post,* November 17, 1938; A. J. Sherman, *Island Refuge: Britain and Refugees from the Third Reich, 1933–1939* (Berkeley: University of California Press, 1973), p. 173; Minutes Franco-British talks of 24 November 1938, *Documents on British Foreign Policy, 1919–1939,* third series, vol. 111 (London: Her Majesty's Stationery Office), pp. 294–296.

113. *New York Times,* November 23, 1938.

Chapter 5

1. I wish to thank my former student Leah E. Weil for her research on Congressional action regarding immigration restriction and the child refugees of Europe, 1938–1941.

2. *Public Opinion Quarterly,* October 1939, pp. 595–596; *Congressional Record,* 76th Cong., 1st sess., vol. 85, 1457–1458, 2338–2341, 2805, 3865–3868, 4817–4819, and appendix, 641–642, 656–666, 835–836, 1073–1074, 1681–1682, 1886–1887, 2057–2059, 2792–2794, 3299; *Admission of German Refugee Children: Joint Hearings Before a Subcommittee of the Committee on Immigration, United States Senate, and a Subcommittee of the Committee on Immigration and Naturalization, House of Representatives,* 76th Cong., 1st sess., April 20, 21, 22, and 24, 1939, pp. 8, 45–49ff. For additional background on this period see David Wyman, *Paper Walls: America and the Refugee Crisis, 1938–1941* (Massachusetts: University of Massachusetts Press, 1968), p. 67ff.

3. *New York Herald Tribune,* February 11, 1939, as quoted in *German Refugee Children,* p. 11.

4. *Galveston News,* February 20, 1939, as quoted in *German Refugee Children,* p. 21. See also *Sioux City Journal,* February 18, 1939; *Ashville* (North Carolina) *Times,* February 23, 1939; *Washington Evening Star,* February 16, 1939, in *German Refugee Children,* pp. 12, 17, 34.

5. *Cincinnati Enquirer,* May 25, 1939, as quoted in *Congressional Record,* 76th Cong., 1st sess., vol. 84, p. 2793; *New York Daily News,* March 16, 1939, as quoted in *German Refugee Children,* p. 31; *St. Petersburg* (Florida) *Evening Independent,* March 24, 1939, in *German Refugee Children,* p. 38.

6. *Washington Post,* February 13, 1939, as quoted in *German Refugee Children,* p. 9.

7. *Miami Herald,* February 21, 1939, as quoted in *German Refugee Children,* pp. 22–23 (emphasis added); *Christian Century,* November 30, 1938, pp. 1456–1459.

8. *Nation,* July 1, 1939, p. 3, as cited in Wyman, p. 85ff; *New York*

Sun, as quoted in *Congressional Record,* 76th Cong., 1st sess., vol. 84, p. 1681; *Pathfinder,* February 25, 1939; *Montgomery Advertiser,* February 17, 1939; *Fort Wayne Journal Gazette,* February 19, 1939, in *German Refugee Children,* pp. 14, 17, 20. Even the bill's supporters felt compelled to argue that not only Jews would be aided. Sidney Hollander, president of the National Council of Jewish Federations, testified in support of the bill. In his testimony he observed that "statements have been made . . . that if this bill is passed, it will benefit primarily Jewish children. . . . If it were [true], I doubt if I would as strongly urge the passage of the bill." David Brody, "American Jewry, the Refugees and Immigration Restriction (1932–1942)," *Publications of the American Jewish Historical Society,* June 1956, vol. 45, p. 343.

9. *Pensacola News,* February 21, 1939, as quoted in *German Refugee Children,* p. 27.

10. *Dayton Daily News,* February 20, 1939, as quoted in *German Refugee Children,* p. 33.

11. Those who offered this view bolstered their argument against the Wagner—Rogers bill by citing Roosevelt's speech at the White House Conference on Children which had been held during April, the same month that the first hearings on the bill took place. *Admission of German Refugee Children: Hearings Before the Committee on Immigration and Naturalization, House of Representatives,* 76th Cong., 1st sess., on H.J. Res. 165 and H.J. Res. 168, May 24, 25, 31, and June 1, 1939, p. 67.

12. *Congressional Record,* 76th Cong., 1st sess., vol. 84, part 14, A-3237; Wyman, pp. 95–96; Henry Cantril, *Public Opinion* (Princeton: Princeton University Press, 1951), p. 1081.

13. *Congressional Record,* 76th Cong., 1st sess., vol. 84, part 14, A-3237; Wyman, pp. 95–96.

14. Cantril, p. 1150; *Reader's Digest,* May 1939. Of the Jews polled, 26 percent were against any change in the quotas.

15. *New York Times,* June 2, 1939, p. 1, June 3, 1939, p. 3, June 5, 1939, p. 1, June 6, 1939, p. 1, June 7, 1939, p. 1, June 8, 1939, p. 1; *Los Angeles Times,* June 1, 1939, p. 1.

16. *Washington Post,* June 3, 1939; *Greensboro* (North Carolina) *News,* June 5, 1939, *Bakersfield Californian* June 5, 1939.

17. *Philadelphia Record,* June 5, 1939; *New York Herald Tribune,* June 3, 1939; *Memphis Commercial Appeal,* June 3, 1939; *Pittsburgh Post Gazette,* June 14, 1939; *Fresno* (California) *Bee,* June 8, 1939.

18. *New York Herald Tribune,* June 3, 1939; *Richmond* (Virginia) *Times Dispatch,* June 14, 1939; *Reno* (Nevada) *State Journal,* June 3, 1939.

19. *Richmond* (Virginia) *Times Dispatch,* June 14, 1939. Also placing blame on Cuba were the *Muncie* (Indiana) *State,* June 10, 1939; *South Bend* (Indiana) *Tribune,* June 3, 1939; *Utica Observer Dispatch,* June 7, 1939; *Brooklyn Eagle,* June 4, 1939; and *Pittsburgh Post Gazette,* June 3, 1939.

20. *Louisville Courier Journal,* June 9, 1939. The *Washington Star,* June 17, 1939, also argued that Cuba had committed no act of inhospitality or harshness.

21. *Seattle Times,* June 5, 1939.

22. *Columbia* (South Carolina) *State,* June 3, 1939.

23. *Christian Science Monitor,* June 2, 1939.

24. *Bridgeport* (Connecticut) *Post,* June 4, 1939; *Evansville* (Indiana) *Courier,* June 6, 1939; *Charlotte* (North Carolina) *News,* June 3, 1939; *Christian Science Monitor,* June 2, 1939; *Richmond* (Virginia) *News Leader,* May 30, 1939.

25. *St. Louis Post Dispatch,* June 4, 1939.

26. *Cleveland Plain Dealer,* June 19, 1939; *St. Louis Globe Democrat,* June 18, 1939.

27. *Baltimore Sun,* June 3, 1939; *Chattanooga* (Tennessee) *News,* June 8, 1939; *Milwaukee Post,* June 6, 1939; *Danville* (Illinois) *Commercial News,* June 4, 1939; *New York Post,* June 6, 1939; *New York Mirror,* June 5, 1939.

28. *New York Times,* June 8, 1939, p. 24.

29. *Greensboro* (North Carolina) *Press,* June 5, 1939; *Dallas Times Herald,* June 13, 1939; *Butte* (Montana) *Post,* June 5, 1939.

30. *Cleveland Plain Dealer,* June 5, 1939; *Milwaukee Journal,* June 2, 1939; *Cleveland News,* June 21, 1939; *Buffalo Courier Express,* June 2, 1939.

31. *Hartford* (Connecticut) *Courant,* June 3, 1939; *Frederick* (Oklahoma) *Leader,* June 13, 1939; *Canton* (Ohio) *Repository,* June 14, 1939.

32. *Baltimore Sun,* June 20, 1939; *Philadelphia Record,* June 5, 1939; *Des Moines Register,* June 14, 1939; *Charleston* (South Carolina) *Post,* June 19, 1939; *Gary* (Indiana) *Post Tribune,* June 16, 1939; *Charlotte* (North Carolina) *News,* June 20, 1939; *Berkeley Gazette,* June 12, 1939; *Kansas City* (Missouri) *Times,* June 17, 1939.

33. *Boston Globe,* June 17, 1939.

34. *Watertown* (New York) *Times,* June 3, 1939; *Washington Star,* June 4, 1939.

35. *Springfield* (Illinois) *State Register,* June 5, 1939.

36. *Missoula* (Montana) *Missoulian,* June 7, 1939; *Seattle Times,* June 5, 1939.

37. *Hartford* (Connecticut) *Times,* June 3, 1939.

38. *Bridgeport* (Connecticut) *Times Star,* June 6, 1939.

39. *Greensboro* (North Carolina) *Record,* June 9, 1939.

40. *Syracuse* (New York) *Herald,* June 5, 1939.

41. *Newsweek,* September 12, 1939, p. 17; *Time,* September 12, 1939, p. 30.

Chapter 6

1. Dieckhoff to Hans-Georg Machensen, November 24, 1937, Dieckhoff to Weizsacker, December 20, 1937, *DGFP,* series D, I, pp. 649, 658–661. Sander Diamond, *The Nazi Movement in the United States, 1924–41* (Ithaca: Cornell University Press, 1974), pp. 21–22, n. 2.

2. Diamond, p. 23.

3. Donald M. McKale, *The Swastika Outside Germany* (Kent, Ohio: Kent State University Press, 1977); Ladislas Farago, *The Game of the Foxes* (New York: McKay, 1971); John Rogge, *The Official German Report* (New York: Thomas Yoseloff, 1961).

4. *FRUS,* vol. 1, November 27, 1937, p. 174; Dieckhoff to Weizsacker, November 8, 1938, *Les Instructions Secrètes de la Propaganda Allemande* (Paris: La Petit Parisien, n.d.), as cited in Alton Frye, *Nazi Germany and the American Hemisphere, 1933–1941* (New Haven: Yale University Press, 1967), pp. 31, 213. Diamond, p. 39.

5. John Roy Carlson, *Under Cover: My Four Years in the Nazi Underworld of America* (New York: Dutton, 1943).

6. Rogge, p. 17.

7. McKale, pp. 89–90.

8. *Los Angeles Examiner,* January 16, 1934.

9. *Chicago Daily News,* March 22, 1934; *Boston American,* April 4, 1934.

10. *New York Post,* March 27, November 27, 1934.

11. *Investigation of Nazi and Other Propaganda: Report Pursuant to House Resolution No. 198,* 74th Cong., 1st Sess., report no. 153, February 15, 1935; *New York Times,* August 19, 1935; Rogge, p. 16ff.; McKale, pp. 90–91; Diamond, pp. 180ff.

12. For dissolution of FONG see Diamond, pp. 179–201, 222; McKale, p. 91.

13. *Saturday Evening Post,* May 27, 1939, p. 5ff.

14. Diamond, p. 39; *The Brown Network: The Activities of the Nazis in Foreign Countries* (New York: Knight Publications, 1936).

15. For Kuhn's report on the meeting with Hitler see the Bund's yearbook, *Kämpfendes Deutschtum: Jahrbuch des Amerika-deutschen Volksbundes auf das Jahr 1937* (New York, 1937), pp. 55–56, as cited in Diamond, p. 256; *Nation,* March 20, 1937, p. 312, June 5, 1937, pp. 636–637, July 24, 1937, p. 86.

16. *Literary Digest,* August 14, 1937, p. 17.

17. "Hitler Speaks and the Bund Obeys," *Look,* October 10, 1938; McKale, p. 141; Diamond, pp. 286, 306; German Embassy to Foreign Ministry, December 20, 1937, *DGFP,* Series D, I, pp. 642, 659, 661, 696.

18. Diamond, p. 310; Dies to Roosevelt, August 15, 1942; J. Edgar Hoover to the Attorney General, August 17, 1942, Dies file, 10B, Franklin D. Roosevelt Library, Hyde Park, N.Y. *Nation,* October 15, 1938, p. 366; William E. Leuchtenberg, *Franklin D. Roosevelt and the New Deal 1932–1940,* (New York: Harper & Row, 1965), pp. 280–281; Frye, pp. 140–151; *DGFP,* series D, IX, pp. 625–626. *Providence* (Rhode Island) *Bulletin,* n.d., 1940, by American correspondent of London's *New Statesman and Nation,* in American Jewish Committee clipping file, no. 189, YIVO Institute, New York. The quotation of the U.S. Attorney is from Leon G. Turrou, *Nazi Spies in America* (New York: Random House, 1938), p. 285.

19. Dieckhoff to Weizsacker, November 8, 1938, *DGFP,* series D, I, p. 368; McKale, p. 143. For the speeches of rally leaders see *Six Addresses on the Aims and Purposes of the German American Bund, Madison Square Garden, February 20, 1939* (New York, 1939), as cited in Diamond, p. 326; *New York Times,* February 21, 1939, p. 1. For reports from German officials to Berlin regarding the rally, see Borches to Berlin, February 27, 1939, *DGFP,* series D, IV, pp. 675–678; Frye, p. 91.

20. *The Nation* called the meeting a "disgusting exhibition." *Nation,* March 4, 1939, April 1, 1939, pp. 374–375; *New York Times,* February 26, 1939; *Saturday Evening Post,* May 27, 1939, p. 7; Diamond, p. 328. For additional press reports on Bund activities see citations from the *Baltimore Sun, Cincinnati Times Star, Boston Herald, Atlanta Constitution, Springfield* (Massachusetts) *Union, New York Post,* and *St. Joseph News Press* in *Contemporary Jewish Record,* March–April 1939, p. 54ff. For a lengthy bibliography of materials on the Bund and other fifth-column groups see Thomas Huntington, "The Trojan Horse Bibliography," *Bulletin of the New York Public Library,* vol. 44 (October 1940), pp. 741–744.

21. Diamond, p. 306; *New York Times,* November 27, 1940.

22. David S. Wyman, *Paper Walls: America and the Refugee Crisis, 1938–1941* (Amherst: University of Massachusetts Press, 1968), pp. 185–186; Leuchtenberg, p. 300.

23. Conference on National Defense, May 30, 1940, Roosevelt Press Conferences, vol. XV, 420–21, as cited in Richard Polenberg, *One Nation Divisible: Class, Race and Ethnicity in the United States Since 1938* (New York: Penguin, 1980), p. 43.

24. J. Edgar Hoover, "Enemies Within," *American Magazine,* August 1940, pp. 18–19, 143–145.

25. *American Magazine,* September 1940, p. 44ff., November 1940, p. 16ff., December 1940, p. 24ff., April 1941, pp. 14–15, 120–121.

26. *New York World Telegram,* June 4–13, 1940; *Pittsburgh Press,* June 3–4, 1940; *New York Post,* September 16–21, 1940; *New York Journal American,* September 22–30, 1940.

27. A series by Bruce Catton of NEA Service, Inc., published in *New York World Telegram,* November 27, 28, 29, 1940. A gauge of the panic spreading in America was this statement by Attorney General Frank Murphy in September 1940: "Unless we are pudding headed we will drive from the land the hirelings here to undo the labors of our Fathers." It is particularly noteworthy that Murphy would make such a statement, since he was considered a strong supporter of civil liberties. J. Woodford Howard, *Mr. Justice Murphy* (Princeton, 1968), p. 207, as quoted in Richard Polenberg, *One Nation Divisible: Class, Race, and Ethnicity in the United States Since 1938,* (New York: Penguin, 1980), p. 44. The State Department was voicing similar arguments: see *FRUS,* 1940, vol. II, p. 242ff.

28. "The Five Columns and Mrs. Crowley," *America,* July 6, 1940, pp. 345–346; "What the Nazis Want Us to Believe," *America,* September 14, 1940, p. 623; "Hunting for Hitlers Can Become a Mania," *America,* September 21, 1940, p. 651.

29. "America vs. Fifth Columnists: A Symposium," *Survey Graphic,* November 1940, pp. 545–550.

30. J. Edgar Hoover, "Big Scare," *American Magazine,* August 1941, p. 24ff.

31. *McCall's,* November 1940, reprinted in *La Notizia,* November 22, 1940.

32. *Fortune,* July 1940, insert, as cited in Wyman, p. 185; *New York World Telegram,* June 4–13, 1940; *New York Mirror,* July 3, 1940; *New York Herald Tribune,* July 6, 1940; *New York Journal American,* September 30, 1940.

33. "Is There a Führer in the House?" *New Republic,* August 12, 1940, pp. 212–213; Heywood Broun, "I Can Hear You Plainly," *New Republic,* October 10, 1939. Coughlin was known to use Nazi materials for his broadcasts. A six—page illustrated article in *Look* in September 1939 argued that Coughlin not only parroted Nazi preachings but was intimately connected with Kuhn and the Bund. The article was written by William Mueller, who was identified by *Look* as an "investigator—journalist, authority on the German-American Bund, and a Catholic." "Father Coughlin and the Nazi Bund," *Look,* September 26, 1939; *Public Opinion Quarterly,* October 1939, p. 604; Charles Herbert Stember et al., *Jews in the Mind of America* (New York: Basic Books, 1966), pp. 127–128.

34. Donald Drummond, *The Passing of American Neutrality* (Ann Arbor: University of Michigan Press, 1955), pp. 372–376.

35. "Who Is the Fifth Column?" *Survey Graphic,* October 1940, pp. 503–508; *Nation,* June 22, 1940, pp. 745–746, June 29, 1940, July 27, 1940, p. 73, August 24, 1940, p. 153, August 31, 1940, pp. 103–104; Polenberg, p. 42; *Congressional Record,* 76th Cong., 3d sess., 76, part I, 680 part 6, 6773.

36. *New York Herald Tribune,* October 10, 1940, p. 24.

37. *Saturday Evening Post,* May 29, 1941, pp. 12, 89; Wyman, p. 190.

38. *Life,* June 17, 1940.

39. *Los Angeles Times,* September 15, 1941.

40. Edwin James, as cited in *Milwaukee Journal,* April 25, 1940. For similar attitudes see *Augusta* (Maine) *Kennebec Journal,* April 25, 1940; *Tulsa* (Oklahoma) *World,* April 25, 1940; *Springfield* (Illinois) *Journal,* March 19, 1941.

41. Heinz Pol, "Spies Among Refugees?" *New Republic,* August 31, 1940, p. 167.

42. *New York Journal American,* September 23, 1940; "What Is the Fifth Column?" *Survey Graphic,* October 1940, pp. 503–508.

43. *Congressional Record,* 76th Cong., 1st sess., vol. 84, part 10, 10455–10456; *Congressional Record,* 76th Cong., 3d sess., vol. 87, part 8, 8347, 9036; Wyman, pp. 185–190, 269; *New York Journal American,* May 23, 1940; *Nation,* July 5, 1941, p. 3, July 19, 1941, p. 45.

44. *Investigation of Un-American Propaganda Activities in the United States: Hearings Before a Special Committee on Un-American Activities, House of Representatives,* 77th Cong., 1st sess., part 14, 8481, 8489–8490; Wyman, p. 191; *Dayton Journal,* February 27, 1941.

45. *New York Herald Tribune,* June 19, 1941; *Philadelphia Bulletin,* June 19, 1941.

46. *New York Journal American,* June 28, 1941 (emphasis added).

47. *Philadelphia Record,* June 19, 1941.

48. The headlines accompanying the story generally reinforced the State Department's charge. *The Washington Post:*

U.S. BARS REFUGEES NAZIS CAN COERCE
Acts to End Espionage Forced by Threats to Torture Relatives

The *Post,* by using the phrase "end espionage" in its headline, made it appear as if the State Department acted because of actual cases of refugees spying and not because it wanted to prevent a potential problem from being realized. The *Washington Times Herald* did a somewhat similar thing:

REFUGEES TERRORIZED INTO SPYING
FOR GERMANY TO SAVE KIN, CHARGE

The *Philadelphia Inquirer* used refugees and spies as synonymous terms:

STATE DEPARTMENT ACTS TO BAR ENTRY OF FOREIGN AGENTS

The *Baltimore Sun*'s headline was more reserved. It described the move as a "precaution" against espionage and sabotage. *Washington Post*, June 19, 1941; *Washington Times Herald*, June 19, 1941; *Philadelphia Inquirer*, June 19, 1941; *Baltimore Sun*, June 19, June 20, 1941.

49. *Nation*, July 19, 1941, p. 45.

50. *New Republic*, August 19, 1941, p. 208; *PM*, February 11, 1941. Some journals showed far greater sympathy for political refugees than they did for "racial" or "religious" refugees, particularly if they were Jews. *Christian Century*, which even in the immediate aftermath of *Kristallnacht* stood firmly against increased immigration of Jews to the United States, came out strongly in favor of the entry of British children and the immigration of "Spanish and German *political* refugees." *Christian Century*, November 30, 1938, June 3, August 21, 1940, February 5, 1941.

51. *Fortune*, July 1940, insert; William L. Langer and S. Everett Gleason, *The Challenge to Isolation, 1937–1940* (New York: Harper & Row and Council on Foreign Relations, 1952), p. 51; Frye, pp. 31, 140–144.

52. Dieckhoff, March 10, 1941, *DGFP*, series D, XII, pp. 258–259; Thomsen to Berlin, May 4, 1940, *DGFP*, series D, IX, p. 282. See also Thomsen to Berlin, September 18, 1939, *DGFP*, series D, VIII, p. 89, and May 22, 1940, *DGFP*, series D, IX, p. 410. For earlier reports of German sensitivity to German–American Bund activities and American public opinion see Dieckhoff to Berlin, June 2, 1938, *DGFP*, series D, I, p. 454ff., and Dieckhoff to State Secretary Weiszacker, November 8, 1938, *DGFP*, series D, IV, p. 638; Frye, p. 156.

53. Frye, p. 156.

Chapter 7

1. The book which propelled both the discussion of American policy during the war and the question of "When did they know?" into the public arena was Arthur Morse's *While Six Million Died* (New York: Hart Publishing, 1967). Yehuda Bauer took issue with Morse's contention that the information was kept from Wise in "When Did

They Know?" *Midstream*, April 1968, pp. 51–58. Most recently the question of the "secrecy" of the Holocaust has been examined in Walter Laqueur's *The Terrible Secret: Suppression of the Truth About Hitler's "Final Solution"* (Boston: Little, Brown, 1980).

2. Martin Gilbert, *Auschwitz and the Allies* (New York: Holt, Rinehart and Winston, 1981).

3. *Saturday Evening Post*, April 5, 1941, p. 12; *Illustrated*, February 15, 1941; *Collier's*, February 27, 1943, p. 29ff.; *New York Times*, October 30, 1941. In February 1942 German editors were told not to report on the "Jewish question" in Eastern Europe. They were also not to even reprint official communiqués which had already been published in newspapers in occupied territories. *Zeitschriftendienst*, February 27, 1942, as cited in Laqueur, p. 215. Although the Germans devoted an overwhelming percent of their propaganda activities to making antisemitic charges, they assiduously tried to prevent mention of the issue of the *Endlösung*, or Final Solution. Michael Balfour, *Propaganda in War, 1939–1945: Organizations, Policies and Publics in Britain and Germany* (London: Routledge & Kegan Paul, 1979), p. 302.

4. Interview with Percy Knauth, February 18, 1985.

5. *New York Times*, October 24, 1941; *Washington Star*, October 23, 1941.

6. George Creel, "Beware the Superpatriots," *American Mercury*, September 1940, pp. 33–41; *Time*, September 18, 1939, p. 59; *Peoria Journal Transcript*, March 9, 1940.

7. Harold Lavine and James Wechsler, *War Propaganda in the United States* (New Haven: Yale University Press, 1940), pp. 241–243, 270.

8. *New York Times*, October 31, 1939, p. 1; *San Francisco Chronicle*, October 31, 1939, p. 1.

9. *Dayton* (Ohio) *News*, July 21, 1941; *China Weekly Review*, July 21, 1941; *Dallas Times-Herald*, July 28, 1941; *Pittsburgh Sun-Telegraph*, November 23, 1941; Frederick Oeschner, *This Is the Enemy* (Boston: Little, Brown, 1942), p. 340.

10. See for example *In Fact*, August 4, 1941, p. 3, August 11, 1941, p. 1, February 23, 1942, pp. 3–4, February 15, 1943, p. 2.

11. *New York Journal American*, November 10, 1941.

12. Sigrid Schultz, *Germany Will Try It Again* (New York: Reynal & Hitchcock, 1944), p. 186; interview with Richard C. Hottelet, December 20, 1984.

13. *Augusta* (Georgia) *Chronicle*, May 20, 1940; *Cincinnati Enquirer*, May 20, 1940; *Los Angeles Times*, November 12, 1939, p. 5.

14. *New York Times*, October 31, 1939, p. 5. See also *New York Times*, October 22, 1939, p. 2E.

15. Tolischus predicted that if a "solution of the Jewish problem" was carried out in Poland "on the German model," the implications would be "ominous." *New York Times,* September 13, 1939, p. 5, October 27, 1939, p. 3, October 31, 1939, p. 1, November 1, 1939, p. 5, November 4, 1939, p. 2; *San Francisco Chronicle,* November 1, 1939, p. 5; *Los Angeles Times,* November 1, 1939, p. 3.

16. *New York Times,* November 1, 1939, p. 2, November 4, 1939, p. 2; *New Republic,* November 15, 1939, p. 90.

17. *Christian Century,* November 30, 1939, p. 1456; *Time,* April 24, 1939, p. 26; *Life,* August 21, 1939, pp. 22–23; *San Francisco Chronicle,* October 31, 1939, p. 1; *New York Times,* November 1, 1939, p. 22, January 6, 1940, p. 2, January 23, 1940, pp. 1, 5, February 4, 1940, March 16, 1940, p. 3; *Milwaukee Journal,* February 29, 1940; *Fort Worth Star Telegram,* March 9, 1940; *Cincinnati Enquirer,* March 22, 1940; *Greenville* (South Carolina) *News,* March 22, 1940; *Chicago Tribune,* March 28, 1940.

18. Schultz, pp. 185–186.

19. Oeschner, p. 131.

20. *Life,* January 8, 1940, p. 58, February 12, 1940, p. 4.

21. *Chicago Tribune,* March 28, 1940. Kirk to the Secretary of State, February 16, 1940, DS 822.4016/2156; Kirk to the Secretary of State, March 20, 1940, DS 862.4016/2158; and Berle to the Secretary of State, February 27, 1940, DS 862/4016/2162.5.

22. *Buffalo Courier Express,* April 6, 1940; *Newark Star Ledger,* May 7, 1940.

23. For an example of this type of reasoning see Richard W. Whitaker, "Outline of Hitler's 'Final Solution' Apparent by 1933," *Journalism Quarterly,* Summer 1981, p. 179ff.

24. Edgar Ansel Mowrer, *Germany Puts the Clock Back* (New York: Morrow, 1933), p. 239; *Spectator,* March 8, 1940; H. R. Knickerbocker, *Is Tomorrow Hitler's?* (New York: Reynal & Hitchcock, 1941), pp. 65, 362.

25. Michael Marrus and Robert Paxton, *Vichy France and the Jews* (New York: Basic Books, 1981), p. 4; *Time,* October 28, 1940, p. 23; *Newsweek,* October 28, 1940, p. 23.

26. *The Nation,* November 9, 1940, p. 443; *PM,* September 6, 1940.

27. *Christian Science Monitor,* March 17, 1941; *New York Herald Tribune,* February 19, 1941; *Illustrated,* February 15, 1941.

28. *Saturday Evening Post,* April 5, 1941, p. 12ff.

29. *PM,* June 17, 1941.

30. *New York Herald Tribune,* June 14, 1941; *Charleston Mail,* June 18, 1941; *Schenectady Union Star,* June 19, 1941; *Miami Herald,* June 20, 1941; *Dubuque* (Iowa) *Telegraph Herald,* June 21, 1941; *Augusta Herald,*

July 2, 1941; Henri Baudry and Joannes Ambre, *Condition Publique*, 110–111, as cited in Marrus and Paxton, pp. 167, 169–171. For examples of French sensitivity to foreign press reports see *New York Times*, January 11, January 26, and February 23, 1941, all as cited in Marrus and Paxton, p. 393, n. 195.

31. Interview with Howard K. Smith, February 27, 1985.

32. For an analysis of the mobile killing operation, see Raul Hilberg, *The Destruction of the European Jews* (New York: Harper & Row, 1979), pp. 177–256. For some examples of military personnel who were aware of the killings, see R. Ch. Freiherr von Gersdorff, *Soldat im Untergang* (Berlin, 1977), pp. 96–99, and Peter Hoffmann, *Widerstand, Staatsstreich, Attentat* (Munich, 1970), 317, as cited in Laqueur, pp. 19–20. For a discussion of the various ways in which the news of the killings reached the German public, see Laqueur, chap. 1.

33. *Washington Star*, August 8, 1941; *New York Post*, August 1941, no day, original clipping found in the Division of Intelligence Information, National Archives, Washington, file no. H–275867.

34. *New York Times*, October 26, 1941, p. 6; *New York Journal American*, November 13, 1941, p. 1, November 29, 1941, p. 2.

35. Memos, Morris to Hull, September 8, 1941, DS 862.4016/2202, and September 30, 1941, DS 862.4016/2204.

36. *New York Herald Tribune*, August 22, October 27, November 6, 1941; *Philadelphia Record*, September 7, 1941; *Christian Science Monitor*, November 26, 1941; *Baltimore Sun*, October 18, 1941; *New York Herald Tribune*, October 27, 1941; *New York World Telegram*, October 5, 1941; *New York Journal American*, November 5, November 6, 1941.

37. *New York Times*, September 23, 1941, p. 9; *Philadelphia Record*, October 22, 1941; *PM*, October 22, 1941; *Utica Observer Dispatch*, October 24, 1941; *Baltimore Sun*, November 18, 1941; DS 862.4016/2206; Oeschner, pp. 131–132, 134, 139.

38. *Chicago Tribune*, October 19, 1941; *Detroit Free Press*, November 16, 1941.

39. *New York Times*, October 13, 1941; *Baltimore Sun*, October 16, 1941.

40. *Chicago Tribune*, October 19, 1941; *Amsterdam* (New York) *Recorder and Democrat*, October 24, 1941; *Utica* (New York) *Observer Dispatch*, October 24, 1941.

41. *New York Journal American*, November 6, 1941, *Los Angeles Times*, September 13, 1941, September 15, 1941, p. 2; *New York Herald Tribune*, November 7, 1941, p. 4, November 8, 1941, p. 3; *New York Times*, September 9, 1941, p. 5, September 21, 1941, p. 1, September 23, 1941, p. 5.

42. *Detroit Free Press*, November 16, 1941.

43. *New York Times,* March 16, 1940, p. 3, August 8, 1940, p. 11, October 7, 1941, p. 5.

44. *Philadelphia Record,* October 22, 1941.

45. *Akron Beacon Journal,* April 26, 1940; *Buffalo Courier Express,* April 6, 1940; *Chicago Tribune,* November 3, 1941. For background on Frank see Hilberg, pp. 133–134.

46. *New York Times,* November 1, 1939, p. 2, January 6, 1940, p. 2, January 23, 1940, p. 5, September 7, 1941, p. 14, December 12, 1941; *New York Journal American,* November 27, 1941, p. 30.

47. *New York Journal American,* November 5, 1941, p. 8; *New York World Telegram,* November 5, 1941, p. 15.

48. *Chicago Tribune,* November 3, 1941, p. 5, November 16, 1941, p. 10.

49. *New York Journal American,* November 17, 1941, p. 32; *Baltimore Sun,* November 18, 1941, p. 10; *New York Times,* August 25, 1941, p. 5, October 13, 1941, p. 8, March 1, 1942, p. 28, May 31, 1942, p. 18; *New York Herald Tribune,* November 27, 1941, p. 6.

50. *New York Herald Tribune,* November 6, 1941, p. 3, November 7, 1941, p. 4, November 8, 1941, p. 3.

51. *New York Journal American,* November 9, 1941, p. 1; *New York Herald Tribune,* November 9, 1941, p. 1; *St. Louis Post Dispatch,* November 8, 1941, p. 1; *Chicago Tribune,* November 9, 1941, p. 16; *Boston Globe,* November 10, 1941; *San Francisco Chronicle,* November 9, 1941, p. 1; *Los Angeles Times,* November 9, 1941, p. 13.

52. Oswald Garrison Villard, *The Disappearing Daily: Chapters in American Newspaper Evolution* (New York: Knopf, 1944), p. 86.

53. Lochner's story was carried in many major newspapers including the *Baltimore Sun,* October 28, 1941, *New York Times,* October 28, 1941, and *Washington Star,* October 28, 1941.

54. *Springfield* (Ohio) *News Sun,* October 19, 1941.

55. *Miami Herald,* November 16, 1941; *Detroit Free Press,* November 16, 1941.

56. *New York Herald Tribune,* November 8, 1941.

57. *New York Herald Tribune,* November 20, 1941 (emphasis added); *Christian Science Monitor,* March 14, 1942; *New York Times,* June 11, 1942.

58. *New York Sun,* December 23, 1941; *Washington Times Herald,* January 11, 1942.

59. *New York Herald Tribune,* December 5, 1941.

60. *San Antonio Light,* December 19, 1941; *Chicago Herald American,* December 1, 1941.

61. *Christian Science Monitor,* November 29, 1941.

62. *New York Times,* March 1, 1942, p. 28.

Chapter 8

1. *New York Times,* May 18, 1942, p. 4.

2. *New York World Telegram,* June 1, 1942, p. 3; *New York Herald Tribune,* June 2, 1942, p. 2; *New York Journal American,* June 1, 1942, p. 3.

3. Frederick Oeschner, *This Is the Enemy* (Boston: Little, Brown, 1942), p. 130; Wallace R. Duel, *People Under Hitler* (New York: Harcourt, Brace, 1942), p. 111; *St. Louis Post Dispatch,* June 11, 1942; Louis P. Lochner, *What About Germany?* (New York: Dodd, Mead, 1942), p. 124.

4. *St. Louis Post Dispatch,* June 11, 1942.

5. Louis Lochner, CBS radio interview, September 22, 1942, as cited in Joyce Fein, *"American Radio's Coverage of the Holocaust: 1938–1945,"* senior thesis, Hampshire College, Spring 1984, p. 54.

6. *Atlanta Constitution,* July 20, 1942.

7. *Philadelphia Inquirer,* June 13, 1942, p. 1; *New York Herald Tribune,* June 13, 1942, p. 7; *New York Times,* June 13, 1942, p. 7.

8. *Los Angeles Times,* June 16, 1942, p. 2; *New York Journal American,* June 16, 1942, p. 3; *London Evening Standard,* June 16, 1942; *New York Times,* June 16, 1942 (emphasis added).

9. "Report of the Bund Regarding the Persecution of the Jews," in "When Did They Know?" *Midstream,* April 1968, pp. 57–58; Martin Gilbert, *Auschwitz and the Allies* (New York: Holt, Rinehart and Winston, 1981), pp. 39–42.

10. *Daily Telegraph and Morning Post,* June 25, 1942; *London Times,* June 30, 1942; *Daily Mail,* June 30, 1942; *Manchester Guardian,* June 30, 1942; *Daily Telegraph,* June 30, 1942; *Montreal Daily Star,* June 30, 1942; Gilbert, p. 43; Andrew Sharf, *The British Press and Jews Under Nazi Rule* (London: Oxford University Press, 1964), pp. 92–93.

11. *New York Times,* June 27, 1942, p. 5; June 30, 1942, p. 7.

12. *Los Angeles Times,* June 30, 1942, p. 3; *Atlanta Constitution,* June 30, 1942, p. 2; *Miami Herald,* June 30, 1942, p. 2; *New York World Telegram,* June 29, 1942, p. 4.

13. *Chicago Daily Tribune,* June 30, 1942, p. 6.

14. *New York Journal American,* June 29, 1942, p. 1 (emphasis added).

15. *Jewish Frontier,* August 1942, November 1942; Marie Syrkin, "Reaction to News of the Holocaust," *Midstream,* May 1968, pp. 62–64.

16. Fein, pp. 49–50.

17. *New York Herald Tribune,* June 30, 1942, p. 1.

18. *St. Louis Post Dispatch,* June 26, 1942, sec. C, p. 1.

19. *New York Times,* July 2, 1942, p. 6.

20. *New York Times,* July 9, 1942, p. 8, July 23, 1942, p. 6.

21. *New York Times,* May 5, 1942, pp. 1, 9, 20, May 7, 1942, p. 7, May 24, 1942, p. 5, June 1, 1942, p. 4.

22. Interview with Percy Knauth, February 18, 1985; interview with C. Brooks Peters, February 12, 1985; David Halberstam, *The Powers That Be* (New York: Knopf, 1979), pp. 216–217; Oswald Garrison Villard, *The Disappearing Daily: Chapters in American Newspaper Evolution* (New York: Knopf, 1944), p. 86.

23. *Saturday Review of Literature,* September 14, 1944, pp. 17–18; Gay Talese, *The Kingdom and the Power* (New York: Bantam Books, 1970), pp. 72, 113–114. For an example of how the *New York Times* creates and reflects public opinion in another area, see Donald O. Dewey, "America and Russia, 1939–1941: The Views of the *New York Times,*" *Journalism Quarterly,* vol. 44 (Spring 1967), pp. 62–70.

24. *New York Times,* June 11, 1942, p. 1; *New York Herald Tribune,* June 12, 1942, p. 18.

25. *Chicago Tribune,* June 14, 1942, p. 1, June 16, 1942, p. 6; *New York Times,* June 14, 1942, pp. 1, 9, June 16, 1942, p. 6, June 27, 1942, p. 5. *Miami Herald* did the same on June 15, 1942, p. 1. *Los Angeles Times,* June 16, 1942, p. 2.

26. *New York Times,* June 14, 1942, p. 1.

27. *New York Times,* July 29, 1942, p. 7.

28. *Toronto Globe,* July 29, 1942; Gilbert, pp. 44, 55.

29. *Newsweek,* August 10, 1942, p. 40. See also *New York World Telegram,* July 27, 1942, p. 22; *Los Angeles Times,* June 18, 1942, p. 2, August 22, 1942, sec. II, p. 4; and *Miami Herald,* June 18, 1942, p. 13.

30. *Daily Express,* July 28, 1942.

31. *Chicago Tribune,* July 26, 1942; *New York World Telegram,* July 27, 1942, p. 22.

32. Saul S. Friedman, *No Haven for the Oppressed: United States Policy Toward Jewish Refugees, 1938–1945* (Detroit: Wayne State University Press, 1973), p. 140. See also *Congress Weekly,* August 14, 1942, p. 2; *New York Times,* July 22, 1942, p. 1; *New York Herald Tribune,* July 22, 1942; *Christian Science Monitor,* July 23, 1942; *New York Journal American,* July 22, 1942; *Chicago Tribune,* July 22, 1942, p. 7, July 23, 1942, p. 17, July 24, 1942, p. 6; *Miami Herald,* August 3, 1942; Fein, pp. 49–50. The *Los Angeles Times* did publicize the Los Angeles

rally and made it clear that it was designed to protest the "terrible mass murders of Jews." *Los Angeles Times,* August 5, 1942, p. 10, August 7, 1942, p. 13, August 9, 1942, sec. II, p. 8, August 11, 1942, sec. II, p. 2, August 12, 1942, sec. II, p. 8, August 13, 1942, sec. II, p. 1, August 22, 1942, sec. II, p. 4. For a discussion of the struggle to establish a Jewish division see Monty Penkower, *The Jews Were Expendable* (Urbana: University of Illinois Press, 1983).

33. *Los Angeles Times,* June 23, 1942, sec. II, p. 4, June 26, 1942, sec. II, p. 4, July 4, 1942, July 14, 1942, p. 1, August 8, August 11, September 25, 1942; *Christian Science Monitor,* August 5, 1942, p. 16.

34. *Christian Science Monitor,* October 3, 1942.

35. *PM,* September 9, October 22, 1941; *New York Times,* September 2, September 7, 1941.

36. *New York Herald Tribune,* November 15, 1941, p. 5; *Chicago Tribune,* October 19, 1941.

37. *Springfield News Sun,* October 19, 1941.

38. *St. Louis Post Dispatch,* August 24, 1942, p. 2; *Christian Science Monitor,* August 19, 1942, p. 2, August 25, 1942.

39. *Manchester Guardian,* August 31, 1942, as quoted in Walter Laqueur, *The Terrible Secret: Suppression of the Truth About Hitler's "Final Solution"* (Boston: Little, Brown, 1980), p. 75.

40. Laqueur, p. 245, n. 18; *Christian Science Monitor,* August 19, 1942, p. 2.

41. *Economist,* December 19, 1942.

42. *New York World Telegram,* August 4, 1942, p. 6; *New York Herald Tribune,* July 27, 1942; *Christian Science Monitor,* July 28, 1942.

43. *Newsweek,* August 10, 1942; Foreign Office Papers, 921/10, 921/7, as cited in Gilbert, p. 99.

44. *St. Louis Post Dispatch,* August 23, 1942, p. 3; *New York Times,* August 29, 1942, p. 14.

45. *New York Times,* February 18, 1944, p. 7, July 19, 1944, p. 5; *New York Herald Tribune,* February 18, 1944. On the reaction of the Hebrew press see Y. Gelber, "Haitonut Ha'ivrit be'Erez Yisrael al Hashmadat Yehudei Europa" (The Hebrew Press and the Destruction of European Jewry), in the collection of articles *Dapim le'heker hashoa ve'hamered* (Tel Aviv, 1969).

46. *London Times,* August 3, 1942, p. 5.

47. Some papers found it hard to abandon the idea that Jews were simply suffering along with other hostage peoples. *Los Angeles Times,* February 22, 1942; *Christian Science Monitor,* February 22, October 7, 1942.

48. *Philadelphia Inquirer*, November 25, 1942; memo, Paul C. Squire to Secretary of State, September 28, 1942, DS 862.4016/2242.

49. *Dallas News*, November 25, 1942, p. 1; *Denver Post*, November 25, 1942, p. 1; *Miami Herald*, November 25, 1942, p. 1; *New York Herald Tribune*, November 25, 1942, p. 1; *Los Angeles Examiner*, November 25, 1942, p. 1; *St. Louis Post Dispatch*, November 25, 1942, p. 1; *Los Angeles Times*, November 25, 1942, p. 2; *San Francisco Examiner*, November 25, 1942, p. 5; *New York Journal American*, November 25, 1942, p. 3; *Baltimore Sun*, November 25, 1942, p. 3; *Chicago Tribune*, November 25, 1942, p. 4; *Washington Post*, November 25, 1942, p. 6; *New York Times*, November 25, 1942, p. 10; *Atlanta Constitution*, November 25, 1942, p. 20; David S. Wyman, *The Abandonment of the Jews: America and the Holocaust, 1941–1945* (New York: Pantheon Books, 1984), p. 363, n. 1. See also *Philadelphia Inquirer*, November 25, 1942, and *PM*, November 26, 1942. The *Los Angeles Times* did run Wise's story as a sidebar to an article by James MacDonald on how the Nazis were "wiping out Jews in cold blood." *Los Angeles Times*, November 25, 1942, p. 2; Fein, p. 55.

50. *New York Times*, December 18, 1942.

51. Roosevelt's personal representative to Pope Pius XII to the Vatican Secretary of State, *FRUS*, 1943, vol. III, p. 775 (emphasis added).

52. *Chicago Tribune*, November 25, 1942, p. 4; *Washington Post*, November 25, 1942; *New York Herald Tribune*, November 25, 1942, p. 1; *Baltimore Sun*, November 25, 1942, p. 3; *New York Journal American*, November 25, 1942, p. 3; *Los Angeles Examiner*, November 25, 1942, p. 1.

53. *New York Times*, November 25, 1942, p. 10.

54. *PM*, November 25, 1942, pp. 1, 13, November 26, 1942, p. 12.

55. DS 740.00 116 European War 1939/694 PS/DG, as cited in Laqueur, pp. 225–227; memo, DS 862.4016/2251.

56. *New York Journal American*, November 24, 1942, p. 2; *Washington Post*, November 25, 1942, p. 6; *New York Times*, November 25, 1942, p. 10, November 26, 1942, p. 16.

57. *New York Journal American*, December 1, 1942, sec. B, p. 1; *Chicago Tribune*, December 1, 1942, p. 19; *Baltimore Sun*, December 1, 1942, p. 6; *New York Times*, December 2, 1942, p. 12, December 3, 1942, p. 10; *New York Herald Tribune*, December 2, 1942, p. 7, December 3, 1942, p. 12.

58. *New York Times*, December 2, 1942, p. 24; *Atlanta Constitution*, December 1, 1942, p. 8; *Los Angeles Times*, December 3, 1942, sec. II, p. 4.

59. For examples of *The Christian Century*'s attitude see *Christian Century*, December 9, 1942, p. 1519; December 30, 1942, p. 1611, May 5, 1943, p. 548, September 8, 1943, p. 1004, September 13, 1944, p. 1045. For attitude of *Christian Century* on Palestine, see Hertzel

Fishman, *American Protestantism and a Jewish State* (Detroit: Wayne State University Press, 1973). Martin E. Marty has written an impassioned defense of *Christian Century*'s editorial position during these years. He attributes its hostility to Wise to the friendship of the editor of the journal, Charles Clayton Morrison, with many Reform and "thus, anti-Zionist" rabbis. While Marty correctly cites a number of occasions when the journal did speak out on behalf of persecuted Jews, there were many other occasions when its position was ambivalent at best. Martin E. Marty, "The *Century* and the Holocaust," *Christian Century,* April 10, 1985, pp. 350–352.

60. *Christian Century,* March 3, 1943, p. 253; March 10, 1943, p. 284; September 8, 1943, pp. 1004–1005, February 16, 1944, p. 205, September 13, 1944, p. 1045, September 27, 1944, p. 1113.

61. Adolf Held memorandum on "Visit to the President," as cited in Eliyho Matzozky, "An Episode: Roosevelt and the Mass Killings," *Midstream,* August-September 1980, pp. 17–19.

62. *New York Times,* December 9, 1942, p. 20; *Washington Post,* December 9, 1942, p. 18; *PM,* December 9, 1942, pp. 18–19; *Los Angeles Examiner,* December 12, 1942, p. 2; *San Francisco Examiner,* December 9, 1942, p. 7; *Los Angeles Times,* December 9, 1942, p. 5; *New York World Telegram,* December 8, 1942, p. 10; *St. Louis Post Dispatch,* December 9, 1942, p. 29; Wyman, *Abandonment,* pp. 73, 365, n. 50.

63. For text of declaration see *Department of State Bulletin,* publication 1852, vol. VII, no. 182 (December 19, 1942). *New York Times,* December 18, 1942, p. 1; *San Francisco Examiner,* December 18, 1942, p. 3; *Los Angeles Times,* December 18, 1942, p. 4; *Washington Post,* December 18, 1942, p. 10; *New York Herald Tribune,* December 18, 1942, p. 17; *New York World Telegram,* December 18, 1942, p. 28; *Los Angeles Examiner,* December 18, 1942, p. 16; *St. Louis Post Dispatch,* December 18, 1942, sec. III, p. 1; *Atlanta Constitution,* December 18, 1942, p. 2.

64. *Los Angeles Times,* December 20, 1942, p. 2; *Washington Post,* December 20, 1942, p. 8; *St. Louis Post Dispatch,* December 20, 1942, p. 9; *Los Angeles Examiner,* December 20, 1942, p. 22; *New York Times,* December 20, 1942, p. 23; *New York Herald Tribune,* December 20, 1942, p. 30; *Chicago Tribune,* December 20, 1942, p. 18, December 25, December 27, 1942.

65. *Newsweek,* December 28, 1942, p. 46; *Time,* December 28, 1942, p. 24; *American Mercury,* February 1943, pp. 194–203; *Reader's Digest,* February 1943, pp. 107–110.

66. Edward J. Bliss, *In Search of Light: The Broadcasts of Edward R. Murrow, 1938–1961* (New York: Knopf, 1967), pp. 56–57.

67. *Christian Science Monitor,* December 18, 1942, p. 22. During this period the *Christian Science Monitor* ran a number of exclusive stories

with "Somewhere in Europe" datelines which argued that the German people were experiencing a sense of "guilt" and "remorse" for the treatment being accorded to the "peoples of the occupied countries." See *Christian Science Monitor*, December 4, 1942.

68. *Atlanta Constitution*, December 1, 1942, p. 8, December 18, 1942, p. 2, December 28, 1942, p. 16.

69. *London Times*, December 7, 1942; *Spectator*, December 11, 1942.

70. *London Times*, December 4, 1942, p. 3, December 5, 1942, p. 5. See also December 18, 1942, pp. 4, 8. Sharf, p. 93.

71. Foreign Office note to Cabinet Committee on Refugees, February 18, 1943, PRO CAB 95/15, as quoted in Bernard Wasserstein, *Britain and the Jews of Europe, 1939–1945*, (London: Institute of Jewish Affairs, 1979), pp. 186–187.

72. *Manchester Guardian*, December 5, December 8, 1942; *Christian Science Monitor*, December 14, 1942, p. 8; *London Times*, December 7, 1942.

73. *FRUS*, 1942, vol. I, pp. 66–67.

74. *Manchester Guardian*, December 8, December 10, 1942; *Daily Telegraph and Morning Post*, December 2, December 11, 1942; *Glasgow Daily Record*, December 2, 1942; *London Observer*, December 6, December 13, December 26, 1942; *Daily Mail*, December 11, 1942; *Evening Standard*, December 14, 1942; *Daily Herald*, December 16, 1942; *Glasgow Evening News*, December 17, 1942; *London Daily Herald*, December 21, 1942; *London Times*, December 12, December 21, 1942— all as cited in Sharf, pp. 93–100. *Spectator*, December 11, 1942.

75. *Jewish Telegraphic Agency [JTA] Daily News Bulletin*, December 21, December 29, 1942.

76. *Manchester Guardian*, December 10, 1942; *London Times*, December 12, 1942.

77. *New York Times*, December 2, 1942, p. 24, December 18, 1942, p. 26; *Los Angeles Times*, December 3, 1942, sec. II, p. 4; *New York World Telegram*, December 11, 1942, p. 26.

78. *Atlanta Constitution*, December 22, 1942, p. 4; Wyman, *Abandonment*, p. 64. For copy of letter to members of Loyal Americans of German Descent soliciting support for ad, see August Rust-Oppenheim, December 29, 1942, DS 862.4016/2253.

79. *New York Post* as cited in *JTA Daily News Bulletin*, December 20, 1942; *New Republic*, December 21, 1942, August 30, 1943; *Nation*, January 2, January 9, February 6, February 27, March 13, June 5, 1943.

80. Information had reached Switzerland earlier regarding disappearance and executions. It had come via Stockholm from sources that Herschel Johnson, the American Consul, described as reliable. Memo, July 21, 1942, DS 862.4016/2237.

81. For the BBC's record of wartime actions see Asa Briggs, *The History*

of Broadcasting in the United Kingdom, vol. III, *The War of Words* (London: Oxford University Press, 1970); Wasserstein, p. 295.

82. Drew Pearson, "Washington Merry-Go-Round," *Washington Post,* October 22, 1942. During the fall of 1942 the Allies were receiving confirmation of the murder plan from a variety of different sources. The initial sources were Jewish organizations, the World Jewish Congress office in Geneva in particular. But over the next few months the Allies also heard from other organizations and individuals. References to these communiqués are to be found in the State Department files. DS 862.4016/2242. See also Penkower, chap. 3, and Richard Breitman and Alan M. Kraut, "Who Was the Mysterious Messenger?" *Commentary,* October 1983, pp. 4–10.

83. Memo, DS 862.4016/2235; DS 862.4016/2238.

84. DS 740.00016 European War 1939/694, as cited in Laqueur, p. 252, n. 18; memo, December 7, 1942, DS 862.4016/2251; Wyman, *Abandonment,* p. 74.

85. Memos, Franklin Mott Gunther to State Department, April 19, October 3, November 2, 1941, in *FRUS,* 1941, vol. II, pp. 868–870; Henry L. Feingold, *The Politics of Rescue: The Roosevelt Administration and the Holocaust, 1938–1945* (New Brunswick: Rutgers University Press, 1970), p. 179.

86. Paul Squire to Cordell Hull, October 29, 1942, DS 860.4016/10–2942. During this period the news of *"Judenrein"* cities, such as Vilna, appeared in the neutral press and was reprinted in the Yiddish press. On September 16 the Swiss paper *Die Nazion* reported that the "last 14,000 Jews remaining in Vilna have recently been deported and are now *'spurlos'* [without a trace] missing." Louis Segal to Cordell Hull, September 23, 1942, DS 862.4016/2240.

87. *FRUS* 1942, vol. I, p. 66.

88. Foreign Office papers 371/30923, C 12201, folio 186, as cited in Gilbert, p. 97; John P. Fox, "The Jewish Factor in British War Crimes Policy in 1942," *English Historical Review,* vol. XCII (January 1977), p. 92. In December 1942 the British Political Warfare Executive issued a number of directives to the BBC to pay particular attention to "Hitler's plan to exterminate the Jews." Mention was made of Treblinka, Belzec, and Sobibor as "extermination camps." Michael Balfour, *Propaganda in War: Organizations, Policies and Publics in Britain and Germany* (London: Routledge & Kegan Paul, 1979), pp. 299–300. This was the first time in the war that the Nazi persecution of the Jews was made a central theme of British propaganda to Europe. Wasserstein, p. 174; Laqueur, pp. 222–223.

89. Arthur D. Morse, *While Six Million Died: A Chronicle of American Apathy* (New York: Hart, 1967), p. 33; Laqueur, pp. 226–227.

90. Wasserstein, pp. 181–182; Balfour, pp. 303–304. The British were

also concerned about the effect that a declaration would have on postwar policy, particularly in relation to the punishment of war criminals. In order to avoid some of the problems which had arisen in connection with punishment after World War I, they did not want to make a public declaration commiting the government to punishment until they were sure such a policy would be put into effect. Fox, passim.

91. Foreign Office Papers 371/34551, as cited in Laqueur, pp. 83, 245, n. 18.

Chapter 9

1. *Manchester Guardian,* February 16, February 17, 1943; *Christian Science Monitor,* February 16, 1943, p. 9; *Los Angeles Times,* February 15, 1943, p. 3; *Washington Post,* January 17, January 24, 1943, February 14, 1943, p. 2, February 15, 1943, p. 2; *New York Times,* January 15, January 27, 1943. In mid-January additional information was sent to Stephen Wise by Gerhart Riegner, the Swiss representative of the World Jewish Congress, via the State Department. Riegner opened his report with the statement "Poland mass executions now confirmed by different sources," and then went on to describe a steadily worsening situation in various parts of Europe. Special Gestapo agents had been sent to Berlin and Holland to speed up deportations as those in Vienna were nearly completed. Memo, DS 862.4016/2256a.

2. *Los Angeles Times,* February 15, 1943, p. 3; *Washington Post,* February 15, 1943, p. 2.

3. *Collier's,* February 27, 1943, pp. 29–33; *New York World Telegram,* February 11, 1943, p. 15; *Christian Science Monitor,* February 16, 1943, p. 9.

4. *Washington Post,* February 15, 1943, p. 2; *Los Angeles Times,* February 15, 1943, p. 3; *New York World Telegram,* February 15, 1943, p. 13; *Atlanta Constitution,* February 15, 1943, p. 18; *New York Times,* February 14, 1943, p. 37.

5. *Christian Science Monitor,* March 4, 1943, p. 11.

6. Ibid.

7. *Los Angeles Times,* March 19, 1943, pp. 3, 7; *Washington Post,* March 19, 1943, p. 2, March 21, 1943, p. 2; *Manchester Guardian,* March 20, 1943; *Los Angeles Times,* March 20, 1943, Sec. II, p. 4; *New York Herald Tribune,* March 21, 1943.

8. *Los Angeles Times,* March 2, 1943, p. 7; *New York Herald Tribune,* March

2, 1943, p. 1; *Christian Science Monitor,* March 2, 1943, p. 7; *New York Journal American,* March 2, 1943, p. 1; *Newsweek,* March 15, 1943, p. 36; *Time,* March 8, 1943.

9. Though they often attracted large crowds, some numbering as high as 20,000, the paucity of editorial comment they generated disappointed the organizers. Stephen Wise to Dear Editor, March 9, 1943, World Jewish Congress papers, U185/3, as cited in David S. Wyman, *The Abandonment of the Jews: America and the Holocaust, 1941–1945* (New York: Pantheon Books, 1984), pp. 89, 367, n. 43, 368, n. 60.

10. *New York Herald Tribune,* February 22, 1943, p. 16; *Los Angeles Times,* February 22, 1943, p. 8; *Philadelphia Inquirer,* February 23, 1943, p. 15; *New York Times,* March 10, 1943, p. 10; *Philadelphia Evening Bulletin,* April 23, 1943, p. 12, as cited in Wyman, *Abandonment,* pp. 86–87, 367, n. 33.

11. *New York Times,* March 10, 1943, p. 12, April 13, 1943, p. 17; *Newsweek,* March 15, 1943, p. 36; *Christian Science Monitor,* March 10, 1943, p. 2; *Miami Herald,* April 17, 1943, p. 10A; Wyman, *Abandonment,* pp. 91–92.

12. *New York Times,* March 3, 1943, p. 22, March 4, 1943; *New York Herald Tribune,* March 3, 1943, p. 18, March 4, 1943, sec. II, p. 3; *New York Sun,* March 3, 1943, p. 20; *Nation,* March 13, 1943, pp. 366–367; *New York Post,* March 6, 1943, p. 21.

13. *FRUS,* 1943, vol. 1, pp. 144–145.

14. *Christian Century,* March 3, 1943, p. 253, March 10, 1943, p. 284; *Contemporary Jewish Record,* February 1943, pp. 235–236; *Free World,* March 1943, pp. 196–197; *America,* March 13, 1943, p. 630; *Christian Science Monitor,* March 11, 1943; *American Mercury,* February 1943, pp. 194–199; *Reader's Digest,* February 1943, pp. 107–110; *Los Angeles Times,* March 11, 1943, sec. II, p. 4.

15. *Newsweek,* March 8, 1943, p. 40.

16. *Christian Science Monitor,* March 19, 1943, p. 18 (emphasis added).

17. *JTA Daily News Bulletin,* March 10, 1943; *Contemporary Jewish Record,* June 1943, pp. 276 ff.; memo, DS 862.4016/2290.

18. Wyman attributes the lack of press interest in the resolutions to the fact that they were so feeble. *New York Times,* March 10, 1943, p. 12, March 19, 1943, p. 11; Wyman, *Abandonment,* p. 95.

19. *London Times,* January 25, 1943; *The* (London) *Observor,* February 7, 1943; Bernard Wasserstein, *Britain and the Jews of Europe, 1939–1945* (London: Institute of Jewish Affairs, 1979), pp. 186–187; *Christian Science Monitor,* March 21, 1943, p. 1; Henry L. Feingold, *The Politics of Rescue: The Roosevelt Administration and the Holocaust, 1938–1945.* (New Brunswick: Rutgers University Press, 1970), p. 177.

20. In an aide-memoire to the State Department the British Embassy acknowledged that His Majesty's Government, while well aware of the problems of rescue, could not "make a merely negative response to a growing international problem [which was] disturbing the public conscience." The British Embassy to the Department of State, January 20, 1943. *FRUS*, 1943, vol. I, p. 134. See also Chargé d'Affaires Matthews to Secretary of State, February 20, 1943. *FRUS*, 1943, vol. I, pp. 138, 403–404.

   In addition to these persistent demands to know what was being done to help the Jews, there was also a growing interest in England regarding the punishment of war criminals. As John Fox has demonstrated, the two issues were clearly linked in the mind of the British government. John P. Fox, "The Jewish Factor in British War Crimes Policy in 1942," *English Historical Review*, vol. XCII, no. 362 (January 1977), pp. 82–106.

21. *Washington Post*, February 14, 1943, p. 2, February 15, 1943, p. 2, February 28, 1943, p. 4; *Los Angeles Times*, February 14, 1943, p. 3, February 28, 1943, p. 3; *New York World Telegram*, February 15, 1943; *Atlanta Constitution*, February 15, 1943; *Christian Science Monitor*, February 16, 1943. Compare with English press: *London Times*, February 13, 1943; *Daily Mirror*, February 15, 1943; *Daily Herald*, February 15, 1943; *Manchester Guardian*, February 17, 1943.

22. *Manchester Guardian*, February 16, 1943.

23. Wasserstein, pp. 186–187.

24. Secretary of State Cordell Hull to President Roosevelt, March 23, 1943. *FRUS*, 1943, vol. I, pp. 146–147.

25. *FRUS*, 1943, vol. I, p. 139.

26. *FRUS*, 1943, vol. I, pp. 137, 145.

27. *New York Times*, April 19, 1943, p. 18; *New York Herald Tribune*, April 19, 1943; *New York World Telegram*, April 21, 1943, p. 30.

28. *Nation*, March 13, 1943, pp. 366–367.

29. From the very outset of discussion of some form of a meeting, caution was voiced about "the danger of raising false hopes." *FRUS*, 1943, vol. I, pp. 134–137, 174; Feingold, p. 190ff.; *New York Journal American*, April 19, 1943, p. 6.

30. *San Francisco Examiner*, April 14, 1943, p. 3.

31. *New York Journal American*, April 19, 1943, p. 6; *New York Times*, April 20, 1943, p. 1.

32. Martin Gilbert, *Auschwitz and the Allies* (New York: Holt, Rinehart and Winston, 1981), p. 281; *St. Louis Post Dispatch*, April 22, 1943, p. 3; *New York World Telegram*, April 19, 1943, p. 15.

33. *Christian Science Monitor*, April 19, 1943, p. 7.

34. Memorandum by Harry Hopkins on meeting between Roosevelt, Hopkins, Hull, Welles, Eden, Halifax, and Strang on March 27, 1943, in Robert E. Sherwood, *Roosevelt and Hopkins* (New York, Harper & Brothers, 1948), p. 717.

35. *New York Journal American,* April 27, 1943, p. 8; *State Department Bulletin,* vol. VIII, no. 386 (April 26, 1943), as cited in Feingold, pp. 196ff., 336, n. 101.

36. *Los Angeles Times,* April, 18, 1943, sec. II, p. 4, April 27, 1943, sec. II, p. 4. During the war Roosevelt often barred reporters from covering his overseas conferences. Sometimes when reporters were allowed to attend, their access was severely restricted. Reporters were particularly upset when they were denied the right to report on events of "little security concern." Graham J. White, *FDR and the Press* (Chicago: University of Chicago Press, 1979), pp. 44, 169, n. 30, n. 31.

37. *Christian Science Monitor,* April 19, 1943, p. 1; *New York Times,* April 20, 1943, p. 1.

38. *New York World Telegram,* April 19, 1943; *New York Journal American,* April 23, 1943; *Christian Science Monitor,* March 31, 1943, p. 1. Five correspondents were officially accredited by the State Department to be present in Bermuda during the conference. They included Robert Edward Vivain (Reuters), H. O. Thompson (United Press), Richard Massock (Associated Press), Ida Landau (Overseas News Agency), and Lee Carson (International News Service). *FRUS,* 1943, vol. I, p. 152; *Christian Science Monitor,* April 26, 1943, p. 1, April 30, 1943, p. 8.

39. *San Francisco Chronicle,* April 19, 1943, p. 3, April 20, 1943, p. 6; *New York Times,* April 22, 1943, p. 10; *Christian Science Monitor,* April 19, 1943, p. 1, April 30, 1943, p. 7; *New York Herald Tribune,* April 23, 1943, p. 8.

40. *St. Louis Post Dispatch,* April 22, 1943.

41. *New York Times,* April 19, 1943, p. 1; *New York Herald Tribune,* April 19, 1943, p. 1; *Christian Science Monitor,* April 19, 1943, p. 1; *San Francisco Chronicle,* April 20, 1943, p. 6; *New York Journal American,* April 20, 1943, p. 4; *Chicago Tribune,* April 19, 1943, p. 8; *San Francisco Examiner,* April 20, 1943, p. 10; *Los Angeles Times,* April 20, 1943, p. 11.

42. *New York Herald Tribune,* April 20, 1943, p. 1; *New York Journal American,* April 20, 1943, p. 4; *New York Times,* April 20, 1943, p. 11.

43. *PM,* April 25, 1943, p. 8; *St. Louis Post Dispatch,* April 22, 1943, p. 2b; *Christian Science Monitor,* April 19, 1943, p. 1, April 22, 1943, p. 8; *Chicago Tribune,* April 20, 1943, p. 5; *San Francisco Chronicle,* April 30, 1943, p. 3; *New York Times,* April 20, 1943, p. 1; *New*

York Herald Tribune, April 18, 1943, p. 40, April 19, 1943, p. 1, April 20, 1943, p. 1, April 22, 1943, p. 4, April 23, 1943, p. 8; *New York Journal American*, April 20, 1943, p. 4; *New York World Telegram*, April 22, 1943, p. 11.

44. *Christian Science Monitor*, April 22, 1943, p. 8; *St. Louis Post Dispatch*, April 22, 1943, p. 36.

45. *FRUS*, 1943, vol. I, p. 172. Long Mss, April 7, 1943, Long to Law, as cited in Feingold, p. 196. For details on Long's attempts to prevent the conference from really pursuing changes in Allied rescue policy, see Feingold, pp. 197–207. *FRUS*, 1943, vol. I, pp. 158–159, 174; *Christian Science Monitor*, April 26, 1943, p. 1, April 27, 1943, p. 1; *New York World Telegram*, April 26, 1943, p. 23; *Los Angeles Times*, April 27, 1943, sec. A, p. 4; Beck to Long, *FRUS*, 1943, vol. I, p. 164; Wyman, *Abandonment*, p. 117.

46. U.S. House of Representatives, *Problems of World War II and Its Aftermath*, part 2, *The Palestine Question* (Washington: Government Printing Office, 1976); *New York Times*, December 3, 1943, p. 3.

47. *New York Herald Tribune*, April 30, 1943, p. 8; *New York Times*, April 30, 1943, p. 9; *New York World Telegram*, April 29, 1943, p. 27.

48. Saul S. Friedman, *No Haven for the Oppressed: United States Policy Toward Jewish Refugees, 1938–1945* (Detroit: Wayne State University Press, 1973), pp. 170–180; *New York Post*, April 23, 1943; *Department of State Bulletin*, vol. VIII, no. 351 (April 17, 1943), as cited in Feingold, p. 198.

49. *Nation*, June 5, 1943, pp. 796–797.

50. *Free World*, July 1943; *New York Times*, April 29, 1943.

51. *New York Journal American*, April 23, 1943, p. 2.

52. *Christian Science Monitor*, April 30, 1943, p. 8; *New York Herald Tribune*, April 29, 1943, p. 8. Saul Friedman points out that the details of what was discussed were not released until 1963, when State Department records on the conference were declassified. Friedman, p. 183.

53. *New Republic*, August 30, 1943; *New York Post, New York Herald Tribune, Boston Globe*—all as quoted in *JTA Daily News Bulletin*, May 4, May 10, 1943.

54. *New York Times*, May 4, 1943, p. 17; *American Hebrew*, May 7, 1943, as cited in Feingold, p. 338, n. 3.

55. *PM*, April 16, 1943, p. 6, April 19, 1943, pp. 14–15, April 25, 1943, p. 8, April 26, 1943; *Christian Science Monitor*, April 22, 1943, p. 8.

56. *PM*, May 2, 1943, p. 2.

57. *PM*, May 9, 1943, p. 2.

58. *New York Times*, April 30, 1943, p. 9; *San Francisco Chronicle*, April 30, 1943, p. 3.

59. *Chicago Tribune,* April 30, 1943, p. 1.

60. *Christian Science Monitor,* April 17, 1943.

61. *The War Diary of Breckinridge Long,* cd. Fred L. Israel (Lincoln: University of Nebraska Press, 1966), June 23, 1943, p. 316.

62. *New York Herald Tribune,* April 20, 1943; *New York Journal American,* April 20, 1943.

63. *New York Times,* April 22, 1943, p. 1; *Christian Science Monitor,* April 22, 1943, p. 1.

64. *New York Times,* April 23, 1943, p. 9, May 7, 1943, p. 7, May 15, 1943, p. 6, June 4, 1943, p. 7.

65. *New York Times,* April 21, 1944, p. 18.

Chapter 10

1. Memo, Harrison to Hull, March 4, 1943, DS 862.4016/2259; May 17, 1943, DS 862.4016/2269. Riegner and Richard Lichtheim cabled Wise via the State Department that contrary to press reports, the number of Jewish victims was closer to 4 million than the 3 that had been reported. July 29, 1943, DS 862.4016/2280.

2. *New York Herald Tribune,* August 30, 1943, p. 4; *St. Louis Post Dispatch,* August 30, 1943, sec. III, p. 1.

3. *New York Times,* December 1, 1943, p. 6, December 5, 1943, p. 3; *Newsweek,* October 18, 1943, pp. 41–42; *New York World Telegram,* November 25, 1943, p. 8, December 11, 1943, p. 1.

4. The *Baltimore Sun* adopted a vastly different approach to the same story and instead stressed that the Nazis had been "decent" to American Jews and that they had been given "sufficient" food. *New York Times,* March 18, 1944, p. 3; *Baltimore Sun,* March 19, 1944.

5. *New York Times,* February 11, 1944, p. 5, February 12, 1944, p. 6.

6. *New York Times,* February 17, 1944, p. 9.

7. *New York Times,* February 18, 1944, p. 7.

8. *New York Times,* March 2, 1944, p. 4.

9. *New York Times,* March 14, 1944, p. 4.

10. *New York Times,* March 5, 1944, p. 6.

11. *New York Times,* February 6, 1944, sec. IV, p. 8.

12. Ben Bagdikian, *The Media Monopoly* (Boston: Beacon Press, 1983), p. 130.

13. *Washington Post,* March 15, 1944; *Christian Science Monitor,* March 21, 1944, p. 6.

14. *Washington Post,* July 15, 1944, p. 2.

15. *New York Times,* May 10, 1944, p. 5; *Washington Post,* April 11, 1944, p. 8.

16. *New York Times,* May 4, 1944, p. 11, May 10, 1944, p. 5, May 17, 1944, p. 5.

17. *New York Times,* May 17, 1944, p. 5, May 18, 1944, pp. 1, 5, June 2, 1944, p. 6. See also *New York Times,* May 4, 1944, p. 11, June 9, 1944, p. 5.

18. *Christian Science Monitor,* May 20, 1944, p. 11; *New York Times,* July 2, 1944, p. 12.

19. *New York Times,* July 13, 1944, p. 3.

20. Ibid.

21. *New York Herald Tribune,* August 30, 1943, p. 1, September 3, 1943, p. 5; *St. Louis Post Dispatch,* August 30, 1943, sec. III, p. 1, September 3, 1943, p. 7; *New York Journal American,* August 30, 1943, p. 1; *New York World Telegram,* August 30, 1943, p. 17. The proposals by the Bergson-backed Emergency Committee to Save the Jewish People had called for reprisal raids and had not mentioned a Jewish national home in Palestine. *Los Angeles Examiner,* August 30, 1943, p. 6, September 2, 1943, p. 7, September 4, 1943, p. 12; *New Republic,* August 2, 1943, p. 124. For discussion of role of Bergson and those around him see Monty Noam Penkower, "In Dramatic Dissent: The Bergson Boys," *American Jewish History,* March 1981, pp. 281–309. Debate regarding the activities of American Jews in general and the tactics of the Peter Bergson–Ben Hecht group in particular conjures up many of the same passions which existed at the time. Elihu Matz, "Personal Actions vs. Personal Relations," *Midstream,* April 1981, pp. 41–48; Lucy S. Dawidowicz, "American Jewry and the Holocaust," *New York Times Magazine,* April 18, 1982, p. 47ff. For a critique of Dawidowicz's arguments, including her comments on the Bergson group's activities, see David Wyman, "Letters to the Editor," *New York Times Magazine,* May 23, 1982, p. 94.

22. *New York Herald Tribune,* September 4, 1943, p. 12; *New York Journal American,* September 4, 1943, p. 4; *New Republic,* August 30, 1943, pp. 299–316; *Christian Century,* September 8, 1943, pp. 1004–1005.

23. *New York Times,* September 7, 1943, p. 16, October 21, 1943, p. 18, November 1, 1943, p. 5, November 24, 1943, p. 13; *New Republic,* August 30, 1943, p. 298; *Nation,* December 18, 1943, p. 739; David Wyman, *The Abandonment of the Jews, 1941–1945* (New York: Pantheon Books, 1984), p. 375, n. 17.

24. *New Republic,* August 30, 1943, p. 309.

25. *Los Angeles Examiner,* September 4, 1943, p. 12; December 11, 1943, p. 1; *New Republic,* August 2, 1943, p. 124.

26. *Time,* October 18, 1943, p. 21; *Los Angeles Examiner,* October 6, 1943, p. 13; *New York Times,* October 7, 1943, p. 14; *Washington Post,* October 7, 1943, p. 1; *Washington Star,* October 7, 1943, p. 6; *Washington Times Herald,* October 7, 1943, p. 3; *New York Post,* October 6, 1943. The *Los Angeles Times* and *New York Herald Tribune* were among the many papers which ignored the event.

27. Palestine Statehood Group Papers, Yale Manuscript and Archives, box 4, folder 1, as cited in Sarah E. Peck, "The Campaign for an American Response to the Nazi Holocaust, 1943–45," *Journal of Contemporary History,* vol. 15 (April 1980), pp. 367–400.

28. See, for example, *Los Angeles Examiner,* December 11, 1943, p. 8; *Los Angeles Times,* December 11, 1943, p. 8; *New York Times,* December 11, 1943, p. 1; *Christian Science Monitor,* December 11, 1943, p. 8; *Chicago Tribune,* December 11, 1943, p. 8. Wyman, *Abandonment,* pp. 197, 383, n. 1.

29. "Aid by the United States to European Refugees: Testimony of Breckinridge Long," *Interpreter Releases,* January 10, 1944, pp. 1–15; U.S. Congress, House, Committee on Foreign Affairs, *Hearings, Resolution Providing for the Establishment by the Executive of a Commission to Effectuate the Rescue of the Jewish People of Europe,* 78th Cong., 1st sess., 1943, pp. 44–45; Saul S. Friedman, *No Haven for the Oppressed: United States Policy Toward Jewish Refugees, 1938–1945* (Detroit: Wayne State University Press, 1973), p. 188ff.; Henry Feingold, *The Politics of Rescue: The Roosevelt Administration and the Holocaust, 1938–1945* (New Brunswick: Rutgers University Press, 1970), p. 230; *New York Herald Tribune,* December 11, 1943. When Long's testimony was released to the press, the State Department, expecting it to quiet criticism of the American record on immigration, distributed it to the diplomatic representatives of other countries. *FRUS,* 1943, vol. I, pp. 237–238. *Nation,* December 25, 1943, p. 748; *New Republic,* December 20, 1943, p. 867; *New York Times,* December 11, 1943, p. 1, December 12, 1943, p. 8, December 31, 1943, p. 14.

30. *Nation,* December 25, 1943, p. 748; *New Republic,* December 20, 1943, p. 867; *PM,* December 20, 1943, pp. 1, 3; *New York Post,* December 11, 1943, pp. 1, 3, December 13, 1943, p. 23; *New York World Telegram,* December 13, 1943, p. 21. For additional Hearst editorial attention to this issue see also *Los Angeles Examiner,* December 11, 1943, p. 1; *New York Journal American,* December 22, 1943, p. 9, December 28, 1943, p. 16; *New York Times,* December 12, 1943, p. 8. Wyman, *Abandonment,* p. 383, n. 18, n. 19.

31. *New York Times,* February 6, 1944.

32. *Los Angeles Times,* January 23, 1944, p. 4; *Christian Science Monitor,* January 24, 1944; *Washington Post,* January 25, 1944; *New York Post,*

January 25, 1944. When Morgenthau originally received the report from his subordinates, it was entitled "Report to the Secretary on the Acquiescence of this Government in the Murder of the Jews." When he gave it to Roosevelt, the title was changed to "Personal Report to the President." Michael Mashberg, "Documents Concerning the American State Department and the Stateless European Jews, 1942–1944," *Jewish Social Studies*, vol. 39 (Winter-Spring 1977), pp. 163–179. Morgenthau had already complained about the State Department's behavior. On November 24 Morgenthau wrote to Hull complaining about the State Department's delay in approving transfer licenses to help evacuate Jews from Roumania. He declared the three and a half months delay "most difficult to understand." DS 862.4016/2297.

33. *New Republic*, February 7, 1944, p. 164; *New York Post*, March 9, 1944. Mowrer was not the only one who believed that the President had acted because of political exigencies. The British thought so as well. John Pehle, Director of the WRB, wrote Under Secretary of State Edward R. Stettinius in March 1944 of the importance of convincing the British that the establishment of the WRB was not "a political move in an election year." *FRUS*, 1944, vol. I, p. 1005. The *Christian Science Monitor* was more positive about the WRB's potential. January 24, 1944, p. 11.

34. *New York Daily Mirror*, January 28, 1944; *Los Angeles Examiner*, January 28, 1944, p. 12; *Washington Post*, January 25, February 8, 1944; *Christian Science Monitor*, January 24, 1944; *PM*, February 7, 1944.

35. David Halberstam, *The Powers That Be* (New York: Knopf, 1979), p. 517; "Bystander to Genocide," *Village Voice*, December 18, 1984, p. 30.

36. *Washington Post*, March 12, 1944; *New Republic*, March 20, 1944, p. 366.

37. *Christian Science Monitor*, March 24, 1944, p. 1; *New York Times*, March 25, 1944, p. 1; *New York Herald Tribune*, March 25, 1944, p. 1; *Washington Times Herald*, March 25, 1944, p. 1; *Los Angeles Times*, March 25, 1944, p. 1. For other warnings see *New York Times*, June 18, 1944, p. 24, June 27, 1944, p. 6, July 10, 1944, p. 9, July 15, 1944, p. 3; Wyman, *Abandonment*, pp. 256, 397.

38. *Baltimore Sun*, March 25, 1944; *New York Times*, March 25, 1944 (emphasis added). Anne O'Hare McCormick, writing in the *New York Times*, explained Roosevelt's willingness to speak out in this manner as motivated by the Administration's concern over the criticism of its paltry rescue efforts. The critiques were "so vocal that the policy makers cannot ignore it." The British were opposed to a statement by Roosevelt and let the Americans know of their opposition. Pehle pointedly criticized them for their opposition. Feingold, p. 252.

39. Wyman, *Abandonment,* p. 256.

40. *New Republic,* April 3, 1944, p. 452.

41. *New York Post,* April 5, 1944, p. 24, April 15, 1944, p. 10, April 21, 1944, p. 4, April 22, 1944.

42. It is unclear who proposed the idea to the WRB, though there is indication that the proposal came from Peter Bergson. Two weeks after the creation of the Board, Bergson gave Josiah DuBois, a WRB staff member, a memorandum with proposals for action. The memorandum called for the establishment of temporary havens for refugees who had reached a "safe" area. By moving them to these havens, the way would be cleared for additional refugees to enter the "safe" areas. Papers of the WRB, box 7, "Memorandum Submitted by the Washington Emergency Committee to Save the Jewish People of Europe," February 7, 1944, Franklin D. Roosevelt Library, Hyde Park, N.Y. Sharon Lowenstein, "New Deal for Refugees," *American Jewish History,* March 1982, pp. 325–341. Actually a similar idea had been proposed by State Department official Philip W. Bonsal in April 1942. See *FRUS,* 1942, vol. I, pp. 455–456.

43. *New York Times,* May 4, 1943, p. 18.

44. *Christian Century,* May 24, 1944, p. 636. Even some midwestern papers, which generally were opposed to anything that had even a faint ring of liberalization of immigration laws, supported the idea. In an editorial entitled "Put Up or Shut Up," the *Terre Haute* (Indiana) *Star* espoused the acceptance of free ports and decried America's demand that other countries accept refugee Jews while it "refuse[d] to admit any part of these sufferers to the United States beyond the present small, pre-war quotas." *Terre Haute* (Indiana) *Star,* May 12, 1944. The situation in Hungary, the creation of the WRB, and Grafton's suggestion stimulated public discussion and debate regarding some change in American immigration and rescue policy. *New York Post,* April 28, 1944; *New York Times,* April 1, 1944; *Christian Science Monitor,* April 11, April 12, April 19, 1944.

45. *In Fact,* April 26, 1944, p. 2; *Miami Herald,* June 15, 1944, p. 6A, July 28, 1944, p. 6A, September 28, 1944, p. 4A. For restrictionists and antisemities who opposed plan see Wyman, *Abandonment,* p. 267.

46. *New Republic,* May 15, 1944, p. 666.

47. *Commonweal,* May 12, 1944, pp. 76–77.

48. *New York Times,* April 1, April 19, 1944; *New York Post,* April 28, 1944; *Christian Science Monitor,* April 11, April 12, April 19, 1944; Lowenstein, p. 334. There were other signs that the public attitude might be softening in this regard. A Gallup poll revealed that Americans had changed their opinion regarding the shipment of food to children in German-occupied countries. Whereas in September

1940, prior to American entry into the war, a substantial majority opposed sending food, 65 percent were in favor (13 percent neutral and 22 percent opposed) in February 1944. People felt that despite the risks that some of the food might fall into enemy hands, everything possible should be done to help the children. The WRB thought the statistic significant enough to make special note of it and keep it in its file. *Washington Post,* February 12, 1944; United States War Refugee Board, *Final Summary Report of the Executive Director, War Refugee Board* (Washington: Government Printing Office, September 15, 1945), p. 45.

49. On May 25 former New York Governor Al Smith held a news conference to announce that seventy-two prominent Americans had signed a petition urging the President to establish temporary havens for refugees. The supporters included a former Vice President of the United States, an Associate Justice of the Supreme Court, the governors of eighteen states, four Nobel Prize winners, thirteen university and college presidents, and prominent industrialists and labor figures. *Contemporary Jewish Record,* June, 1944, p. 401ff.; U.S., Congress, Senate, S. Res. 297, 78th Cong., 2d sess., 1944, vol. 90, part 4; Lowenstein, p. 337.

50. *New York Times,* May 19, 1944, p. 18; *Christian Century,* May 24, 1944, p. 636.

51. *Nation,* June 10, 1944, pp. 670–671.

52. Roosevelt was obviously not strongly committed to the idea because he continued to suggest that better places could be found overseas— for instance, in the Mediterranean resorts with "numerous hotel facilities." Roosevelt chose the name "Emergency Refugee Shelter" for the havens because it denoted the transitory nature of the refuge. The refugees were to be sheltered on an emergency and temporary basis only. Actually by the time *The Nation* published Stone's letter the President had already indicated that he favored the idea, but his statement, the magazine noted, was so "indefinite" that it believed Stone's pleas for public pressure were as "valid as they were before Mr. Roosevelt spoke." *Newsweek,* June 12, 1944, p. 32; *Nation,* June 10, 1944, p. 670; *New York Post,* June 1, 1944; *New York Times,* June 10, 1944, p. 1, June 13, 1944, p. 1; *Washington Post,* June 13, 1944; Wyman, *Abandonment,* pp. 263–265.

53. *PM,* August 2, 1944, p. 2; *Chicago Tribune,* August 5, 1944, p. 1; *New York Times,* August 5, 1944, p. 1; *New York Herald Tribune,* August 5, 1944, p. 1; *Washington Post,* June 11, 1944; Sarah E. Peck, "The Campaign for an American Response to the Nazi Holocaust," *Journal of Contemporary History,* vol. 15 (1980), p. 399; Wyman, *Abandonment,* p. 266. The arrival of the refugees may have aroused some concerns.

It may have well been pure coincidence that the *New York Herald Tribune* chose to publish three days prior to the arrival of the Oswego-bound refugees a lengthy editorial extolling the fact that immigration had fallen since 1931. It attributed this "wholesome development" to the restrictions and "selectivity" of American immigration laws. Two months later it published an even more strident editorial on the same theme. The potential arrival of a group of refugees and the liberation of portions of Europe may have forced the *New York Herald Tribune* to focus on those who would "flock" to these shores and not on those facing destruction. *New York Herald Tribune*, August 2, October 3, 1944. For newspaper coverage of the refugees' arrival see the collection of newspaper clippings in papers of the War Relocation Authority, Emergency Refugee Shelter, Temporary Havens in the United States, folder 5, record group 210, National Archives, Washington.

54. *Washington Post*, March 22, 1944, p. 2; *New York Herald Tribune*, March 22, 1944; Martin Gilbert, *Auschwitz and the Allies* (New York: Holt, Rinehart and Winston, 1981), p. 234.

55. *New York Times*, June 4, 1944, p. 6.

56. *Los Angeles Times*, June 17, 1944, p. 3; *New York World Telegram*, June 16, 1944.

57. *New York Times*, June 20, 1944, p. 5, June 25, 1944, p. 5; *Washington Times Herald*, June 20, 1944.

58. For a detailed history of the release of the report see Gilbert, chap. 25.

59. The articles published on July 3 gave the higher figure in the range, 1,715,000; subsequent articles all referred to 1,750,000. Apparently the Lithuanian Jews were inadvertently dropped from the original list of victims. When they were added, the toll reached 1,750,000. *New York Times*, July 3, 1944, p. 3, July 6, 1944, p. 6; *Christian Science Monitor*, July 3, 1944, pp. 3, 7; *Washington Star*, July 3, 1944, p. 2; *Los Angeles Times*, July 9, 1944, p. 15; *Washington Times Herald*, July 9, 1944; *Seattle Times*, July 3, 1944, p. 2; *Kansas City Star*, July 3, 1944, p. 12; *PM*, July 6, 1944.

60. *New York Times*, July 3, 1944, p. 3.

61. *Christian Science Monitor*, July 3, 1944, p. 3; *Los Angeles Times*, July 9, 1944, p. 5.

62. *Washington Post*, July 7, 1944, p. 2; *Washington Times Herald*, July 9, 1944.

63. Brigham's article ran the length of an entire column, while another story on the page on Eden's warning to the Hungarians about harming the Jews was three-quarters of a column long. *New York Times*, July 6, 1944, p. 6.

64. *New York Herald Tribune,* July 6, 1944, p. 3; *Washington Post,* July 7, 1944, p. 2. Other reports on Auschwitz that appeared during this period included a *Christian Science Monitor* report on July 10 by a staff correspondent stationed in London that the "extermination and massacres of the Hungarian Jewish community" had already begun. *PM* carried one of the more extensive descriptions of conditions in Auschwitz based on information it had received from the Czechoslovakian government in exile. This information was based on the eyewitness report which had reached Switzerland in mid-June. A Czech diplomat, who described the report as "so revolting" that he was barely able to force himself to read it, told *PM* that though a few details in it might be incorrect, it was "indisputably clear" that terrible cruelties were being "carried out [in a] wholesale, systematic . . . deliberately organized" fashion. *Christian Science Monitor,* July 10, 1944, p. 7; *PM,* July 6, 1944.

65. *Christian Science Monitor,* July 6, 1944, pp. 1, 7.

66. *Christian Science Monitor,* August 12, 1944, p. 11. *Christian Century,* September 27, 1944, p. 1113.

67. *New York Times,* July 19, 1944, p. 5; *New York Herald Tribune,* July 19, 1944, p. 4; *Chicago Tribune,* July 19, 1944, p. 10; *Christian Science Monitor,* July 20, 1944, p. 7.

68. Allied leaders had spoken out on this issue. The press tended to pay their warnings more attention than it paid the actual reports on Hungarian Jews. The *Washington Post* and *Los Angeles Times* both placed the story of Hull's warning on the front page, while the *New York Times, New York Herald Tribune,* and *Baltimore Sun* carried it on page 3. *New York Times,* July 10, 1944, pp. 5, 10, July 15, 1944, p. 3; *New York Herald Tribune,* July 10, 1944, pp. 9, 10, July 15, 1944, p. 3, July 19, 1944; *Baltimore Sun,* July 15, 1944, p. 3; *Los Angeles Times,* July 10, 1944, p. 6, July 15, 1944, p. 1; *Washington Post,* July 15, 1944, p. 1; *Washington Post,* July 15, 1944; *Chicago Tribune,* July 10, 1944, p. 7; *Christian Science Monitor,* July 10, 1944, p. 7. For a description of widespread oppression in Hungary see column by Paul Winkler, "Pogroms in Hungary," in *Washington Post,* July 15, 1944, p. 6. Earlier protests by Allied leaders had also been covered by the press. *Washington Post,* June 13, 1944, June 22, 1944, p. 5; *New York Times,* June 13, 1944, p. 1, June 22, 1944, p. 9, June 27, 1944, p. 6; *New York Herald Tribune,* June 27, 1944.

69. *Nation,* July 31, 1944; *Christian Science Monitor,* July 25, 1944, p. 9, July 29, 1944, p. 1.

70. *New Republic,* July 31, 1944, p. 117.

71. *PM,* July 31, 1944.

72. *Washington Post,* July 25, 1944.

73. The *Washington Post* printed a letter from the director of the American League for a Free Palestine which contained the text of a cable sent to Winston Churchill demanding that as many Hungarian Jews as possible be saved by allowing them entry into Palestine. *Washington Post,* August 1, 1944, p. 8.

74. *PM,* August 2, 1944; *New York Times,* August 1, 1944, p. 17, August 9, 1944, p. 13, August 18, 1944, p. 5; *Chicago Tribune,* August 1, 1944, p. 3, August 9, 1944, p. 5; *Washington Times Herald,* August 5, 1944; *Washington Post,* August 18, 1944, p. 3; *Baltimore Sun,* August 18, 1944, p. 4; *New York Herald Tribune,* August 18, 1944; *Chicago Tribune,* August 18, 1944, p. 7.

75. *New York Post,* August 24, August 29, 1944; *Washington Post,* September 2, 1944; *Nation,* August 26, 1944, p. 229; *New Republic,* September 4, 1944, p. 261.

76. *New York Post,* August 7, 1944.

77. *New York Daily News,* August 14, 1944.

78. *New York Herald Tribune,* June 20, 1944; *New York Post,* August 7, 1944; *New York World Telegram,* June 16, 1944; *New York Times,* August 22, 1944, p. 10; *New York Times,* September 4, 1944; *PM,* September 3, September 4, September 5, 1944; *Washington Post,* August 30, 1944, p. 2.

Chapter 11

1. Charles Herbert Stember, *Jews in the Mind of America* (New York: Basic Books, 1966), p. 141; Vernon McKenzie, "Atrocities in World War II—What We Can Believe," *Journalism Quarterly,* vol. 19 (September 1942), pp. 268–276; *New York Post,* April 2, 1943, p. 29.

2. *Washington Post,* March 21, 1943, sec. B, p. 7.

3. *New York Post,* April 2, 1943, p. 29.

4. Arthur Koestler, "The Nightmare That Is a Reality," *New York Times Magazine,* January 9, 1944, pp. 5, 30; *Christian Century,* February 16, 1944, pp. 204–206.

5. *Saturday Evening Post,* October 28, 1944, pp. 18,19,96; *In Fact,* February 14, 1944, p. 3; Koestler, pp. 5, 30.

6. *New York Times,* October 27, 1944. The December 1944 Gallup poll asked people if they believed the stories that the Germans had murdered many people (the question did not mention Jews) in concentration camps; 76 percent responded affirmatively, while 24 percent did not believe it to be so. A follow-up question which was asked of those who had responded in the affirmative illustrated

the depth of confusion even among those who were willing to acknowledge that many had died:

Nobody knows, of course, how many may have been murdered but what would be your best guess?

100,000 or less	27%
100,000 to 500,000	5
500,000 to 1 million	1
1 million	6
6 million or more	4
Unwilling to guess	25

Although three-quarters of those polled accepted the charge "many were murdered" as true, they were strikingly ignorant about the number of victims in light of the fact that by this time tolls of well over 3 million were commonly cited. This number had been confirmed by varied sources, including governments in exile, the Inter-Allied Information Committee, church groups, Jewish and non-Jewish rescue organizations, the press, and, most importantly, the detailed eyewitness report on Auschwitz which had been re-leased the previous month by the WRB. The report had been widely featured by newspapers all over the country, which considered it the official confirmation for which they had been waiting. Most of the headlines cited the death toll as being between 1,750,000 and 2,000,000. It was not until 1945 that Americans adopted more "realistic notions" of the number killed. By May 1945 the median estimate of the number of those killed was 1 million. This again included all victims, since the question did not mention Jews. *Washington Post,* December 3, 1944. George H. Gallup, *The Gallup Poll: Public Opinion, 1935–1971* (New York: Random House, 1972), vol. I, p. 472. Henry Cantril, *Public Opinion* (Princeton: Princeton University Press, 1951), p. 383; Stember, p. 141.

7. *Washington Post,* April 16, 1945, p. 1; April 19, 1945, p. 2.

8. Studs Terkel, *The Good War* (New York: Pantheon Books, 1984), p. 144; *Washington Post,* April 23, 1945, p. 6, April 27, 1945, p. 6, April 28, 1945, pp. 1, 2.

9. *Washington Post,* April 28, 1945, p. 4; *New York World Telegram,* April 3, 1945, p. 1.

10. *St. Louis Post Dispatch,* May 20, 1945, p. 1d; *Editor & Publisher,* May 5, 1945, p. 40. The recollections of the soldiers are from the Fred R. Crawford Witness to the Holocaust Project, Emory University,

Atlanta, Georgia, and are cited in Robert H. Abzug, *Inside the Vicious Heart: Americans and the Liberation of Nazi Concentration Camps* (New York: Oxford University Press, 1985), p. 138.

11. *The Nation,* May 19, 1945 p. 579, reprinted in James Agee, *Agee on Film I* (New York: Grosset & Dunlap, 1969), pp. 161–162; Milton Mayer, "Let the Swiss Do It!" *Progressive,* May 14, 1945, as cited in Abzug, pp. 136–137, 186.

12. *New Statesman and Nation,* April 28, 1945, p. 267; Alexander Kendrick, *Prime Time: The Life of Edward R. Murrow* (Boston: Little, Brown, 1969), p. 278; David Halberstam, *The Powers That Be,* (New York: Knopf, 1979), pp. 43–44.

13. *Time,* March 8, 1943, p. 29; *Newsweek,* September 13, 1943, p. 40.

14. *San Francisco Examiner,* April 23, 1945, p. 7; *New York Times,* August 4, 1944, p. 5.

15. Bill Lawrence, *Six Presidents, Too Many Wars* (New York: Saturday Review Press, 1972), pp. 90–91.

16. *New York Times,* November 29, 1943, p. 3; Lawrence, p. 95 (emphasis added).

17. *St. Louis Post Dispatch,* November 29, 1944, p. 1; *Newsweek,* December 6, 1943, p. 22; *Los Angeles Examiner,* November 29, 1943, p. 1; *New York World Telegram,* November 29, 1943, p. 10.

18. *New York Times,* November 29, 1943, p. 3 (emphasis added); *Los Angeles Examiner,* November 29, 1943, pp. 1, 2 (emphasis added).

19. *New York Journal American,* November 29, 1943, p. 1, December 11, 1943, p. 1; *New York World Telegram,* November 29, 1943, p. 10.

20. *Manchester Guardian,* November 29, 1943.

21. *Los Angeles Examiner,* November 29, 1943, pp. 1, 2.

22. Lawrence's skepticism may also help explain why the *New York Times* used the figure of 50,000 in its headline and not the 100,000 figure that the *New York World Telegram* and *New York Journal American* did. *St. Louis Post Dispatch* November 29, 1943, p. 1; *Los Angeles Times,* November 29, 1943, p. 1; *Los Angeles Examiner,* November 29, 1943, p. 1; *New York Journal American,* November 29, 1943, p. 1; *New York Times,* November 29, 1943, p. 3.

23. *New York Journal American,* December 11, 1944, p. 1. In a strange quirk of journalistic practice the paper ran the story twice, once on November 29 and again on December 11.

24. Lawrence, p. 92; *Los Angeles Times,* November 29, 1943, p. 1.

25. *New York Times,* August 30, 1944, p. 1, August 31, 1944, p. 16; Lawrence, p. 102.

26. *New York Times,* August 31, 1944, p. 16; Lawrence, p. 102.

27. *Atlanta Constitution,* August 30, 1944, p. 1; *San Francisco Examiner,* August 30, 1944, p. 1; *New York Sun,* August 30, 1944, p. 3; *New York World Telegram,* August 30, 1944, p. 9; *New York Herald Tribune,* August 30, 1944, p. 4; *Chicago Tribune,* August 30, 1944, p. 6; *Baltimore Sun,* August 30, 1944, p. 3; *Miami Herald,* August 30, 1944, p. 2; *Los Angeles Examiner,* August 30, 1944, pp. 1, 4; *Los Angeles Times,* August 30, 1944, p. 4; *Life,* August 28, 1944, p. 34, September 18, 1944, pp. 17–18.

28. *St. Louis Post Dispatch,* August 30, 1944, p. 1; *New York Herald Tribune,* August 30, 1944, p. 4.

29. *Newsweek,* September 11, 1944, p. 64; *Time,* August 21, 1944, pp. 36, 38, September 11, 1944, p. 36.

30. *Saturday Evening Post,* October 28, 1944, pp. 18–19, 96.

31. *Christian Century,* September 13, 1944, p. 1045.

32. Michael Balfour, *Propaganda in War, 1939–1945: Organizations, Policies, and Publics in Britain and Germany* (London: Routledge & Kegan Paul, 1979), pp. 332–334.

33. *The Christian Century,* September 13, 1944, p. 1045; Martin Gilbert, *Auschwitz and the Allies* (New York: Holt, Rinehart and Winston, 1981), pp. 299–301.

34. Walter Laqueur, *The Terrible Secret: Suppression of the Truth About Hitler's "Final Solution"* (Boston: Little, Brown, 1980), p. 91. An example of this attitude was to be found in the aide-memoire sent by the British embassy to the Department of State on January 20, 1943, in which the British proposed some kind of private conference to deal with the refugee problem. The British stressed that "the refugee problem cannot be treated as though it were a wholly Jewish problem which could be handled by Jewish agencies or by machinery only adapted for assisting Jews. There are so many non-Jewish refugees and there is so much acute suffering among non-Jews in Allied countries that Allied criticism would probably result if any marked preference were shown in removing Jews from territories in enemy occupation. There is also the distinct danger of stimulating anti-semitism in areas where an excessive number of foreign Jews are introduced." *FRUS,* 1943, vol. I, p. 134. The British claimed that antisemitism had been "revived by the authoritative disclosures of the Nazis' systematic massacres of the European Jews" and therefore it seemed best not to focus on them. Ian McLaine, *Ministry of Morale* (London, 1979), pp. 164–166, as cited in Laqueur, p. 92. For discussion of American attitudes toward Jews during the war see Stember, pp. 142–145.

35. *PM,* April 30, 1943, p. 8.

36. The statement by Roosevelt, Churchill, and Stalin is contained in the report by Justice Jackson to the President on *International Conference on Military Trials,* Department of State Publications, 3080, 1949, pp. 11–12 (emphasis added). For discussion of the implications of the statement see Raul Hilberg, *The Destruction of European Jewry* (New York: Harper, 1979), p. 682. The Allied policy resulted in what today can only be described as rather absurd decisions. When the Nazis interned American civilians who had been stranded in Europe when the war broke out, they separated the American Jews from other American citizens. Two camps were created, one for the Jews and one for the non-Jews. Although the reason for the existence of the two camps was known to the State Department, it refused to officially acknowledge the fact that Jews had been separated from non-Jews. As far as it was concerned, "there were simply two American men's camps in Germany." *Baltimore Sun,* March 19, 1944.

37. *Washington Post,* April 24, 1945, p. 1; Henry L. Feingold, *The Politics of Rescue: The Roosevelt Administration and the Holocaust, 1938–1945* (New Brunswick: Rutgers University Press, 1970), p. 227; Arthur Sweetser to Leo Rosten, February 1, 1942, as cited in Eric Hanin, "War on Our Minds: The American Mass Media in World War II," Ph.D. diss., University of Rochester, 1976, pp. 104–105; Christopher Lasch, *The Culture of Narcissism: American Life in an Age of Diminishing Expectations* (New York: Warner Books, 1979), pp. 76, 246; Jacques Ellul, *Propaganda: The Formation of Men's Attitudes,* translated by Konrad Kellen and Jean Lerner (New York: Knopf, 1965), p. 53.

38. *Christian Science Monitor,* January 30, 1943, pp. 2, 11 (emphasis added).

39. *New York Times,* January 24, 1940, p. 20, January 30, 1940, p. 18. In March 1940 the *Greenville* (South Carolina) *News* also condemned the "ruthless . . . persecution of the Polish people" and the "deliberate program of exterminating the Polish people." It too failed to cite the Jews. That same month the *Fort Worth Star Telegram* believed that the Jews would fare better than the Poles, who could be expected to "dig their own graves and occupy them." *Cincinnati Enquirer,* March 22, 1940; *Greenville News,* March 22, 1940; *Fort Worth Telegram,* March 9, 1940; *Asheville Citizen,* November 22, 1941.

In 1942 Victor Bienstock, the popular syndicated columnist, described the Nazis as bent on the extermination of Poland and its incorporation into the Reich. The sole difference, he argued, between the Poles and Jews was a matter of degree: the Jews would be killed more rapidly than the Poles; otherwise both groups faced the same ultimate fate. *New York Post,* January 5, 1942; *Philadelphia Record,* January 4, 1942.

40. *Los Angeles Times,* January 30 1943, sec. II, p. 4.

41. *Time,* August 21, 1944, pp. 36, 38; *Atlanta Constitution,* August 30, 1944, p. 4; *Los Angeles Times,* August 30, 1944, p. 4; *St. Louis Post Dispatch,* August 30, 1944, p. 1: *Los Angeles Examiner,* August 30, 1944, p. 1.

42. *Saturday Evening Post,* October 28, 1944, p. 96; *New York Herald Tribune,* August 30, 1944, p. 4; *Atlanta Constitution,* August 30, 1944, pp. 1, 3.

43. *Newsweek,* September 11, 1944, p. 64; *Life,* September 18, 1944, p. 17; *St. Louis Post Dispatch,* August 30, 1944, pp. 1, 12; *Time,* May 7, 1945, pp. 32, 35.

44. *Life,* August 28, 1944, p. 34.

45. Stephen E. Ambrose, *Eisenhower: Soldier, General of the Army, President Elect, 1890–1952* (New York: Simon & Shuster, 1983), p. 400.

46. Those participating included Julius Ochs Adler, vice president and general manager, *New York Times;* Malcolm Bingay, editor, *Detroit Free Press;* Amnon Carter, editor, *Fort Worth Star Telegram;* Norman Chandler, general manager, *Los Angeles Times;* William L. Chenery, publisher, *Collier's;* E. Z. Dimitman, executive editor, *Chicago Sun;* John Hearst, publisher of the Hearst papers; Ben Hibbs, editor, *Saturday Evening Post;* Stanley High, associate editor, *Reader's Digest;* Ben McKelway, editor, *Washington Star;* Glen Nevill, executive editor, *New York Daily Mirror;* William I. Nichols, editor, *This Week Magazine;* I. K. Nicholson, president and editor, *New Orleans Picayune;* Joseph Pulitzer, editor and publisher, *St. Louis Post Dispatch;* Gideon Seymour, executive editor, *Minneapolis Star-Journal;* Duke Shoop, Washington correspondent, *Kansas City Star;* Beverly Smith, associate editor, *American Magazine;* Walker Stone, editor, Scripps-Howard Newspaper Alliance; and M. E. Walter, managing editor, *Houston Chronicle.*

47. *St. Louis Post Dispatch,* May 18, 1945, p. 1 (emphasis added).

48. *Miami Herald,* April 28, 1945, pp. 1, 2 (emphasis added).

49. *St. Louis Post Dispatch,* May 6 1945, pp. 1,6; *Chicago Tribune,* May 6, 1945, p. 7; *Miami Herald,* May 6, 1945, p. 11; *New York Journal American,* May 6, 1945, p. 5.

50. *St. Louis Post Dispatch,* May 15, 1945; *San Francisco Examiner,* May 12, 1945.

51. *St. Louis Post Dispatch,* April 29, 1945, p. 3a; *Miami Herald,* May 6, 1945, p. 5b.

52. *St. Louis Post Dispatch,* May 6, 1945, p. 1.

53. Senator Barkley, the majority leader of the Senate, did report to the Senate that in Buchenwald Jews had a much higher rate of death than did other prisoners.

54. *St. Louis Post Dispatch,* May 1, 1945, p. 2b.

55. *San Francisco Examiner,* April 19, 1945, p. 4, May 1, 1945, p. 14 (emphasis added). For other examples of what Hearst papers said, see *New York Journal American* May 1, 1945, p. 14 and *Chicago Herald American,* May 1, 1945. *Washington Post,* April 19, 1945, p. 2.

56. Walker Stone, a columnist with the *New York World Telegram,* described the inhabitants of Buchenwald and Dachau as including "German citizens, whose only crime was resisting the Nazi political machine, preaching Christianity from German pulpits, or *having Jewish blood." New York World Telegram,* May 10, 1945, p. 17 (emphasis added).

57. *St. Louis Post Dispatch,* May 13, 1945, p. 2a.

58. *New York Times,* April 18, 1945, reprinted in Louis L. Snyder, ed., *Masterpieces of War Reporting: The Great Moments of World War II* (New York, Julian Messner, 1962), p. 432; *Miami Herald,* April 21, 1945, p. 1, May 4, 1945, p. 1.

59. *New York Sun,* May 2, 1945, p. 8; *Baltimore Sun,* May 1, 1945, p. 2; *New York World Telegram,* April 30, 1945, p. 1.

60. *St. Louis Post Dispatch,* April 24, 1945, p. 3a.

61. *New York World Telegram,* April 30, 1945, p. 2; Percy Knauth, *Germany in Defeat* (New York: Knopf, 1946), p. 32; *Time,* April 30, 1945, pp. 40, 43.

62. Hilberg, p. 681. As the Allies approached some of the camps, the Germans, in a last macabre act, evacuated the Jewish prisoners in order to keep them from falling into the hands of the liberators. For a map of the route of the death march from Auschwitz to the camps in Germany and the evacuations from these camps as the Americans and British approached, see Martin Gilbert, *The Macmillan Atlas of the Holocaust* (New York: Macmillan, 1982), pp. 222–224. *Chicago Tribune,* April 25, 1945, pp. 1, 10.

63. Benjamin West, *Behavlei Klaia [In the Throes of Destruction]* (Tel Aviv, 1963), p. 47, as cited in Yehuda Bauer, *A History of the Holocaust* (New York: Franklin Watts, 1982), p. 199.

64. See, for example, *New York Herald Tribune,* January 7, 1942, p. 1; January 8, 1942, p. 3; *St. Louis Post Dispatch,* January 7, 1942, p. 1; Laqueur, pp. 69–70.

65. The OSS Department of Research and Analysis called attention to the way the Russians avoided focusing on Jews in a lengthy memorandum entitled "Gaps in the Moscow Statement of Atroci-

ties." The memorandum emphasized that "non-Aryans" had been consciously omitted from the Russian reports. Laqueur, p. 69.

66. *Time*, September 11, 1944, p. 36.

67. *St. Louis Post Dispatch*, January 7, 1942, p. 1; *PM*, January 7, 1942; *Philadelphia Record*, January 8, 1942; *Providence Evening Bulletin*, January 7, 1942; *Washington* (D.C.) *News*, January 2, 1942; *Washington Times Herald*, January 11, 1942.

68. Interview with Henry Shapiro, February 7, 1985.

69. Lawrence, p. 100.

70. *Washington Post*, March 31, 1944, p. 3; *New York Times*, May 8, 1944, p. 8.

71. *St. Louis Post Dispatch*, February 2, 1945, p. 2.

72. Foreign Office papers 371/51185, WR 874, as cited in Gilbert, *Auschwitz and the Allies*, p. 337.

73. *San Francisco Examiner*, May 8, 1945, p. 12; *Atlanta Constitution*, May 8, 1945, p. 17; *New York Sun*, May 7, 1945, p. 4; *St. Louis Post Dispatch*, May 7, 1945, p. 10a; *Soviet Monitor*, no. 5999, "Special Bulletin: The Oswiecim Murder Camp," as cited in Gilbert, *Auschwitz and the Allies*, p. 338.

74. Gilbert, *Auschwitz and the Allies*, p. 337.

75. Leonard Dinnerstein, "The U.S. Army and the Jews: Policies Toward the Displaced Persons After World War II," *American Jewish History*, March 1979, pp. 353–366. See also Leonard Dinnerstein, *America and the Survivors of the Holocaust* (New York: Columbia University Press, 1982).

76. The American legation in Bern which first received the report in June did not give it a high priority and delayed transmitting the full text. Wyman believes that had the full report arrived earlier, it would have strengthened rescue efforts. David S. Wyman, *The Abandonment of the Jews: America and the Holocaust, 1941–1945* (New York: Pantheon Books, 1984), p. 324.

77. Virginia Mannon to John Pehle, November 16, 1944, War Refugee Board Records, box 6, Franklin Roosevelt Library, Hyde Park, N.Y.; DS 840.48 Refugees, July 5, 1944. The summary of the report was received by the War Refugee Board in the summer of 1944. The full report was received in October.

78. For a detailed analysis of McCloy's role including his response to Pehle's suggestion that camps be bombed, see Gilbert, *Auschwitz and the Allies*, pp. 238, 248, 256, 303, 326–328.

79. *New York Herald Tribune*, November 26, 1944.

80. *Louisville* (Kentucky) *Courier Journal,* November 26, 1944.

81. *Philadelphia Inquirer,* November 26, 1944.

82. *New York Times,* November 26, 1944.

83. *Washington Post,* November 26, 1944.

84. War Refugee Board, *German Extermination Camps: Auschwitz and Birkenau* (Washington: Executive Office of the President, 1944), preface.

85. *New York Herald Tribune,* November 26, 1944. The following papers carried the Associated Press dispatch concerning the WRB's report on November 26, 1944: *Baltimore Sun, Washington Star, New York Journal American, Detroit News, St. Louis Globe Democrat, Nashville Tennessean, Rochester Democrat and Chronicle, Columbia* (South Carolina) *State, Madison* (Wisconsin) *Capital Times, Bridgeport* (Connecticut) *Post, Huntington* (West Virginia) *Herald Advertiser, Macon* (Georgia) *Telegram News, Buffalo* (New York) *Courier Express, Jacksonville* (Florida) *Times-Union, Providence* (Rhode Island) *Journal, Roanoke* (Virginia) *Times, Raleigh* (North Carolina) *News and Observer, Worcester* (Massachusetts) *Telegram, Greensboro* (North Carolina) *News.* The *Pittsburgh Post-Gazette* carried it on November 27.

86. *Washington Times Herald,* November 26, 1944; *Louisville Courier Journal,* November 26, 1944; *Wheeling* (West Virginia) *News Register,* November 26, 1944; *New York World Telegram,* May 3, 1945, p. 9.

87. *Chicago Tribune,* November 26, 1944.

88. Elmer Davis to John Pehle, November 23, 1944, War Refugee Board Records, box 6, "German Extermination Camps," Franklin D. Roosevelt Library; statement by John Pehle to McGill University Hillel Holocaust Conference, September 22, 1975.

89. *Yank,* January 28, 1944, p. 9, August 24, 1944, p. 17; Virginia Mannon to John Pehle, November 16, 1944, War Refugee Board Records, box 6, "German Extermination Camps," Franklin D. Roosevelt Library.

90. Terkel, p. 283.

91. *New York Times,* April 28, 1945, p. 6; *St. Louis Post Dispatch,* April 29, 1945, p. 1; *Atlanta Constitution,* April 30, 1945, p. 12; Joseph Pulitzer, "A Report to the American People," *St. Louis Post Dispatch,* May 20, 1945, sect. D, p. 1.

92. *St. Louis Post Dispatch,* April 29, 1945, p. 3a.

93. *New York World Telegram,* May 8, 1945, p. 13.

94. Denny's article for *New York Times Magazine,* reprinted in *St. Louis Post Dispatch,* May 11, 1945, p. 2c.

95. *St. Louis Post Dispatch,* May 5, 1945, p. 3a. For Julius Ochs Adler's reaction see the *New York Times* April 28, 1945, p. 6. Interview with Richard C. Hottelet, December 21, 1984.

96. *Miami Herald,* April 28, 1945, p. 5B.

97. McKenzie, p. 271.

98. *Baltimore Sun,* April 20, 1945, p. 12; *San Francisco Examiner,* April 23, 1945, p. 7.

99. *New York Times,* May 18, 1942, February 17, 1945.

100. *Newsweek,* December 4, 1944, p. 59; *Chicago Herald American,* May 1, 1945; *Life,* May 7, 1945, pp. 32–37 (emphasis added).

101. Wyman, *Abandonment,* p. 314.

102. *Basler Deutscheszeitung,* as quoted in *St. Louis Post Dispatch,* May 1, 1945, p. 2b.

103. *Baltimore Sun,* April 7, 1945, p. 1.

104. Gilbert, *Macmillan Atlas,* pp. 215, 223.

105. *Miami Herald,* April 29, 1945, p. 10.

106. *Atlanta Constitution,* February 8, 1945, p. 10.

107. Ibid.; *Washington Evening Star,* July 15, 1944; *New York Times,* July 8, 1944, p. 10, January 1, 1945; *PM,* December 18, 1944; *Nation,* July 15, 1944, p. 58.

108. *Christian Century,* May 9, 1945, p. 575.

109. *San Francisco Examiner,* April 23, 1945, p. 7. A similar assessment of the problem was offered by William Ebenstein in 1945. He noted that if a few hundred or even a few thousand people had been killed by the Germans, people would have easily believed, but told that "many millions of Jews and Christians . . . have been systematically burned and slaughtered . . . people naturally refuse to believe it." William Ebenstein, *The German Record: A Political Portrait* (New York: Farrar & Rinehart, Inc., 1945), p. 238.

110. *Life,* October 11, 1943, p. 93. See also *Time,* September 6, 1943, p. 26.

111. Terkel, p. 466.

112. For a discussion and insightful analysis of a broad range of the diplomatic action and inaction regarding the Holocaust see Monty Noam Penkower, *The Jews Were Expendable* (Urbana: University of Illinois Press, 1983).

113. British officials sometimes demonstrated stronger resistance to Jewish requests than did American. In January 1945 an official of the Refugee Department of the Foreign Office, an office which was known to be well informed, wrote that "sources of information are nearly always Jewish whose accounts are only sometimes reliable and not seldom highly colored. One notable tendency in Jewish reports on this problem is to exaggerate the numbers of deportations and deaths." I. L. Henderson minute, January 11, 1945, PRO FO 371/51134 (WR 89/14/48), as cited in Bernard Wasserstein,

Britain and the Jews of Europe, 1939–1945 (London: Institute of Jewish Affairs, 1979), p. 178.

114. Gilbert, *Auschwitz and the Allies,* pp. 99, 312; Wyman, *Abandonment,* p. 266.

115. Alexis de Tocqueville, *Democracy in America,* vol. II (New York: Vintage Books, 1954), pp. 119–120.

INDEX